dBASE IV™
Programming
Techniques

W. Edward Tiley

CORPORATION

LEADING COMPUTER KNOWLEDGE

dBASE IV™
Programming Techniques

DEDICATION

Dedicated to Wil, Dylan, Devon, and Marlene:
four people who put a welcome dose of chaos into my life

Also dedicated to Kim and Richard

Publishing Director

David Paul Ewing

Acquisitions Editor

Terrie Lynn Solomon

Product Line Director

William Coy Hatfield

Editors

Mary Bednarek
Virginia Noble
Mark Simpson

Technical Editors

William McGirr
David W. Solomon

Indexer

Sherry Massey

Book Design and Production

Dan Armstrong   Jon Ogle
Cheryl English   Cindy L. Phipps
David Kline   M. Louise Shinault
Lori Lyons   Peter Tocco
Jennifer Matthews

Composed in Garamond and Universal Monospace I
by Que Corporation

ABOUT THE AUTHOR

W. Edward Tiley

Ed Tiley lives and teaches in Tallahassee, Florida. He is the founder of Data-Train, a vertical-market software house that specializes in custom-written dBASE language applications and applications for vacation-property managers.

Mr. Tiley is the author of *Using Clipper* and coauthor of the *dBASE IV Handbook*, 3rd Edition, both published by Que Corporation.

CONTENTS AT A GLANCE

TABLE OF CONTENTS

II	**Developing dBASE IV Applications**

4	**Writing dBASE IV Programs** 105

5	**Managing Data Entry** 121

ACKNOWLEDGMENTS

Tim Lebel, Patty Masai, Ralph Wakefield, and Rick Knight of Ashton-Tate. Thanks for the help.

Midge Watson. Thanks for the hours.

Que Corporation thanks Bill Hatfield for his many contributions to this book, including assisting in the overall development, providing technical support to the editors, and supplying additional material for Chapter 17.

Que Corporation thanks David Solomon for contributing to Appendix A.

TRADEMARK
ACKNOWLEDGMENTS

Que Corporation has made every attempt to supply trademark information about company names, products, and services mentioned in this book. Trademarks indicated below were derived from various sources. Que Corporation cannot attest to the accuracy of this information.

1-2-3 is a registered trademark of Lotus Development Corporation.

3Com is a registered trademark of 3Com Corporation.

Clipper is a trademark of Nantucket, Inc.

COMPAQ and COMPAQ MS-DOS 3.2 are registered trademarks of COMPAQ Computer Corporation.

CompuServe Information Service is a registered trademark of CompuServe Incorporated and H&R Block, Inc.

dBASE, dBASE II, dBASE III, and Ashton-Tate are registered trademarks, and dBASE III Plus, dBASE IV, RapidFile and Framework II are trademarks of Ashton-Tate Corporation.

Epson FX-85 is a trademark of Epson America, Inc.

HotShot Graphics is a registered trademark of SymSoft Corporation.

HP is a registered trademark and LaserJet is a trademark of Hewlett-Packard Co.

InSet is a registered trademark of INSET Systems Inc.

Macintosh is a registered trademark of Apple Computer, Inc.

MS-DOS and Microsoft Paintbrush are registered trademarks of Microsoft Corporation.

NetWare and Novell are registered trademarks of Novell, Inc.

PC Paintbrush is a registered trademark of ZSoft Corporation.

PFS is a registered trademark of Software Publishing Corporation.

PS/2 and IBM PC XT are trademarks of International Business Machines Corporation.

WordPerfect is a registered trademark of WordPerfect Corporation.

FORM.COD, copyright © 1988, Ashton-Tate Corporation. All rights reserved. Reprinted by permission.

CONVENTIONS USED IN THIS BOOK

Certain conventions were followed to help make *dBASE IV Programming Techniques* easy to use.

The names of menus and options selected from menus appear in boldface type. Note the following example:

Select **Print database structure** from the **Layout** menu.

dBASE IV commands and functions, program listings, and all on-screen messages and information appear in a special typeface. Consider the following examples:

The `DEFINE WINDOW` command includes several options.

Use the `DTOC()` function in the command.

The command `@10,10 SAY "Hello"` places the word `Hello` on the tenth line of the screen.

In dBASE IV command lines that show the syntax of the command, several additional conventions apply.

Text in capital letters represents keywords of the command.

Italicized elements, such as file names or expressions, that are enclosed in angle brackets (‹›) represent information you must supply. Just substitute the appropriate information for the italicized element. Don't type the brackets when you enter this information. For example, note the following command line:

`SAVE TO` ‹*name of memory file*›

After you type the `SAVE TO` portion of the command, you should enter the name of the memory file to which you want to save the variables. Do not type the angle brackets (‹›).

Elements in square brackets ([]) are optional. If you include these optional elements, do not type the square brackets. Notice the following command:

```
DEFINE MENU ‹menu name›
    [MESSAGE ‹character expression›]
```

dBASE paradigm conventions require that the default value appear in uppercase letters in the display of command syntax. In the following syntax line, for example, the default value for the system memory variable `_alignment` is `"LEFT"`:

```
_alignment = "LEFT"/"right"/"center"
```

Introduction

dBASE IV™ is the latest version of Ashton-Tate's ever popular database management software. dBASE IV combines an improved, interactive user interface with significant extensions to the dBASE programming language.

dBASE IV is more powerful than ever. For some, the power and complexity of such a product is overwhelming and intimidating; for others, this power becomes an opportunity.

People who create database management systems using dBASE IV are in great demand. You can become a dBASE IV programmer by using the techniques in this book. You learn to put the power of dBASE IV into the hands of users who know little or nothing about dBASE IV yet need the power of a data management application.

dBASE IV Programming

A dBASE IV *application*, as the term is used in this book, is a set of procedures and programs. The application can be used by persons not familiar with dBASE IV to gather information, manipulate information into a usable form, and output information for use in an organization's business.

It is inefficient for a business to hire an individual to answer the phone and take orders, and then spend three weeks training that person to operate the computer system needed for the job.

It is more efficient to create a program or series of programs that applies dBASE IV software techniques to a particular situation, such as taking orders; tracking memberships; and creating invoicing, billing, and inventory records for an organization. The employee can learn to use the application in a few days; that same employee might take several weeks to learn dBASE IV.

Creating these applications is the job of the dBASE IV programmer. If you find yourself in the position of designing programs for others to use, this book will get you on the right track to writing programs that have professional quality.

Who Should Read This Book

Working with dBASE IV is a little like learning to play chess. The fundamentals are simple and straightforward. The complexity of chess becomes apparent when you actually sit down to play chess with someone who is just a little bit better than you are. Thirty-two chessmen on sixty-four alternately colored squares represent billions and billions of possible combinations that can accommodate a wide variety of defensive and offensive playing strategies.

Like chess, dBASE IV starts simply. You create a data file and place information in the file. Then you select information to answer questions and print out the results in reports. Using the dBASE IV Control Center and entering commands one at a time at the dot prompt are powerful methods for tracking information that is easy to use and fairly quick to learn. The complexity of dBASE IV becomes apparent when you are asked to create data files and information tracking procedures for someone else to use. At this point, you decide to become a dBASE IV programmer.

To many people, the image of a computer programmer is that of an absent-minded professor who wears Earth shoes and carries a plastic pen caddy in a shirt pocket. In reality, however, most computer programmers are everyday business persons who have a job to do and who want it done quickly, accurately, and with a minimum of user training. If you find yourself about to step through that threshold and begin to design database applications for others to use, this book is for you.

To become a truly successful chess player, however, you need the ability to look ahead several moves into the future to anticipate what will happen later if you do something now. The same qualities are helpful in writing dBASE IV programs; you need to be able to stand back and take in "the big picture."

You need to anticipate how the design of a data file affects data entry and reports. The major factor, however, in becoming a good dBASE programmer is having the foresight to anticipate problems. When you design programs for others to use, you must design the program code to keep potential problems from becoming real problems.

Once you become familiar with a few concepts, you will realize that creating a database management application is a simple process. How far you extend the process is up to you. Like learning to play chess, how much you are willing to excel is strictly a personal decision.

Just as there are various levels of chess players, there are various levels of dBASE IV programmers and programming techniques. You can create something as simple as a keyboard macro, or you can go a step further and create an information tracking system with the dBASE IV Applications Generator. You can even immerse yourself in dBASE IV and create applications from scratch that might eventually be sold to a business for thousands of dollars.

What You Should Know

This book is not intended as an introduction to dBASE IV. To get the most from this book, you need a basic familiarity with creating and manipulating dBASE IV data files from the dot prompt and the Control Center. You should be familiar with the most frequently used dBASE commands and functions and have a basic understanding of how to control the dBASE IV environment with the SET commands.

If you need a basic introduction to dBASE IV, refer to the *dBASE IV Handbook,* 3rd Edition, by George Tsu-der Chou and W. Edward Tiley, published by Que Corporation. Other Que titles that can serve as reference when working with dBASE IV include *dBASE IV Tips, Tricks, and Traps*, 2nd Edition, by George Tsu-der Chou and Steve Davis; *dBASE IV Applications Library*, by Thomas W. Carlton; *dBASE IV Que Cards*; and *dBASE IV Quickstart*.

How This Book Is Organized

The information presented in this book is divided into 17 chapters and 5 appendixes. Each chapter takes a specific topic and presents information that can help you master each aspect of dBASE programming.

Part I, "Getting Started with dBASE IV Programming," includes Chapters 1 through 3. Part I gives you information on making the transition from being a dBASE IV user to becoming a dBASE IV programmer.

Chapter 1, "Designing Database Management Applications," presents the fundamentals of data management design. You learn the importance of planning applications in advance and designing efficient data structures. The process of establishing indexing procedures is also covered.

Chapter 2, "Working with dBASE IV Macros," deals with keyboard macros. You learn how to record, edit, save, and use macros to automate dBASE IV operations at their most fundamental level.

Chapter 3, "Using the Applications Generator," introduces the dBASE IV Applications Generator and shows you how to create simple database applications quickly and efficiently. You learn to generate a Quick Application, build a complete application, and modify an application.

Part II, "Developing dBASE IV Applications," consists of Chapters 4 through 13. Part II teaches you the basics of creating dBASE IV applications.

Chapter 4, "Writing dBASE IV Programs," introduces the dBASE IV program files. This chapter defines the dBASE IV program and shows you how to write a program that produces a mailing list of customers. The dBASE IV memory variables are also introduced.

Chapter 5, "Managing Data Entry," introduces the programming techniques needed for accepting data entry from users. You learn how to use the `@...SAY...GET` command to create data-entry screens that can be used in the mailing list application introduced in Chapter 4.

Chapter 6, "Creating Programs That Make Decisions," discusses the commands and variables that control the program's execution. You learn the importance of including commands that evaluate program conditions and how to integrate the `IF`, `DO CASE`, and `DO WHILE` constructs into the mailing list application.

Chapter 7, "Building dBASE IV Menus and Screens," expands the information on dBASE IV screen-handling techniques. You learn how to create BAR and POPUP menus and to control the screen with windows as you continue to refine the mailing list application.

Chapter 8, "Modular Programming in dBASE IV," shows you how to write modular programs. You learn to create procedures and user-defined functions to get the most power from your dBASE IV programming. You learn also how to build a library of procedures and functions for use in all your applications. The complete code for the mailing list application developed in Chapters 4 through 7 is presented at the end of Chapter 8.

Chapter 9, "Six Steps to Good Programming," explains how to apply the programming concepts introduced in previous chapters in developing a systematic approach to writing programs and applications. The topics covered include controlling the environment, using data files and indexes, processing data, and documenting your programs.

Chapter 10, "Handling Multiple Data Files," shows you how to write programs that use subroutines to handle multiple data files. You learn how to add records to a file and how to edit records in two files simultaneously.

Chapter 11, "Writing Programs That Produce Reports," discusses several ways to create programs that produce output. You learn how to use the dBASE IV system memory variables to make printing simple and easy.

Chapter 12, "Ensuring Data Integrity," shows you how to write programs that require greater accuracy in data entry through advanced data-validation techniques.

Chapter 13, "Using Sample Programs as Models," presents a sample application that will help you design and write programs of your own. Several modules are included to illustrate how an application is put together from individual pieces of code.

Part III, "Exploring Advanced Topics," consists of Chapters 14 through 17. This section explores the techniques of refining applications and distributing them to the end user.

Chapter 14, "Debugging dBASE IV Programs," presents the dBASE IV debugger. You learn how to invoke and run the interactive debugger in finding and correcting errors in your applications. A number of debugging tips are provided as well.

Chapter 15, "Networking with dBASE IV," shows you how to create applications that can be run on multiuser local area networks (LANs). The topics covered include locking procedures, commands, and functions used in networking, data security, and transaction processing.

Chapter 16, "Distributing Programs with the RunTime Module," shows you how to use the RunTime module to distribute your programs and applications to users who do not have dBASE IV. You learn how to use the BUILD and dBLINK utilities, as well as how to BUILD a sample RunTime application.

Chapter 17, "Using the dBASE IV Template Language," introduces the dBASE IV Template Language, a special programming language that directs the operations of the Applications Generator and the code generators that create screen formats, report formats, and label formats. The compiler, interpreter, and debugger included with the Template Language are also presented.

Several appendixes supplement the information in the chapters.

Appendix A, "dBASE IV Commands and Functions," is a summary of commands and functions helpful to users and programmers of dBASE IV.

Appendix B, "Menu Structure of the Applications Generator," is a detailed explanation of choices available with the Applications Generator. (See Appendix E for a visual map of these menus.)

Appendix C, "Sample Code from the Applications Generator," is a line-by-line commentary of a sample code produced by the Applications Generator (see Chapter 3).

Appendix D, "Differences between dBASE III Plus and dBASE IV," is a summary of major differences between the two latest versions of dBASE.

Appendix E, "dBASE IV Control Center Command Menu," is a visual map of all the menus and choices available with the dBASE IV Control Center.

A Word of Encouragement

Learning to pass on the power of dBASE IV to users who are not familiar with dBASE is not as difficult a task as it may first seem. Remember that at some point in your life you could not read, ride a bicycle, perform 8th grade mathematical computations, or drive a car. Once mastered, however, these everyday human tasks became second nature to you. Creating dBASE IV applications is the same. With a little effort and a little bit of time, you too will be creating sophisticated data management applications quickly, easily, and efficiently.

Part I

Getting Started with dBASE IV Programming

Includes

Designing Database Management Applications

Working with dBASE IV Macros

Using the dBASE IV Applications Generator

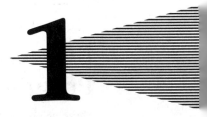

Designing Database
Management Applications

This chapter presents the basic concepts involved in designing dBASE IV applications for others to use. A dBASE IV *application* is simply a more formal description of a dBASE IV *program*. The distinction, used primarily by programmers, is strictly technical. From a structural standpoint, programs are just one of the tools that are combined to create the total solution to a data management problem. Ideally, all individual parts combine seamlessly to provide users with an application that anticipates their needs.

The major difference between using an applications program and using dBASE IV at the dot prompt or Control Center is one of pre-planning. As you work at the dot prompt or Control Center, you can be spontaneous. As you discover what needs to be done to your data, you can add to your routine. This approach doesn't work, however, when you are writing programs and applications. As a designer, you can never forget to include a needed function, so the importance of planning is stressed in this chapter and the rest of the book.

You learn how to plan and document a dBASE IV application based on your research of the user's needs. As you learn to build the application step-by-step, you are introduced to the various dBASE IV objects (data files, data-entry screens, reports, and labels) that combine to create applications.

The use of indexing to allow flexibility and easy access to the data is also covered. You learn to plan and design effective menus and screens for the user and how to prevent errors from getting into the system.

Whether you are a new programmer or an advanced dBASE user, this chapter will introduce you to the process of designing dBASE IV applications.

Becoming a dBASE IV Programmer

There are several paths to becoming a dBASE IV programmer. One of the most common is to simply become recognized as someone who is good with dBASE. Co-workers will ask you for help and support, and before you know it, you are creating applications for others to use.

Another path arises out of necessity. One day, you realize that you need to create a small application for someone else to use because you simply don't have the time to do it yourself anymore.

Whatever the reason, you decide to take the step of becoming a dBASE IV programmer. Becoming a dBASE IV programmer is a natural progression from being a dBASE IV user. As a dBASE IV user, you have acquired a basic familiarity with concepts and command structures. Formatting information with functions has become second nature to you. Soon, you begin to write programs that surprise even you with their power.

Whether you realize it or not, while you have been working at the Control Center and the dot prompt, you have been creating database applications. You create a data structure, set an index format so that you can easily retrieve information, design a report template, create a filter to exclude extraneous information, and send the output to a printer. The only difference between your database management application and any other is that yours was probably never written down; yours was stored in your "gray RAM." As you perform each step from the Control Center or the dot prompt, you simply decide what needs to be done next and issue the proper command.

When you begin to design systems, keep in mind three major goals:

1. Take time to plan your application.

    If you spend time planning your application, you avoid a number of potential pitfalls. Among these are poorly designed menu structures, in which the user's choices seem to have been hung onto the menus in a haphazard fashion; cumbersome program segments that try to accomplish too many tasks at once; and inadequate *overhead* (the capacity for the application to grow over the next few months or years).

2. Keep the application simple for your users.

    Design your applications so that they are arranged logically. The term "user-friendly" may be overused, but you have the responsibility to provide a user interface that doesn't intimidate inexperienced users.

3. Make sure that the results are accurate.

   It doesn't matter how attractive the screens look or how well the reports are formatted if the answers on the bottom line of the report are incorrect. Make sure that your programs are as free as possible of opportunities to get bad data entered into the system. Always check and re-check results for accuracy.

Keep these goals in mind as you work through this chapter and the rest of the book.

Planning dBASE IV Applications

Whoever first said "a little planning goes a long way" was probably a designer of database management systems. It is impossible to overemphasize the importance of planning your application before you actually start to build it. The more planning you do, the more organized your effort will be; building the application will also be a faster process. Remember that there are three basic steps in designing a database application:

1. Gathering information

2. Working with the information

3. Outputting the information

Before you design the application, you should have some idea of its projected output, so that you can design the method and format of the output before you design the input. If you know what the final result should be, you will know which pieces to put together to achieve that result. The next sections detail the process of gathering and working with the information so that the most effective application can be designed to serve your users.

Gathering Information

Whether you are an employee of the company, a part of the organization's MIS department, or an outside consultant, you should approach building an application as if you were an outsider who knows nothing about the problem to be addressed by the application. The first step in this process is to listen.

Managers and users often have very different views about a new application. Managers tend to see a new application as a reporting tool that distills information into a summarized form on a timely basis. Users in the trenches are more interested in being able to access data on a different level. The manager may want to know the total number of accounts receivable and which accounts are severely delinquent. The accounts-receivable clerk, on the other hand, wants to access information on an account-by-account basis so that customer questions can be answered and decisions about credit limits can be made.

Many times your application is a user's first experience with computers. The user may be fearful and mistrusting of management's intentions. Some will think that management is less interested in improving the quality of work than in monitoring the worker. Others will be gung-ho, ready for a new experience.

It is your job to listen to all divergent viewpoints and strike a balance in the application, attempting to serve the needs of both groups.

Make it a point to talk to everyone in the organization whose job will be affected by the new application. Listen to their expectations and try to get a handle on their attitude toward the project. Many times you can reassure users who have negative attitudes by allaying their suspicions.

As you talk to each user, gather as much information as possible about how the job is currently being performed. Collect sample forms that can give you an idea of how the paperwork is being handled manually. Obviously a computerized application differs from a paper-oriented application, but there are many parallel concepts. In many ways the two differ only in terms of the way data is stored. Standard business forms (such as invoices, inventory reports, and ledgers) have become standard because they serve a real purpose. Your application will probably still produce these same types of documents. The purpose of computerization is to produce the information easier and faster, not replace the system entirely. The closer you can relate the application to the paper system it is replacing, the more secure and accepting users will feel about the necessary changes.

Working with the Information

In some ways a database management system is like a jigsaw puzzle. Like the puzzle, the application is made up of many small pieces that interlock and combine to create the whole. These pieces (objects) can include data files, data-entry screens, report and label formats, and menu structures. Each should be designed to complement the others. In later chapters you learn how to create program objects that complement the data structures used in your applications, but for now, concentrate on the file structures and their relationships: these form the foundation on which all else is built.

Documenting the Application

After you have talked with everyone who will use the application, sit down and sketch out how the application is to be be built. A contractor would never build an office park without a blueprint. You should never begin building an application without a blueprint of your own.

Draw out the design of the menu structure, define the tasks the application needs to accomplish, and then place these designs into a model of the menu structure. Use the current forms and reports as guides for designing entry screens and reports that will be both informative and easy to use.

If you plan well enough, you can actually write a rough draft of the user's manual. While this may seem like putting the cart before the horse, the technique can serve two important purposes. First, the draft can be used as a blueprint, outlining the appearance of the finished product. Second, the draft can be used as a specifications document. If the manual specifies that a feature is included in the application, it will be harder to forget to include it. If the documentation does not include a feature, it will be harder for users to claim that an agreed-upon feature has been left out. A specifications document also gives you "closure" on a project. If you are charging a flat fee for the software, the specifications document can show that you are finished so that you can collect your fee. Or, the specifications document can support an increase in your fee because of additions to the original specifications.

Planning for the Future

It is axiomatic that given a bit, users will want a kilobyte. Many times the persons in charge of getting the application built for the organization have little if any experience in specifying computer programs. How well they anticipate the application's uses will depend on their own level of computer literacy.

Many times they will ask, "Can you...", rather than say, "We need...". You must accept the responsibility for building enough overhead into the application to accommodate future expansion.

It is not unusual for users to come to you (even before the application is finished) asking the question, "If it does this so well, can you also make it do that?"

Try to anticipate these expansions. Ask yourself the hard questions. If the user decides that the data gathered in the application should tie in with accounting software, does the data structure contain all necessary information? Have you designed the inventory module so that it can be used as a basis for adding automated ordering at a later time? Does the customer information in the invoicing module have the capacity to also include information that the marketing staff will want?

Obviously it is impossible to anticipate all future directions the user might want to take. If, however, you try to anticipate the future, you will be better prepared to accommodate the almost certain requests for expansion of the system.

Building the Application

This book presents examples of program code that illustrate how applications are built. Most deal with solutions that are representative of retailing situations because most people are familiar with the underlying concepts involved in buying and selling. Building an application begins as a foundation. Some basic concepts separate good data structures from bad ones. The following sections show you how to build solid data structures that the application can stand on.

Planning Data Structures

The foundation of an application is its data structure. How reports are written, how entry screens appear, and the speed and efficiency of the overall application greatly depend on the way data is written to the disk.

dBASE IV can modify data structures easily (without the loss of data stored in them), but once you have built a significant portion of the application, changing structures usually means changing major objects that use the data. Extra work for you and delays for the project are often the result.

If, for example, you include in a data file a numeric field that is one or two digits too small, it is fairly simple to use the MODIFY STRUCTURE command to increase the field's capacity. No data is lost. Unfortunately, each time you alter a field, you also need to modify every place in the application (such as reports and entry screens) where the field is used in order to reflect these changes to the data structure.

Before beginning the actual design of data files, make sure that you have done your homework. If your application is meant to replace a paper system or to augment current manual systems, take time to learn the old way of doing things. Find out how each step of the process is performed, what information is gathered in each step of the process, and what information is passed on from one process to the next.

Your application will be more favorably received by users if it does not represent too radical a departure from the "way things have always been." You may not want to totally clone the manual system, but you can usually leave enough of the old landmarks in place so that users don't get the feeling that they must totally relearn their jobs.

When designing a new system, mentally picture how that process would be performed if it were a manual process already in place.

Creating Data Files

Figure 1.1 displays a data file that holds names and addresses for mailing. The screen also shows some of the most common mistakes you can make in designing a data structure. Notice that both fields one (`NAME`) and three (`CTSTZIP`) combine information that can be used more flexibly if separated out into other fields. In the case of field one, the data can be more easily used if the first name, middle initial, and last name are placed into separate fields. Similarly, the city, state, and ZIP should be placed in different fields to make sorting and extracting from the list an easier process.

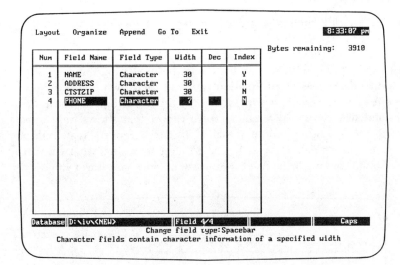

Fig. 1.1

An improperly designed mailing-list file.

If the first name, middle initial, and last name are all entered into a single field, it is difficult to index the database on the last name. If the name field is 30 characters long and contains the name John Q. Public, the value of the field is "John Q. Public   " because dBASE IV records are made up of fixed-length fields. When a character field is not filled completely, it is padded with spaces. To extract only the last name from such an arrangement, you can use the following statement:

```
? SUBSTR(TRIM(FIELD_NAME),AT(". ",FIELD_NAME)+2)
```

The method works but requires extra effort and development time. Success also depends on whether the data has been properly entered by the user, a condition never to be taken for granted. If the user forgets to type the period after the middle initial, or if the name in the field is something like "J. Worthington

Fullbright," an error will result. Compare all this trouble and grief with the simplicity of outputting just the last name when the fields are properly divided, as in the following statement:

```
? LAST_NAME
```

Likewise, it is difficult to put the data in figure 1.1 into ZIP-code order because the city, state, and ZIP code are all in the same field. Trying to create a report that includes only those customers that live in California, or only those customers who live in ZIP-code area 22079, requires extra data-manipulation.

This type of data structure also slows things down considerably because of the extra workload on the computer and the user.

Figure 1.2 shows a better method for dividing the name and geographic information. Because the name is now broken into first, last, and middle initial, and because city, state and ZIP are stored in separate fields, it is easier for the user to extract data when performing a complex query. By modifying the data structure so that individual pieces of information reside in their own fields, the user can, for example, print a report that includes only those customers whose first name is Tom and who reside in Michigan, or a report that shows only those persons named Jones whose middle initial is J. These reports may not be needed (or even contemplated) now, but it is safest to assume that the data structures you build today will be used tomorrow in ways you never intended.

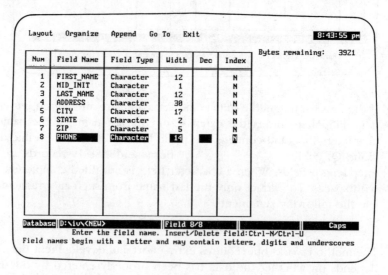

Fig. 1.2

A well-designed mailing-list file.

30 characters of disk space are used to store a name. You can more easily retrieve the name later if you store the name, whether it is in one field or four, as component parts. A good rule of thumb is that data stored in files should be

broken up into the smallest logical components possible. By storing the city, state, and ZIP code in three fields, you make it possible for the application to extract the data in more useful ways.

Designing Efficient Data Structures

Because dBASE IV (.DBF) data files have a fixed record-length structure, you should design data structures to avoid wasting disk space. A field width of 25 takes up 25 bytes of disk space whether the field is filled in or not. Design data structures that do not duplicate the same data over and over.

This is where there is a significant departure between the way information is stored in .DBF files and the way information is stored on paper records. A printed order form, for example, has space at the top so that the user can write in information such as the person who is making the order, the date the order is taken, the sales person, and payment terms. Below this area is a space in which the user can write in information about individual items being ordered. This information typically includes part numbers, quantity, item description, unit cost, and extended cost (such as quantity × unit cost). Other blanks on the form are available for such items as discounts, back orders, and shipping information. Only a limited number of lines, however, is available on the form to write in information about the individual items. If the customer orders more items than there are lines, you simply staple another form to the original and keep taking the order.

Storing the same information in database records is a different proposition. If you design the order-form data file as one big file with many groups of fields to simulate the item lines of its paper counterpart, you are also designing a number of inefficiencies into the data structure.

First, customer information is repeated each time an order is made by that customer. If the customer makes frequent orders, substantial disk space is wasted. In addition, if the customer's address or telephone number is changed, each order record must be edited to reflect the new information.

Second, the order form must be large enough to accommodate the ordering of a large number of items. If the customer orders only a few items, disk space is wasted. If the customer orders more items than the order record can hold, a second or third order record must be created, and customer information is repeated. Because the order is spread over two or more records, it is easy to miss this fact and fill only one order at a time. This can result in each order being filled separately, wasting time and shipping expenses.

Third, the design makes it much harder to search through the data and find out if Customer X ordered Item Y.

A better approach is to use the relational capabilities of dBASE IV and break ordering information into three files: one for customer information, one for order information, and one for information about individual items.

The customer database would include name and address information about each customer, as well as an individual account number which can be used to identify a particular customer only (see fig. 1.3).

Fig. 1.3

Basic customer information for a database.

```
Structure for database: D:\PDB\CUSTOMER.DBF
Number of data records:        0
Date of last update   : 01/26/89
```

Field	Field Name	Type	Width	Dec	Index
1	ACCT_NO	Character	5		Y
2	COMPANY	Character	30		N
3	ADDRESS	Character	30		N
4	CITY	Character	17		N
5	STATE	Character	2		N
6	ZIP	Character	5		Y
7	CREDIT_LIM	Numeric	8	2	N
** Total **			98		

The order database would include information such as the date of sale, payment terms, salesperson, and tax-exempt numbers. It would also include a field to hold the customer's account number and a unique order number that identifies the individual transaction (see fig. 1.4).

Fig. 1.4

The base data structure for the invoice.

```
Structure for database: D:\PDB\INVOICE.DBF
Number of data records:        0
Date of last update   : 01/26/89
```

Field	Field Name	Type	Width	Dec	Index
1	ACCT_NO	Character	5		Y
2	INVOICE_NO	Character	7		Y
3	PUR_DATE	Date	8		N
4	SAL_PER	Character	10		N
5	SHIP_NAME	Character	30		N
6	SHIP_ADDR	Character	30		N
7	SHIP_CITY	Character	17		N
8	SHIP_STATE	Character	2		N
9	SHIP_ZIP	Character	5		N
10	DATE_SHIPD	Date	8		N
** Total **			123		

A third database would be used to hold information, such as quantity, cost, and description, about each item ordered. The file would also contain a field holding the order transaction number so that each record in the database can be tied back to the proper order information in the second file (see fig. 1.5).

```
Structure for database: D:\PDB\INV_ITEM.DBF
Number of data records:        0
Date of last update   : 01/26/89
Field  Field Name  Type        Width   Dec   Index
    1  INV_NO      Character      7            N
    2  ITEM_NO     Character     10            N
    3  QTY         Numeric        3            N
    4  PRICE       Numeric        8     2      N
    5  B_ORDERED   Logical        1            N
** Total **                     30
```

The advantages to this configuration are many. The customer information needs to be entered into the system only once. Any changes need to be entered into only one record.

Because the items are stored in a separate file, no disk space is wasted. The single order record contains all information necessary to find the other information. Because it is indexed on the invoice number and contains the account number, the "driver" record can then be used to locate the rest of the information needed to print the invoice.

Each item record contains information about one specific purchase only, but because it is indexed on the invoice number, the application can read the invoice number from the invoice file and perform a SEEK to assemble all items in the order. The index can also be used later to research how many times an individual item has been ordered, and in what quantities. This information can be useful when deciding how many units of an item to place into inventory.

As a side benefit, the accuracy of data stored by the application is improved. Typing errors are less likely if you set up the ordering module so that the user enters a customer account number only (instead of the entire customer information). The application can then be designed to look into the customer database for items such as the name and address.

In the same way, you can increase accuracy in the application by having the module take the part number as an entry, looking up the pricing and description that are stored in a file containing information about all items in stock, and transferring that information into the order.

Lookups reduce typing, thus increasing speed and efficiency. You also minimize the chances of users entering incorrect prices or descriptions into the system.

Accessing data in the most efficient manner is an important feature of the application; the key to this efficient access is the index, which is covered in the next section.

Indexing dBASE IV Data Files

If you have been using dBASE IV (or dBASE III Plus) at the dot prompt, you are probably familiar with indexing. If you are like most new dBASE programmers, however, you probably have not given much thought to how indexing is used in applications.

You can use indexing to change the order in which records in a data file are presented based on a key expression. A *key expression* is the field or combination of fields on which the sort is produced. Like the sorting process, the records are put into a different order. Unlike sorting, however, the physical order in which the records are written to disk remains unchanged.

The dBASE IV SORT command is actually a throwback to an earlier time when the order of records had to be physically rearranged in order for the user to access the data in a certain manner.

Today, the dBASE IV INDEX command is preferred to the SORT command. dBASE IV provides two types of index files: the .NDX file and the .MDX file. The .NDX file, which is compatible with versions of dBASE III and III Plus, uses a file to store the information needed to order the data records in one fashion. Unless you must maintain compatibility with dBASE III and dBASE III Plus file structures, however, use the index arrangement provided with dBASE IV.

New with dBASE IV is the .MDX file—a multiple-index file capable of storing as many as 47 different index structures, which can be used to present data in different orders. Each of these separate index arrangements is known as a TAG. Conventions for naming TAGs are the same as those for naming fields in the data file. Each name can include up to 10 characters and can contain letters, numbers, and the underscore character. The TAG name, however, must begin with a letter.

Following is the syntax for the INDEX command:

```
INDEX ON <key expression> TO <.NDX filename>/TAG <tagname>;
  [OF <.MDX filename>] [UNIQUE] [DESCENDING]
```

dBASE IV files can be indexed on any valid dBASE expression. The key expression can be a single field or a combination of fields within the data structure. When you index on a combination of fields, all fields must be converted into a single type. Remember that a valid dBASE IV expression is any calculation whose result can be stored as a memory variable or in a field.

Creating .NDX Index Files

Index files with the .NDX extension are compatible with earlier versions of dBASE III. When you open a data file with the USE command, you can at the same time open as many as 10 (in dBASE III Plus, the limit is 7) .NDX files. In the following example, the customer data file is opened as well as four .NDX files, which provide the order of the records:

```
USE CUSTOMER INDEX CUST_ID, COMPANY, NAME, ZIP
```

Only the first index file in the list, called the *Master Index*, actually controls current ordering of the records. You open the other index files to make sure that they remain up-to-date whenever new records are added or deleted or when field values, which would change the key expression for the index, are edited. To create the CUST_ID index file, use the following commands:

```
USE CUSTOMER

INDEX ON CUST_ID TO CUST_ID
```

These commands tell dBASE IV to create a single .NDX file that puts in order the records of the field CUST_ID and names the index file CUST_ID.

Creating .MDX Index Files

When you use the CREATE or MODIFY STRUCTURE commands, the data structure is displayed in a table similar to that shown in figure 1.6. Notice that the far right-hand column has the header Index. Space is also provided for answering Y for yes and N for no. When you CREATE or MODIFY a data structure, if you enter a Y in any of the index fields, a production .MDX file is created automatically.

By default, a production .MDX file has the same name as its corresponding data file. The existence of the .MDX production index file is noted in the header of the data file. When the data file is opened, the production .MDX index file is automatically opened at the same time. An .MDX file can have as many as 47 index TAGs.

You will seldom approach this limit, however, because too many active index TAGs affect the execution speed of dBASE IV applications. Any field in the data file (except memo fields) in which a Y has been entered in the index column creates an individual TAG to be included in the .MDX index file. To add a TAG to the production .MDX file at a later time, use the following commands:

```
USE CUSTOMER

INDEX ON CITY TAG CIT
```

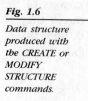

Fig. 1.6

*Data structure
produced with
the CREATE or
MODIFY
STRUCTURE
commands.*

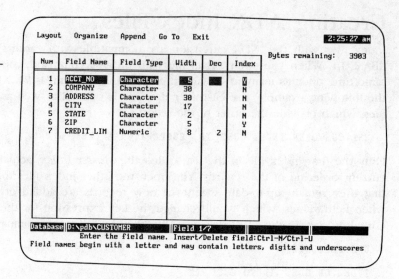

You can simply erase .NDX index files from the disk when no longer needed, but you must use the DELETE TAG command to remove unwanted TAGs from the .MDX file.

Indexing on Multiple-Field Expressions

Many times you want to create index files (.NDX) or TAGs in which the key expression is made up of more than one field from the data file. For example, an alphabetical listing of customers can be indexed by last name, and within the last name groupings, by first name. Bill Jones then appears in the order before Frank Jones. The following commands index in this fashion:

```
INDEX ON LAST_NAM+FIRST_NAM TAG FULL_NAM   && Creates a TAG

INDEX ON LAST_NAM+FIRST_NAM TO FULL_NAM    && Creates an .NDX file
```

When you use multiple fields to form a key expression, all fields must be converted into the same data type. For example, to list customers in order of how long they have been customers, you use the DTOS() function to change the date to a string. If you include the last name in the key expression, those customers who became customers on the same date would be listed alphabetically within that date group. Notice the string in the following example:

```
INDEX ON DTOS(BEG_DAT)+LAST_NAM TAG LEN
```

The DTOS() function is necessary to properly order date fields. If you use the DTOC() function, the date 12/10/89 appears after the date 12/01/90. Sorting on a character field starts evaluation with the leftmost character. 12/10 is therefore placed after 12/01 regardless of the year because the year is farther to the right.

The DTOC() function is useful for such operations as inserting a character date into a string for display purposes. The DTOS() function is more useful than DTOC() for sorting because it places the year first (leftmost). The DTOS() function converts the date field to a yyyy/mm/dd format, thus sorting/indexing the date fields appropriately. Even though dates are displayed as mm/dd/yy, the century is stored (you can SET CENTURY ON to have it displayed). It can then be used with the DTOS() function.

dBASE expressions used as index keys are limited to 220 characters. The calculated result of the expression is limited to 100 characters.

Describing the Index Structure

Logically the records in a data file are divided into points in the file called *nodes*.

Nodes can be thought of as being arranged in a pyramidal fashion (see fig. 1.7). The capstone or top of the pyramid is the node that corresponds to the record at the midpoint of the data file. Each of the other nodes descend from this midpoint and correspond to a record in the data file. In other words, each node acts as a pointer, showing where the record can be found in the data file.

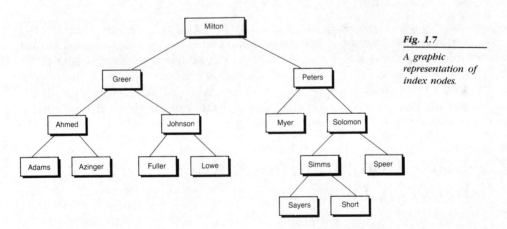

Fig. 1.7

A graphic representation of index nodes.

If you index a data file of customers based on the last name, the record representing the median value of all values in the last-name field becomes the first node or capstone of the pyramid (see "Milton" in fig. 1.7). Half the records in the index have a value less than the primary node, and half the records have a value greater.

When the FIND or SEEK command is issued, dBASE IV first positions an index pointer at the primary node to determine if the FIND or SEEK expression is greater or less than the value of the field. If the expression is less than the value of the primary node, the bottom half of the data file can be ignored. If the expression is greater than the value of the primary node, the record will be in the bottom half of the file. Each evaluation moves the index pointer one step closer to the target record.

The next node to be evaluated would be the quarter point of the values in the first half of the data file. The index pointer moves to this node, determines whether or not the SEEK (FIND) expression is greater or less than the value of that node, and then moves in that direction. This process continues until the proper record is found or it is determined that no node in the index contains the search expression.

As you can see, the very first positioning of the index pointer eliminates the search through half of the database. The second positioning eliminates another quarter of the total number of records in the data file. Each subsequent positioning of the index pointer eliminates from the search half of the remaining records. After evaluating only three records, 7/8ths of the total number of records in the data file have been eliminated as a possible match of the search expression. This rapid search of the data file makes it possible to position the record pointer on the desired record in very short order. Compare this to the LOCATE command, which sequentially evaluates each record in the data file to see if its value matches the LOCATE expression.

For example, if you issue the command SEEK "Fuller", "Milton" becomes the first record to be evaluated. Because Fuller comes before Milton in alphabetical order, all records that come after Milton can be ignored. Greer is next to be evaluated. Since Fuller comes before Greer, all the records left in the search with a value greater than Greer can be ignored. With each evaluation, half the records that remain can be eliminated. In this case, the record for Fuller is found after only four evaluations.

Using Common Index Keys between Files

In the invoice example presented previously, customer and invoice databases share a field that contains the customer's account number. Additionally, the invoice and items databases share a field that links them by the order number. You can use those fields and indexes to link data files together.

These fields forge the relationships between the files, making it possible to assemble information from all three files in order to print an invoice.

Be mindful of these relationships as you design data structures. This capability to link files together gives dBASE IV applications the flexibility and the power to create output that can be tailored to any need.

Four basic relationships can exist between two data files. These relationships are covered in the next sections.

One-To-One Relationships

The one-to-one relationship seems simple, but it is relatively rare. If, by design, for every record in file A there is a matching and corresponding record in file B, the two files are said to have a one-to-one relationship.

In practice, there are few reasons for creating a one-to-one relationship. In most cases, it is better if these two data structures are combined into one data file. Then, when you position the record pointer, you do not need to select the other data file and position the record pointer there as well.

At times, one-to-one relationships are unavoidable—for example, when the number of fields that must be maintained exceeds the limit of 255, or when the number of bytes of storage needed for the record exceeds the limit of 4,000. This is a rare occurrence because data structures of that size tend to be poorly designed. However, once in a blue moon, it is necessary to split the information between two data files.

One-To-Many Relationships

The one-to-many relationship is the most common relationship found in dBASE IV data structures. The relationship between the order file and the items file in the invoice example is a one-to-many relationship. For each order, several records in the item file may be linked to the order file.

Another example of a one-to-many relationship is the relationship between the customer database and the invoice database. Only one customer can have a particular account number, but it is likely that the customer will have multiple invoices in the invoice database.

Many-To-One Relationships

As an example of a many-to-one relationship, imagine a file that contains the proper two-letter abbreviations of each of the fifty states. The file is used as a lookup in data validation. As the user enters addresses into a data file, a second data file is used as a lookup table to ensure that the user has entered an approved abbreviation. Many customers from Minnesota may be on file, yet in the lookup file, the abbreviation for Minnesota is found only once.

Random Relationships

Random relationships fortunately are fairly rare. In programming, random relationships are the hardest of the four types to deal with because of the number of different possibilities in which the data may appear or be used. Another term for the random relationship is many-to-many.

Random relationships most often occur in statistical analysis and scientific fact finding. One example is a database application in which patients with various diseases are matched against another database of the various drugs and combinations of drugs used to treat these diseases. The application tries to find a statistical pattern of success rates between the two. In business applications, these types of relationships are relatively rare.

Building Menus and the User Interface

dBASE IV applications are intended to be menu-driven. Users access data through the application's menu structure, which presents various options and tasks to be performed. The user interface you build will help shield users from having to deal with the actual operations of dBASE IV. Remember that one of your goals in creating an application is to keep users from having to learn dBASE IV commands.

The menu structure is therefore an essential part of an application. The menu becomes the user's first impression of your work and reflects the quality of the application.

To be effective, the menu structure must be consistent, well-organized, and intuitive. Each level of the menu structure should be the same type (light-bar vs. typed choices); operate in the same manner; and accept user input in the same way, preferably in the same screen locations.

This consistent user interface is a real plus; once users learn how the menus work and where things are placed, they don't need to think about the interface and instead can concentrate on the underlying concepts of the program. This feature was one reason for the immediate success of Lotus Development's 1-2-3 program. Once you learn how to use the menus in one section of the Lotus program, you can teach yourself to use other sections. The menus are laid out so consistently that the user's intuitive guesses about unfamiliar territory are nearly always correct.

Planning Menus

When you design a database management application, outline the individual tasks to be performed by the application (such as adding records, editing records, and printing reports). You can then design the menu structure so that these tasks are offered to the user logically. That is, all data-entry tasks for a particular data file are grouped under one menu choice; all reports that can be printed are grouped under another; housekeeping functions are presented together; and in general, similar functions and tasks can be found in the same place in the menu structure. And of course, all menus work the same way.

In Chapter 7, you learn how to put together the commands in order to build a consistent menu system. The following sections, however, present an overview of the planning required for effective menu design.

Determining User Needs

The average user performing a database management task has very specific ideas about what makes a good program versus a bad program.

First and foremost, most computer users want to avoid having to become computer literate. "Just tell me how to get to the menu, and keep me away from all that other stuff," they will say. The incredible success of the Apple Macintosh computer system is based largely on the fact that users do not need to learn commands. Macintosh users can point at a choice with a mouse or other pointing device and then push a button. The success of the Macintosh interface has had a ripple effect throughout the computer industry, even touching dBASE IV.

Even though dBASE IV has no mouse support, its menu structure is loosely based on the Mac's menu interface. As you use the dBASE IV Editor, the Control Center, or any other work surfaces that use menus, you see a consistent user interface that is both easy to learn and powerful. As a programmer, take the time to study these menus so that you can create interfaces that work as well.

Your users will probably be no different from the norm. They do not want to learn dBASE IV fundamentals. They could care less about the structure of the database. They are only interested in entering and editing their data, and printing out a report that gives them the answer they are looking for.

Designing the User Interface

Three main elements go into a good user interface; the menu structure, the entry screens (including prompting for responses), and error trapping. These features are covered in the next sections.

Menu Structures

Three major menu types are available to you as a programmer: text-style menus (the user selects an action by pressing a specific key), horizontal-bar menus, and vertical pop-up menus.

Creating light-bar menus is quick and easy in dBASE IV. In previous dBASE versions, the programmer needed to paint the choices available to the user along with a prompt that indicated which keystroke activated which choice. Occasionally you will find it necessary to use the older style of interface when the system you are writing for does not support inverse video. Fortunately these machines are dying out quickly, and you may never encounter one.

An easier method is to use the BAR and POPUP menus introduced with dBASE IV. Both types of menus provide painted, on-screen prompts that the user can highlight by using the arrow keys. If the user presses Enter while a choice is highlighted, the task attached to that menu item is run. When the item has been run, the menu again takes over, offering the user the chance to continue. You have been using examples of these throughout dBASE IV. For example, when you create a report with the `CREATE REPORT` command, the menu at the top of the screen is a BAR menu. The dialog boxes that appear when you highlight a choice on the BAR menu are POPUPs.

The only real difference between BAR and POPUP menus is their orientation. The prompts on BAR menus are usually on one line of the screen, and choices are highlighted with the left/right arrow keys. Prompts on POPUPs are stacked vertically, and choices are highlighted with the up/down arrow keys.

By placing a BAR menu across the top of the screen and positioning POPUPs under each BAR prompt that appears when the corresponding BAR prompt is chosen, you can simulate the Macintosh-style menus used in dBASE IV.

More important than the mechanics of the menus, however, is the grouping of individual tasks attached to the menus. Are the menus placed where they will have the most impact? Are the tasks attached to them logically grouped? Ask yourself these questions before you begin building the menus for your application.

See Chapter 7 for more detailed information about building menus.

Data-Entry Screens

The design of data-entry screens is crucial to the success of the user interface. Even though entry may be accepted in two or more databases, all entry screens should look like they belong together; in fact, they do.

There are two ways to create entry screens: with the `CREATE SCREEN` command or by hand-coding the commands to accept user entry.

If a large number of items is to be entered, it is better to include a two-page entry screen than to cram it all onto the computer screen at once. Simple, uncomplicated screens are much easier to work with. Whenever possible, leave a blank line between entry areas. This feature reduces eyestrain and fatigue, making it possible for the user to work longer and more efficiently.

Figure 1.8 shows the standard dBASE IV data-entry screen for the file CUSTOMER.DBF. The screen appears when the file is first opened and you issue either the APPEND or EDIT commands without an entry screen. Note that the user is prompted to fill in the entry area with the actual field name, the entry boxes are single-spaced, and everything is jammed up into the top-left corner of the screen.

Fig. 1.8

The standard dBASE IV entry screen for the CUSTOMER.DBF file.

The screen in figure 1.9, on the other hand, has been crafted with the CREATE SCREEN command to sit just above the center of the screen. The screen is symmetrical and has descriptive prompts that tell the user what to enter in each area. Screens built with the CREATE SCREEN command are activated with the SET FORMAT command.

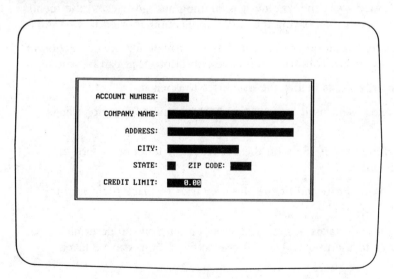

Fig. 1.9

The CUSTOMER.DBF file controlled by a .FMT (FORMAT) file.

Put yourself "in your users' shoes" when designing applications. If you enter information four or five hours a day, which screen would you rather have? The answer is obvious.

Screen design affects staying power. Are users able to work for long stretches without undue fatigue and eyestrain? Screen design also affects data integrity. Tired users make more typing errors, thus introducing more errors into the data to be stored. Remember that a single item of data may be used frequently; if this item is in error, all its uses are in error also.

Error Trapping

As a programmer, part of your job is to foresee where things can go wrong and trap these possibilities before they trigger an error message from dBASE IV. You can insulate the user from dBASE IV by making sure that your application anticipates what can go wrong and does something before the user reaches the dBASE IV error-handling routines.

For example, make sure that whenever your application performs a SEEK or FIND, the EOF() condition is also tested. The EOF() function returns a value of true (.T.) whenever the record pointer falls below the last record in the data file. In dBASE IV, the record pointer can be positioned at the end of the file without triggering an internal error. The error condition is not triggered until some sort of manipulation is attempted on the non-existent record.

If your application tests to ensure that the record pointer is positioned on a valid record before performing some action (for example, data entry with the @...SAY...GET command), you can determine how the situation is handled. The application may abort the routine it is running and go back to the menu. But this is much better than having the entire application aborted by dBASE IV.

You have available several other opportunities to provide for the correction of errors before they occur. Following are some conditions that can be tested:

❑ That a data file exists before the user tries to open it

❑ That the expression used in a SEEK or FIND command will not trigger an error

❑ That the printer is on-line with the ISPRINTER() function before the user sends output

❑ That data types are tested before the user tries to place them into the data file

You can catch these mistakes before they are acted on. You can determine what message is shown to the user and which corrective actions can be taken.

The ON ERROR Command

Another feature available with dBASE IV, the ON ERROR command, enables you to intercept unforeseen error conditions and control the reaction to these errors.

Usually the procedure involves calling a special program that you have written which is designed to keep dBASE IV from closing down your application. For example, in the program code, just before your application opens a data file, you can place the following command:

```
ON ERROR DO NO_OPEN
```

Attached to the application is a program file, NO_OPEN, which has two functions: tell the user what went wrong; then shut down the module that caused the error and take the user back to the menu.

Once the danger of a file-opening error has passed, you cancel the error-handling routine with the following command:

```
ON ERROR
```

The ON ERROR command given without an argument cancels the last ON ERROR statement given. You can also activate an alternate error-trapping program by issuing the ON ERROR command with a different argument. The new ON ERROR command replaces the active ON ERROR condition with another routine more suited to the current activities of the application.

Summary

In this chapter you saw the responsibilities involved in creating data management applications that will be used by others. Your job as a programmer is to take a complex task and make it simple for even the least computer-literate user to manage. It is a big responsibility, but fortunately the tools available with dBASE IV make things much simpler as well.

Applications must be well planned and data structures should be designed with non-obsolescence in mind. The application should also shield users from the intricacies of dBASE IV.

Indexing your data files properly provides the basic relationships between them and makes finding data a much quicker process. Anything you can include as part of your application's user interface that makes the application simpler and easier to use will not only be appreciated by the user but will also make your application more readily accepted by even the staunchest anti-computer personnel using the application.

You learned to arrange menus logically, grouping related tasks together and designing entry screens so that the information to be typed is clearly labeled and arranged to reduce eyestrain. You also learned to provide for errors and error-handling before errors occur.

The next chapter focuses on the capability of dBASE IV to record and play back macros.

2

Working with dBASE IV Macros

A macro, the simplest form of a dBASE IV program, resembles a DOS batch file. dBASE IV's macro capability allows you to transfer to disk for permanent storage those routines you perform on a regular basis. This method is called *recording* a macro.

Even though macros are extremely limited in creating applications, they are presented in this chapter for a more complete understanding of dBASE IV's features. You will find macros occasionally useful as a way of simulating the ability to stuff keystrokes into the typeahead buffer. You may also want to record some macros that will automate a few simple tasks for your users while you get their application ready.

In this chapter, you learn to record, store, edit, and play back macros. Macros enable you to automate many simple tasks, as well as support end users who are experimenting with macros on their own.

Understanding dBASE IV Macros

Within dBASE IV or any other computer language, a *program* can be defined as a recorded set of instructions that cause a computer system to perform a specific task or set of tasks. Implied are the properties of repeatability and predictability; whenever you call up the program, you can be certain in advance of the program's actions.

Most programs act exactly the same way every time they are invoked; the only variations are those caused by choices made by the user. A small percentage of programs, however (examples include kaleidoscopes or computer games that simulate card games), include planned randomness as part of their operation. Theoretically, this planned, random activity causes the program never to run exactly the same way twice. The underlying principle, however, is that the *actions* are planned. Therefore, a computer program can also be defined as a repeatable set of instructions.

In many ways, a macro can be compared to a tape recording of keystrokes. You record the keystrokes needed to perform a job and then save them so that they can be played back repeatedly.

The problem with macros is that they are absolutely literal. For macros recorded at the Control Center, the highlight bar must always be in exactly the same place when the macro is played back; otherwise, errors can occur. The macro can be built to leave the Control Center, go to the dot prompt, and then return to the Control Center with the highlight bar in the correct place, but this procedure is time-consuming.

If you support dBASE IV users as well as develop applications, you should be familiar with dBASE IV's macro capabilities. Teaching beginning and intermediate users to automate data management tasks with macros eliminates your need to write programs to handle the simplest tasks. You can then concentrate on more pressing problems.

On occasion, a macro fits a certain situation quite nicely, and you may find macros helpful in your own day-to-day activities even if you don't find overwhelming reasons to include macros in all your applications. Macros do not eliminate the need to create applications, but they can be useful as short-term substitutes for data management tasks that are not complex.

Writing dBASE IV Macros

Macros are extremely simple to create and use. You tell dBASE IV to begin recording a macro and then perform the steps you want repeated. After you have completed the steps of the task that needs to be repeated on a recurring basis, you tell dBASE IV to stop recording. For example, a task sequence might include opening a data file, specifying a screen format, and issuing the APPEND command. You then save the recorded instructions to a *macro library*, a disk file that stores macros. A macro library saved to disk can be restored from the disk into memory at any time; any macro (the library can contain a maximum of 35) in the macro library can be run.

Recording Macros

A macro can be recorded almost anywhere in dBASE IV: at the Control Center and outside the Control Center. You can even record a macro while a program is running. In fact, some of your more advanced users may record macros to automate repetitive tasks rather than use applications.

Recording a Macro at the Control Center

The most complete macro control is available at the Control Center. To access the **Macros** menu at the Control Center, press F10 to highlight **Tools**, or press Alt-T to display the **Tools** dialog box. Pressing M or highlighting **Macros** and pressing Enter takes you to the **Macros** menu (see fig. 2.1). To begin recording a macro, place the highlight bar on **Begin Recording** and press Enter; alternately, press B.

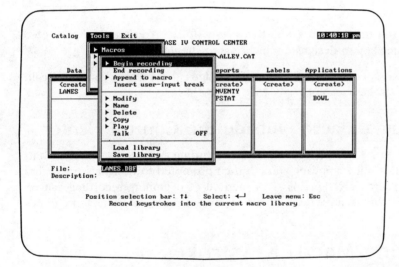

Fig. 2.1

Recording a macro at the Control Center.

Next, dBASE IV wants to know which keystroke combination is to invoke the macro.

Remember that macros are stored in macro libraries; each library can hold a maximum of 35 macros. As many as nine macros in each library can be attached to a function key that is used in combination with the Alt key. To invoke these macros any time, hold down the Alt key and press the corresponding function key. Figure 2.2 shows a macro library containing three macros. One macro is attached to the F8 key. To run this macro, the user holds down the Alt key and presses F8. You can also attach one macro to each letter of the

Fig. 2.2

Choosing a key that begins the macro playback.

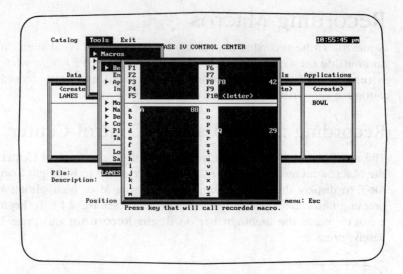

alphabet. To run these macros, you first press Alt-F10. You are then prompted to press a letter key to designate which macro should be executed.

After you have specified the key that designates this macro, you can begin recording keystrokes.

Recording a Macro Outside the Control Center

Outside the Control Center, you can begin recording a macro by pressing Shift-F10. A POPUP window appears; you are then prompted to designate a key that triggers the macro (see fig. 2.3). This method of beginning recording can be invoked from almost anywhere in dBASE IV, including during a program's operation.

Recording Macro Keystrokes

Once you have assigned a key to the macro, you are free to begin the straightforward process of recording the macro. You simply enter the keystrokes and/or commands you want executed; dBASE IV stores the keystrokes in memory. When you later run the macro, dBASE IV duplicates them exactly. By simply executing the normal tasks of a dBASE IV session, you are creating a "program" that can be run repeatedly.

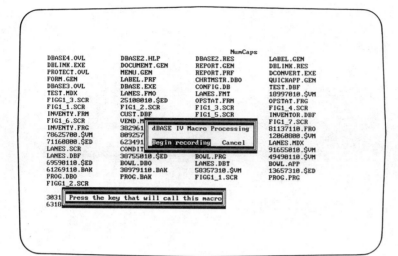

Fig. 2.3

Recording a macro outside the Control Center.

Pausing for User Input

For two or more sets of similar tasks, you can record the macro so that it can be used for either task. For example, if you have more than one database with exactly the same structure, you can use one report form to output the data from any of those data files. By pressing Shift-F10 while recording a macro, you can include the code to suspend the macro; you or another user can then enter variable information. When you press Shift-F10, the macro picks back up and continues execution.

Figure 2.4 shows the POPUP window that enables you to insert a user-input break. Three choices are available from the POPUP menu: **End recording**, **Insert user-input break**, and **Continue recording**.

If you choose **Insert user-input break**, all keystrokes up to the user-input break will be played when the macro executes. At that point, the macro will be suspended and the user will be prompted to resume macro execution by pressing Shift-F10.

Ending a Macro Recording

When you reach the point where the macro should end, press Shift-F10. The POPUP window shown in figure 2.4 appears; you can end the recording by choosing **End recording** from the menu. If you pressed Shift-F10 in error, not meaning to end the recording or to insert a user-input break, you can also choose **Continue recording**.

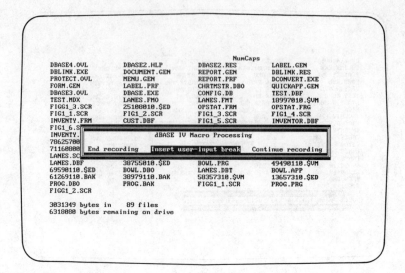

Fig. 2.4

Placing a user-input break into a macro.

Troubleshooting Macro Recording

During the recording process, all the keystrokes you executed are saved, except for those keystrokes that are part of the macro-definition process. For example, when you press Shift-F10, the keystrokes that tell the macro to stop recording are not recorded as part of the macro. All other keystrokes, however, are recorded. This can present a problem when creating macros that deal with menus and lists of files. There are a few pitfalls here that must be avoided.

When recording a macro at the Control Center, take special care placing the highlight bar. For example, if you begin recording a macro at the Control Center with the highlight bar positioned on <**create**> in the **Data** column, you can safely assume that pressing the right-arrow key three times to move the highlight bar to the **Reports** column will work correctly. However, there is no guarantee that pressing the down-arrow key three times will always select the same report.

If a newly created report falls into the alphabetical sort at or near the top of the column, the macro will become outdated; it will still choose the third report in the list, regardless of that report's name. When choosing a file name in any column in the Control Center, type the name of the intended file while the highlight bar is somewhere in that column. By being exact and typing the full file name, you can be sure that the macro will always choose the same file.

For example, assume that you have four label files—LB1, LB2, LBD1, and LBD2—shown in the **Labels** column of the Control Center. Place the highlight bar anywhere in the column. When you type L to begin specifying a file name, the highlight bar jumps to the first entry starting with the letter L. When you type B, the highlight bar does not move because all four entries have B as the second character. If you next type 2, the highlight bar jumps to the file LB2. If, on the other hand, you type D, the highlight bar jumps to LBD1. As you type the file name, the highlight bar homes in on the proper entry. By typing all the letters in the file name, you assure yourself of activating the proper file in the Control Center.

Use this technique also whenever you deal with a list or menu that includes a variable number of choices. Many menu items on the Control Center menu are conditional; you can move the highlight bar to these choices only under certain conditions. If one prompt on the menu is accessible unexpectedly (due to some underlying environmental change), using the arrow keys to select a menu item when recording a macro can cause the wrong prompt to be selected when the macro runs. For this reason, it is better to use the shorthand method of choosing menu items (each prompt in a window has a different character as its first letter) at the Control Center by pressing the first letter of the desired menu prompt. For example, you choose **Settings** in the **Tools** menu at the Control Center by pressing Alt-T-S.

Editing a Macro Recording

Sometimes, a change in a file name or a modification to the macro's task can cause the macro to fail to perform correctly. In this case, you have two choices. You can re-record the macro or you can edit the macro itself.

If you re-record by using a key already attached to a macro, dBASE IV will pop up a window requiring you to confirm that the old version will be overwritten.

To edit the macro itself, access the **Tools** menu at the Control Center and choose **Macros**. Select the **Modify** option from the **Macros** menu.

dBASE IV stores macros as character strings. Keystrokes such as the up-arrow key are recorded as key words surrounded in braces ({}). Because they are stored as character strings, you edit macros by using either the text editor supplied with dBASE IV or another editor you specified in your CONFIG.DB file.

The **Modify** option of the **Macros** menu displays a POPUP window that displays the keystrokes used to access each macro and the number of bytes (characters) contained in each macro (see fig. 2.5). This feature helps you keep track of the size of your macros. The number on the right-hand side of the column displays the number of bytes in each macro. In the library displayed in figure 2.5, 42 bytes are assigned to the F8 keystroke, and 29 bytes are assigned to the letter Q.

Fig. 2.5

Choosing a macro to edit.

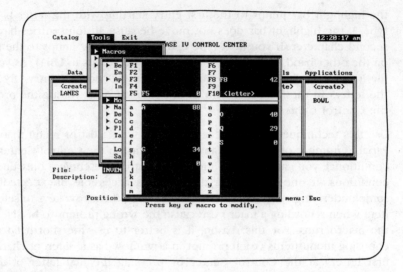

Once you have chosen a macro to edit, dBASE IV invokes your text editor and you can edit the macro.

Figure 2.6 displays most of the dBASE IV macro key words. These keywords represent cursor movement and function-key keystrokes. You use the key words to tell dBASE IV about special keystrokes during macro execution. For example, every time you press the up-arrow key while recording a macro, the up-arrow key word (shown on the left of line 1 in figure 2.6) is inserted into the macro character string. Most macro key words are self-explanatory. They are simply the name of the key surrounded by braces.

Fig. 2.6

A list of macro key words.

```
{uparrow}{downarrow}{rightarrow}{leftarrow}{PgUp}{PgDn}{Home}{End}{Ins}{Del}    <
{Enter}                                                                          <
{F1}{F2}{F2}{F3}{F4}{F4}{F5}{F6}{F7}{F8}{F9}{F10}{Tab}{Shift-Tab}{Alt-F1}        <
{Alt-F2}{Alt-F3}{Alt-F4}{Alt-F5}{Alt-F6}{Alt-F7}{Alt-F8}{Alt-F9}{Alt-F10}       <
{Ctrl-F1}{Ctrl-F2}{Ctrl-F3}{Ctrl-F4}{Ctrl-F5}{Ctrl-F6}{Ctrl-F7}{Ctrl-F8}        <
{Ctrl-F9}{Ctrl-F10}{Shift-F1}{Shift-F2}{Shift-F3}{Shift-F4}{Shift-F5}{Shift-F6}<
{Shift-F7}{Shift-F8}{Shift-F9}{InpBreak}{{}}^@^@^@^@^@^@^@^@^@^@^@^@^@^@^@^@^@^@^*
```

The final line of figure 2.6 illustrates several conventions to be used when editing macros. The key word to the right of {Shift-F9} is the macro key word that signifies an input break, which pauses the macro for user input. Notice the two left curly braces and two right curly braces immediately to the right of the macro key word {InpBreak}. The set of braces is used as a delimiter to tell dBASE IV that a special keystroke is about to occur. Whenever you need to include a curly brace as a literal keystroke, place two curly braces into the macro string. This tells dBASE IV that the upcoming is a character keystroke and that the brace is a literal entry—not the beginning of macro key word.

Once you make the necessary changes to your macro string and save them with the appropriate commands, the macro is again ready for use in its modified form. Be sure, however, to save the macro library to disk to make the changes permanent. Saving with the text editor only will not save the macro to disk. The next section discusses the procedures for saving the macros in macro libraries.

Saving Macros in Macro Libraries

A macro library is a disk file that contains the macro strings of up to 35 macros. To save macros to disk, you can choose **Menu** from the **Macros** menu at the Control Center. You can also save a macro library to disk by using the following command at the dot prompt:

SAVE MACROS TO ⟨*filename*⟩

This command writes to disk a file with the extension .KEY. The library file will contain any currently defined macros already in memory. To read or load a macro file into memory, move the highlight bar to **Load Library** in the **Macros** menu at the Control Center or use the following command at the dot prompt:

RESTORE MACROS FROM ⟨*filename*⟩

Remember that if you RESTORE MACROS from the disk into memory without saving the macros currently in memory, the macros in memory will be lost. At times, however, you want to create a quick macro for a single use. If you do not save that macro to disk as part of a library, it will be released when you restore a library from disk or exit dBASE IV.

Adding to Macro Recordings

Unfortunately, you must be in the **Macros** menu at the Control Center to tell dBASE IV to add new material to the end of a previously recorded macro. You may have trouble if the macro was originally recorded at a location other than the Control Center, such as at the dot prompt. The keystrokes needed to leave the Control Center and go to the dot prompt are also appended to the macro.

There are two ways to work around this problem, however. If you only need to get back to the dot prompt and then begin recording keystrokes to be added to the macro, you can simply perform the keystrokes necessary to return to the dot prompt, and then record the macro as usual. Once you finish, edit that macro and remove the unneeded key strokes.

The second method is a bit more complex. First, you need to edit the macro you want to add to the original. While that macro string is in the editor, mark it as a block and save it to disk as a text file. Then abandon the edit and edit the first macro. Position the cursor at the bottom of the macro string (but before the ^@ symbols if they appear in your text editor) and read into that macro string the text file you created during the previous edit.

Deleting and Copying Macros

From the **Macros** menu, you can choose to **Delete** or **Copy** previously recorded macros (see fig. 2.7). There is no shortcut method for performing either of these actions; the process must be performed at the Control Center. To delete a macro that is no longer needed, choose **Delete** and press Enter. You are asked to press the keystroke attached to the macro you want to delete. When you press the appropriate letter, the macro is deleted.

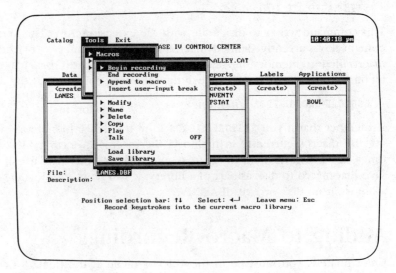

Fig. 2.7

The Macros menu at the Control Center.

At times, you may want to change a macro slightly without losing the original. In these cases, it is a simple matter to copy an existing macro and attach the copy to a different key. You can then edit the copy without modifying the original. Figure 2.8 shows a sample screen that prompts you to identify the macro to copy.

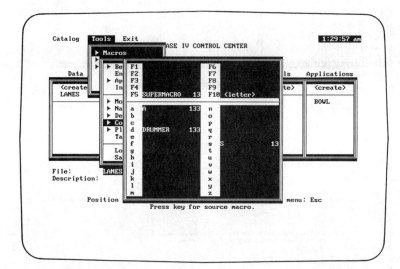

Fig. 2.8

Choosing a macro to copy.

Recording a Sample Macro

This section illustrates the mechanics of a sample macro recording.

Figure 2.9 shows the Control Center screen as it appears before a macro is invoked. Three data files are listed. LANES.DBF is a small data file that tracks the condition of the automatic pinsetting machinery for the Shur-Strike Family Bowling Center. Three possible reports that detail some aspect of the information can be run.

The macro's task is to open LANES.DBF, present the user with a list of reports from which to choose, print the report, close the file, and return control to the keyboard.

NOTE: In order for the macro to operate properly, the highlight bar must be positioned in the **Data** column, and no files can be open.

Figure 2.10 shows the contents of the macro's character string as it is seen during the **Modify** process. To re-create this macro, create a data file named LANES and some report formats to play with. Begin recording a macro and press the keystrokes listed in figure 2.10 exactly as they appear.

Fig. 2.9

The Control Center at the beginning of macro recording.

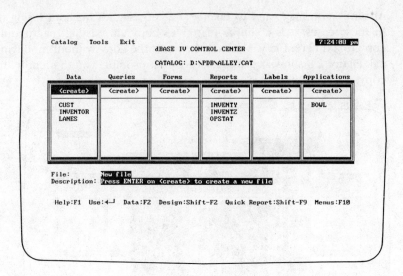

Fig. 2.10

The keystrokes of the macro.

```
lanes{Enter}
u{rightarrow}{rightarrow}{rightarrow}{InpBreak}{Enter}
pb{leftarrow}{leftarrow}{leftarrow}lanes{Enter}
c^0^0^0^0^0^0^0^0
```

Take a moment to go over the keystrokes documented in figure 2.10.

First, the name of the data file (lanes) is entered letter for letter. (Remember, the highlight bar needs to be in the **Data** column when the macro is invoked.) The lanes entry positions the highlight bar on the proper data file. The {Enter} key word confirms the selection of lanes.

The first entry on the next line (the letter u) is the response to the POPUP window that offers the user the opportunity to USE the data file. Once this keystroke is registered, the next three keystrokes (the right-arrow key three times) move the highlight bar to the **Reports** column.

A user-input break is then inserted. While the macro is suspended, the user can either type the name of the desired report or press the up/down-arrow keys to highlight the proper report. The user next presses the highlight bar and then Shift-F10. The macro resumes and issues {Enter} to confirm the report choice.

The keystrokes p and b are responses to POPUPs that appear during the printing phase of the macro's execution. These keystrokes signal dBASE IV to **Print the report** and to **Begin printing**.

After the printing is completed, the macro issues three left-arrow keystrokes, moving the highlight bar back to the **Data** column.

The macro then closes the lanes data file by typing the name explicitly and issuing an {Enter}. The c is a response to the POPUP that allows you to choose to close the file.

Once these actions have been completed, the macro terminates.

Summary

In this chapter, the process of creating dBASE IV macros was introduced. You learned how to record, edit, play, delete, and copy macros, as well as how to store them in libraries.

Aspects of troubleshooting macros were covered, and a sample macro recording was presented.

Spend some time trying out the information in this chapter. Don't spend too much time with macros, however. Ultimately, you will find their value transitory.

Macros are presented in this book so that you can use the information to respond to users' requests for immediate results. You can build a few macros that can automate some of their work, giving you time to get up to speed on programming techniques.

In the next chapter, you learn to use the dBASE IV Applications Generator.

3

Using the dBASE IV Applications Generator

The dBASE IV Applications Generator is a powerful and flexible tool that can put the power of dBASE programming into the hands of nearly every level of dBASE user, including new and intermediate users of dBASE IV, and beginning through experienced dBASE IV programmers.

New users of dBASE IV can use the Applications Generator to generate simple menu-driven applications quickly and easily without knowing any programming commands.

Intermediate users and beginning programmers can use the Applications Generator to assemble complete applications from a menu-driven environment. New programmers can use the Applications Generator to produce quick results while learning the ins and outs of dBASE IV programming. The Applications Generator can also be used to create code for menus which can then be used in programs.

The experienced dBASE IV programmer can control the Applications Generator with the dBASE IV Template Language (supplied with the Developer's Edition of dBASE IV). The programmer can then automate production of standardized modules that supplement programs written from scratch. The dBASE IV *Template Language*, a programming language, is a set of commands recognized by the Applications Generator as instructions for creating an application. The Template Language in effect tells the program (the Applications Generator) how to write programs. Experienced programmers can find more information on the dBASE IV Template Language in Chapter 17.

The material presented in this chapter is a hands-on demonstration of the Applications Generator at work. You learn to create dBASE IV objects, start the Applications Generator, create the Application Object, and navigate the menu structure. The advantages of creating Quick Applications are explored. The chapter then leads you through the steps of creating a sample application as you learn to design menus, chain objects together, and design exit operations. Finally, you learn to generate the program code and create applications that use multiple data files.

Two appendixes supplement this chapter. Appendix B is a complete reference documenting all the menus and options available within the Applications Generator. As you go through the demonstration, refer to Appendix B frequently to discover new ways to use the Applications Generator.

Appendix C contains a printout of the code generated by the demonstration in this chapter. The code is embedded with many comments so that you get a "play-by-play" (line-by-line) description of the program's operation. The printout shows you how the Applications Generator handles the tasks you assign to the application.

Understanding the dBASE IV Applications Generator

The Applications Generator provides a set of menus and a work surface so that you can set specifications for an application. Among other procedures, you can use the Applications Generator to create menus and attach actions to the menu prompts, specify reports, and design screens. In short, you can use the Applications Generator to build a complete application without knowing how to write programs.

The Applications Generator introduces a new concept, and thus a new term, to dBASE IV. The dBASE IV Applications Generator is said to be "object-oriented." An object is one of the basic building blocks of an application (such as data files, menus, screen formats, and report formats).

By combining and linking these objects together, the Applications Generator creates an application that can become (as far as users are concerned) the beginning and end of dBASE IV. Once you have created an application, you can instruct users to type the following command at the DOS prompt to use the application:

```
DBASE <application name>
```

By using this command, users can call the application at the same time they start dBASE IV, avoiding both the Control Center and the dot prompt.

The major advantage of giving users a finished application (as opposed to just giving them dBASE IV) is the inherent capability of a dBASE IV application to shield novice users from the intricacies of dBASE IV. The finished application also provides the safety of a framework; the user can perform only those actions that you, the programmer, have identified and approved.

This feature is particularly important when users are not only new to database management, but new to computers as well. For example, a new user executing the BROWSE command is like a bull in a china shop. The condition of the data file and integrity of data may never be the same again.

Giving users a finished application also reduces the "learning curve." Because you provide a number of prefabricated tasks, teaching someone to do those tasks within the framework of an application is much easier than teaching someone to become adept at dBASE IV.

As a side benefit to you, the programmer, the Applications Generator is an excellent tutor. As the programmer creates objects (such as menus, report forms, and screen formats), these objects are translated into programs written using the dBASE IV command language. By taking apart an application and studying the programming code of its component parts (objects), the programmer can learn much about how dBASE IV programs are written from scratch.

Understand that the code created by the Applications Generator (as it is shipped from the factory) is likely to be quite different in form from an application you write by hand; the factory code needs to be generic and flexible enough to handle many different situations in any hardware environment. The code created by the factory template is capable of supporting a multiuser environment, so you can create network applications without knowing the specifics of network programming.

The application created by the template MENU.GEN (the standard template shipped as part of dBASE IV) creates very simple code, especially in the sections that perform the specific actions you include. At the same time, MENU.GEN wraps the code in a complex package of commands that control such items as SET command environmentals, data-file usage, and menus.

Even the smallest application contains about 900 lines of code. Even if you decide to do things differently in your own programs, the generated code can provide you with a model for handling some problems that arise in everyday programming situations.

The Structure of the Applications Generator

The Applications Generator provides the programmer with a work surface and a menu structure. You enter specifications for an application by moving through the menus and selecting choices. You can create a menu structure for an application, and then attach actions to the items on the menus created. You can perform all these actions without writing a single line of program code.

As you give instructions to the Applications Generator, the entries are stored as a lookup table of variables. After you have specified for the application a menu structure and all the actions attached to the different menu prompts, you instruct the Applications Generator to create the program files. Using a *template* (a special type of program that turns the specifications you have entered into dBASE program code), these programs are written to disk as .PRG files.

Your specifications are stored in a file with the extension .APP so that you can come back later and make changes or additions to the application. When you generate the code again, these modifications are written into the application code.

Once you create the code, you or an end user can run it just as any dBASE program. You can run the application from any of the following three locations:

From the dot prompt: Use the DO command to start program execution.

From the Control Center: Highlight the application's name in the **Applications** column and press Enter.

From the DOS prompt: Enter the command DBASE just as you normally would to begin dBASE IV, adding a space and the name of the application's main .PRG file name (for example, enter the command DBASE ‹*application name*›).

Uses for the Applications Generator

While learning how to program in dBASE IV, you will find several different uses for the Applications Generator.

Primarily you will want to use it to produce results quickly. Even before you learn the ins and outs of programming, you can use the Applications Generator to create custom applications of varying degrees of sophistication. For many programmers, the results obtained with the Applications Generator are good enough to satisfy their needs, and they are content to go no further in learning to create programs.

If you are supporting dBASE IV users as well as creating applications, teaching the users to use the Applications Generator to build their own applications can take a great deal of work off your shoulders so that you can concentrate on more demanding projects.

The Applications Generator is also handy for creating BAR and POPUP menus in an interactive environment. You can then take the code generated by the Applications Generator, extract with your text editor the portions of code used to create menus, and insert them into the programs you write. This method is perhaps more time-consuming than writing the menus by hand, but for a beginner, it can be an invaluable tutorial.

You will also find the Applications Generator handy for a process known as *prototyping*. In prototyping, you build sample parts of an application to show to the person(s) responsible for approving application design. If you are acting as an independent consultant, you can design a small prototype to show your client how you would approach a particular task. If you are an employee in a company, you can show a prototype to your supervisor or department head.

As you become more proficient as a dBASE programmer, you develop individual preferences in the way you create programs, user interfaces, and applications. You also find that you are creating the same types of programs over and over. By using the Template Language (presented in chapter 17), you can customize the way the Applications Generator creates code. The Template Language enables you to automate many of your daily, repetitive programming chores.

Getting Started with the Applications Generator

The best way to get started with the Applications Generator is to use the Applications Generator to develop a sample application.

As your first exercise, imagine that your friend, who owns the Treasure Trove Children's Gift Shop, has come to you for help. The Treasure Trove staff is having problems keeping vendor information current. Your friend tells you that the company needs to keep a list of vendors and account representatives so that inquiries can be made and credit limits can be checked.

After listening to the problem, you determine that the folks at Treasure Trove need a very simple application. The application would provide a file in which vendor information can be entered. The file would include company names and addresses, sales reps, credit arrangements, and the terms of payment when credit has been extended.

The Treasure Trove staff also needs you to design a report that is a simple print-out of their vendors in alphabetical order. They also need you to design a printout of mailing labels.

You need to create four dBASE IV objects before you invoke the Applications Generator. Creating these objects is the subject of the next few sections.

Creating dBASE IV Objects

Although you can generate most objects on-the-fly within the menu structure of the Applications Generator, it is better to create these objects at the dot prompt or at the Control Center after you have sketched them out with pencil and paper. The application is then less likely to be missing a piece that you have to insert later.

Before invoking the Applications Generator, create the following four objects:

1. A data file to hold vendor information

2. A data-entry screen

3. Report objects

4. Label objects

If you have any questions about creating the objects discussed in the following sections, see the *dBASE IV Handbook*, published by Que Corporation.

The Data File

Figure 3.1 shows the file structure for a file named VENDOR. VENDOR contains ten fields whose contents include the following: a unique vendor ID string (ID); the company name (COMPANY); the name of the sales representative assigned to Treasure Trove (REP_NAME); the address, city, state, and ZIP of the vendor (ADDRESS, CITY, STATE, ZIP); the vendor's phone number (PHONE); the credit limit with the vendor (CREDIT_LIM); and terms of repayment (TERMS).

Notice also that three index TAGs are included as part of the production .MDX file (marked as Y in figure 3.1). The first TAG is the vendor ID number (this TAG is not used in this application, but comes in handy later when the application is expanded to include inventory). The second TAG is the company name (used for placing the vendor list in alphabetical order). The ZIP code is also used as an index TAG so that mailing labels can be sorted in ZIP-code order.

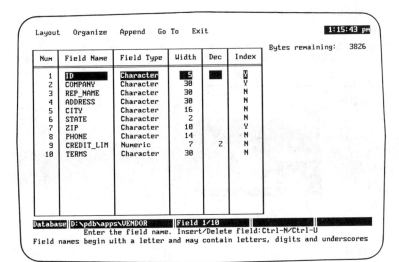

Fig. 3.1

*Structure of the
VENDOR data file.*

The Data-Entry Screen

Figure 3.2 is a sample layout of the VENDOR file as it has been created using
the CREATE SCREEN command at the dot prompt. You can also reach the screen-
creation environment by selecting <**create**> from the **Forms** column at the
Control Center.

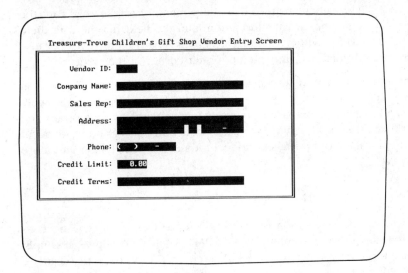

Fig. 3.2

*VENDOR data-
entry screen
controlled by a
format file.*

If you do not create a screen format for your application, dBASE IV displays a standard data-entry screen (see fig. 3.3). The standard screen contains data-entry boxes stacked vertically, with field names serving as prompts to tell the user where to enter information.

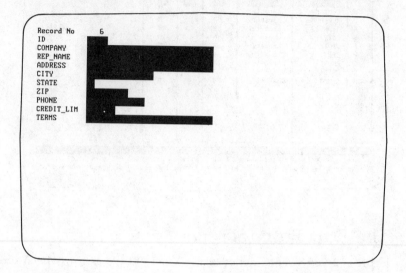

Fig. 3.3

Standard data-entry screen.

Standard data-entry screens can cause two major problems. First, raw field names are used as prompts that tell which information is to be typed into which GET area. Field names are meant to be a memory jog so that you, the programmer, can remember what information is in the field. To the user, field names can be somewhat cryptic. Second, the screen is hard on the eyes because the GET areas are all crammed into the upper-left corner of the screen.

By comparison, the formatted screen is more pleasing to the eye. The reason for creating data-entry screens goes beyond good looks, however. A well-designed entry screen enables users to work longer with less eye strain and fatigue, thus increasing productivity by making data entry faster and more accurate. Tired users make more mistakes and feel the need to take longer and more frequent breaks.

The Report Object

To fully utilize this demonstration of the Applications Generator, you need to include in the application a report form (.FRM). Figure 3.4 shows a sample Vendors List form. The form produces a directory of vendors that can be printed with different index TAGs to provide different SORTs of the information. Remember that an index does not really change the physical order of the

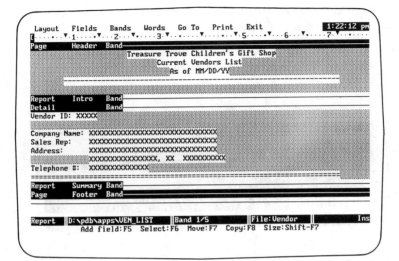

Fig. 3.4

Sample layout of the Vendors List report.

records in the data file, but logically orders the records so that they appear to be sorted in a particular way.

The Label Object

You also want to create a simple .LBL form file for printing mailing labels. At the dot prompt, issue the following command:

```
CREATE LABEL VEND
```

Then place information into the label band that creates labels with the following form:

```
SALES REPRESENTATIVE
COMPANY
ADDRESS
CITY, STATE, ZIP
```

Starting the Applications Generator

To invoke the Applications Generator from the dot prompt, use the CREATE APPLICATION command with an argument—the name of the application to be created. Note the following example:

```
CREATE APPLICATION VENDOR
```

Alternately, you can invoke the Applications Generator at the Control Center by placing the highlight bar in the **Applications** column, highlighting

<**create**>, and pressing Enter. You then fill in the application's name (VENDOR) in the data-entry screen shown in figure 3.5.

With either method, you are presented with a data-entry screen (see fig. 3.5) in which you can enter basic information about the application.

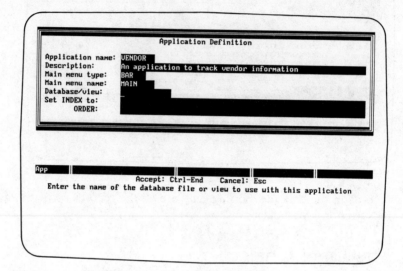

Fig. 3.5

Entry screen for basic application information.

Remember, the major function of the Applications Generator is to gather information at its menu prompts about the application's structure. When you tell the Applications Generator to create code, it translates these bits of information into commands as well as the arguments to the commands that make up the application's programming.

You first need to enter the name of the application; type this information (VENDOR) in the first field. If you began the process at the dot prompt, this line is already filled in with the name you gave as an argument to the CREATE command. If you started the process from the Control Center, you need to fill the line in. For the purpose of this demonstration, make sure that the name in the field is VENDOR (see fig. 3.5).

On the next line, Description, you can place a short description of the application. This message is meant as a memory jog or as a fragment of documentation which enables you to remember something about the application at a later time. The message is included in the application's program header as a comment line. For this example, type the following description and press Enter:

```
An application to track vendor information
```

Most dBASE IV applications are menu-driven. The third line of the application-definition frame specifies the menu type that serves as the main or "first-called" menu. This is the first menu the user sees when the application begins executing. By default, the Applications Generator uses a bar-type (horizontal) menu. You can therefore place the menu prompts across the top of the screen and attach pop-up menus to provide dialog boxes for each prompt across the horizontal-bar menu.

This type of screen is similar to the Macintosh interface. When the user chooses one of the main menu items, a POPUP menu opens underneath it. Although the method presented in this demonstration is the default, you do not need to accept the default. By specifying the main menu as a POPUP menu, you can create a menu within a frame in which the prompts are stacked vertically. Other POPUP menus can be placed to provide a balanced and attractive windowed interface.

In either case, you must give the main menu a name, which is placed in the entry underneath the menu type. For this demonstration, in the Main menu name field, type MAIN and press Enter. The next three entries specify which database or query file is used to provide data to the entry screens and reports. Pressing Shift-F1 (Pick) while the cursor is in the Database/view entry field presents an availability list (see fig. 3.6). You can then highlight the data or query file you want to use.

To choose the field, highlight **VENDOR.DBF** and press Enter.

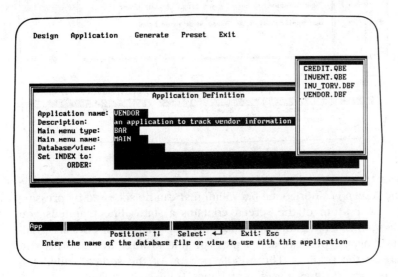

Fig. 3.6

Availability list for the VENDOR application.

Notice the availability list shown in figure 3.6; one of the files, CREDIT.QBE, is not a .DBF file, but a *query-by-example* file. You use a query file to set up a view that includes filters and conditions, so that only a portion of the records in one or more data files becomes available to the user. Later in this chapter, you learn how to use a query file to combine two data files so that you can print a report containing information from each.

Finish entering the data into the screen by typing VENDOR as the index-file name and COMPANY as the index TAG that sets the ORDER. To signal dBASE IV that you have completed entry in this screen, press Ctrl-End.

Creating the Application Object

Once you have pressed Ctrl-End to signify that you have finished entering information into the start-up screen, you are presented with a screen similar to the one shown in figure 3.7.

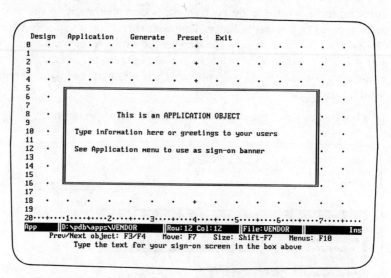

Fig. 3.7

The work surface showing the Application Object.

Take a moment to examine the parts of the screen shown in figure 3.7. At the very top of the screen is a horizontal-bar menu that can be accessed by pressing F10 (Menu). The bottom of the screen contains a status line that tells you about open files/items, a navigation line that tells you what major keys are available for controlling the process, and a message line prompt that informs you where you are in the process. The middle portion of the screen, called the work surface, is marked off as a grid containing 19 lines and a ruler.

In the middle of the screen is a window containing text: this is the *Application Object*. The Application Object is created automatically by the Applications Generator. As you see in the next few sections, you can alter the text of the Application Object but you cannot delete it.

The Application Object is the beginning point of your application. It is used by the Applications Generator to store information about the structure of your application. All other objects and modules of the program attach themselves to this Application Object; it therefore remains on-screen when everything else has been put away.

You can use the Application Object as a sign-on banner for your application, or you can have the application proceed straight to the main menu, bypassing any display of the Application Object. Sign-on banners have several uses. They can alert users to the fact that a program is about to begin running or pass on last-minute instructions. Perhaps the most important use for the sign-on banner, however, is to provide copyright protection for your application. (See the following section on copyright protection for more information.)

To use the Application Object as a sign-on banner, erase the text that is inside the frame of the object and replace it with the text you want as your sign-on banner. Then, access the **Application** dialog box by pressing F10 and highlighting **Application**. Choose **Display sign-on banner** from the menu and press Enter (see fig. 3.8). A POPUP menu appears from which you can choose whether or not to display the Application Object as a sign-on banner.

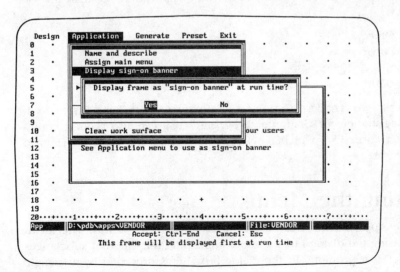

Fig. 3.8

The Application Object chosen as a sign-on banner.

You can move and resize the frame around the Application Object by using Shift-F7 (Size) to make the frame larger or smaller. To reposition the frame once you have properly sized and aligned type within the frame, use the F7 (Move) key. Remember that the Application Object remains on-screen as long as the Applications Generator is operating. To build the application, you simply use the menus to create or open the objects you need.

Providing Copyright Protection

According to legal experts, should you decide to invoke copyright protection for the design of an application, you have a better chance of prevailing in a dispute if a sign-on banner is used to proclaim your copyright interests.

Although failure to do so does not necessarily diminish your rights to a copyright, placing a copyright notice in a sign-on banner is recognized as a prudent method of ensuring that you are fully protected under the United States copyright laws. The sign-on banner is considered an airtight notification to anyone possessing your application that it is copyrighted material.

Your copyright message should include the copyright symbol (©), the year in which the copyrighted material was produced, and the name of the person or organization to whom the copyright is assigned. The word "Copyright" can be substituted for the copyright symbol (©).

For more information on copyrighting of software applications, contact the following agency:

Copyright Office
Library of Congress
Washington, D.C. 20559.
(202) 479-0700.

You can request two circulars: Circular 1, "Copyright Basics," and Circular 61, "Copyright Registration for Computer Programs." You can also request copies of "Application Form TX," which is used in registering copyright interests to computer software.

Navigating the Menus

To access the **Applications Generator** menu, press F10 (Menu). The menu activates, showing the dialog box (a menu containing the different subchoices available under that prompt). In the dialog box, items preceded by a triangle (pointing to the right) produce a submenu, offering more specific options (see fig. 3.9).

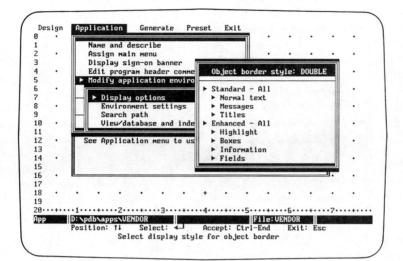

```
   Design  Application   Generate   Preset   Exit
 0    •                                        •    •     •    •       •
 1    •        Name and describe
 2    •        Assign main menu                     •    •     •       •
 3            Display sign-on banner
 4    •        Edit program header comme┌─────────────────────────────┐•
 5            ▶ Modify application enviro│ Object border style: DOUBLE │
 6    •                                   └─────────────────────────────┘
 7    •          ▶ Display options        ▶ Standard - All            •
 8    •            Environment settings   ▶ Normal text
 9              Search path              ▶ Messages                  •
10    •          View/database and inde   ▶ Titles
11                                        ▶ Enhanced - All           •
12    •        See Application menu to us  ▶ Highlight
13                                         ▶ Boxes                   •
14    •                                    ▶ Information
15                                         ▶ Fields                  •
16    •
17
18    •     •      •       •      •     +       •       •      •
19
20┄┄┄┄┄┄┼┄┄┄┄1┄┄┄┄┄┼┄┄┄┄2┄┄┄┄┄┼┄┄┄┄3┄┄┄┄┄┼┄┄┄┄4┄┄┄┄┄┼┄┄┄┄5┄┄┄┄┄┼┄┄┄┄6┄┄┄┄┄┼┄┄┄┄7┄┄┄┄┼┄┄┄
 App   ║D:\pdb\apps\VENDOR          ║          ║File:VENDOR      ║
       Position: ↑↓     Select: ◄┘      Accept: Ctrl-End    Exit: Esc
              Select display style for object border
```

Fig. 3.9

Choices marked with a triangle call submenus.

Pressing the left- or right-arrow keys moves you from one dialog box to the next/previous dialog box. Using the up- or down-arrow keys selects from the prompts contained within the dialog box.

If you know which dialog box you want to see, a shortcut method is available to you. Hold down the Alt key and type the initial of the prompt you want highlighted (for example, pressing Alt-D always opens the menu with the **Design** dialog box displayed).

The **Applications Generator** menu found at the top of the screen is one of the few dBASE IV menus that changes depending on conditions. If only the Application Object is open on the work surface (screen), the menu choice to the right of **Design** is **Application** (see fig. 3.9). Once you have opened an object (such as a POPUP menu), **Application** is replaced by **Menu** and **Item**. These two choices are shown during the time an object is open on the work surface (see fig. 3.10). If the open object is a field, structure, or files list, **Menu** is replaced by **List**. Batch processes are signified by **Batch**.

Before you begin designing the application, take a moment to page through the reference section of **Applications Generator** menus presented in Appendix B. As you work your way through the demonstration, refer frequently to Appendix B to see all options available with the Applications Generator.

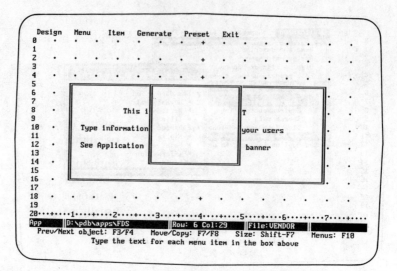

Fig. 3.10

Menu prompts change when an object is open.

Generating Quick Applications

Before building a complete application, you may want to try a *Quick Application* as a trial run. The **Application** dialog box includes the menu choice **Generate quick application** (see fig. 3.11). You use this choice to create a very simple application that provides data entry into a data file, prints one report, and prints one set (style) of mailing labels. You can also include a screen format file to control the display of the data-entry screens. Beyond these features, however, no customization is available.

Fig. 3.11

The Quick Application entry screen.

If you are under pressure to create something "yesterday," the Quick Application can be a lifesaver. Many times the manager of a project is impatient to get data to disk, knowing that getting data entered is one of the most time-consuming aspects of implementing a new application.

You can generate a Quick Application that at least lets users start keyboarding information while you prepare a more comprehensive system. Make sure, however, that the data structures are set before allowing users to key in information. Otherwise, you have to do a fair amount of editing.

You can also use the Quick Application for prototyping data-entry screens and reports. Showing prototypes under the umbrella of a **Generate quick application** menu helps to present that prototype in its most favorable light. Human nature dictates that a nicely packaged item is usually received more favorably than the same item by itself.

For this demonstration, choose **Generate quick application** from the menu (see fig. 3.12). Fill the fields with the names of the four objects that you created before invoking the Applications Generator (the database file, the screen format file, the report format file, and the label format file). Then press Ctrl-End. A confirmation screen appears; you then tell the Applications Generator to create the application.

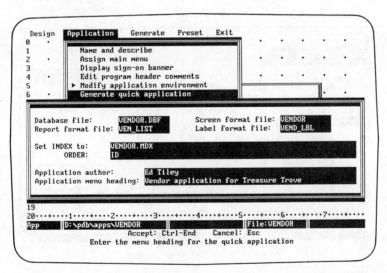

Fig. 3.12

The Quick Application entry screen filled in.

Exit the Applications Generator and call up the Quick Application. Look it over, checking its built-in features and how these features are presented to the user. After you have seen how the Quick Application is packaged, erase the file VENDOR.APP (or transfer it to another subdirectory), start over, and return to this point.

Now that you have seen how the Applications Generator works in its most basic form, you have a better basis for understanding how the choices you select from the **Applications Generator** menus affect the final output.

Creating a Sample Application

At this point, you are ready to begin creating a more customized form of the VENDOR application. Invoke the Applications Generator again and fill in the application information screen as before. This prepares you for designing the main menu.

Designing the MAIN Menu

To create the BAR menu called **MAIN**, access the **Design** dialog box and choose **Horizontal bar menu**. You are presented with a list of existing bar-type menus and the **<create>** prompt (see fig. 3.13). You can choose **<create>** to design new menus from scratch.

You can choose existing menus (those created for past applications) by highlighting the menu name and pressing Enter.

Fig. 3.13

The BAR menu PICK list.

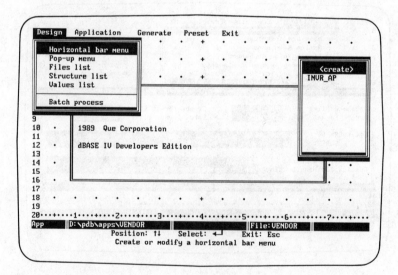

You can duplicate a previously created menu by accessing the **Name and describe** choice from the **Menu** dialog box and entering a new name in the entry screen (see fig. 3.14). When the menu is saved, the new name becomes

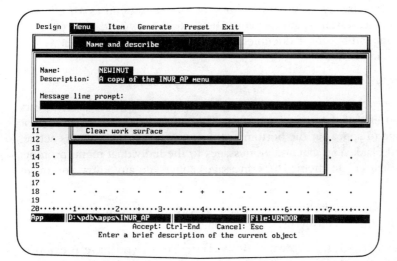

Fig. 3.14

The menu name changed in order to copy it.

the current name and the old version is left on disk unchanged. The new menu starts out as an exact duplicate, retaining all the attributes of the older version.

When you choose **Horizontal bar menu**, you are presented with a screen prompting you to enter three pieces of information: the name of the menu, a description of the menu, and a message to be displayed when the menu is active. The description and message are optional (see fig. 3.15).

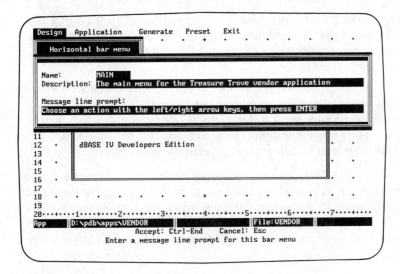

Fig. 3.15

The entry screen for the MAIN menu.

Because you have already assigned the name of the main menu as **MAIN**, type `MAIN` in the `Name` field of this entry screen. The second entry field, `Description`, is used for commenting on or documenting the purpose for this menu. At this point, type the following:

`The main menu for the Treasure Trove vendor application`

Finally, you are prompted to enter a message line prompt. This message appears on the bottom line of the screen whenever this menu is active. If you do not want a message to appear at the bottom of the screen while the menu is active, leave this field blank. You can attach messages to the individual menu prompts in a menu as you create them. These messages supersede any entry you make here.

Once you have filled in the information and checked it for accuracy, signal the end of entry in this screen by pressing Ctrl-End.

In your discussions with the owners of Treasure Trove, you have previously determined that the **MAIN** menu for the VENDOR application should include entries that allow for data editing, printing reports, and mailing labels, and an entry that can be accessed by the user to terminate the application and return to the dBASE dot prompt or the Control Center.

The data-entry portion of the application enables users to add, edit, and delete vendors as well as pack the data file and back up data to disk. The reports module enables users to print the VENDOR list in alphabetical order in order of vendor number as well as print mailing labels in ZIP-code order.

When you press Ctrl-End, an empty frame appears on-screen (see fig. 3.16). You enter in the frame the prompts that will be a part of the menu. Also, the message line instructs you to press F5 to begin defining the BAR menu. Pressing F5 again ends the entry.

Before you begin to design the items that appear on the **MAIN** menu, be aware that the highlight used to show the item as being active to the user will be two spaces wider than the prompt itself. If, for example, the prompt has four letters, the highlight bar showing the prompt as active will be six columns wide. Remember to take this into account when spacing the prompts.

To begin defining the **MAIN** menu, press the right-arrow key, or press the space bar twice to position the cursor a little bit away from the left edge of the frame so that the highlight does not obscure the frame when the first prompt is highlighted. Press F5 to begin defining the first prompt; then type `DATA`. Before moving the cursor to a different location, press F5 to finish defining the item on the menu.

Move the cursor to the right three more spaces, press F5, and type `REPORTS`. Remember to end the entry by pressing F5 again (see fig. 3.17).

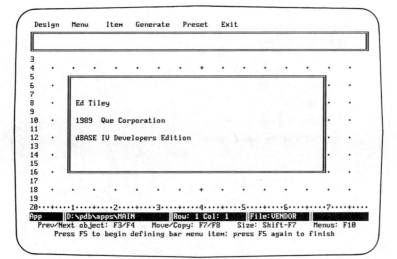

Fig. 3.16

A blank bar-type menu ready to be filled in with prompts.

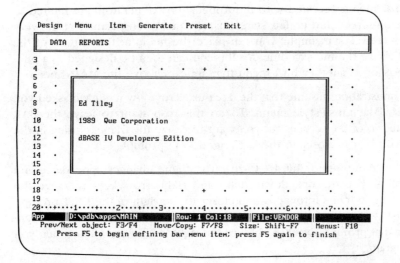

Fig. 3.17

Placing prompts on the MAIN menu.

To enter the final prompt of the menu, choose **Exit**, move the cursor three more spaces to the right, press F5, and then type EXIT (see fig. 3.18). End by pressing F5 again.

Sizing and Placing the Main Menu

Once you have assigned the prompts to your menu, you need to adjust the size of the frame surrounding the menu and possibly move it to a different location on-screen.

Fig. 3.18

*The MAIN menu
with all three
prompts in place.*

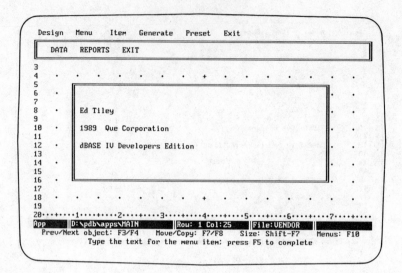

Horizontal-bar menus (created with the Applications Generator) are limited to a single line on-screen, but no law states that the menu must remain at the very top of the screen. For example, you can place the menu at the bottom of the screen, just above the message line. A submenu can then be designed as a pull-up dialog box or as another BAR menu that appears above the **MAIN** menu.

For this demonstration, assume that the Treasure Trove owners have asked you to simulate a Macintosh-style menu. To do this, you want to leave the BAR menu on the top of the screen, but you want to resize the frame, closing in the right side so that it is closer to the last (rightmost) prompt.

To resize the frame, press Shift-F7 (Size). The frame changes appearance and begins to blink. Use the up-, down-, left-, and right-arrow keys to move the image of the menu frame into a position closer to the right of the **EXIT** prompt. Leave at least two extra spaces to the right of the last prompt, so that the highlight bar for that prompt does not obscure the right side of the frame when you run the program.

Figure 3.19 shows the menu frame after resizing. Note that the original borders of the frame remain on-screen for you to use as a gauge. After you press Enter, however, the frame assumes the size you have specified, and the display of the previous borders of the frame disappears.

You can use two tricks when resizing frames around objects. First, do not size the frame so that text placed inside the frame is covered. Second, the sizing operation is performed by moving the lower-right corner in relation to the top-left corner of the frame. If an item inside the frame is too far to the right edge of the frame once you have adjusted the size, you can position that item before pressing Shift-F7 (Size). By moving the item to the left edge of the frame, you give yourself maximum flexibility in determining the position of the right edge of the frame (see fig. 3.20).

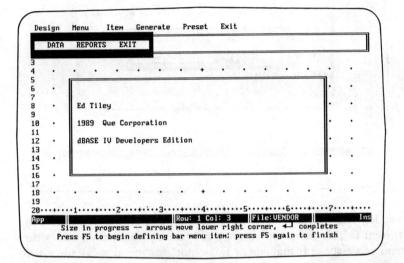

Fig. 3.19

The menu frame after resizing.

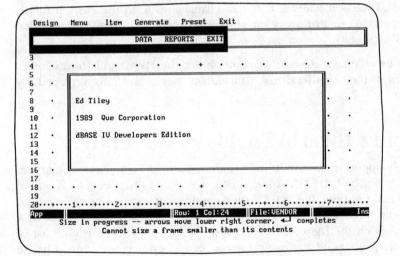

Fig. 3.20

Text that must be moved before resizing.

To move the frame, press F7 (Move). A small pop-up window appears on-screen and offers two choices: **Entire frame** or **Item only**. To move the entire frame and all its contents, choose **Entire frame** (see fig. 3.21). To position an item within the frame, highlight the item you want to move and press F7 (Move), choosing **Item only**.

Fig. 3.21

The whole menu moved by selecting Entire frame.

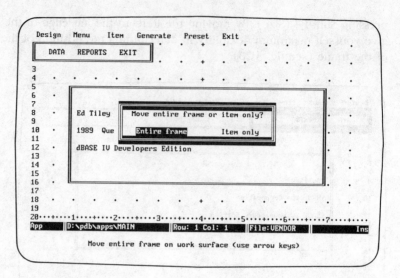

In this instance, leave the **MAIN** BAR menu at the top-left corner of the screen. Because each item in this menu opens a POPUP menu which then offers the user a submenu of database management tasks, put this menu away for a few moments by accessing the **Menu** dialog box and choosing **Put away current menu**. dBASE IV asks if you want to save changes made to the current frame. (Each time you choose **Put away current menu**, you are asked whether you want to save changes.)

Note that once you have closed the menu object, the **Menu** and **Item** choices disappear from the **Applications Generator** menu and are replaced by **Application**.

Designing the DATA POPUP Menu

In this sample application, POPUP menus are used to provide choices that can be made under each of the **MAIN** menu prompts. When the user selects one of the **MAIN** menu prompts, the POPUP menu appears as a dialog box. To design a POPUP menu, access the **Design** dialog box and choose **Pop-up menu**. A files list appears on the right side of the screen. You can choose from a list of previously designed POPUP menus or you can create a new one. Choose <**create**>.

You are presented with a POPUP-menu information screen with three fields to be filled in: Name, Description, and Message line prompt (see fig. 3.22).

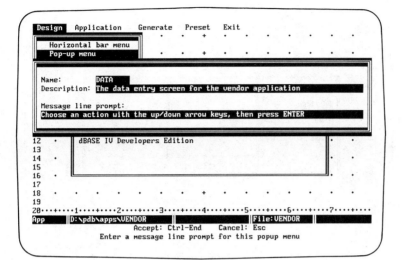

Fig. 3.22

The POPUP entry screen filled in for the data-entry menu.

First, enter the name of the menu as DATA; then provide a description of the menu for later documentation. In this case, type The data entry screen for the vendor application. Finally, enter a message line prompt to be displayed whenever this POPUP menu is active. You can give each prompt its own message. The message shows only if the highlighted prompt does not have a message attached. Once you have entered the information in the three prompts, press Ctrl-End to signal the end of entry.

An empty frame positioned in the center of the screen appears (see fig. 3.23). Note that the navigation line below the status line indicates that the same keys are available to move, copy, and size this frame as were available when you designed the BAR menu.

When you planned the VENDOR application, you decided on the five tasks to be attached to the **DATA** prompt of the **MAIN** menu: adding new vendor records, editing/deleting vendor records, packing the data file (eliminating records marked for deletion), rebuilding the indexes, and backing up the data onto the floppy disk.

Because all these actions are integral to maintaining data files, it is logical that they all appear on the same menu. However, because all but two of these choices are passive (the user highlights the choice, presses Enter, and waits for the results), you can use a "dummy" prompt—such as a line of dashes—to separate the two sets of tasks from one another (see fig. 3.24).

For now, access the **Menu** dialog box and choose **Put away current menu**. The specifications you have set are saved to disk, and the work surface is cleared of everything except the Application Object.

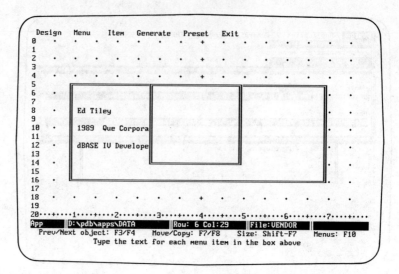

Fig. 3.23

The DATA menu ready to be filled in with prompts.

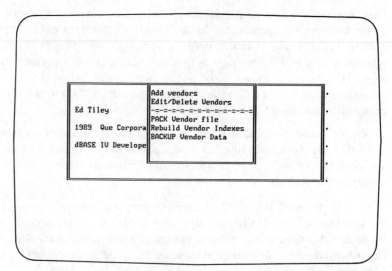

Fig. 3.24

The DATA menu with prompts filled in.

Building the REPORTS POPUP Menu

To complete the VENDOR application, you need one more dBASE IV object: the **REPORTS** menu. To create the **REPORTS** menu, follow these steps:

1. Access the **Design** dialog box and choose **Pop-up menu**.

2. Choose <**create**> from the menu of available POPUPs (see fig. 3.25).

3. Press Ctrl-End to accept the entry-screen information.

4. Enter the following three prompts into the menu frame (see fig. 3.26):

```
Vendors by name
Vendors by ID #
Mailing labels by Zip
```

5. Size the frame for the **REPORTS** menu.

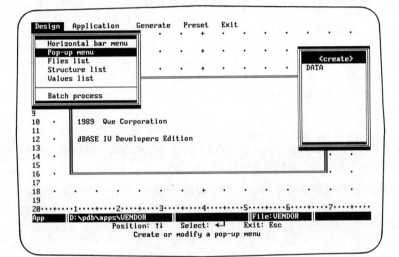

Fig. 3.25

The PICK list for creating the REPORTS menu.

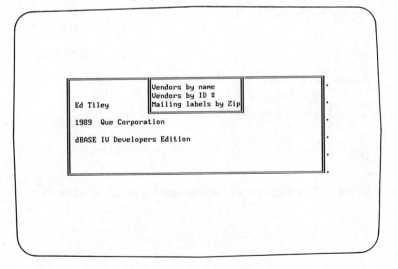

Fig. 3.26

The REPORTS menu prompts.

Once you have worked the POPUP menu into form, access the **Applications Generator** menu dialog box and choose **Put away current menu**. You should now have a clean work surface (the only object showing should be the Application Object).

If the work surface still has open objects other than the Application Object, access the **Application** dialog box and choose **Clear work surface** to put away any objects that are currently still open.

Assembling the Application

Once you have all the objects (such as menus, reports, and screens) to be bound together as a single application, it is a fairly straightforward task to follow the logical chain in assigning actions to the items contained in these objects. In fact, when you become comfortable with the Applications Generator, you can create an application similar to the VENDOR application in less than fifteen minutes.

At this point, you are ready to assemble the VENDOR application by attaching the POPUP menus for data entry and reports to the **MAIN** BAR menu and by attaching actions to each prompt of the POPUPs.

Access the **Design** dialog box and choose **Horizontal bar menu**. Because you have previously created a BAR menu with the name **MAIN**, it appears in the files list that pops up on the right side of the screen (see fig. 3.27).

Fig. 3.27

The PICK list for calling the MAIN menu back to the work surface.

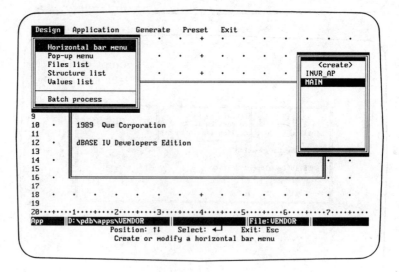

Highlight **MAIN** and press Enter. The BAR menu you designed with the prompts **DATA**, **REPORTS**, and **EXIT** now becomes active. The prompts are placed on the work surface.

Highlight the **DATA** prompt; then press Alt-I to display the **Item** dialog box. Choose **Change action**; the **Action** submenu appears (see fig. 3.28).

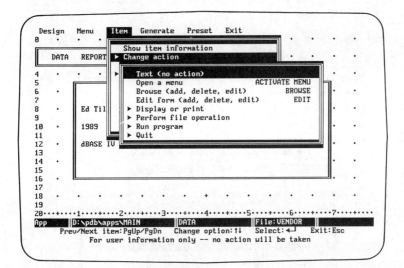

Fig. 3.28

An action assigned to the DATA prompt of the MAIN menu.

You have previously determined the five functions to be attached to the **DATA** prompt of the **MAIN** menu: **Add vendors**, **Edit/Delete Vendors**, **PACK Vendor file**, **Rebuild Vendor Indexes**, and **BACKUP Vendor Data**. You constructed a POPUP menu that offers the user those choices.

To attach that POPUP menu to the **DATA** prompt of the **MAIN** menu, choose **Open a menu**. Define the menu type as POP-UP and the menu name as DATA.

Note that in this instance, the prompt and the menu name are the same word. This is strictly for convenience. There is no requirement that a POPUP menu be named the same as the prompt that invokes it.

Once you have filled in the menu type as POP-UP and the menu name as DATA, press Ctrl-End to attach that action to the menu prompt.

If you want to confirm that the action you have specified will take place when the user chooses **DATA** from the **MAIN** menu, choose **Show item information** from this menu. You are presented with a screen that provides a quick synopsis of the action.

At this point, you have two additional choices: creating a help screen and attaching a message to the prompt. Creating help screens can cut down considerably on the amount of support you must provide your users. Properly written prompt messages can also help users.

Your message and the help screen act as a two-tiered support mechanism. The message tells the user what the menu prompt does or what keystrokes can be entered. The help screen provides a second, more detailed explanation. By effectively combining the two, you provide the user with a quick memory jog and a detailed explanation.

If you want to add a help screen, choose **Write help text** and enter the text. To attach a message to the menu prompt, choose **Assign message line prompt**.

Remember that help screens and messages are of great value to new users. You should include them whenever possible.

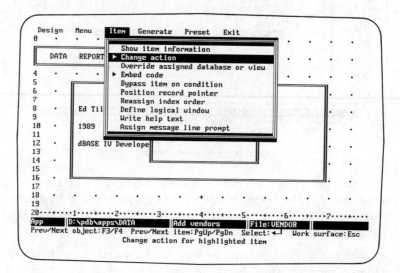

Fig. 3.29

An action assigned to the Add vendors prompt.

You are now ready to specify the actions of the POPUP menu attached to the **DATA** prompt of the **MAIN** menu. Because you will be positioning the POPUP in relation to the **MAIN** menu, do not put the menu away.

Access the **Design** dialog box and choose **Pop-up menu**. Highlight **DATA** and press Enter. The POPUP menu you created previously is now displayed above the Application Object.

To attach an action to each prompt on this menu, highlight your choice and press Alt-I. The **Item** dialog box is displayed. Choose **Change action** (see fig. 3.29). Make certain that **Add vendors** is selected. Check this by looking at the center portion of the status bar, where the prompt text is replicated. If **Add vendors** is not the currently selected choice on the POPUP, press PgUp/PgDn until it is.

The only action you want users to be able to perform from this item on the POPUP is to add vendor records to the file. Choose **Edit form** from the **Action menu** and fill in the information. In the Format file field, enter the name of the VENDOR screen file. Following the example in this chapter, type VENDOR. Make sure that the Mode field is set to APPEND and press Ctrl-End (see fig. 3.30).

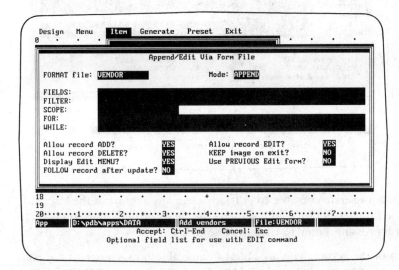

Fig. 3.30

The entry window set to allow only APPENDs.

You can include a message line prompt and help text to be associated with this prompt. The message line is displayed whenever this prompt is highlighted; the help message is displayed whenever the user presses F1 while this item is highlighted.

Because the APPEND command always places new records at the end of the file, you need not choose to position the record pointer.

Once you have placed any help text or message lines you want attached to this menu item, press Ctrl-End. This action ends the specification for this item and returns you to the object so that you can choose the next item on the menu that needs attention.

Next, highlight **Edit/Delete Vendors** and press Alt-I to attach an action to that item.

Choose **Change action** from the **Item** dialog box, and then choose **Edit form** from the menu displayed. You are then presented with an information screen in which you can specify the format file as VENDOR and the mode as EDIT (see fig. 3.31).

Fig. 3.31

*The entry window
set to control
the Edit/Delete
function.*

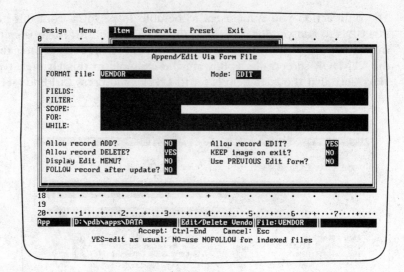

Because you want users to be able to edit or delete any record in the data file, leave blank the middle section of the screen (the fields dealing with items such as FILTERs) by pressing Enter to bypass these fields.

At the bottom of the screen, you are able to determine how you want the edit to proceed. Answer No to `Allow record ADD?`, Yes to `Allow record EDIT?`, Yes to `Allow record DELETE?`, No to `KEEP image on exit?`, No to `Display edit MENU?`, No to `Use PREVIOUS Edit form?`, and No to `FOLLOW record after update?` (see fig. 3.31).

Once these settings are in place, press Ctrl-End to accept them and return to the **Item** dialog box. At this point, you can attach help text and a message line prompt for use when this item is highlighted.

Press Ctrl-End to return to the base object, the menu itself, so that you can highlight the next prompt. Alternately, as a shortcut, you can press the PgDn key while the **Item** dialog box is still displayed. This action selects the next prompt and makes it current.

Because the third line of the menu is simply a line of dashes used to separate different groups of prompts, do not attach an action to this line of the menu. When this menu is activated at run time, the highlight bar skips over this line without allowing the user to stop on the line.

You are now ready to provide actions for the last three prompts on the menu.

Highlight **PACK Vendor file**. Choose **Change action**, which displays the **Action** menu. From the **Action** menu, choose **Perform file operation**.

When you choose **Perform file operation**, another menu pops up. The menu allows you to choose one of a group of different commands used to maintain data in a data files. Highlight **Discard marked records** and press Enter (see fig. 3.32). You are presented with another window asking you to confirm that the discarded records are to be purged from the data file. Press Enter to confirm. You are then returned to the **Item** dialog box.

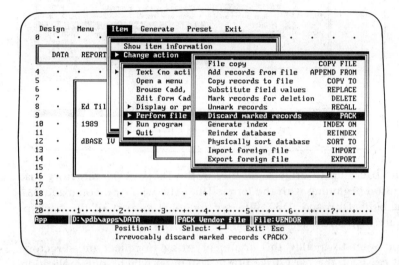

Fig. 3.32

Setting the action of the PACK prompt.

You can enter help text and a message line to be attached to this prompt of this item on the POPUP menu.

Press PgDn to select the next prompt, which reindexes the file. Choose **Perform file operation** again. Highlight **Reindex database** and press Enter (see fig. 3.33). A confirmation window appears; press Enter to confirm.

You are returned to the **Item** dialog box. Pressing PgDn selects the item **BACKUP Vendor Data** and makes it current.

This time, when you choose **Change action**, also choose **Run program** from the submenu presented. Then highlight **Run DOS program**.

You are presented with two entry fields. In the first, type the word BACKUP, the DOS utility used for archiving data on the hard drive to floppy disk. On the parameters line, type the arguments that would be given to the BACKUP command if you entered it at the DOS prompt. In this case, you enter the following argument:

    D:\IV\APPS*.DB? A:

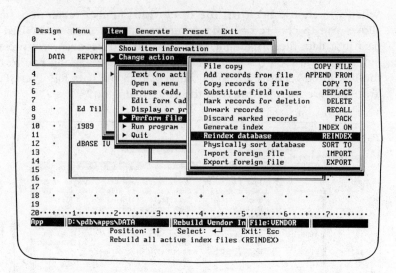

Fig. 3.33

Setting the action of the Rebuild Vendor Indexes prompt.

This command backs up to drive A: all files in the D:\IV\APPS directory that have an extension beginning with the letters DB. (The wild-card command DB? specifies that both .DBF and .DBT files are included as part of the backup. Memo fields are therefore also backed up.)

Obviously you want to modify this argument string to reflect the directory structure that exists on the hard drive of the system on which your application will run.

NOTE: If you include DOS commands in your application, be sure that external DOS commands (see your DOS manual for more information) can be invoked from the current subdirectory. This means that the .EXE or .COM files must be accessible. You can include a copy of the external command in the current directory or in the PATH statement in the AUTOEXEC.BAT file. If for some reason the BACKUP command is not available to the application when this menu item is chosen, the user will receive an error message. Your job is to ensure that the computer environment is capable of accessing the DOS BACKUP command.

Also, different versions of DOS (including OEM versions of the same release, such as COMPAQ MS-DOS 3.2, IBM PC DOS 3.2, and others) have slightly different syntax arrangements. Be sure to test this feature under the running conditions found on the user's system.

Once you have entered the program name and parameters as they are shown in figure 3.34, press Ctrl-End to attach that command to the menu item.

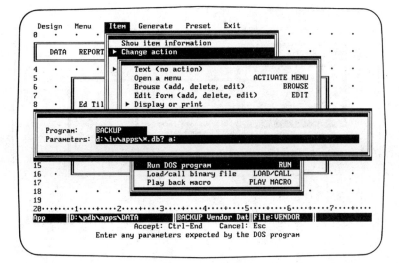

Fig. 3.34

*Setting the action
of the BACKUP
prompt.*

Once you have attached an item to all five items in the **DATA** menu, press Ctrl-End to put away the **Item** dialog box of the **Applications Generator** menu. To complete the design of the menu, properly position the POPUP menu as a dialog box to the **DATA** prompt of the **MAIN** menu.

To position the POPUP, press F7 and choose **Entire frame**. (When you want to move an item within a POPUP or BAR menu, choose **Item only**.) When you choose **Entire frame**, the border around the frame begins to blink. Use the up-, down-, left-, and right-arrow keys to place the frame where you want it to appear when the user chooses **DATA** from the **MAIN** menu.

Figure 3.35 shows the optimum placement for emulating Macintosh-style menus. Once you have placed the menu, press Enter. The object is displayed in its new position.

You have completed design of the **DATA** menu. Access the **Menu** dialog box and choose **Put away current menu**.

Completing the Application Specifications

To complete the VENDOR application, you only need to attach the **REPORTS** POPUP to the appropriate **MAIN** menu prompt, attach actions to the **REPORTS** menu items, and provide the appropriate action for the **EXIT** prompt for the **MAIN** menu.

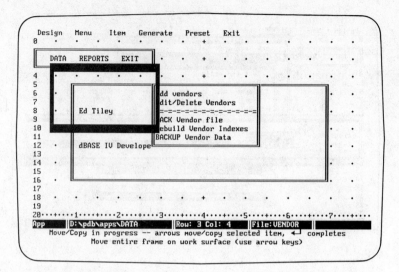

Fig. 3.35

The blank frame showing the menu's placement.

In order to complete the **REPORTS** menu, access the **Design** dialog box, and choose **Pop-up menu**. Highlight **REPORTS** and press Enter.

Like the **DATA** menu, the **REPORTS** menu is positioned in the middle of the screen above the Application Object. You are now ready to attach actions to each of the three prompts.

Make sure that **Vendors by name** is currently selected and then access the **Item** dialog box. Choose **Change action** and then choose **Display or print** from the submenu (see fig. 3.36).

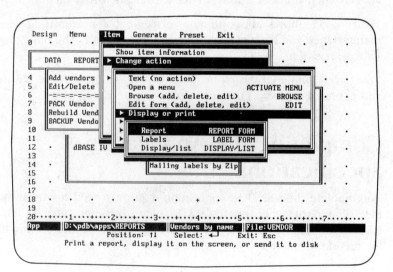

Fig. 3.36

Assigning an action to the Vendors by name report.

All three menu items are assigned an action through this item. When you choose **Display or print**, another screen presents the choices **Report**, **Labels**, or **Display/list** (see fig. 3.36). Choose **Report**.

An information screen for printing a report appears (see fig. 3.37). Enter information into the fields.

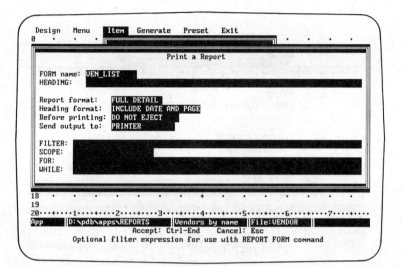

Fig. 3.37

The Print a Report screen.

Because the application, by default, orders the vendors by ID number, choose **Reassign index order** from the **Item** dialog box; specify COMPANY in the Set ORDER to field (see fig. 3.38); and press Ctrl-End.

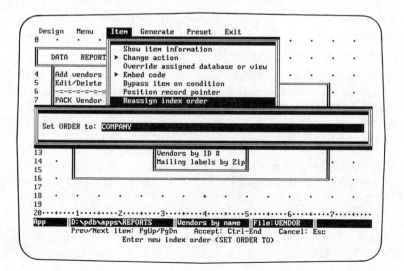

Fig. 3.38

Changing the index order for the report.

You can write help text for this prompt or assign a message line prompt which appears at the bottom of the screen whenever this item on the **REPORTS** menu is highlighted.

Once you have finished the specification for the **Vendors by name** prompt, press PgDn to make the **Vendors By ID #** prompt current. Again assign the action to print a report (see fig. 3.39).

Fig. 3.39

The Print a Report screen with the index changed.

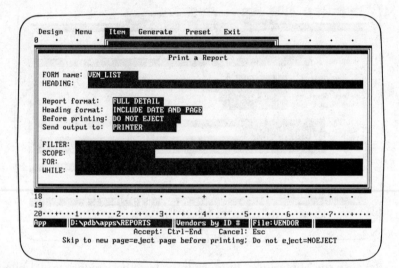

Because the report must be ordered by the ID TAG of the index file, choose **Reassign index order**, enter the TAG name ID in the field, and press Ctrl-End.

The last item that needs action on this menu is **Mailing labels by Zip**. Press PgDn to make that item active and choose **Change action**; then choose **Display or print** from the submenu. Finally choose **Labels**.

Figure 3.40 shows the information screen that appears. Because you want all vendors in the file to be included in the mailing label printing, do not enter information into the FILTER, SCOPE, FOR, or WHILE fields. Fill in the information as it is shown in figure 3.40; then press Ctrl-End to accept the entry or Esc to return to the menu without making any changes.

Next, reassign the order for the mailing labels so that they are printed in ZIP-code order. Choose **Reassign index order** from the dialog box, and enter the field name ZIP in the Set ORDER to field. Press Ctrl-End to accept the entry or Esc to return to the menu without making any changes.

At this point, you are ready to position the **REPORTS** menu so that it appears in the correct place when **REPORTS** is chosen from the **MAIN** menu. Press Esc to

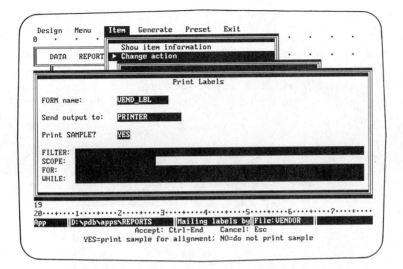

Fig. 3.40

The Print Labels entry screen.

clear the **Applications Generator** menu from the screen and then press F7. Choose **Entire frame** and use the up-, down-, left-, and right-arrow keys to position the menu (see fig. 3.41). Press Enter; the object is displayed on the work surface in the same position as it is displayed at run time.

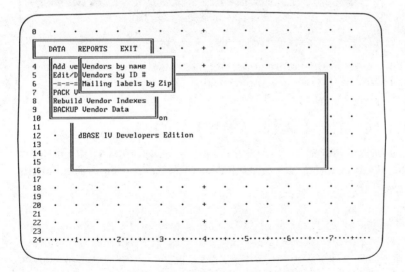

Fig. 3.41

Positioning the REPORTS POPUP.

Next attach the POPUP to the **MAIN** menu prompt using a shortcut method of making the **MAIN** menu the currently selected object. Notice that the navigation line at the bottom of the screen shows that you can cycle from one object to another with the F3/F4 keys. Pressing F3 cycles to the previous object; pressing F4 cycles to the next object.

In this case, press F3; the frame around the **MAIN** menu is highlighted. Move the cursor to **REPORTS** and access the **Item** dialog box. Choose **Change action** and then **Open a menu**. You will be presented with an information screen that enables you to enter the menu type as POP-UP and the menu name as REPORTS (see fig. 3.42).

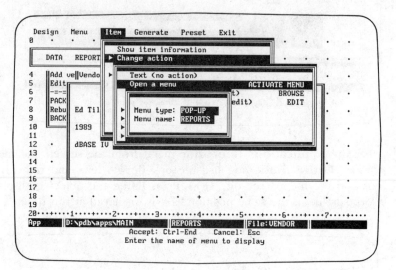

Fig. 3.42

Attaching the REPORTS POPUP to the MAIN menu prompt.

When you have entered this information, press Ctrl-End to accept the entry or press Esc to return to the menu without making any changes.

Designing the EXIT Operation

One more action is required to complete linking all tasks of the VENDOR application to the **MAIN** menu: attach an action to the **EXIT** prompt of the **MAIN** menu.

At this point, you can press PgDn (notice that the prompt in the middle of the status bar changes to **EXIT**). Choose **Change action** and then choose **Quit**. **Return to calling program** is highlighted. To select, press Enter. A confirmation frame appears asking you to confirm the choice. Press Enter again; the action is now attached to the **EXIT** prompt (see fig. 3.43).

If you plan to have users start the applications you create at the same time they start dBASE IV from the dot prompt, you want to choose the quit action that

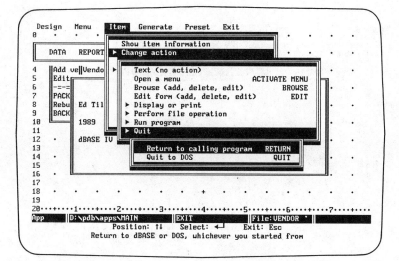

Fig. 3.43

Setting the action of the EXIT prompt.

terminates to DOS. Your users then will not have to type QUIT at the dot prompt in order to exit from dBASE IV.

Almost certainly, in this case, you want to assign a message line prompt informing the user that this choice will terminate the running of the application. Because this choice on the **MAIN** menu does not access a submenu, this prompt is the only clue your user has about the action attached to that choice.

You can also create a help screen so that more details are available when the user presses F1.

Generating the Program Code

You have now completed all the actions required before generating the actual program code. Access the **Menu** dialog box and choose **Clear work surface**. Each object you currently have open presents you with a confirmation box asking if you want them saved or abandoned. In this situation, choose the save in all three cases.

Display the **Generate** dialog box by pressing Alt-G; you are presented with three choices (see fig. 3.44):

1. **Begin generating** causes the Applications Generator to start writing the program code for the application.

2. **Select template** enables you to choose as the model for creating the application any templates you have constructed with the dBASE IV Template Language.

Fig. 3.44

*The Generate
menu.*

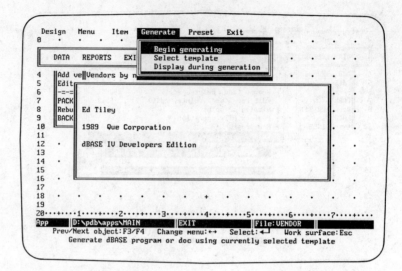

3. **Display during generation** causes the code to be displayed as it
   is being written.

If you have a fast machine, the **Display during generation** choice is relatively
useless because the code scrolls by the window faster than you can read it. The
choice, however, produces an interesting display during the time the code is
being generated, so you may decide to turn the display on.

Choose **Select template**. Notice that the default template is MENU.GEN (see
fig. 3.45). Later you can write templates that do things your way. For now,
press Enter to confirm this choice.

Fig. 3.45

*The Generate menu
showing the
template-selection
screen.*

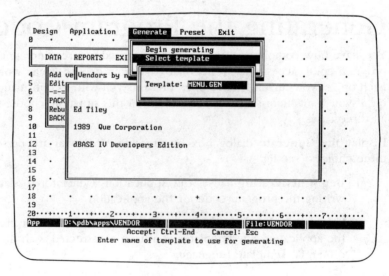

Next, choose **Begin generating** and sit back and watch your application begin to take form. The message line at the bottom of the screen identifies the file with which the Applications Generator is currently working. The middle portion of the status line shows how many lines of code have been generated.

Once the code has been generated, the message line displays the following prompt:

```
Generation is complete, press any key...
```

At this point, pressing any key returns you to the **Applications Generator** menu. Choose **Exit** and then choose **Save and exit**.

You are returned to either the dot prompt or the Control Center (depending on where you invoked the Applications Generator).

To test the VENDOR program, enter the following command at the dot prompt:

```
DO VENDOR
```

Because the application has not previously been run, dBASE IV compiles the program files before executing the application. This step is only performed the first time new code is executed. As long as no changes have been made to the underlying program files, this action is performed only once. You are now ready to test the application.

Testing the Application

When you enter the command `DO VENDOR` and press Enter, the application begins to execute. If you have chosen to activate the sign-on banner, the Application Object is displayed on-screen for a few seconds before the **MAIN** menu is activated.

Once the application begins to execute, put yourself in the place of the users. Access each and every menu prompt and perform the action the menu prompt is attached to. Be certain that the application is performing just as you expected.

Because the code is generated by the Applications Generator, programming errors are unlikely. As always, however, the human element is the weakest link in the chain. You may, for example, have accidentally assigned the same action to two menu items or assigned the wrong action to a menu item. Testing is always a necessary part of creating applications. Once you become proficient with the Applications Generator, you will find that you spend more time testing the application than creating it.

Delivering the Application to the End User

Once you have completely tested your application and know it is working properly, you can make it available to the end user.

You can take either of two paths; the choice depends on whether or not you want the end user to be able to eventually modify the application. For example, in creating the VENDOR application, two program (.PRG) files were created: VENDOR.PRG and MAIN.PRG. During your testing cycle, these two program files have been compiled; the compiled version has been written into files with the same name, bearing the .DBO extension.

Typing DIR *.* at the dot prompt displays all files in the directory. VENDOR.DBO and MAIN.DBO are listed among the files on the disk. All report form, label form, and screen format files (.FRM, .LBL, .FMT) have also been compiled into files bearing corresponding names and extensions (.FRO, .LBO, and .FMO). The O, which has replaced the last letter of the extension, stands for Object. Each of these dBASE IV objects is compiled into *object code*, a compiled version of the commands and functions in the underlying files. Object code is created automatically the first time these objects are run.

To distribute this application to users, copy onto a diskette only those files that bear an extension ending in the letter O, along with any .DBF, .NDX or .MDX files that also belong to the application. (End users will, of course, need to run these in their own copy of dBASE IV, or under the RunTime module supplied with the Developer's Edition of dBASE IV. See chapter 16 for more information on distributing applications using the RunTime module.)

By distributing only object files, you make it more difficult for the end user to make modifications to your code; such modifications can introduce problems or bugs. It is not impossible to make modifications, but the computer literacy and sophistication level needed to modify object code are beyond the ambitions of all but a handful of dedicated computer vandals.

If however, you have reason to give an end user the ability to make an alteration to the application (for example, to make minor modifications in a report form or entry screen), you also want to include the .FRM, .LBL, and .FMT files. These files can then be altered by the user. The alterations are automatically compiled as part of the application when the new version is executed. (For this to take place, the SET DEVELOPMENT ON command must be issued before executing the new object for the first time.)

The RunTime module will not compile these files. For users to be able to make changes, they need the full version of dBASE IV or the dBASE IV Developer's Edition.

Some residual files are left after the Applications Generator has done its work, but these are meant to be reserved in case you need to make modifications to the application at a later date. For example, VENDOR.APP is a file that holds the specifications for the Application Object. MAIN.BAR holds the specifications for the BAR menu you called **MAIN**, and REPORTS.POP and DATA.POP contain the specifications for both of the POPUP menus used in this application.

Make sure you retain these files as a backup; this ensures that you can make modifications to the application at a later time without having to rebuild menu structures from scratch. These specification files and the underlying program files (.PRG) should seldom be given to end users unless the users are ready to accept the responsibility of maintaining and making changes in the application.

Remember that the code for the VENDOR application can be found in Appendix C for your reference. Examine the structure of the code generated by the Applications Generator.

Understanding Application Inheritance

As each module of your application is called into service, it inherits certain conditions from the module that called it (such as environmental SETtings or screen-display defaults). You can use the inheritance effect to give your applications more flexibility.

As each new menu or prompt is accessed by your application, these inherited characteristics are passed on. An object can therefore be used in more than one application. The object inherits environmentals and color characteristics, so you do not have to modify the object to make it fit the application.

By having a menu change its display colors, for example, you can color-code the application; each item called by the menu inherits those color settings.

The active database/view can also be made an inherited characteristic. For example, you can create a menu in which each prompt opens a different data file and then calls a POPUP menu whose items offer the user file-maintenance items (such as **REINDEX**, **PACK**, or **COPY**) that do not depend on the data structure. If the items on the POPUP have the **Override assigned database or view** set as in effect at run time, the same menu can be used for any data file that might be open when the menu is called. You can therefore use the inheritance effect to create menus that can be used in any application you might create in the future.

You can also use the inheritance effect to create an object (a POPUP menu whose menu items are available reports) and call that object from another object that overrides the database/view. For example, choosing **REPORTS** from the **MAIN** menu would call a POPUP that offers a variety of SORTs. Each prompt

SETs the view in a particular way, and then activates the **REPORTS** menu. In turn, each item on the menu would use the view in effect at run time. Once the user has selected the way the data should be sorted, the **REPORTS** menu is called to do the printing. Each of those items in the **REPORTS** menu inherits the database/view in effect at run time.

Creating Applications That Use Multiple Data Files

A week has gone by since you gave the owners of Treasure Trove their application; they now want you to add a new feature.

They ask you to enhance the application so that it can be used to keep track of inventory and to identify which vendors supply which items. After they leave, you pat yourself on the back for being far-sighted enough to have included vendor ID numbers in the original data structure. This makes the job much easier.

One benefit of a relational database is its capability to combine information from two or more files into a report. Applications created by the Applications Generator cannot explicitly manipulate multiple data files, but the applications can use views of those files created by a query.

You know that making this modification only requires three new objects. You need a data file (see fig. 3.46), a query file that links the vendor and inventory data, and a report form geared to the combination of these two files. This report can be created at the dot prompt by SETting the view to the query file (see fig. 3.47) and then issuing the CREATE REPORT command. With the VIEW in effect, all fields in both underlying data files are available to be PICKed as you build the report form (see fig. 3.48). You create a report that displays each item in inventory along with the name of the vendor supplying the item.

The query file is necessary to present the data from both files because the Applications Generator has no provision for having multiple files open at the same time. The query combines the data in the two files into a view that can be used as if it were one data file. Views are read-only, however. You must open the individual source data files in order to make changes to the data.

You also need to create on the **MAIN** menu a menu prompt that lets the folks at Treasure Trove perform data-entry operations on the new file.

```
┌──────────────────────────────────────────────────────────────┐
│  Layout   Organize   Append   Go To   Exit          12:12:16 pm│
│                                          Bytes remaining:  3933│
│  ┌─────┬────────────┬────────────┬───────┬─────┬───────┐       │
│  │ Num │ Field Name │ Field Type │ Width │ Dec │ Index │       │
│  ├─────┼────────────┼────────────┼───────┼─────┼───────┤       │
│  │  1  │ PART_NO    │ Character  │   9   │     │   Y   │       │
│  │  2  │ VENDOR_ID  │ Character  │   5   │     │   Y   │       │
│  │  3  │ DESCRIPT   │ Character  │  30   │     │   N   │       │
│  │  4  │ COST       │ Numeric    │   7   │  2  │   Y   │       │
│  │  5  │ ON_HAND    │ Numeric    │   4   │  0  │   N   │       │
│  │  6  │ ON_ORDER   │ Numeric    │   4   │  0  │   N   │       │
│  │  7  │ LAST_ORDER │ Date       │   8   │     │   Y   │       │
│  │     │            │            │       │     │       │       │
│  │     │            │            │       │     │       │       │
│  └─────┴────────────┴────────────┴───────┴─────┴───────┘       │
│ Database  D:\pdb\apps\INV_TORY   Field 7/7                     │
│        Enter the field name. Insert/Delete field:Ctrl-N/Ctrl-U │
│ Field names begin with a letter and may contain letters, digits and underscores │
└──────────────────────────────────────────────────────────────┘
```

Fig. 3.46

Structure for the INVENTORY data file.

```
┌──────────────────────────────────────────────────────────────┐
│  Layout   Fields   Condition   Update   Exit        12:15:43 pm│
│  Vendor.dbf  │ # ID          │ #↓COMPANY       │ REP_NAME       │
│              │ LINK1         │ AscDict1        │                │
│                                                                │
│  Inv_tory.dbf │#↓PART_NO     │ # VENDOR_ID     │ ↓DESCRIPT      │
│               │              │ LINK1           │                │
│                                                                │
│  ┌View────┬───────────┬───────────┬───────────┬───────────┐   │
│  │INVENT  │Vendor->   │Inv_tory-> │Inv_tory-> │Inv_tory-> │   │
│  │        │COMPANY    │PART_NO    │DESCRIPT   │COST       │   │
│  └────────┴───────────┴───────────┴───────────┴───────────┘   │
│ Query   D:\pdb\apps\INVENT   File 2/2                          │
│  Next field:Tab  Add/Remove all fields:F5  Zoom:F9  Prev/Next skeleton:F3/F4 │
└──────────────────────────────────────────────────────────────┘
```

Fig. 3.47

Query-creation screen showing the combined files.

Fig. 3.48

Layout for the Inventory report from the combined files.

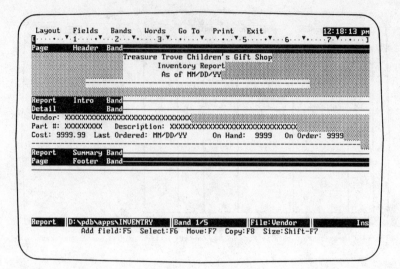

Modifying the VENDOR Application

To modify the VENDOR application, issue the following command:

```
MODIFY APPLICATION VENDOR
```

Then press Enter at the dot prompt.

The Applications Generator opens with the Application Object centered in the middle of the screen. Access the **Design** dialog box and choose **Horizontal bar menu**. From the list, choose **MAIN**. You need to expand the border to accommodate the extra prompt.

Press Shift-F7 (Size) and use the right-arrow key to extend the frame of the menu to the right. Move the cursor onto D in the **DATA** prompt. Make sure you are in the insert mode and then type the prompt VENDOR ENTRY. Use the Delete key to erase the letters DATA (see fig. 3.49). You change the prompt's wording without altering the action attached to it.

When you press Delete to erase the second A, the highlight disappears. The cursor will be one character to the left of Y in ENTRY. Tap the left-arrow key to make sure that when the cursor is on the prompt, both words are highlighted.

While **ENTRY** is highlighted, access the **Item** dialog box and choose **Show item information** to ensure that the menu item's action is to open the menu **DATA**. Clear the **Item** dialog box in order to place the next prompt, **INVENTORY ENTRY**.

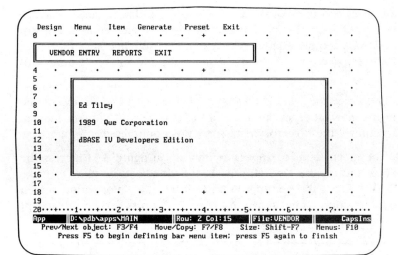

Fig. 3.49

Altering the DATA prompt.

Use the right-arrow key to move one character past the **VENDOR ENTRY** prompt. Then (making sure Insert is still on) insert three spaces with the space bar, press F5 to begin defining an item, and type INVENTORY ENTRY. When you have typed the last character, press F5 to complete the definition. Press Shift-F7 and the left-arrow key to resize the frame (see fig. 3.50).

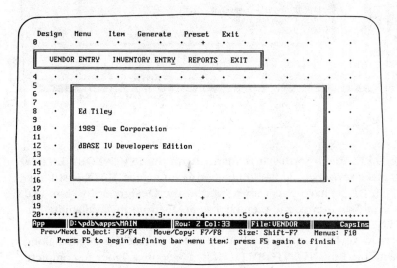

Fig. 3.50

Adding the INVENTORY ENTRY prompt to the menu.

Next you want to make a copy of the **DATA** POPUP so that it can be used to edit the inventory file. Access the **Design** dialog box and choose **Pop-up menu**. Choose **DATA** and press Enter. The data menu now becomes the active object. Press Alt-M to access the **Menu** dialog box and choose 'Name and describe**.

In the Name field, enter the name INVENTRY and press Ctrl-End to accept the entry. This menu is now an exact duplicate of the **DATA** POPUP menu and can be modified to control the inventory data-entry tasks quite easily.

After you edit the menu items to appear as they do in figure 3.51, access the **Menu** dialog box and choose **Override assigned database or view** to make the INV_TORY.DBF file active for this POPUP. When the information screen resembles the information frame shown in figure 3.52, press Ctrl-End to accept the entry.

Fig. 3.51

Altering the new menu to handle inventory items.

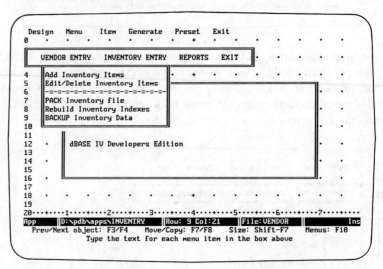

Reposition the **DATA** menu so that it is aligned with the **INVENTORY ENTRY** menu prompt. Make sure that the horizontal-bar menu named **MAIN** is still displayed on-screen. If you have put it away, access the **Design** dialog box and choose **Horizontal bar menu**, and then choose **MAIN** from the availability list. Make the **INVENT** menu active again by pressing F4 several times. Then use F7 and the right-arrow key to position the POPUP menu so that it is aligned along the left edge with the I in **INVENTORY** (see fig. 3.53); press Enter to complete the move.

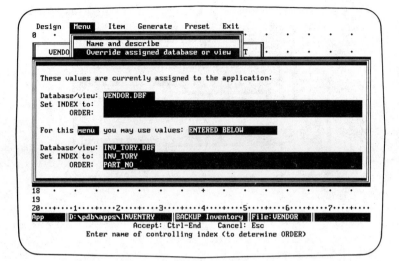

Fig. 3.52

Making the INVENTORY file active for all the actions of the menu.

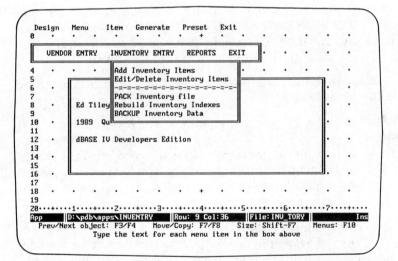

Fig. 3.53

Placement of the new menu.

Use F3/F4 to make **MAIN** the currently selected object. Make sure that the **INVENTORY ENTRY** prompt has **Open a menu** as its action and that the menu it opens is **INVENT** (see fig. 3.54).

All that remains is to modify the **REPORTS** POPUP menu to include the new report. Access the **Design** dialog box, choose **Pop-up menu**, and select **REPORTS** from the files list.

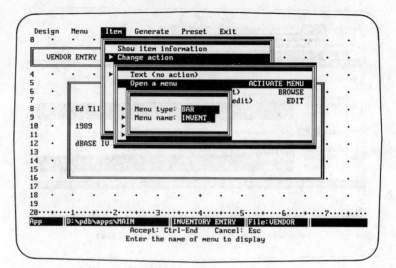

Fig. 3.54

Attaching the new POPUP to the MAIN menu.

Using the Shift-F7 (Size) key, expand the frame of the menu and move the **Mailing labels by ZIP** down one line with the F7 (Move) key. To move just the prompt, make sure the **Mailing labels by ZIP** is highlighted before pressing F7 (Move). Then choose **Item only** rather than **Entire frame**.

Next add the prompt **Inventory Report** to the menu in the blank line left by moving the **Mailing labels by ZIP**.

Your screen should resemble the one shown in figure 3.55. Before you can generate the modified report, you have only one task left: to attach an action to the menu item. Press Alt-I to display the **Item** dialog box and choose **Change action**; then choose **Display or print**. From the resulting menu, choose **Report**. When you have filled in the information frame as it appears in figure 3.56, press Ctrl-End to accept the entry.

Next choose **Override assigned database or view** from the **Item** dialog box so that the entries entered below the values field will be in effect for the time this item is open. If you cannot remember the name of the query file you created to join the two files, remember that Shift-F1 (Pick) presents you with an availability list.

When you have edited the information frame to appear as it does in figure 3.57, press Ctrl-End to accept entry; you can also attach help text and/or a message line prompt to this item.

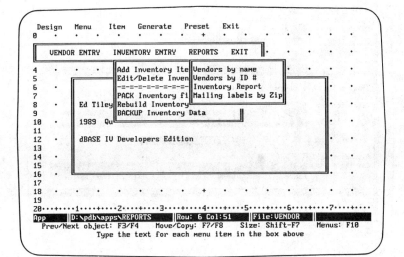

Fig. 3.55

Adding a new line to the REPORTS menu.

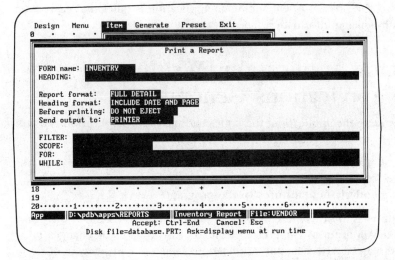

Fig. 3.56

Attaching the Print a Report form to the menu prompt.

When you finish specifying the item, access the **Menu** dialog box and choose **Clear work surface**. This puts away (saves to disk) all the objects you have been working with, leaving only the Application Object on the work surface. Next access the **Generate** dialog box and begin generating the code.

You will be informed that VENDOR.PRG already exists and asked to confirm the overwrite. Press Y and then press Enter; the new application replaces the old one on disk. Once the code is generated, exit the Applications Generator. At the dot prompt, enter the following command to test the new application:

```
DO VENDOR
```

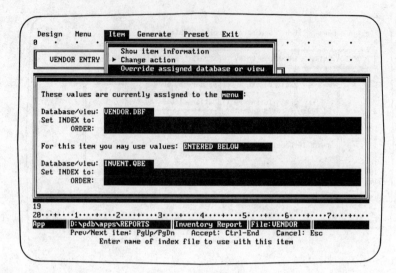

Fig. 3.57

Setting the Database/view for the Inventory report.

As you can see, the process of enhancing an application is quick and easy, even when it requires using information from more than one data file.

Enhancing Applications Written by the Applications Generator

Once you generate the application, the code that makes the application run will be contained in the files VENDOR.PRG and MAIN.PRG just as before.

You can modify this code using either the dBASE IV editor or your text editor. These changes can be as simple as modifying some environmentals or as complex as adding entirely new features to the program.

A note of caution is in order here, however. Once you have modified the code, it is out of the Applications Generator's control. Any updates or changes must be performed manually because the Applications Generator is unaware of these changes. The Applications Generator simply drops them from the application if you regenerate the code with the Applications Generator.

As you gain experience and confidence, however, this becomes less important. For most situations, assembling applications by hand gives you extra control over the way the application executes.

Summary

In this chapter, you learned to create an application using the menus provided with the Applications Generator. You also learned to create dBASE IV objects (data files, entry screens, reports, and labels) and the Application Object. The process of creating BAR and POPUP menus and attaching actions to the menu prompts is covered in detail.

To give you practice, you learned to create Quick Applications for trial runs and for prototyping.

The importance of careful testing of your application is stressed as well as the process of delivering the application to your end user.

By now, you should be more comfortable with using query files to combine data from two or more files. You now have the tools to create applications that use multiple data files, and you learned how to modify and enhance applications written by the Applications Generator.

The most important topic covered, however, is that pre-planning can help you create the best possible application. The importance of planning becomes even more evident as you begin writing applications from scratch.

The next chapter introduces you to writing programs from scratch, thus giving you complete control over how an application executes. Until you have absorbed that material, produce applications with the Applications Generator so that your users can get started while you are getting up to speed.

Part II

Developing dBASE IV Applications

Includes

Writing dBASE IV Programs

Managing Data Entry

Creating Programs That Make Decisions

Building dBASE IV Menus and Screens

Modular Programming in dBASE IV

Six Steps to Good Programming

Handling Multiple Data Files

Writing Programs That Produce Reports

Ensuring Data Integrity

Using Sample Programs as Models

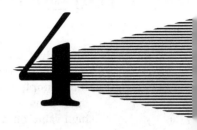

Writing
dBASE IV Programs

In Chapters 2 and 3, you were introduced to the fundamentals of creating macros and applications for others to use. These two techniques are useful, but there are disadvantages to both. Macros can help you automate simple routines. They cannot, however, make decisions based on the condition of data and execute the proper commands to suit the situation. Likewise, the Applications Generator is an extremely powerful tool, but to take full advantage of its power, you need to know how to write programs in both dBASE IV and in the dBASE IV Template Language. By knowing how to write programs, you can tap all the potential of dBASE IV.

Learning to write programs using the commands and functions of the dBASE IV command language enables you to take full advantage of the power and flexibility of dBASE IV. By writing your own programs, you take total control of the application. You specify exactly what is shown on-screen and when. You provide users with the exact tasks to be performed. You ensure that data written to the database is as correct as possible because you specify the data validation routines the application must perform before the data is accepted.

Beginning with this chapter and continuing through chapter 8, you learn to create a simple application that produces a mailing list of customers. Each of the next few chapters presents a new aspect of the mailing list application. The completed application is presented at the end of Chapter 8.

In this chapter, you build a program that imports outside data into a data file and then discards any duplicate records that may have been introduced to the data file.

About half the applications you create will require some sort of data import from sources outside of dBASE IV, either because the data was purchased (as in the example used in this chapter) or because different hardware/software configurations were used to create the data in the first place. Users tend to put a high value on data that has previously been created by another program or system. In most cases, the cost of rekeying far exceeds the cost of converting data.

The chapter also shows you how to take control of dBASE IV by using the dBASE IV command language and programming techniques. You learn how to control the dBASE IV environment through the use of memory variables and macro substitution. You also learn how to bind several operations into a compiled application.

Using the dBASE IV Command Language

dBASE IV programs are (in simple terms) ASCII files containing the commands and functions that perform a task(s) automatically. The dBASE IV command language is extremely flexible and powerful, making it easy to create applications that perform complex operations with a minimum of development time.

For the most part, you already know the dBASE IV command language. Included in the language are the same commands you enter at the dot prompt. In a program environment, however, the command language offers extra tools (commands used only in programs) to help you control the computer's actions.

To create a dBASE IV program, use the MODIFY COMMAND command at the dot prompt. dBASE IV program names follow all standard DOS conventions concerning file names. For example, to create a program called ADD_CUST, you issue the following command:

```
MODIFY COMMAND add_cust
```

Using Text Editors in Programming

dBASE IV provides a built-in text editor that is especially designed for writing programs and accepting data entry in memo fields. The files created by the built-in editor are saved to disk in pure ASCII format. Figure 4.1 displays the work surface and menu structure of the dBASE IV text editor.

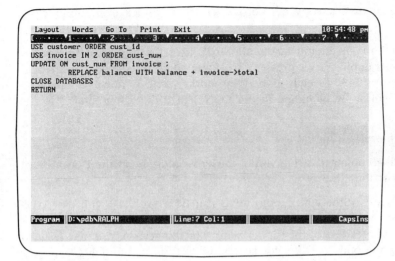

```
   Layout   Words   Go To   Print   Exit                    10:54:48 pm
[.....1......2......3......4......5......6......7.......]
USE customer ORDER cust_id
USE invoice IN 2 ORDER cust_num
UPDATE ON cust_num FROM invoice ;
         REPLACE balance WITH balance + invoice->total
CLOSE DATABASES
RETURN




Program  D:\pdb\RALPH          Line:7 Col:1                CapsIns
```

Fig. 4.1

The dBASE IV built-in text editor.

You can use as a program any file written to disk in pure ASCII format (sometimes also called a DOS text file) that bears the extension .PRG. You can create the file in your text editor or word processor, and then call dBASE IV and run the program.

Moving back and forth between dBASE IV and your word processor, however, can take a lot of time and disk accessing. With dBASE IV, you can use the text editor of your choice in place of the built-in editor. You then use the dBASE command MODIFY COMMAND to edit any files using your favorite text editor. If you want to substitute the text editor of your choice for the dBASE editor, however, you must alter the CONFIG.DB file.

Text editors are used in two situations in dBASE IV: in response to the command MODIFY COMMAND and when accepting entry in a memo field.

In response to MODIFY COMMAND, which allows you edit any text file, dBASE opens either the built-in editor or any editor that has been specified in the CONFIG.DB file. The following line in the CONFIG.DB file specifies the text editor of your choice:

    TEDIT = <*command*>

command is the command string you would type at the DOS prompt to invoke the editor of your choice. Make sure, however, that the computer can find the editor's files through the DOS PATH command before loading dBASE IV.

Alternately, you can include a path as part of the CONFIG.DB entry, as in the following example:

    TEDIT = \WP\WP

This example invokes a copy of WordPerfect that resides in a subdirectory named WP.

For accepting entry in memo fields, dBASE IV uses the built-in editor as the default. If, for example, a user presses Ctrl-Home while the data-entry cursor is in a memo field, dBASE IV calls its built-in editor. You can, however, specify a different text editor by including in the CONFIG.DB file a line similar to the following:

```
WP = <command>
```

command is the command string you or a user would type at the DOS prompt in order to start the editor.

Using an alternate editor with memo fields can be a problem with early versions of dBASE IV because the screen does not repaint after the editor terminates, leaving whole areas of the screen blank. For this reason, you may want to insist on using the built-in editor for accepting entry in memo fields.

Designing the Mailing List Application

The owners of the Treasure Trove Children's Gift Shop (see Chapter 3) have come to you with yet another problem to solve. They have decided to contract with a company, the Monolith Mailing List Company. Monolith will provide Treasure Trove with lists of prospective customers in each of the three cities in which Treasure Trove shops are located.

The lists will be delivered on diskette(s) in a BASIC format comma-delimited file. The folks at Treasure Trove want you to create an application they can use to read the records into a database, eliminate duplicates, and print mailing labels. They want to be able to extract the prospects in their database so that they can target different mailings to different groups of customers based on residence, income level, and the number of children in the family.

Some mailings will be produced in-house; larger mailings of printed material will be handled by Treasure Trove's printer.

To have dBASE IV import data from most sources, you include the APPEND FROM command. Among others, dBASE IV can read files such as Lotus 1-2-3 files, Data Interchange Format files (DIF), Standard Data Format (SDF) files, and comma-delimited files.

The comma-delimited file is more or less a common denominator because almost every data management software package written in the last ten years can create a comma-delimited file.

The folks at Treasure Trove provide you with a file specification showing the structure of the data as it is to be supplied by the company selling the lists (see fig. 4.2).

Fig. 4.2

The file specification sheet for the Treasure Trove Children's Gift Shop.

Monolith Mailing List Company
File Specification Sheet: Treasure Trove Children's Gift Shop

All mailing lists will be supplied on diskette in a comma-delimited format. Each field will be separated by a comma from the field that follows. Each entry on the mailing list will be followed by a hard carriage return.

The fields will be comprised as follows:

TITLE	4
FIRST NAME	12
MID. INITIAL	1
LAST NAME	12
STREET ADDRESS	30
CITY	17
STATE	2
ZIP CODE	10
INCOME CODE	1
# CHILDREN	2

The number following each field name represents the maximum character length of the field.

Explanation of yearly income codes:

1 = Under 15,000
2 = 15,001 to 25,000
3 = 25,001 to 35,000
4 = 35,001 to 50,000
5 = 50,001 to 100,000
6 = Over 100,000

A sample line from the file might look like the following:

"Dr.","Henry","L","Jacobs","234 West St.","Wilson","AL","32456-3332",2, 3

After giving the problem some thought, you decide that for the Treasure Trove application to be really useful, you need to create an application that will allow the Treasure Trove staff to import the monthly list from Monolith. The application will also provide an entry screen in which employees can add names, edit records that are in the file, delete selected records, and purge duplicates based on street address and ZIP-code fields.

You also want to offer the user a printing module that will include the following capabilities: a list of all prospects, as well as the capability to produce mailing labels according to the following formats: print all the labels; print labels by city, and print labels by income code.

All the routines in the application will be bound together by a menu so that Treasure Trove employees can use the system easily, with a minimum of training.

Each of the next few chapters presents a new concept that will help you more fully develop the mailing list application for the Treasure Trove staff. The final result, the completed application, is presented at the end of Chapter 8.

For now, you have several tasks at hand. They include creating the data and index files, designing an entry screen, creating label formats, and designing a menu to bind all the operations together.

Creating the Data File

Your first task is to create the data file to hold the prospects. Figure 4.3 shows the structure of the MAILLIST.DBF data file.

Fig. 4.3

The structure of the MAILLIST.DBF file.

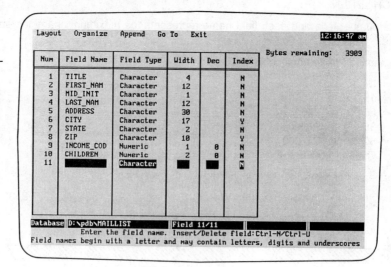

Importing Data into the Database

When developing an application, it is best to create the programs that will be combined as small, single-task modules. The advantage of this method is that you can concentrate on one aspect of the problem at a time. Additionally, small routines are easier to debug and maintain.

The following code, which imports data from the comma-delimited files supplied by the mailing company, is short and simple:

```
USE maillist
APPEND FROM monthly.dta DELIMITED
CLOSE DATABASES
```

This code opens the data file, adds the information to a file called MONTHLY.DTA, and then closes the data file.

Eliminating Duplicate Prospects

A handy dBASE IV feature, which is included in its INDEXing capabilities, is the creation of UNIQUE indexes. While the MAILLIST.DBF file is open, issue the following command:

```
INDEX ON zip + address TAG dup_find UNIQUE
```

A UNIQUE index contains only those records whose key expressions are totally different. If two records have the same key expression, only the first will be recorded in the index, logically eliminating those records with duplicate keys.

By INDEXing on the expression zip + address, only one label will be printed for each address found in the data file because no two households within any ZIP-code area can possibly have the same street address.

Figure 4.4 shows the output of the DISPLAY STATUS command after the index TAGs have been created.

Because testing your programs is essential, you want to put some test data into the file. Be sure to include one or two duplicate records to make sure that the purge portion of the program is operating correctly.

Figure 4.5 displays the result of the LIST command when the ORDER is set to the TAG ZIP. Notice that there are two duplicate pairs of records. Figure 4.6 shows the result of the LIST command when the ORDER is set to the TAG dup_find. Only one of each of the duplicate records is LISTed.

Fig. 4.4

Using the DISPLAY STATUS command to show file and environmental information.

```
Currently Selected Database:
Select area:  1, Database in Use: D:\PDB\MAILLIST.DBF   Alias: MAILLIST
Production   MDX file:  D:\PDB\MAILLIST.MDX
           Index TAG:       CITY  Key: CITY
           Index TAG:       ZIP  Key: ZIP
           Index TAG:       DUP_FIND  Key: zip+address (Unique)

File search path:
Default disk drive: D:
Print destination:  PRN:
Margin =     0
Refresh count =    0
Reprocess count =    0
Number of files open =    5
Current work area =    1

ALTERNATE  - OFF   DELIMITERS - OFF   FULLPATH   - OFF   SAFETY      - ON
AUTOSAVE   - OFF   DESIGN     - ON    HEADING    - ON    SCOREBOARD  - ON
BELL       - ON    DEVELOP    - ON    HELP       - OFF   SPACE       - ON
CARRY      - OFF   DEVICE     - SCRN  HISTORY    - ON    SQL         - OFF
CATALOG    - OFF   ECHO       - OFF   INSTRUCT   - ON    STATUS      - OFF
CENTURY    - OFF   ENCRYPTION - OFF   INTENSITY  - ON    STEP        - OFF
Press any key to continue...
```

Fig. 4.5

A LISTing of data showing duplicates.

```
Record#  TITLE FIRST_NAM   MID_INIT LAST_NAM   ADDRESS
CITY            STATE ZIP          INCOME_COD CHILDREN
    2  Mr.   Raoul       S        Hernandez  2523 Simmons Ln.
Walton Beach   FL    32345-3444        3      2
    7  Mr.   Ralph       D        Williams   984 Western Academy Rd.
Dothan         AL    32422-5433        5      4
    3  Ms.   Sheila      H        Brown      123 Whittaker Ln
Walton Beach   FL    32412-0223        2      2
    1  Ms.   Sheila      H        Brown      123 Whittaker Ln
Walton Beach   FL    32412-0223        2      2
    7  Mr.   Ralph       D        Williams   984 Western Academy Rd.
Dothan         AL    32412-5433        5      4
    5  Dr.   Phillip     R        Johnson    143 Southside Dr.
Dothan         AL    32432-3473        5      1
    8  Mr.   William     D        Billings   123 EZ St.
Walton Beach   FL    32345-6766        6      2
    9  Ms.   Wanda       C        Pesco      534 Cleese Ln.
Dothan         AL    32493-3343        3      3
    6  Dr.   Phillip     R        Johnson    143 Southside Dr.
Dothan         AL    37832-3473        5      1
    4  Ms.   Melinda     K        Fillmore   7543 Carmine Dr.
Walton Beach   FL    32354-9874        2      3
```

Note that the UNIQUE index does not erase duplicate records but hides them from the actions of dBASE IV commands. The records still take up disk space in the data file. You need to include in the application a routine that APPENDs the new information and then removes any duplicate records.

Be aware of this trick: when you use the COPY TO command with a UNIQUE index as the master (controlling) index, only those records seen by the index are transferred.

Fig. 4.6

A LISTing of data showing duplicates removed by the UNIQUE index.

You face a design decision at this point. Do you include two routines: one to bring in the new data and another to purge duplicate records? Or do you combine the two actions in one routine?

Generally you want your program to be broken up into the simplest modules possible. In this case, however, you want to make sure that no duplicate records exist when the labels are printed. It makes sense, then, to combine the two actions in one routine. That way the user cannot forget to perform the purge before printing the mailing labels.

At the dot prompt, issue the command MODIFY COMMAND new_data. Then enter the lines of code listed in figure 4.7.

```
***** Program: NEW_DATA.PRG *****
* A program that appends information from a file called
* MONTHLY.DTA' and purges any duplicate records
USE maillist ORDER dup_find
APPEND FROM monthly.dta DELIMITED
COPY TO temp
SET SAFETY OFF
ZAP
SET SAFETY ON
APPEND FROM TEMP
ERASE temp.dbf
CLOSE DATABASES
RETURN
***** End of program *****
```

Fig. 4.7

The program NEW_DATA.PRG.

The commands in NEW_DATA.PRG open the data file and APPEND information from a comma-delimited file. The program then creates a temporary data file and copies all the records (except duplicates) into the file.

Any time a command attempts to overwrite a data file or to perform a ZAP (which is the equivalent of the DELETE ALL command followed by the PACK command), dBASE IV requests confirmation before proceeding. SETting SAFETY OFF suppresses this confirmation process. Because the ZAP is programmed, and an inexperienced user might not understand the confirmation prompt, it is best to suppress the confirmation.

Once the data file has been purged, all the records in the temporary file are brought back into the database. This technique effectively removes all duplicate records. The temporary file is then deleted, and the database is closed.

Because the .MDX file is opened at the same time the data file is opened with the USE command, no provision for keeping the indexes current is necessary. When indexes are open (either .NDX or .MDX files), dBASE IV automatically keeps the indexes current with the records in the data file.

To test the program, issue the following command at the dot prompt:

```
DO new_data
```

Understanding the dBASE IV Compiler

Before actually executing the commands in your program, dBASE IV compiles the commands into a special file called an *object file*.

To fully understand how a dBASE IV application is assembled from its individual parts of program code, first understand that all dBASE IV .PRG programs are compiled into .DBO files when they are executed for the first time. The extension .DBO stands for *dBASE object*. These files are also recompiled whenever the code changes so that the object file reflects any modifications to the program code.

Previous versions of dBASE have worked interpretively. Interpretive processing is similar to the way dBASE IV processes commands entered at the dot prompt and the way BASIC programs are run.

First, the command string is parsed to determine any errors in syntax. If errors exist, an error condition is triggered.

If there are no syntax errors, the command string is converted into machine language: the zeros and ones a microprocessor can "understand." Then, and only then, is the command executed by the database engine.

With previous versions of dBASE, typing DO ‹*prog_nam*› at the dot prompt opens the program file (.PRG). The first command is then read into the interpreter. Each line of code is checked for syntax, translated, and then executed.

The major drawback to this method is that once the program has become perfected so that it runs bug-free, the first two steps are redundant. If the program works properly today, you can pretty much count on the fact that it will work properly tomorrow, too. Checking syntax and translating the command into machine language is therefore a waste of time once it has been performed the first time.

dBASE IV, on the other hand, compiles your programs before running them. This compilation process first performs syntax checks on each of your command lines and then translates them into machine language. The result is an object file which is written to disk with the extension .DBO. This is the object code actually run when you invoke that program a second, third, or subsequent time.

The compiling process speeds execution many times over. In most cases, it takes much longer to check and translate a command than it does to execute it. By compiling the code, you eliminate the two slowest steps in the process. Compared to previous dBASE versions, dBASE IV programs execute as much as ten times faster once they have been compiled.

Modifying the Mailing List Application

One shortcoming of the routine presented with NEW_DATA.PRG is that the data being brought into the database has to be in a file called MONTHLY.DTA. It is unreasonable to expect that each month's data will be contained in files with the same name.

What is needed here is some interaction with the user of the program. This beginning step toward creating a user interface relies on manipulating the screen and memory variables in order to do the job.

The easiest way to deal with this problem is to allow the user to tell the program which file to use when APPENDing the new records. To do this, you can include in the program a memory variable to hold the name of the file as typed by the user.

Using Memory Variables

Memory variables are named areas in RAM in which data can be stored temporarily. Variables have the same data types as fields. with one exception: a memo field cannot be created as a memory variable. Some commands, such as `ACCEPT` and `INPUT`, can create variables, but most of the time you use either the `STORE` or = commands to initialize (create) memory variables. Notice the following example:

```
STORE 123 TO varl
```

Alternately, you can use the following form:

```
varl = 123
```

Both commands store the numeric value one hundred twenty-three (123) to a variable named varl. To retrieve the stored value, you need only refer to the variable name, as in the following example:

```
? varl
```

This command outputs the value of the variable and not the string "varl".

Chapter 6 contains more detailed information about memory variables. For now, just keep in mind that for a variable to be legal, its contents must be able to be stored as a field within a data file.

Using Macro Substitution

Another important use of variables is to store a piece of information in RAM that can later be retrieved and used to supply an argument to a command. The benefit of this feature is that a program can be written to be as flexible as possible. For example, instead of having one file name embedded in the code, the ability to substitute a variable value for the argument of a command allows the program to use any file the user types into the variable.

In most cases, dBASE IV allows you to use a macro substitution of a variable as an argument to a command.

NOTE: Macro substitution is not related to recording macros. (See Chapter 2 for information on dBASE IV macros.) Macro substitution is a method of telling dBASE IV to use the value of a variable as part of a command. You signal a macro substitution by placing an ampersand (&) in front of the variable's name. Notice the following example:

```
USE &fil_name
```

In the preceding line, dBASE IV substitutes the value of the variable fil_name into the command string, rather than trying to open a file called FIL_NAM.

The program NEW_DATA.PRG can be amended (see fig. 4.8) to allow the user to specify a file name.

```
***** Program: NEW_DATA.PRG *****
* A program that appends information from a file specified
* by the user and purges any duplicate records. The code has been
* modified to accept any file name.
ACCEPT "Enter the name of the file with new records: " TO new_fil
USE maillist ORDER dup_find
APPEND FROM &new_fil DELIMITED
SET SAFETY OFF
COPY TO temp
ZAP
SET SAFETY ON
APPEND FROM TEMP
ERASE temp.dbf
CLOSE DATABASES
RETURN
***** End of program *****
```

Fig. 4.8

The program NEW_DATA.PRG modified to allow appended information from a file specified by the user.

Suppressing dBASE IV Screen Messages

When you run the program NEW_DATA, a number of messages are painted on-screen by dBASE IV. Figure 4.9 shows the messages generated by the commands in the NEW_DATA program file as it runs. These messages may be acceptable and even desirable when you enter commands interactively at the dot prompt, but you want to suppress them when your programs are running.

Not only are these messages distracting to users, they can interfere with program execution. As each message is displayed, the screen is scrolled up a line. On-screen messages which you have included to guide the user through a procedure can be scrolled off the top of the screen and lost.

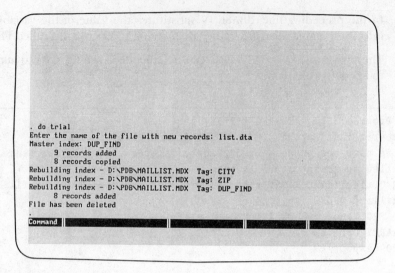

Fig. 4.9

A trial run of NEW_DATA.PRG executing with SET TALK ON in effect.

```
. do trial
Enter the name of the file with new records: list.dta
Master index: DUP_FIND
        9 records added
        8 records copied
Rebuilding index - D:\PDB\MAILLIST.MDX   Tag: CITY
Rebuilding index - D:\PDB\MAILLIST.MDX   Tag: ZIP
Rebuilding index - D:\PDB\MAILLIST.MDX   Tag: DUP_FIND
        8 records added
File has been deleted
.
```
```
Command
```

You should suppress these messages whenever possible. Therefore, you should begin nearly every program/application you write with the following three SET commands:

SET STATUS OFF	Clears the status bar usually present on line 21 of the screen.
SET SCOREBOARD OFF	Prevents dBASE IV from displaying the settings of the Insert, Num Lock, and Caps Lock keys on line 0 (the top line) of the screen when the status bar is turned off.
SET TALK OFF	Suppresses all messages (except error messages) normally presented by dBASE IV.

It is your responsibility as a designer to keep your users informed about what is going on. Shielding users from the intricacies of dBASE IV, including confusing messages, is also your responsibility.

Figure 4.10 is a version of NEW_DATA.PRG which has been modified to take full control of the screen by suppressing messages.

When the SET commands are added to NEW_DATA.PRG, the screen has a much cleaner appearance when the program executes (see fig. 4.11). Only one prompt, that created by the ACCEPT command, appears on-screen. Placing a CLEAR command before the RETURN in the code will erase that line from the screen. When the program is finished, only a dot prompt will appear on-screen.

```
***** Program: NEW_DATA.PRG *****
* A program that appends information from a file specified by the
* user and purges any duplicate records. This version of the
* program also takes full control of the screen. The code has
* been modified a second time.
SET TALK OFF
SET STATUS OFF
SET SCOREBOARD OFF
ACCEPT "Enter the name of the file with new records: " TO new_fil
USE maillist ORDER dup_find
APPEND FROM &new_fil DELIMITED
SET SAFETY OFF
COPY TO temp
ZAP
SET SAFETY ON
APPEND FROM TEMP
ERASE temp.dbf
CLOSE DATABASES
RETURN
***** End of program *****
```

Fig. 4.10

The program NEW_DATA.PRG modified to take full control of the screen.

```
Enter the name of the file with new records: list.dta
.
```

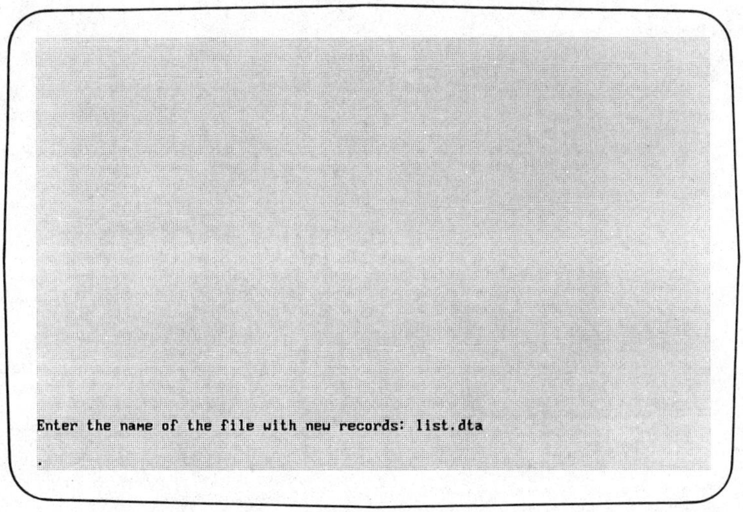

Fig. 4.11

A trial run of NEW_DATA.PRG executing with SET TALK OFF in effect.

Summary

In this chapter, you learned to create a simple dBASE IV program. You learned to enter program commands into an ASCII file so that they can be compiled into "object code" by the dBASE IV compiler. To run the program, use the DO command.

You also learned how to use a memory variable to ACCEPT information from the user, and how to use the macro-substitution function to tell dBASE IV to use the value of the variable as an argument to a command.

You learned how and why to take control of the screen in order to suppress the messages that dBASE IV would otherwise paint on-screen as your program executes.

In the next chapter, you learn how to accept entry from the user utilizing the a...SAY...GET command and how to use variables more effectively. These skills will help you complete the mailing list application.

Managing Data Entry

I n Chapter 4, you were introduced to the principles of designing an application that produces a mailing list of customers. Effective data-entry screens
are needed for this application so that the Treasure Trove staff can add, edit,
and delete prospects in the MAILLIST.DBF database. To accomplish this task,
the application must provide users with effective and efficient data-entry.

In this chapter, you learn to create programs that control data entry. The
`@...SAY...GET` command and the mechanics of `APPEND`ing records and positioning the record pointer for edits and deletions are presented.

The chapter also introduces the optional arguments to the `@...SAY...GET` command as well as the process of accepting entry into memo fields.

Constructing Data-Entry Programs

One way to create data-entry programs is to construct a report format file and
then use the `APPEND` and `EDIT` commands. These commands are excellent tools
for someone working "a la carte" at the dBASE IV dot prompt, but present some
weaknesses that make them less attractive when you are designing applications
for users who are unfamiliar with dBASE IV. Remember that one objective in
building applications is to create an environment in which users follow the
rules of the application, not necessarily the rules of dBASE IV.

The major problem with the `APPEND` command is that the user has to know to
press Enter in the first field (leaving it blank) in order to terminate the process.
All too often, new users forget this and press PgDn or some other key, thus
placing blank records into the database. This error can have an impact on their
confidence. It can also make them believe that the reports are not acting correctly (because the first ten lines are always blank). In reality, the report form
is not wrong; it is just that the first ten records in the file are blank.

121

The shortcomings of the EDIT command are more pronounced. First, there is the issue of placing the record pointer. If the file is indexed by last name, and the user wants to edit the record for Hector Villas, the user must press many PgDns to get there. To some extent, the BROWSE command can help position the record pointer, but you then give up the data-validation benefits that are built into the dBASE language. Additionally, your users need to know that pressing Ctrl-U marks records for deletion.

To solve potential data-entry problems fostered by the APPEND and EDIT commands, you want to create data-entry program modules that are easy to use yet provide the maximum in data validation. You can produce these modules by using the @...SAY...GET command within programs.

@...SAY...GET, one of the most frequently used commands in the dBASE IV language, is useful both for accepting data from the keyboard as well as for outputting data to the screen and printer. @...SAY...GET and its options are covered in the following sections.

Understanding the @...SAY...GET Command

The backbone of dBASE IV data-entry operations is the @...SAY...GET command. Its main function is to place on-screen a prompt that tells the user what information to enter and then provide a place in which to type the information. Nine optional clauses can be added to the @...SAY...GET command. The clauses provide features such as entry formatting, data validation, and color settings.

The syntax of the @...SAY...GET command is as follows:

```
@ <row>,<col> [SAY <exp>
    [PICTURE <expC>[[FUNCTION <function list>]]
[GET <variable/field>
    [[OPEN] window <window name>]
    [PICTURE <expC>]
    [FUNCTION <function list>]
    [RANGE [<low>][,<high>]]
    [VALID <condition> [ERROR <expC>]]
    [WHEN <condition>]
    [DEFAULT <exp>]
    [MESSAGE <expC>]]
    [COLOR [<standard>][,<enhanced>]]
```

Understanding the Syntax of @...SAY...GET

The syntax of the main portion of the `@...SAY...GET` command is discussed in the next sections.

@ <row>, <col>

The first portion of the `@...SAY...GET` command positions the left edge of whatever expression is to be painted on-screen. An `@...SAY` without a `GET` clause is often used to paint information on-screen or to send report information to the printer.

The *row* argument specifies the line on the screen or on the printed page at which the prompt is to appear. The functions `ROW()` and `PROW()` (or a numeric expression) can be substituted to position the prompt on the proper row.

The *col* argument specifies the column (measured from the left margin) at which the prompt should begin. The `COL()` and `PCOL()` functions (or a numeric expression) can be substituted to provide a number which is used as the column to begin placement. Note the following example:

```
@10,10 SAY "Hello"
```

This command places the word `Hello` on the tenth line of the screen, ten columns to the right of the left margin (see fig. 5.1).

```
                          Caps



                                              Fig. 5.1
                                              ─────────
                                              Placing a message
                                              on-screen.



   HELLO
```

SAY <exp>

The `SAY` portion of the command specifies the expression to be painted on-screen (or printed in a report). The expression is most often a character string; however, almost any legal dBASE IV expression can be used.

The `SAY`ed expression can be made up of more than one field or variable. In these cases, you must convert each of the individual parts of the compound expression that returns a single data type, as in the following example:

```
@10,10 SAY "Today's date is: " + DTOC(DATE())
```

The expression "Today's date is: " + DTOC(DATE()) returns a character string (see fig. 5.2).

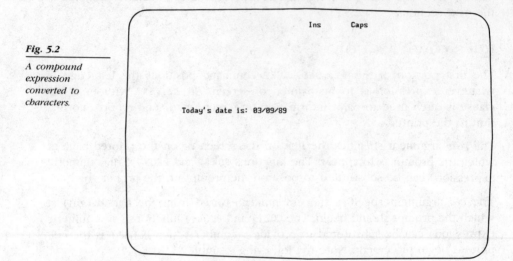

Fig. 5.2

A compound expression converted to characters.

GET <variable/field>

The GET clause of @...SAY...GET specifies the location of the variable/field when the READ command is issued. There are two ways to issue the GET: with a SAY statement or without. The following two statements produce exactly the same effect (see fig. 5.3):

```
@10,10 SAY "Enter last name: " GET elnam
```

or

```
@10,10 SAY "Enter last name: "
@10,27 GET elnam
```

You can perform a GET on a variable or field in which the prompt is already painted on-screen. You do not need to include the SAY portion in an @...GET command.

To create multiple-page entry screens, include the @...SAY...GET commands as part of a format file. You use the command SET FORMAT TO to activate the GETs. To create the pages, you insert READ commands at the points where the page breaks will occur. Users can press PgUp or PgDn to cycle among the different screens.

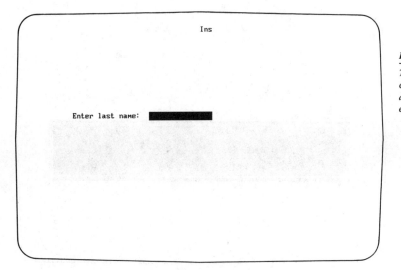

Ins

Enter last name: ▮▮▮▮▮▮▮▮▮▮▮▮

Fig. 5.3

The @...SAY...GET command used for accepting data entry.

Exploring the Options of the @...SAY...GET Command

A number of options are available with the @...SAY...GET command. Take a few minutes to look at each option covered in the following sections.

OPEN WINDOW <window name>

The OPEN WINDOW clause is used to control the editing of memo fields in the entry screen. A memo field can be displayed in one of two ways: as a TAG or a WINDOW. If you do not include the OPEN portion of the clause in the command, the memo field appears in the entry screen as a small GET box with the word memo inside. When the cursor is placed on this field, pressing Ctrl-Home opens up the editor so that entry can be made into the memo field.

If you specify the OPEN portion of the clause, the memo field is displayed as a window that remains open on-screen during the data-entry process (see fig. 5.4). The window must be named with the DEFINE WINDOW command. The syntax for the DEFINE WINDOW command is as follows:

```
DEFINE WINDOW mem1 FROM 11,5 TO 15,75
@10,10 SAY "Memo field: " GET memfield OPEN WINDOW mem1
READ
```

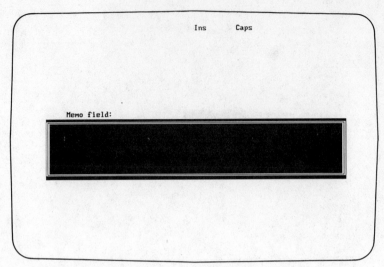

Fig. 5.4

*Using a WINDOW
to accept entry
into a memo field.*

PICTURE <expC> and
FUNCTION <function list>

The PICTURE and FUNCTION clauses of the @...SAY...GET command are used to format SAY output or to provide an edit mask that controls input in the GET portion of the command.

The FUNCTION clause specifies conditions that apply to the entire SAY or GET, such as capitalizing all the characters in the entry. The PICTURE clause specifies a template that formats or controls entry on a character-by-character basis.

The PICTURE and FUNCTION clauses in the SAY portion of the command are seldom used for data-entry screens. Their main use is in formatting information sent either to the screen or the printer for reports.

These clauses, however, work exactly the same way as the PICTURE and FUNCTION clauses that are applied to the GET portion of the @...SAY...GET command. Tables 5.1 and 5.2 list the PICTURE and FUNCTION symbols recognized by the dBASE IV @...SAY...GET command.

Table 5.1
PICTURE Clause Symbols of the @...SAY...GET Command

Symbol	Function
!	Converts alphabetic characters to uppercase without affecting any other characters.
#	Restricts input to digits, blanks, and plus and minus signs.
$	Displays the current currency symbol in place of leading zeros in numeric fields.
*	Displays asterisks in place of leading zeros in numeric fields. Used to separate numeric periods. The comma only appears if there is a digit to its left.
.	Specifies decimal placement.
9	Allows only the characters 0-9 in character data. Allows only the numbers 0-9, plus signs, and minus signs in numeric data.
A	Allows only alphabetic characters.
L	Allows only logical data. Restricts entry to the letters t, T, f, F, y, Y, n, N.
N	Restricts data entry to letters and numeric digits.
X	Allows any character.
Y	Used in logical fields to force Y and N as the only valid responses (eliminates T or F). Responses are automatically converted to uppercase.

Table 5.2
FUNCTION Clause Symbols of the @...SAY...GET Command

Symbol	Function
!	Allows any character; converts alphabetic characters to uppercase.
^	Displays numeric data in scientific notation (for example, $1.85 + 10^2$).
$	Displays numeric data in currency format.
(	Encloses negative numbers in parentheses.
A	Restricts the entire field to alphabetic characters only.

Table 5.2—*Continued*

Symbol	Function
B	Aligns text flush left within the GET box or SAY area.
C	Displays the string CR (credit) after a positive numeric value; used only in reporting.
D	Conforms data entry of dates to the SET DATE command status.
E	Presents date fields in European date format (dd/mm/yy).
I	Centers text within the GET area.
J	Aligns text flush right within the GET box or SAY area.
L	Displays leading zeros in numeric data.
M	Restricts legal entries into the field to multiple choice. Users can cycle through the available choices by using the space bar.
R	Allows literal characters to be displayed in the GET area but not written to the data file.
S‹*n*›	Limits the size of the GET area on screen. If the variable/field in which entry is being made is wider, the entry inside the box scrolls horizontally.
T	Trims leading and trailing spaces from a variable/field.
X	Displays DB (debit) after a negative numeric value.
Z	Suppresses the painting of zeros in the GET area when a numeric value is equal to zero.

The PICTURE and FUNCTION clauses can be combined in the PICTURE expression to restrict user entry to only acceptable character types. The PICTURE clause provides a template that validates entry on a character-by-character basis. Notice the following example:

```
@10,10 SAY "Enter identification code: " ;
GET id_code PICTURE "@! A9999"
```

NOTE: Remember that the semicolon is used to break a command onto two or more lines for easier reading; the semicolon does not affect the command's operation.

In the preceding example, the PICTURE clause provides a template that restricts entry into the GET box to only five characters. The first character must be alphabetic and the last four characters must be numeric digits. The function ə! provides automatic capitalization of the alphabetic characters allowed in this variable/field.

Generally, you include the FUNCTION as part of the PICTURE clause. However, in some cases, you want a formatting function to apply but do not need to specify a template that restricts character-by-character entry. In these cases, the FUNC-TION clause can stand alone. The following line, for example, restricts entry to alphabetic characters only:

```
ə10,10 SAY "Enter Name: " GET nam FUNCTION "@A"
```

RANGE <low>, <high>

The RANGE clause of the ə...SAY...GET command specifies low and high ranges for acceptable values. For example, in a numeric field, you can include the following clause:

```
RANGE 3,12
```

This clause limits user input into this variable/field to a numeric entry between 3 and 10 inclusive. To specify the lower boundary only, use the following form:

```
RANGE 3,
```

To specify the upper boundary only, use the following form:

```
RANGE ,12
```

Date and character information may also be subject to RANGE checking.

VALID <condition> [ERROR <expC>]

The VALID clause of the ə...SAY...GET command provides more sophisticated error checking based on a condition. This condition can be either explicitly stated as part of the clause or be contained within a user-defined function. In either case, the result of the evaluation must have a logical return value of True (.T.) or False (.F.). Note the following example:

```
ə10,10 SAY "Enter account code: " GET acct VALID $ "aAbBcCdD"
```

Only the letters A, B, C, or D (either upper- or lowercase) are accepted by the GET.

The VALID clause (a new feature in dBASE IV) can also refer to a user-defined function, which can be designed to test the entry as well as to perform certain types of actions.

The ERROR clause, a companion to the VALID clause, can specify an ERROR message to be displayed on the bottom line of the screen when an entry is rejected. See the following example:

```
@10,10 SAY "Account #: " GET acct VALID VERIFY();
ERROR "Try again. That account not found."
```

See Chapter 8 for more information on user-defined functions.

WHEN <condition>

You can use the WHEN clause of the @...SAY...GET command to specify a logical condition that returns the value of True or False. The WHEN specifies whether a particular entry box should be skipped. If the condition evaluates as true (.T.), the user can move the cursor into the GET area and type an entry.

If the condition returns a value of false (.F.), that particular GET is skipped, as in the following example:

```
@10,10 SAY "Enter Credit Limit: " GET lim ;
WHEN UPPER(has_credit) = "YES"
```

If the user has entered YES in the field that determines whether or not credit will be extended, a credit limit can be entered. If the has_credit field has a value other than "YES", the user cannot move the cursor into the GET area.

DEFAULT <exp>

The DEFAULT clause of @...SAY...GET specifies a value which will be pre-planted in the GET area. The value must be of the same data type as the variable/field. This clause of the @...SAY...GET is activated only when APPEND is used to accept entry into a screen controlled by a .FMT file. If SET CARRY is ON, the CARRY value supersedes the default value. Notice the following example:

```
@10,10 SAY "Enter Name: "GET nam DEFAULT "Tom"
```

MESSAGE <expC>

The MESSAGE clause of @...SAY...GET places an instructional message on the bottom line of the screen when the cursor is in that particular GET area (see fig. 5.5). You can then provide instructions to be displayed on the bottom of the screen whenever the cursor is positioned in the GET area. See the following example:

```
@10,10 SAY "Cost: " GET cst;
MESSAGE "Enter Unit Cost "
```

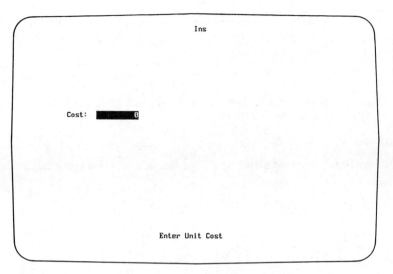

Fig. 5.5

Using a message to instruct the user.

COLOR <standard>, <enhanced>

The COLOR clause of the @...SAY...GET command alters the screen display of individual prompts and GET areas.

The standard color pair is used to paint the SAY expression onto the screen. The enhanced color pair is used to paint the GET area onto the screen.

Standard color codes as specified in the SET COLOR TO command are used in this clause. Table 5.3 lists the letter codes used to specify colors in the SET COLOR command.

Table 5.3
Color Codes for the SET COLOR TO Command

Color	Letter
Black	N
Blue	B
Green	G
Cyan	BG
Blank	X
Red	R
Magenta	RB
Brown	GR
White	W

Use an asterisk (*) to indicate blinking characters and a plus sign (+) to indicate high intensity. For example, to alter the color of only the prompt, use the following form:

```
COLOR W+/D,
```

To specify only the color pair used in the GET area, without altering the color of the prompt, use the following form:

```
COLOR ,N/BG
```

The following line paints the command bright white on a blue background; the GET area is black on cyan:

```
@10,10 SAY "Enter Name: " GET nam COLOR W+/B, N/BG
```

Creating Data-Entry Screens

There are two ways to assemble the @...SAY...GET commands to create data-entry screens. The first is to hand-code each one. This requires a great deal of planning and some experimentation to place everything the way you want it to appear.

You can purchase a screen layout sheet from a computer supply store to help your planning. The sheet includes a grid so that you can draw out your screen design before you write the code. Regular graph paper can be substituted but is not as convenient.

Another method is to use the CREATE SCREEN command to create screen format files. Within the work surface provided by the CREATE SCREEN command, you can visually lay out the prompts and GET areas. After saving the screen layout to disk, you can take the @...SAY...GETs and bring them into your own program files with the text editor. These commands can then be modified to give you a screen with a professional and hand-crafted look in relatively little time.

When you use the CREATE SCREEN command to create screen format files, the files are written to a file with the name you specified and the extension .FMT. A second, compiled version of this file is given the extension .FMO. The .FMT version of the file written in the dBASE language is similar to the one reproduced in figure 5.6. Figure 5.7 shows how the screen-creation work surface looks just before you save the screen.

A large portion of the file is taken up with commands that control environmental issues such as how SET TALK and SET STATUS are set going in and coming out of the routine.

For the moment, you can ignore these commands. The commands of primary interest at the moment are the @...SAY...GETs used to accept data entry.

```
*-- Name....: MAIL.FMT
*-- Date....: 2-24-89
*-- Version.: dBASE IV, Format 1.0
*-- Notes...: Format files use "" as delimiters!
***********************************************************************
*-- Format file initialization code -----------------------------

IF SET("TALK") = "ON"
   SET TALK OFF
   lc_talk = "ON"
ELSE
   lc_talk = "OFF"
ENDIF


*-- This form was created in EGA25 mode.
SET DISPLAY TO EGA25


lc_status=SET("STATUS")
*-- SET STATUS was OFF when you went into the Forms Designer.
IF lc_status = "ON"
   SET STATUS OFF
ENDIF


*-- @ SAY GETS Processing. ---------------------------

*--  Format Page: 1

@ 4,22 SAY "Treasure Trove Mailing List Program"
@ 5,10 TO 17,70 DOUBLE
@ 7,15 SAY "Title & Name: "
@ 7,29 GET title PICTURE "XXXX"
@ 7,34 GET first_nam PICTURE "XXXXXXXXXXX"
@ 7,47 GET mid_init PICTURE "X"
@ 7,48 SAY ". "
@ 7,50 GET last_nam PICTURE "XXXXXXXXXXX"
@ 9,16 SAY "    Address:"
@ 9,29 GET address PICTURE "XXXXXXXXXXXXXXXXXXXXXXXXXXXXXX"
@ 11,29 GET city PICTURE "XXXXXXXXXXXXXXXXX"
@ 11,47 GET state PICTURE "@! AA"
@ 11,50 GET zip PICTURE "99999-9999"
@ 13,33 SAY "Income Code: "
```

Fig. 5.6

The MAIL.FMT program.

Fig. continues

Fig. continued

```
@ 13,46 GET income_cod PICTURE "9"
@ 15,22 SAY "Number of Children in the Family:"
@ 15,56 GET children PICTURE "99"

*-- Format file exit code ------------------------------

*-- SET STATUS was OFF when you went into the Forms Designer.
IF lc_status = "ON"              && Entered form with STATUS ON.
SET STATUS ON                    && Turn STATUS "ON" on the way out.
ENDIF

IF lc_talk = "ON"
    SET TALK ON
ENDIF

RELEASE lc_talk,lc_fields,lc_status
*-- EOP: MAIL.FMT
```

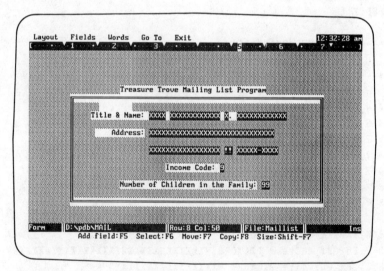

Fig. 5.7

Sample entry screen produced by the MAIL.FMT code.

When you issue the @...SAY...GET command, the prompt you specify and the entry area are painted on-screen. You can issue up to 2,000 GETs in a format file. When you issue the READ command, the GETs are activated and processed in the order in which they were issued.

Because the format file is written in dBASE, you can create the file, and then extract only the @...SAY...GET commands which can then be placed in your program.

Using the standard template in the Applications Generator, you would include the following command:

```
SET FORMAT TO mail
APPEND
```

You can, however, have more control over the data-entry portions of your application. You can write a program (see fig. 5.8) that takes the @...SAY...GETs from the format file and combines them with the APPEND BLANK command (which puts a new blank record at the bottom of the data file) and the READ command (which activates the GETs).

With the program ENTRY.PRG, the data file is opened, a blank record is placed at the end of the file, and then the data is accepted from the user. When the user presses Enter in the last field or presses PgDn at any time, the READ is terminated and the data file is closed. The program then terminates.

```
***** Program: ENTRY.PRG *****
* A simple data-entry program
USE maillist ORDER zip
APPEND BLANK
@ 4,22 SAY "Treasure Trove Mailing List Program"
@ 5,10 TO 17,70 DOUBLE
@ 7,15 SAY "Title & Name: "
@ 7,29 GET title PICTURE "XXXX"
@ 7,34 GET first_nam PICTURE "XXXXXXXXXXX"
@ 7,47 GET mid_init PICTURE "X"
@ 7,48 SAY ". "
@ 7,50 GET last_nam PICTURE "XXXXXXXXXXX"
@ 9,16 SAY "     Address:"
@ 9,29 GET address PICTURE "XXXXXXXXXXXXXXXXXXXXXXXXXXXXXX"
@ 11,29 GET city PICTURE "XXXXXXXXXXXXXXXX"
@ 11,47 GET state PICTURE "@! AA"
@ 11,50 GET zip PICTURE "99999-9999"
@ 13,33 SAY "Income Code: "
@ 13,46 GET income_cod PICTURE "9"
@ 15,22 SAY "Number of Children in the Family:"
@ 15,56 GET children PICTURE "99"
READ
CLOSE DATABASES
RETURN
***** End of program *****
```

Fig. 5.8

The program ENTRY.PRG.

The PICTURE clauses provide templates in which only specified characters can be typed. For example, because the ! function has been included, only alphabetic letters, which are automatically capitalized, are accepted as entries into the STATE field. The ZIP field likewise only accepts numbers. The dash in the PICTURE template prevents entry into that spot, storing the dash as part of the value in the data file.

Using the SET Command

Three variations of the SET command can be used to vary the appearance of your entry screens. These variations include the following:

```
SET INTENSITY

DELIMITERS TO

SET DELIMITERS on/OFF
```

These commands can be used to alter the way GETs appear on-screen. The commands turn off the enhanced color setting or reverse video on monochrome screens (SET INTENSITY OFF); specify characters used to surround the GET area (SET DELIMITERS TO); and turn on the delimiters you have specified (SET DELIMITERS ON).

The following code produces the screen shown in figure 5.9.

```
CLEAR
SET TALK OFF
USE maillist
APPEND BLANK

@5,15 SAY "    Enter title: " GET title
@7,15 SAY "Enter first name: " GET first_nam
@9,15 SAY " Enter last name: " GET last_nam
READ

CLOSE DATABASES
RETURN
```

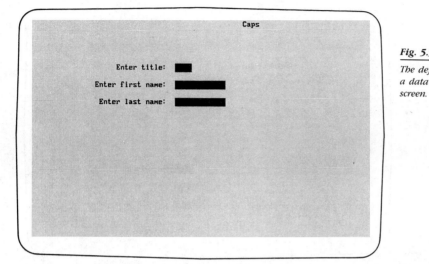

Fig. 5.9

The default look of a data-entry screen.

The addition of the SET commands to the sequence produces the screen in figure 5.10.

```
CLEAR
SET TALK OFF
SET INTENSITY OFF
SET DELIMITERS TO "[]"
SET DELIMITERS ON

USE maillist
APPEND BLANK

@5,15 SAY "    Enter title: " GET title
@7,15 SAY "Enter first name: " GET first_nam
@9,15 SAY " Enter last name: " GET last_nam
READ

CLOSE DATABASES
SET INTENSITY ON
SET DELIMITERS TO
SET DELIMITERS OFF
RETURN
```

Fig. 5.10

A data-entry screen using delimiters.

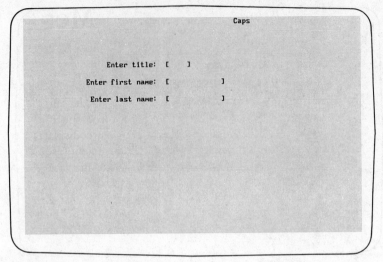

This method of formatting the data-entry screen can prove invaluable when you are programming for an older system that cannot produce color or inverse video, or when you are trying to simulate the appearance of another program that does not use reverse video.

In the preceding examples, the delimiters were specified as the flat bracket characters ([]). To use the same symbol both before and after the GET area, include only one character between the quotes, as in the following example:

```
SET DELIMITERS TO ":"
```

Changing the CONFIG.DB File

Many times applications are designed to be used on more than one machine. If one machine has a video card that cannot display reverse video, you do not have to maintain two versions of the program, nor do all users have to forego color and reverse video for highlights. You only need to alter the CONFIG.DB file on the one problem machine by including the following commands in the CONFIG.DB file:

```
INTENSITY = OFF
DELIMITERS = ":"
DELIMITERS = ON
```

Placing these lines in the CONFIG.DB file sets them as the default method of presenting GETs.

Accepting Entry into Memo Fields

In previous versions of dBASE, the programmer had to create a format file in order to accept entry into memo fields. With dBASE IV, this requirement has been eliminated.

You have two options for handling memo fields in data-entry programs: as TAGs or in WINDOWs. To use memo fields as TAGs, you specify the the memo field just as you would any other field. The procedure displays the GET area as a small box (TAG) containing the word memo. When the user presses Ctrl-Home, an editing window in which information can be entered opens up (see fig. 5.11).

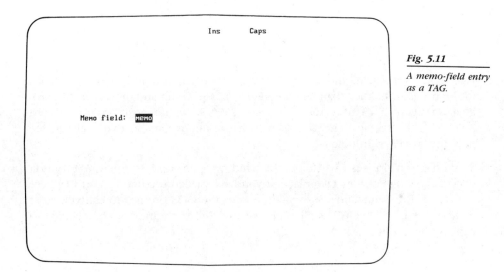

Ins   Caps

Memo field: MEMO

Fig. 5.11

A memo-field entry as a TAG.

The second method is to use the OPEN WINDOW clause of the @...SAY...GET command. This method requires you to first DEFINE a WINDOW that is placed on-screen by the OPEN WINDOW clause. It displays the contents of as much of the memo field as will fit in the WINDOW (see fig. 5.12). To type in the memo field, the user must press Ctrl-Home.

In both methods, the user ends entry into the memo field by pressing Ctrl-End.

For purposes of this demonstration, add a memo field called comment to MAILLIST.DBF (created in Chapter 4) and modify the file ENTRY.PRG so that it contains the commands listed in figure 5.13.

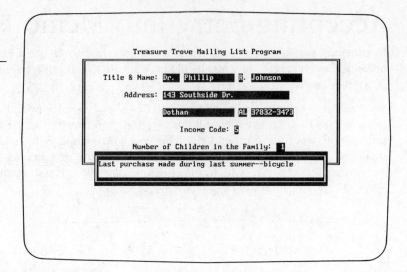

Fig. 5.12

Sample entry screen showing a memo-field WINDOW.

```
                    Treasure Trove Mailing List Program

         Title & Name: Dr.  Phillip      R. Johnson

             Address: 143 Southside Dr.

                      Dothan             AL 37832-3473

                      Income Code: 5

              Number of Children in the Family: 1

         Last purchase made during last summer--bicycle
```

Figure 5.12 represents the screen that appears when you add these commands to the program. Rather than use the APPEND BLANK command, however, the program in figure 5.13 uses the command GOTO 3, which positions the record pointer in the memo field to a record that contains data so that you can see how the screen will look.

When the user presses Ctrl-Home, the window opens up into the dBASE IV text editor, allowing entry to take place. If you have placed the line WP = cmd (where cmd equals the command you would enter at the DOS prompt to call your text editor) in your CONFIG.DB file, you can use the text editor of your choice to edit the memo field.

Summary

In this chapter, you learned how to use the @...SAY...GET command to create data-entry screens. You learned about data validation and how to control user entry with the PICTURE and FUNCTION clauses.

Examples demonstrated how the @...SAY...GET command can be used to provide data validation and instructions to the user, all in one command line.

You also learned how to create format files and then extract the @...SAY...GET commands, bringing them into your data-entry program for customization.

The chapter also discussed two methods used in taking input into memo fields. Memo fields can be included in data-entry programs as TAGS or as WINDOWs. Using WINDOWs for memo fields give your data-entry screens a more professional appearance.

```
***** Program: ENTRY.PRG *****
* ENTRY.PRG modified for accepting entry into a memo field
USE maillist ORDER zip
GOTO 3                      && Positions the record pointer to a
                            && record with an entry already typed
                            && into the fields so that you can see
                            && how it works.


DEFINE WINDOW memwin FROM 16,13 TO 19,67


@ 4,22 SAY "Treasure Trove Mailing List Program"
@ 5,10 TO 17,70 DOUBLE
@ 7,15 SAY "Title & Name: "
@ 7,29 GET title PICTURE "XXXX"
@ 7,34 GET first_nam PICTURE "XXXXXXXXXXX"
@ 7,47 GET mid_init PICTURE "X"
@ 7,48 SAY ". "
@ 7,50 GET last_nam PICTURE "XXXXXXXXXXX"
@ 9,16 SAY "    Address:"
@ 9,29 GET address PICTURE "XXXXXXXXXXXXXXXXXXXXXXXXXXXXXX"
@ 11,29 GET city PICTURE "XXXXXXXXXXXXXXXX"
@ 11,47 GET state PICTURE "@! AA"
@ 11,50 GET zip PICTURE "99999-9999"
@ 13,33 SAY "Income Code: "
@ 13,46 GET income_cod PICTURE "9"
@ 15,22 SAY "Number of Children in the Family:"
@ 15,56 GET children PICTURE "99"
@ 16,13 GET comment OPEN WINDOW memwin
READ

RELEASE WINDOWS memwin

CLOSE DATABASES
RETURN
***** End of program *****
```

Fig. 5.13

The program ENTRY.PRG modified for accepting entry into a memo field.

In the next chapter, you learn how to control your entry screens with the dBASE IV control constructs, so that your users can have some degree of control over data-entry processes.

Creating Programs
That Make Decisions

Thus far, all the programs presented in this book have been little more than dBASE IV batch files. Like a batch file, the first line in the program is executed, then the second, then the third, and so forth until the last command in the file is reached. After all lines in the program have been executed, the program terminates and passes control back to the dot prompt or another program.

These batch-style programs can sometimes be useful in an application, but you will soon find that you need more control. The real power of a computer program is its capability to make decisions and perform appropriate commands based on a given situation.

Chapter 4 presents NEW_DATA.PRG, a program that adds new prospects to the Treasure Trove mailing list. In this program, the user has no control over the program; the user has no way to tell the program to recycle so that additional prospects can be entered. In the program's current form, the user chooses to add a prospect from the menu, enters the information, and is then returned to the menu. The modules for editing and deleting prospect records have not yet been built; these modules must position the record pointer and take instructions from the user about how to proceed.

To build these modules, you need to use memory variables and a group of dBASE IV commands called control structures. The control structure commands provide *conditional branching*, a process that enables you to include in your programs two or more sets of commands that may or may not be executed, depending on the circumstances existing at the time the program is running.

These commands (IF...ENDIF, DO CASE...ENDCASE, DO WHILE...ENDDO, and SCAN...ENDSCAN) give your programs the capability to evaluate a condition and takë the proper action. By chapter's end, you will be familiar enough with these commands to complete the data-entry modules of the Treasure Trove mailing list application.

Creating Memory Variables

Memory variables are small pieces of random-access memory (RAM) that have been carved out to store temporarily any values not stored in data files. The five basic types of memory variables include character, floating point, numeric, logical, and date.

Each of these variables corresponds to a data type found in data-file structures. To qualify as a legal memory variable, the variable must be capable of being stored as a field in a data file. Note that there are no variables of the memo type.

Each memory variable must be given a name. Variable names follow the same rules as field names: they must begin with a letter, are limited to 10 characters, and can contain only letters, numbers, and the underscore character (_).

Using the PRIVATE and PUBLIC Commands

Memory variables fall into two groups: PUBLIC and PRIVATE. To understand PUBLIC and PRIVATE memory variables, remember that a dBASE IV application can be considered a chain of programs. The first-called program is the highest-level program. That program calls another program which, in turn, calls another, and so on, creating a chain of modules that go from the highest level to lower levels.

Memory variables can be created by any program in the application regardless of its level. Usually when one of these programs terminates, all memory variables created on that level are RELEASEd (erased from memory) before control is passed back to the next higher level.

If a lower-level module declares a memory variable to be PUBLIC, that variable is not RELEASEd when the lower-level module terminates; rather, the variable remains in memory and its value is available to any program module in the application until it is RELEASEd.

Memory variables can also be declared as PRIVATE. In later chapters, you learn to develop program modules that can be used in more than one application. The PRIVATE command enables you to create a memory variable that has the same name as a variable that exists in a higher-level module. By declaring the lower-level variable PRIVATE, you protect higher-level variables with the same name from having their value changed by the lower-level variable.

If, for example, program A creates a memory variable called subtotal, and then calls program B, the variable and its value are available to program B. Changes made to the value of subtotal remain even after program B terminates because subtotal is not released from memory until program A terminates.

To protect the value of subtotal from being changed while program B is running (assuming that program B uses a variable called subtotal), you can use the PRIVATE command in program B to create a second variable called subtotal.

Because program B declared it PRIVATE, anything done to the value of subtotal in program B does not affect the variable called subtotal created by program A. When program B terminates, the variable is RELEASEd, and the original variable called subtotal is left unchanged.

This technique enables you to write modules that can be plugged into any application without worrying that a higher-level module uses the same variable name in its code.

Using the STORE and = Commands

The PUBLIC and PRIVATE commands create memory variables, but they are initialized as logical variables with the value .F.. To provide a usable value for the variable, you need to include a STORE or = statement in the program.

The STORE and = commands have two functions: creating memory variables and assigning values to variables.

When dBASE IV encounters a STORE or = command, it first checks to see whether the variable exists. If dBASE IV doesn't find a variable by the same name, it creates the variable and then assigns the value. If the variable named is already in use, dBASE IV assigns it a new value.

Variables created by the STORE and = commands are always PRIVATE unless they have been previously declared PUBLIC.

The STORE and = commands also set the variable type. The variable type (such as data, numeric, date, or logical) is always adjusted to agree with the type of data being placed in the variable.

The following examples of code create new memory variables or give a new value to variables that already exist.

The following command initializes a character variable whose content is the string "Jim":

```
var = "JIM"
```

The following form of the command initializes a numeric memory variable whose value is equal to 12:

```
var = 12
```

In the final example, the STORE command is used:

```
STORE "Jim" TO var1
```

This command performs exactly the same function as var1 = "Jim"

With the STORE form of the command, you can initialize more than one memory variable at a time, as long as all those variables have the same initial value.

The following command creates four numeric variables with the value of zero:

```
STORE 0 TO subtotal,total,tax,balance
```

Either of the next two command lines initializes three memory variables of the date type whose values would be blank.

```
STORE CTOD(" / / ") TO ddat,edat,due_dat
```

or

```
STORE { / / } TO ddat, edat, due_dat
```

Understanding the Uses of Memory Variables

Memory variables are useful for storing several types of information. These include storing user entry to determine program flow; storing values to be used by the SEEK and FIND commands; storing information about the dBASE IV environment; and storing messages and other character expressions so that they can be substituted as arguments to commands.

You can use memory variables to store user entry to determine program flow. For example, you can allow the user to answer Yes or No to determine whether the program should continue.

Memory variables can store values to be used by the SEEK or FIND commands. In this way, you can allow the user to enter an account number or other identifying value and then have the program SEEK the proper record.

You can store information about the dBASE IV environment in memory variables. As an example, you can use the SET() function to store the setting for SET CONFIRM to a variable so that the environment can be restored when the program is finished running.

Messages and other character expressions can be stored in memory variables and later substituted as arguments to commands. For example, you can put the character strings for color settings into a variable so that the program can use the variable's value to change screen colors during program execution.

Giving Variables a Value

The intended use of a variable determines how it is given its value. Variables that are meant to be given a value only by the program are simply stated in the program code with the STORE and = commands. Variables that are meant to be given a value by the user are usually initialized as blanks and then filled in with an @...SAY...GET command.

Notice the following example:

```
var = "Error 142 That file cannot be found."
```

In the preceding code, the variable var can be passed to a subroutine that displays error messages to the user and tries to correct the problem. The value of var is never changed by the user.

The next example illustrates a variable that is given a value by the user.

```
STORE SPACE(5) TO cust_id
@10,10 SAY "Enter the customer account number: " GET cust_id
READ
```

In the preceding code, the variable cust_id is initialized by the STORE command and is given a value of five spaces. This value regulates the width of the entry area and makes it appear blank during the GET issued by the @...SAY...GET command. Once the variable has been given a value by the user, it can be used to direct program flow. For example, SEEK cust_id positions the record pointer to the record specified by the user.

Variables can also be given a value based on the return value of a function which can be used to determine current environmental values while a program is executing. Note the following example:

```
var = SET("TALK")
var = DATE()
```

In the preceding code, the variables take on the values returned by the functions SET() and DATE(). In this manner, values can be stored in memory like snapshots, waiting to be referred to later.

Using dBASE IV Control Structures

To appreciate the way variables are used in programs, you should have an understanding of the dBASE IV program-structure commands (also called constructs) which use memory variables extensively. Once values are stored in memory, those values can be referred to by the control constructs, which use variable and data values to determine the program's actions. Including these constructs in dBASE IV routines lets you take the step up from writing batch files to creating real programs.

In the data-entry program introduced in Chapter 5, each line of program code was executed in order from first to last. To be truly effective, programs must be able to look at a condition and determine which procedure or portion of the program needs to be executed next. In dBASE IV programs, these conditions are usually the values of variables or fields.

A truly useful program must be able to distinguish its surroundings and, based on an evaluation of some condition, be able to branch off into the proper direction. That is why many texts call the results of these constructs conditional branching. Conditional branching is the basis of computer programming in every language.

In dBASE IV, the major control constructs include the following commands: IF...ENDIF, DO CASE...ENDCASE, DO WHILE...ENDDO, and SCAN...ENDSCAN. Within these commands is the capability to decide which piece of program code is actually executed depending on the value of a memory variable, a field, or an environmental condition such as a value created by the SET command. These major control constructs are discussed in the following sections.

Using the IF Command

The IF command is the most basic of the dBASE IV constructs that allow for conditional branching. The basic format of the command establishes a condition that can be evaluated as a Yes or No answer (True or False).

If the condition evaluates as True (.T.), the program lines that follow the IF statement are executed.

The IF command opens up a program structure that must be terminated. For every IF, there must be a corresponding ENDIF that terminates the structure.

If the condition is True, all lines of program code between the IF and the ENDIF are executed. If the condition returns a value of False, the commands between the IF and the ENDIF are ignored. Consider the following example:

```
var1 = 8
IF var1 < 10
   @10,10 SAY "The value of the variable is less than 10."
   @12,10 SAY "These two lines will be painted on the screen."
ENDIF
```

In the preceding example, notice the three-space indentation of the two lines of program code that are part of the IF...ENDIF structure. dBASE IV does not require you to indent code nested inside a control structure like IF...ENDIF. One of your jobs as a programmer, however, is to modify your program code later. Proper indentation of program code within constructs provides visual clues to the logical structure of the program.

By indenting the two lines inside the control structure, you can see at a glance that these lines of code run together as a group. Indenting this way makes your programs easier to read and follow.

Notice also that a value is placed into a memory variable before the IF command is issued. In this example, the memory variable is given the value of 8 in the line directly before the IF command. The proximity of this variable to the IF statement is for illustration only. In practice, if you could assign a value just before an IF is performed, you would not need the IF command because you would already know the value and could decide what to do long before the program is run. Rather, it is the value of some pre-existing condition (such as the value of a calculation in another module or the value of the current record) that is evaluated by the IF during program execution.

Also notice that the comparison used in an IF statement is a valid dBASE IV expression. Consider the next line:

```
IF var1 < 10
```

In the preceding line, var1 < 10 is a valid dBASE IV expression. This means that the expression can be placed in a variable. The expression var1 < 10 returns a logical (True/False) value when it is computed.

Only two conditions can exist in the expression var1 < 10: the statement is either True or False. If the comparison var < 10 is True, dBASE IV executes the first line of code directly following the IF statement and continues with each subsequent line until it reaches the ENDIF. In this case, the statement is True, and both commands positioned between the IF and the ENDIF are executed.

Providing a Branch for Conditions

An additional component to the IF...ENDIF control structure is available to provide for an alternate set of instructions if the comparison is False. Notice the following code:

```
var = 8
IF var <10
   @ 10,10 SAY "The value of the variable is less than 10."
   @ 12,10 SAY "These two lines will be painted on the screen."
ELSE
   @ 10,10 SAY "Because the comparison returns a value of False."
   @ 12,10 SAY "This code is executed as an alternative."
ENDIF
```

In the preceding example, the ELSE clause is used to provide a second set of program instructions that run if the condition evaluates as False.

If the condition evaluates as True, all lines of program code following the IF statement are executed in turn until the ELSE statement is reached. If the condition evaluates as False, all statements following the ELSE statement up to the ENDIF are executed.

To understand constructs, remember that a program pointer (similar to the record pointer) moves along the lines of your program. The line on which the program pointer is positioned is executed next.

With the IF command, the program pointer first positions itself on the IF statement and waits to see what value is returned as a result of the evaluation. If the value is True, the pointer is positioned on the next line of code and works its way down until it reaches either an ELSE or an ENDIF.

If the condition evaluates as False, the program pointer moves to the ELSE statement (if one exists) or to the ENDIF statement. Encountering either of these two commands causes the pointer to position and execute the line that follows.

The commands placed into the IF...ENDIF control structure can be any legal dBASE IV commands, including those that call other programs.

Making Subcomparisons

You often need to make subcomparisons within an IF...ENDIF control structure. Making these subcomparisons is called nesting.

Nesting IF...ENDIF control structures provides a powerful tool for manipulating data. The following code illustrates a nested IF...ENDIF:

```
IF age <18
   IF gender = 'M'
      @10,10 SAY "This boy is a minor."
   ELSE
      @10,10 SAY "This girl is a minor."
   ENDIF
ELSE
   IF gender = 'M'
      @10,10 SAY "This is a man."
   ELSE
      @10,10 SAY "This is a woman."
   ENDIF
ENDIF
```

In the preceding example, three IF...ENDIF control structures are nested together to produce one result.

In this case, the variables age and gender are evaluated. First, age is evaluated to see whether the person's age is less than 18. If this condition is True, that person is a minor, and the second comparison which falls between the leftmost IF and the leftmost ELSE commands is executed.

The code that falls between those two commands is itself an IF...ENDIF control structure. This code determines whether the value of the memory variable gender is equal to the character string M. If so, the program executes the next statement which expresses the fact, "This boy is a minor.". If the gender variable is not equal to the character string M, the program knows that this minor child is female, and the message This girl is a minor. is painted on-screen.

If, however, the original condition, IF age <18 returns a value of False, the IF...ENDIF which falls under the leftmost ELSE command is instead executed.

The code under the ELSE is used to determine the gender, as in the preceding section. You can assume that this comparison will take place only if the age variable comparison is False.

Note that all four possible actions are mutually exclusive, and each message is designed to paint in exactly the same place. Only one of those four commands can be run because only one pair of comparisons can be True whatever the values of age and gender.

Making Compound Evaluations

In certain programming situations, you need to evaluate two or more conditions to establish which branch of the program should be executed.

You can combine multiple evaluations into one expression whose result is True or False by using any of the following three operators: .AND.; .OR.; and .NOT..

The following code illustrates the .AND. operator:

```
IF age > 18 .AND. gender = 'M'
    @10,10 SAY "This is an adult male."
ENDIF
```

There are two sides to the evaluation in the preceding code. First, the age condition is evaluated. Then the gender value is evaluated. For this compound expression to return a value of True, both individual expressions must be True. If either returns a False value, the entire expression is False.

The .OR. operator returns a value of True if either of the individual expressions is True, as in the following example:

```
IF age > 18 .OR. gender = 'M'
    @10,10 SAY "This is an adult of either gender or a minor boy."
ENDIF
```

There are two sides to the preceding evaluation. First age is evaluated; then gender is evaluated. For this compound expression to be True, only one of the two sides must be true. To be False, both sides of the .OR. statement must be False.

The .NOT. operator is used as an inverter. If you want an IF statement to run when the return value is False, use the .NOT. operator to invert the expression's value, as in the following example:

```
IF .NOT. EOF()
    @10,10 SAY "The record pointer is not at the end of file yet."
ENDIF
```

If the value of the EOF() function is True (.T.), the .NOT. inverts the value to True. The message line is therefore only executed when the record pointer is positioned on a valid record.

Nesting Compound Evaluations

Like IFs, compound comparisons can be nested to establish precedence or grouping for complex evaluations. You can also use parentheses to form even more complex comparisons. Notice the following code:

```
IF (age > 18 .OR. gender = 'M') .AND. .NOT. EOF()
    @10,10 SAY "This is an adult of either gender or a minor boy."
    @12,10 SAY "Also the record pointer is not at end of file."
ENDIF
```

In the preceding comparison, the first expression is a compound expression which evaluates the age and gender variables. For this expression to be True, one of the individual comparisons to the right of the .AND. operator must be True, and the value of the EOF() function must be False. Otherwise the code in the structure is not executed.

If both age and gender comparisons are False, or if the value of EOF() is True, the entire expression is False. Even if both the age and gender comparisons are True, a value of True for the EOF() function causes the entire expression to be False.

Using the DO CASE Structure

Often you want your program to be able to branch out in more than the two directions provided with the IF...ELSE...ENDIF construct. At those times, you want to use a DO CASE control construct to provide avenues to multiple branches. The following example illustrates that DO CASE...ENDCASE works much like IF...ENDIF.

```
DO CASE
    CASE choice = "A"
        @10,10 SAY "You have chosen A."
    CASE choice = "B"
        @10,10 SAY "You have chosen B."
    CASE choice = "C"
        @10,10 SAY "You have chosen C."
    OTHERWISE
        @10,10 SAY "You have not chosen A, B, or C."
ENDCASE
```

First, the structure is opened with the DO CASE statement. This differs from the IF...ENDIF only in that the initial line doesn't propose the first comparison as it does in the IF statement.

With DO CASE...ENDCASE, a comparison is proposed by each CASE statement. If the return value of the evaluation is True, the commands following that CASE statement are executed.

If no CASE statement returns a value of True, the statements attached to the OTHERWISE statement (if one exists) are executed.

If no OTHERWISE statement is offered, and none of the CASE statements evaluate as True, no lines of program code within the DO CASE control structure are executed; rather, the line following the ENDCASE is the next line of code to be executed.

The `ENDCASE` statement terminates the `DO CASE...ENDCASE` control structure. For every `DO CASE`, there must be a corresponding and terminating `ENDCASE`.

Nesting is also possible within the `DO CASE` control structure. You can nest either `IF...ENDIF` control structures or other `DO CASE...ENDCASE` control structures within the `DO CASE...ENDCASE` control structure.

Compound comparisons can also be used in the `DO CASE...ENDCASE` control structure.

Using the DO WHILE Structure

One of the most powerful features of a programming language, including dBASE IV, is its capability to repeat sections of program code for as many repetitions as are needed.

For example, you may want to position the record pointer on the first record in a data file, perform a calculation, and then print the result. For each record in the data file, there should be one line of data output in the report. Alternately, you may want to perform those actions on only the next five records in the file.

The `DO WHILE...ENDDO` construct is used to set up multiple repetitions of sections of program code.

Like the `IF...ENDIF` control structure, the first line of a `DO WHILE...ENDDO` also presents a comparison. As long as that comparison returns a value of True, the instructions between the `DO WHILE` and the `ENDDO` continue to execute. Notice the following example:

```
USE cust ORDER cust_no
DO WHILE .NOT. EOF() && This command sets up a comparison that
                     && tells the dBASE IV database engine to
                     && continue repeating the commands inside
                     && the control structure as long as the
                     && record pointer is not at the end of file.

    ?first_nam, last_nam
    SKIP
ENDDO
CLOSE DATABASES
```

In the preceding example, the `DO WHILE .NOT. EOF()` sets up the condition that drives the control structure. As long as the `EOF()` function continues to return a value of False (.F.), the commands that fall between the `DO` and the `ENDDO` are executed repeatedly.

In the preceding example, every record in the data file is acted on by the commands inside the `DO WHILE...ENDDO`. For every record in the data file, the person's name is outputted. The control structure terminates only when the `EOF()` function indicates that there are no more records to process. Upon termination, the program pointer falls to the line of code directly following the `ENDDO` statement.

Eliminating Records from Processing

On occasion, you may want only some records to be processed, based on a certain evaluation of the data. For example, you may only want to select those records that identify past due accounts.

Because you cannot always determine in advance how many repetitions will be needed, or which records meet the criteria of a conditional evaluation, you can nest a comparison within the `DO WHILE...ENDDO` that contains the `LOOP` clause of the control structure. The `LOOP` command passes control back to `DO WHILE` condition, which is re-evaluated. If the condition is still true, the following commands execute.

For example, if you want to alter the previous control structure to ignore all customers whose last name is Smith, you substitute the following code:

```
USE cust
DO WHILE .NOT. EOF()
    IF last_nam = "Smith"
        SKIP
        LOOP
    ENDIF
    ? first_nam,last_name
    SKIP
ENDDO
```

In this example, the first operation inside the control structure is the evaluation of the last_nam field. If last_nam equals Smith, the record pointer is positioned at the next record in the data file, and control is passed back, with the `LOOP` command, to the first line following the `DO WHILE`. Programmers call this type of control structure a *loop*.

If last_nam equals Smith, the record pointer moves on and the loop is repeated. The command that displays the name is not executed if the name equals Smith.

If however, the comparison returns a False (the name is other than Smith), the `LOOP` command is not executed. The command that displays the first and last name is executed, the record pointer is moved to the next record, and the LOOP is processed again. This allows you to exclude records from processing based on a comparison.

Using an EXIT To Terminate the Loop

In other situations, certain conditions can indicate a need to terminate the DO WHILE...ENDDO control structure. This termination is executed with the EXIT command.

With the preceding example, if you wanted to terminate the loop when you reached the first customer whose balance was greater than $1,000, the program code might look like the following:

```
USE cust
DO WHILE .NOT. EOF()
    IF last_nam = "Smith"
        SKIP
        LOOP
    ENDIF
    IF bal > 1000
        EXIT
    ENDIF
    ? first_nam,last_nam
    SKIP
ENDDO
```

You now have two ways to terminate the DO WHILE...ENDDO control structure. Either the record pointer will reach the end of file, or a record will have a balance field whose value is greater than 1,000.

If the comparison involving the balance field is True, the EXIT command is executed. The EXIT command passes control of the program to the line of code immediately following the ENDDO.

Setting Up a Specific Number of Repetitions

Occasionally you need to repeat a set of instructions a specific number of times. To do this, you can assign a number to a variable and either increment or decrement the value of that variable to trigger the comparison in the DO WHILE statement. Notice the following code:

```
reps = 5
DO WHILE reps <> 0
    reps = reps - 1
    ?"The program loop is still running"
ENDDO
```

In the sample code, dBASE IV paints the message five times. Each time dBASE IV rolls through the loop, the value of the variable reps is decremented by 1 (its value is reduced by 1). As long as the value of the variable reps is not equal to 0, the loop will continue to repeat.

When the value of the variable reps becomes equal to 0, the comparison in the DO WHILE line is no longer True, and control is passed to the first line of code following the ENDDO.

Creating Infinite Loops

One of the oldest programming practices in the dBASE language is beginning a program loop with a comparison that will never return a False value. Theoretically, this practice creates a program loop that runs forever. However, by placing a conditional statement inside the loop, you can trigger the loop's termination. Notice the following code:

```
USE cust
DO WHILE .T.   && This form of the command is a shorthand
               && way of saying "Loop forever."
   ? first_nam, last_nam
   SKIP
   IF EOF()
      EXIT
   ENDIF
ENDDO
CLOSE DATABASES
CLEAR
RETURN
```

When the record pointer falls to the end of file, and the value of the EOF() function becomes True, the code inside the IF structure is executed. That code consists solely of the EXIT command, which passes control of the program to the line immediately following the ENDDO.

Remember that for every DO WHILE there must be a corresponding and terminating ENDDO.

Nesting DO WHILEs

Technically, it is possible to nest DO WHILE...ENDDO control structures. Such nesting, however, is seldom necessary and can be detrimental to your mental health because it makes debugging a program more difficult.

A better method is to place DO WHILE...ENDDO control structures into subroutines which are then called with the DO command. This technique creates a program that performs actions in more than one file. A good example is a program that prints all the invoice numbers for each customer in the accounts file (see figs. 6.1 and and 6.2).

PRIN_IT.PRG (see fig. 6.1) opens the needed data files, SETs the printer on, and then prints the header for the first record in the data file. After printing the header, the program puts the account number in a variable and then calls a second program that has its own loop to run.

INVCES.PRG (see fig. 6.2) uses the account number (in the variable) to perform a SEEK to find the first record in the index with that account number. If none is found, no invoices exist for that customer; the program prints a message reporting that fact and terminates.

Fig. 6.1

The program PRIN_IT.PRG.

```
***** Program: PRIN_IT.PRG *****
* This program controls the record pointer and
* data processing for the customer file.
USE cust ORDER acct
USE inv IN 2 ORDER cust_id
SET PRINTER ON
DO WHILE .T.
   ? "Customer: " + comp_name
   var = acct_no
   DO invces
   ?
   SELECT 1
   SKIP
   IF EOF()
      EXIT
   ENDIF
ENDDO
CLEAR
CLOSE DATABASES
SET PRINTER OFF
RETURN
***** End of program *****
```

```
***** Program: INVCES.PRG *****
* A program that examines the invoices to determine
* whether any belong to the current customer
SELECT 2
SEEK var
IF EOF()
   ? "This customer has no invoices on file."
   RETURN
ENDIF
DO WHILE .T.
   ? "Invoice number: "+ TRIM(ino)
   SKIP
   IF EOF() .OR. cust_id <> var
      EXIT
   ENDIF
ENDDO
RETURN
***** End of program *****
```

Fig. 6.2

*The program
INVCES.PRG.*

If at least one invoice exists, the information is printed and the record pointer is moved to the next record. A test is performed to make sure that the record pointer has not gone to the end of file or that the account number in the next record is different. If the record pointer is at a record for the same customer, the loop is repeated. When the records run out or the record no longer has the account number of the same customer, the loop is terminated.

Control passes back to the program named PRIN_IT.PRG, a blank line is added to the report, and the record pointer is moved to the next customer record.

The two programs go back and forth printing all invoice numbers for all customers until all customer records have been exhausted. Then and only then does the higher-level program, PRIN_IT.PRG, terminate.

If you made a mistake in the program code (seldom are programs correctly programmed the first time), it is much easier to find the mistake if each program segment is short and simple. Nesting one DO WHILE inside the other often makes finding which part of the program has the error much more difficult. If the program crashes, the error message usually tells you which program module was at fault. You can usually find the problem more easily if you have small modules of code because you are starting your search much closer to the problem code.

Using the SCAN Command

The `SCAN...ENDSCAN` command is similar in many ways to the `DO WHILE...ENDDO` control structure. The `SCAN` control structure allows you to set up a condition for selecting only those records in the data file that should be processed. Notice the following example:

```
USE cust INDEX co_name
SET PRINTER ON
SCAN FOR balance > 500
    ?co_,first_nam,last_nam,phone_no,balance
ENDSCAN
SET PRINTER OFF
```

In this example, the `FOR balance > 500` comparison is used to determine whether information from that record is to be outputted into the report. Each record in the data file is evaluated in turn. Only those records for which the comparison returns a value of True are processed by the commands inside the `SCAN...ENDSCAN` control structure.

Like the `DO WHILE...ENDDO` control structure, the `SCAN...ENDSCAN` control structure uses the `LOOP` and `EXIT` commands to provide additional control. These two commands are used exactly as in a `DO WHILE...ENDDO` control structure. (See the section on the `DO WHILE` command for more details.)

The `SCAN...ENDSCAN` construct has one major weakness. Like the `LOCATE` command, the `SCAN...ENDSCAN` command processes each record in the data file sequentially. This process can be very slow if the file contains a large number of records. This lack of speed is probably acceptable if all or most of the records in the file will be processed. If, however, the first record that meets the condition is toward the end of file, it is probably better to position the record pointer with a `SEEK` and include a `SCOPE` clause in the `SCAN` condition line. See the dBASE IV Language Reference manual for more information about including a `SCOPE` clause in the `SCAN...ENDSCAN` construct.

Completing the Mailing List Application

Now that you have a basic understanding of variables and control constructs, you can complete the programs that produce the data-entry screens for the mailing list application presented in Chapter 5.

In Chapter 5, a memo field was added to the data file to illustrate the process of dealing with memo fields. The memo field has now been removed from the data file's structure; it was not intended that a memo field be included in the prospect file.

In the next sections, you learn to construct the programs for adding, editing, and deleting prospects in the mailing list database.

Completing the Module for Adding Prospects

Chapter 5 presents the program that enables users to add new prospects to the mailing list. The program's weakness is that only one prospect can be added at a time; the program RETURNs as soon as the last field is filled in. This continuous return to the menu after each prospect is added to the file can be annoying to operators when several new prospects must be added.

The solution is to place the code inside a DO WHILE loop so that the program can ask the user whether more prospects are to be added. If more prospects are to be added, the program must clear the screen of the old information, APPEND a new record to the file, and accept entry into the new record. The program continues in this fashion until the user signals that there are no more records to add.

The code for the program AD_PROSP.PRG is presented in figure 6.3; the program as it appears on-screen is displayed in figures 6.4 and 6.5.

The SET commands have been added to AD_PROSP.PRG so that you can test the code in the same environment in which it will ultimately run. In the real application, these commands are issued by the highest-level program.

Other than the SET commands, much of the code here is recognizable from the simple batch-style program presented in Chapter 5.

The program opens the data file and APPENDs a blank record just as its predecessor did. But now a DO WHILE loop is opened so that the user can add more than one record.

After entry is made in the last field, a variable called confirm is initialized and given the value of a single space. An @...SAY...GET is then performed to ask the user whether another record is to be added. Notice that the (Y/N) in the prompt tells the user which keystrokes are expected (see fig. 6.5).

Fig. 6.3

The program
AD_ PROSP.PRG.

```
***** Program: AD_PROSP.PRG *****
* A program that adds prospects to the mailing list
SET TALK OFF
SET SCOREBOARD OFF
SET STATUS OFF
CLEAR
USE maillist ORDER zip
APPEND BLANK
DO WHILE .T.

   @ 4,22 SAY "Treasure Trove Mailing List Program"
   @ 5,10 TO 17,70 DOUBLE
   @ 7,15 SAY "Title & Name: "
   @ 7,29 GET title PICTURE "XXXX"
   @ 7,34 GET first_nam PICTURE "XXXXXXXXXXX"
   @ 7,47 GET mid_init PICTURE "X"
   @ 7,48 SAY ". "
   @ 7,50 GET last_nam PICTURE "XXXXXXXXXXX"
   @ 9,16 SAY "    Address:"
   @ 9,29 GET address PICTURE "XXXXXXXXXXXXXXXXXXXXXXXXXXXXX"
   @ 11,29 GET city PICTURE "XXXXXXXXXXXXXXXX"
   @ 11,47 GET state PICTURE "@! AA"
   @ 11,50 GET zip PICTURE "99999-9999"
   @ 13,33 SAY "Income Code: "
   @ 13,46 GET income_cod PICTURE "9"
   @ 15,22 SAY "Number of Children in the Family:"
   @ 15,56 GET children PICTURE "99"
   READ
   STORE ' ' TO confirm
   @19,22 SAY "Add another prospect? (Y/N) ---> " GET  confirm
   READ
   IF UPPER(confirm) = 'Y'
      CLEAR
      APPEND BLANK
      LOOP
   ELSE
      EXIT
   ENDIF
ENDDO
CLEAR
CLOSE DATABASES
RETURN
***** End of program *****
```

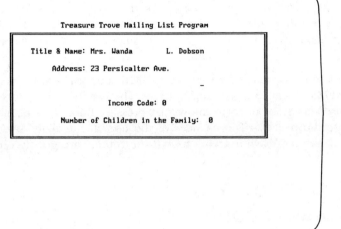

Fig. 6.4

The screen produced by AD_PROSP.PRG.

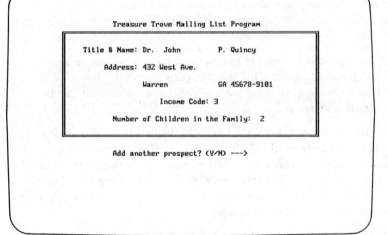

Fig. 6.5

The LOOP prompt produced by AD_PROSP.PRG.

The response is converted to uppercase with the UPPER() function and compared to the character string 'Y' by the IF statement. The code inside the IF...ENDIF construct executes only if the user presses Y. Another record is created at the end of the file, and the LOOP command sends the program pointer back up to the DO WHILE statement. All of the code is repeated. This cycle continues as long as the user answers Y to the confirmation prompt. Because the IF condition tests only for the Y keystroke, anything other than a response of Y causes the program pointer to drop out of the loop to the commands just below the ENDDO.

These commands clean up the screen, put away the files, and terminate the program. Control of the program pointer is then passed back to wherever the program was called. If the caller was another program (it is intended that this calling program will be a menu in the finished application), that program will resume.

This approach to data entry is far superior to SETting a format file as active and issuing the APPEND command. The prompt asks whether the user wants to continue. The user does not need to know that pressing Enter in a blank screen will terminate the process. The chances of the user accidentally APPENDing a completely blank record while trying to exit the routine are greatly reduced.

Completing the Module for Editing Records

Creating a program that allows the user to edit records that already exist in the data file is a complicated task. In this application, the records do not have a field that contains a unique value for each record. In a customer file, each customer has a unique account number, and inventories have unique part numbers.

Trying to give each prospect a unique number or character string is impractical in this case. Unfortunately, the mailing list company supplying lists to Treasure Trove does not include in the mailing list a telephone number that can be used to single out a particular record.

Fortunately, a little ingenuity can go a long way in dBASE programming. The module for editing records is decidedly more complex than the module for simply adding new records. The extra effort is worth it, however, because the user must always come first. Your responsibility is to shield the user from having to learn dBASE IV. If you include a BROWSE in the application, you lose any data-validation standards you have established.

The module for editing records requires a significant amount of developmental work but will pay dividends later. Programmers never throw away code; once a module is developed, it can serve as a model for later applications. Whenever programmers run into a similar problem, they invariably reach back for something they have written before to see whether it can be modified to fit the current situation. The module for editing records falls into this category. This code can be used in nearly every application that requires editing records that lack a unique key. You use the code to modify only the data-file name and the @...SAY...GET commands specific to this application.

To create the module for editing records, you must create a new index TAG which indexes the records on the last name of the prospect. Open the MAILLIST.DBF data file at the dot prompt and issue the following command:

```
INDEX ON last_nam TO TAG last_name
```

This line adds to the .MDX file another TAG that can be used to find records according to the last name of the prospect.

Planning Programs Using Pseudocode

It is sometimes useful to write out, in English statements, the steps required to perform a programming task. These statements can describe the process before you actually write the program code. You therefore create a blueprint to use as a map or specification sheet.

Creating such a description can help you sort out ideas about how to approach a problem. Once you determine what needs to be done, and in what order, the code will fall into place more easily when you actually sit down to write it.

Table 6.1 contains a pseudocode listing that outlines the steps the program must go through so that the user can edit the records in the mailing list file.

Table 6.1
Pseudocode for the Module for Editing Records

1. Open the data file ordered by the last name TAG.

2. Paint a data-entry screen in which the user can type the name for the search.

3. Perform a SEEK to position the record pointer by using the SET NEAR command. If the name is misspelled, the record pointer will at least be close to the intended record.

4. Make sure that the record pointer is not at the end of file.

5. Open a loop to accept the edit entry.

6. Display the record found.

7. Allow users to move backward or forward through the file to find the record they are searching for.

8. Accept user entry.

9. Ask users whether they want to edit more records.

10. If so, repeat the code, beginning with step 2 of the pseudocode.

11. If not, close the files and terminate the program.

After you outline the necessary steps, you can begin writing the program code one piece at a time.

According to the pseudocode, several steps may need to be repeated. Rather than repeat the same commands in two different places in the program, it is better to place this section of code in another program file that can be called by the DO command. You need to include the same process in the module for deleting records. (Deleting records is covered later in this chapter.) If you put the code in a separate program file, it can be called into action with the DO command. When you repeat code in several places, each occurrence is compiled separately, enlarging the program code. Any bugs in the code must be corrected in each occurrence of the code. Placing repeating code in a separate module enhances performance by cutting down code size and makes programs easier to debug.

Writing the Module for Editing Records

The module for editing records uses two pieces of code: ED_FND.PRG and ED_PROSP.PRG. ED_FND.PRG (see fig. 6.6) is the repeating section that is placed in a separate module. ED_PROSP.PRG (see fig. 6.8) contains the code for editing the record found by ED_FND.PRG.

Fig. 6.6

The program ED_FND.PRG.

```
***** Program: ED_FND.PRG *****
* A program that accepts user entry of a last name and positions
* the record pointer to the closest match. The program also tests
* to make sure that the record pointer is not at end of file.
CLEAR
STORE SPACE(12) TO l_name
@ 4,22 SAY "Treasure Trove Mailing List Program"
@ 5,10 TO 7,70 DOUBLE
@ 6,15 SAY "Enter the last name of the prospect: " GET l_name
READ
SET NEAR ON
SEEK l_name
SET NEAR OFF
IF EOF()
   @ 6,11 CLEAR TO 6,69
   @ 6,11 SAY "Error. No records found. Press any key to return to menu."
   WAIT ""
   CLEAR
   RETURN
ENDIF
RETURN
***** End of program *****
```

The program ED_FND.PRG contains the code needed to find records and position the record pointer. The code takes care of steps 2-4 of the pseudocode listed in Table 6.1.

First, the program clears the screen and initializes a variable called 1_name. 1_name is the same length as the last name field and is filled with spaces.

Next, the program paints a screen header and a box, and then prompts the user for entry into the 1_name variable (see fig. 6.7).

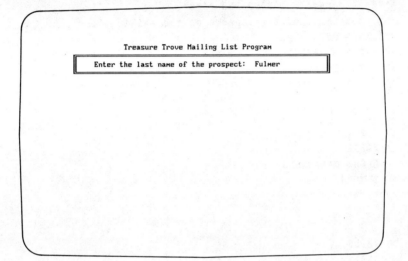

Treasure Trove Mailing List Program

Enter the last name of the prospect: Fulmer

Fig. 6.7

The screen presented by ED_FND.PRG.

The SET NEAR command is used to alter the way a SEEK is normally performed by dBASE IV. Without the SET NEAR, the SEEK expression must find an exact match or the record pointer will fall to the end of the file. By SETting NEAR ON, the record pointer will position itself to the next record with a greater value in the event an exact match does not exist. The record pointer only falls to the end of the file if the SEEK expression is greater than the last key in the index.

The SEEK is performed, and SET NEAR is turned off.

If no records are in the file, or the user enters a key greater than any of the records in the file, the EOF() function will return a value of True (.T.). This condition is tested because trying to edit the phantom (EOF) record triggers a dBASE IV error message. As a developer, it is your responsibility to prevent this situation. If the record pointer is at the end of file, you have a problem.

Because this module runs one level below the actual editing program, the program's RETURN only returns control back to the calling program. The calling program still tries to execute the editing of @..SAY...GETs. This again triggers the error message from dBASE IV. The solution is to inform the user of the problem, but leave the file open for a minute and let the calling program retest the situation when this file terminates. In other words, let the calling program determine whether an error has occurred and have it take the appropriate action.

Figure 6.8 contains the code for the main editing module, ED_PROSP.PRG.

Fig. 6.8

*The program
ED_ PROSP.PRG.*

```
***** Program: ED_PROSP.PRG *****
* A program to edit prospects on the mailing list
SET TALK OFF
SET SCOREBOARD OFF
SET STATUS OFF
USE maillist ORDER last_name

DO ed_fnd
IF EOF()
   CLEAR
   CLOSE DATABASES
   RETURN
ENDIF


DO WHILE .T.
   CLEAR
   @ 4,22 SAY "Treasure Trove Mailing List Program"
   @ 5,10 TO 17,70 DOUBLE
   @ 7,15 SAY "Title & Name: "
   @ 7,29 GET title PICTURE "XXXX"
   @ 7,34 GET first_nam PICTURE "XXXXXXXXXXX"
   @ 7,47 GET mid_init PICTURE "X"
   @ 7,48 SAY ". "
   @ 7,50 GET last_nam PICTURE "XXXXXXXXXXX"
   @ 9,16 SAY "    Address:"
   @ 9,29 GET address PICTURE "XXXXXXXXXXXXXXXXXXXXXXXXXXXXXX"
   @ 11,29 GET city PICTURE "XXXXXXXXXXXXXXXX"
   @ 11,47 GET state PICTURE "@! AA"
   @ 11,50 GET zip PICTURE "99999-9999"
   @ 13,33 SAY "Income Code: "
   @ 13,46 GET income_cod PICTURE "9"
   @ 15,22 SAY "Number of Children in the Family:"
```

Fig. continues

Fig. continued

```
        @ 15,56 GET children PICTURE "99"
        @ 17,12 SAY "  Press PgUp for previous record   PgDn for next record  "
      READ
        IF LASTKEY() = 18
           SKIP -1
           IF BOF()
              @ 18,18 SAY "Top of file. Press any key to return to menu."
              WAIT ''
              EXIT
           ENDIF
           LOOP
        ENDIF
        IF LASTKEY() = 3
           SKIP
           IF EOF()
              @ 18,18 SAY "End of file. Press any key to return to menu."
              WAIT ''
              EXIT
           ENDIF
           LOOP
        ENDIF
        STORE ' ' TO confirm
        @19,22 SAY "Edit another prospect? (Y/N) ---> " GET confirm
        READ
        IF UPPER(confirm) = 'Y'
           CLEAR
           DO ed_fnd
           IF EOF()
              EXIT
           ENDIF
           LOOP
        ELSE
           EXIT
        ENDIF
      ENDDO
      CLEAR
      CLOSE DATABASES
      RETURN
      ***** End of program *****
```

The SET commands at the beginning of the file are included so that you can independently test the module in the same environment as it will run. The highest-level program normally SETs the environment in the application. Once the code is attached to a menu, these commands should be removed.

First, the program opens the data file and ORDERs the file according to the last_name TAG.

The ED_FND subroutine is then performed. When the program pointer returns to the next line, the EOF() situation is retested. At this point, the program is on the correct level to abort. If EOF() is True, the screen is CLEARed, the data file is CLOSEd, and the program is terminated.

If the record pointer is positioned on a valid record, a loop is opened with the DO WHILE command. The @...SAY...GETs, which display the data in the current record, are activated by the READ command.

The next two IF constructs are the heart of this program. Pressing the PgUp or PgDn keys terminates the READ. These two constructs use the LASTKEY() function to determine whether one of these two keys was used to terminate the read. If so, the record pointer is moved one record up or down in the file, depending on which key was pressed (see fig. 6.9). If the record pointer is moved to either the beginning or end of file, and if @...SAY...GETs are READ on the phantom records that exist in both locations, a dBASE IV error will result. To eliminate this possibility, test the BOF()/EOF() conditions before the LOOP command is issued. If the user has gone too far in either direction, the program is terminated. Of course, the user is told why the program is terminated. Remember, your responsibility as a programmer is never to leave a user hanging.

Fig. 6.9

Pressing PgUp enables the user to access the previous record.

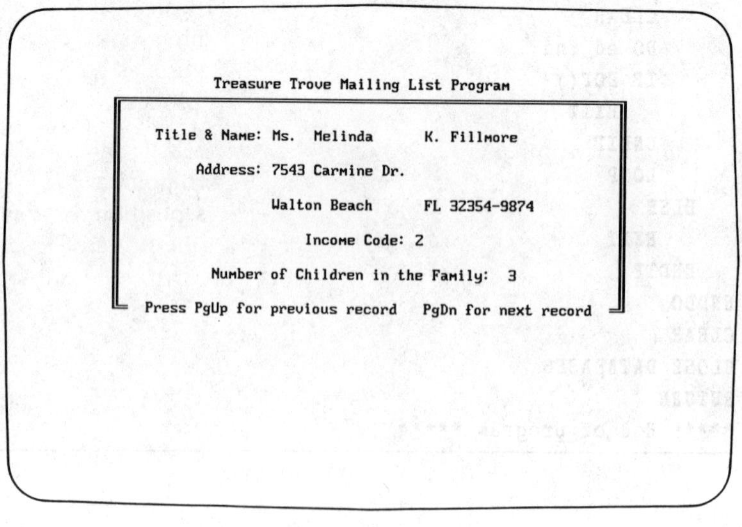

```
                    Treasure Trove Mailing List Program

        Title & Name: Ms.  Melinda      K. Fillmore

             Address: 7543 Carmine Dr.

                      Walton Beach      FL 32354-9874

                      Income Code: 2

             Number of Children in the Family:  3

        Press PgUp for previous record   PgDn for next record
```

The user has been informed of options for moving the record pointer by the ⓐ...SAY which paints a prompt over the bottom of the box that surrounds the entry area (see fig. 6.10). Whenever possible, place these kinds of instructions on-screen. It is sad but true that many users never read the documentation you prepare for the application. You can, however, take some satisfaction in developing applications easy enough to use without reading the manual. (Never use this as an excuse for not documenting an application, however.)

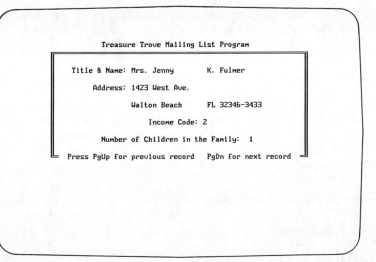

```
                    Treasure Trove Mailing List Program

        Title & Name: Mrs. Jenny        K. Fulmer

            Address: 1423 West Ave.

                     Walton Beach      FL 32346-3433

                  Income Code: 2

        Number of Children in the Family:  1
      Press PgUp for previous record   PgDn for next record
```

Fig. 6.10

The editing screen for the record controlled by ED_PROSP.PRG.

The edits are retained even if the user makes entries into the fields before pressing PgUp or PgDn. The user is given the maximum leeway in deciding how to use the program. The user can scroll through the records making edits sequentially or go to the last field and press Enter. As long as the READ is terminated by a key other than PgUp or PgDn, the user is given the opportunity to enter another search key or to terminate the process.

If the user answers Y, the ED_FND.PRG program is called again, and control is passed back to the top of the loop if the record pointer is positioned to a valid record when the subroutine terminates. This positioning continues until the user either enters an answer other than Y to the prompt or moves the record pointer too far up or down in the file.

Each step outlined in the pseudocode has been covered by program code in the module. By writing down the goals ahead of time, the code is easier to write.

Completing the Module
for Deleting Records

You will find ways of reusing code, therefore spreading out the development time and costs to more than one module/application. The module for deleting records, which is basically a slightly modified version of the module for editing records, is a case in point.

The ED_FND.PRG program is used in this module as well and remains unchanged so that both modules can call upon it.

Figure 6.11 contains the code for the module for deleting records.

Fig. 6.11

The program
DL_PROSP.PRG.

```
***** Program: DL_PROSP.PRG *****
* A program to delete prospects from the mailing list. This
* module is a slightly altered version of ED_PROSP.
SET TALK OFF
SET SCOREBOARD OFF
SET STATUS OFF
USE maillist ORDER last_name

DO ed_fnd
IF EOF()
   CLEAR
   CLOSE DATABASES
   RETURN
ENDIF
DO WHILE .T.
   CLEAR
   @ 4,22 SAY "Treasure Trove Mailing List Program"
   @ 5,10 TO 17,70 DOUBLE
   @ 7,15 SAY "Title & Name: "
   @ 7,29 GET title PICTURE "XXXX"
   @ 7,34 GET first_nam PICTURE "XXXXXXXXXXX"
   @ 7,47 GET mid_init PICTURE "X"
   @ 7,48 SAY ". "
   @ 7,50 GET last_nam PICTURE "XXXXXXXXXXX"
   @ 9,16 SAY "   Address:"
   @ 9,29 GET address PICTURE "XXXXXXXXXXXXXXXXXXXXXXXXXXXX"
   @ 11,29 GET city PICTURE "XXXXXXXXXXXXXXX"
   @ 11,47 GET state PICTURE "@! AA"
```

Fig. continues

Fig. continued

```
@ 11,50 GET zip PICTURE "99999-9999"
@ 13,33 SAY "Income Code: "
@ 13,46 GET income_cod PICTURE "9"
@ 15,22 SAY "Number of Children in the Family:"
@ 15,56 GET children PICTURE "99"
@ 17,12 SAY "  Press PgUp for previous record   PgDn for next record  "
CLEAR GETS
STORE ' ' TO confirm
@21,22 SAY "Delete this prospect? (Y/N) ---> " GET confirm
READ
IF LASTKEY() = 18
   SKIP -1
   IF BOF()
      @ 18,18 SAY "Top of file. Press any key to return to menu."
      WAIT ''
      EXIT
   ENDIF
   LOOP
ENDIF
IF LASTKEY() = 3
   SKIP
   IF EOF()
      @ 18,18 SAY "End of file. Press any key to return to menu."
      WAIT ''
      EXIT
   ENDIF
   LOOP
ENDIF
IF UPPER(confirm) = 'Y'
   DELETE
   PACK
   EXIT
ELSE
   EXIT
ENDIF
ENDDO
CLEAR
CLOSE DATABASES
RETURN
***** End of program *****
```

The code used in this module is exactly the same as ED_PROSP.PRG up to the last @...SAY...GET. At that location, the READ command is replaced by the CLEAR GETS command.

CLEAR GETS is used to display a screen with @...SAY...GETs, including the field values, just as they would be displayed for editing. CLEAR GETS, however, cancels the GETs from memory. Once they have been CLEARed, the next READ command will not activate them.

Because there is no READ here, the IF constructs that test for the LASTKEY() value must be placed under the confirmation prompt's READ command. They still work just as they did in the module for editing records. The only difference is that the confirmation prompt is displayed while the user is moving the record pointer (see fig. 6.12).

Fig. 6.12

The screen produced by the program DL_PROSP.PRG.

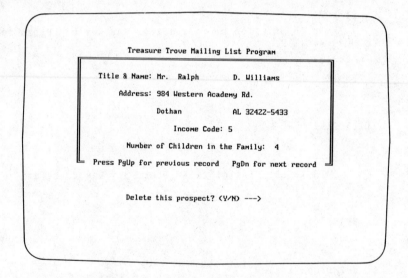

```
                    Treasure Trove Mailing List Program

        Title & Name: Mr.  Ralph         D. Williams

             Address: 984 Western Academy Rd.

                      Dothan              AL 32422-5433

                       Income Code: 5

            Number of Children in the Family:  4
        Press PgUp for previous record    PgDn for next record


            Delete this prospect? (Y/N) --->
```

Pressing Y accepts the deletion; pressing PgUp and PgDn moves the record pointer.

If the deletion is accepted, the current record is marked for deletion, and the file is immediately PACKed before the loop is EXITed. If any key but Y, PgUp, or PgDn is pressed, the loop is EXITed without marking or PACKing any records.

The commands following the ENDDO clear the screen, close the file, and terminate the program.

To complete the mailing list application, you only need to create a menu structure that makes it easy for users to run the application and a label file to print out the information.

Summary

In this chapter, you learned how to create and manage memory variables in your programs. You saw the difference between PRIVATE and PUBLIC variables, as well as the different types of variables available.

You also saw how each of the major control constructs provides for conditional branching. The IF...ENDIF construct enables you to write a program that can branch in two directions depending on the circumstances at the time the program is running.

The DO CASE...ENDCASE construct provides for more than two branches. The DO WHILE...ENDDO construct enables you to write code that can be repeated as many times as needed to accomplish a particular task.

SCAN...ENDSCAN is the construct that enables you to perform actions on every record in the database.

These constructs can provide your users with the maximum flexibility in deciding how to use your programs, even as you retain control over such issues as data validation. In this chapter, you learned to put the constructs into practice by completing the data-entry portions of the mailing list application.

In the next chapter, you learn how to construct several different types of menus, which can be used to provide different user interfaces.

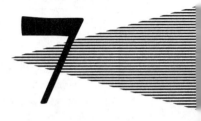

Building dBASE IV Menus and Screens

A n entire class of screen-handling and menu-building commands are new with dBASE IV. These commands create and define horizontal-BAR menus, vertical-POPUP menus, and windows.

In this chapter, you learn the techniques of DEFINEing windows, BAR menus, and POPUP menus. You can then use these techniques to create the menu structure for the mailing list application which was introduced in Chapter 4.

Using Windows in dBASE IV

A *window* can be defined as a named, rectangular section of the screen contained within a border. As many as 20 windows can be DEFINEd in memory at a time.

Windowing has been included in dBASE IV to give programmers the ability to vary screen presentations and to cover other active objects on the screen while another action is displayed.

With windowing, you need fewer commands to produce the user interface. You do not have to DEACTIVATE menus or clear the screen of other information before performing the action. You only need to ACTIVATE a window to cover the part of the screen you want to use. Later in this chapter, you see this technique in detail.

Windows are created in a series of steps. Each window must be DEFINEd and then ACTIVATEd. When the window is no longer needed, it is DEACTIVATEd. The steps in creating windows are covered in the next sections.

Creating dBASE IV Windows

To create a window, you use the DEFINE WINDOW command, adding arguments that specify the name, upper-left corner, and bottom-right corner of the window. You can include arguments specifying the display (color) attributes of the area within the window and the frame. You can specify the border as single-lined, double-lined, or as a panel. You can also specify that no border be included.

Following is the syntax of the DEFINE WINDOW command:

```
DEFINE WINDOW <window name>
    FROM <row1>, <col1>
    TO <row2>,<col2>
    [DOUBLE/PANEL/NONE/<definition string>]
    [COLOR [<standard>],[<enhanced>],[<frame>]]
```

The arguments SINGLE and DOUBLE specify the frame as a single- or double-lined box. The PANEL argument specifies a thick line around the window; NONE sets the frame to the same color as the background color in effect at the time the window is ACTIVATEd.

You cannot paint anything within the border, even if the border is specified as NONE.

To create a window that appears on-screen from the coordinates 4,10 to 8,70, use the following command:

```
DEFINE WINDOW win1 FROM 4,10 TO 18,70 DOUBLE
```

This command creates a window called win1 whose frame extends from line 4, column 10 to line 8, column 70.

To display win1, use the following command:

```
ACTIVATE WINDOW win1
```

The blank window is placed on-screen.

To remove the window from the screen, use the following command:

```
DEACTIVATE WINDOW
```

Windows can be chained one after the other, but only one window can be active at a time. The ACTIVATE WINDOW command suspends any active window until the DEACTIVATE WINDOW command is issued. The DEACTIVATE WINDOW command clears the current window from the screen (but not from memory), and the next, most recently active window is again made the active window.

As an argument to the DEACTIVATE WINDOW command, you can include a list of windows to be DEACTIVATEd or the argument ALL. This form of the command allows you to DEACTIVATE more than one window at a time.

Following is the syntax of the DEACTIVATE WINDOW command:

DEACTIVATE WINDOW <*list of window names*>/ALL

One advantage to using windows in your applications is that the section of screen which is covered by the window is automatically restored when the window is DEACTIVATEd.

Relative Addressing with Windows

Once a window is ACTIVATED, items painted on-screen are positioned relative to the upper-left corner of the window. The following code creates the window shown in figure 7.1:

```
CLEAR
DEFINE WINDOW win1 FROM 4,10 TO 18,70 DOUBLE
ACTIVATE WINDOW win1
@0,0 say "This is the top left corner of the window."
? "This line is relatively positioned as well."
WAIT   "So is this one."
DEACTIVATE WINDOW win1
RETURN
```

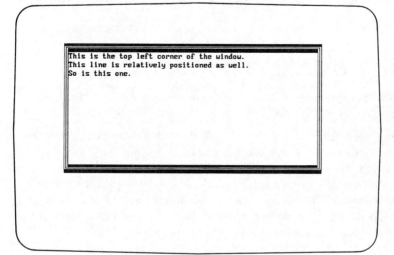

Fig. 7.1

A window showing text items positioned relatively.

All screen display occurs inside the frame of the active window, regardless of its source. You can think of a window as being a screen-inside-a-screen. Any commands that display output are processed as if the window were a miniature screen.

Moving Windows

Windows can be repositioned on-screen with the MOVE WINDOW command. There are two forms of this command. With the first form, you can state the screen coordinates of the top-left corner of the window. Notice the following example:

```
MOVE WINDOW win1 TO 6,16
```

With the second form, you can move the window relative to its current position. See the following line:

```
MOVE WINDOW win1 BY 2,6
```

Both forms of the command move the window so that the upper-left corner is positioned at line 6, column 16. The size of the window remains unchanged. The lower-right corner is repositioned relatively.

The new coordinates of the window become permanently associated with the window. Any subsequent ACTIVATE command positions the window in its new place.

You must be careful whenever you move a window within a program; no part of the window can be moved past the edge of the screen. If the command to move the window moves it past the edge of the screen, an error condition is triggered.

Creating dBASE IV Menus

In addition to windowing, dBASE IV adds to its list of new features two types of window-style menu structures: the BAR menu and the POPUP menu.

You can create three different types of dBASE IV menus: text-based, BAR, and POPUP menus. Text-based menus use no graphics or light bars. Users make choices by typing a letter or number. Text-based menus are often used in applications when the system's video card is unable to display a light-bar menu, or when compatibility with previous versions of dBASE is required. BAR and POPUP menus paint prompts within a frame; the user highlights choices by pressing the arrow keys and activates the choice by pressing Enter.

Creating Text-Based Menus

Previous dBASE versions do not support light-bar menus. Before dBASE IV, the programmer painted prompts on-screen, and then included the ACCEPT or @...SAY...GET command to accept a typed entry (usually a number or a letter) from the user to activate a choice. Notice the following code:

```
SET TALK OFF
SET SCOREBOARD OFF
SET STATUS OFF
CLEAR

DO WHILE .T.

   @ 5,22 SAY "Treasure Trove Children's Gift Shop"
   @ 7,15 TO 15, 65 DOUBLE
   @ 9,25 SAY "A. Add prospects to the file"
   @10,25 SAY "B. Edit prospects in the file"
   @11,25 SAY "C. Delete prospects in the file"
   @12,25 SAY "D. Print mailing labels"
   @14,25 SAY "Q  Quit"
   ?
   ?
   ACCEPT "          Make choice here: " TO chc
   DO CASE
      CASE UPPER(chc) = "A"
         DO ad_prosp
      CASE UPPER(chc) = "B"
         DO ed_prosp
      CASE UPPER(chc) = "C"
         DO dl_prosp
      CASE UPPER(chc) = "D"
         DO reports
      CASE UPPER(chc) = "Q"
         RETURN
      OTHERWISE
         ? CHR(7)
         @ 6,22 SAY "Invalid entry. Please try again."
   ENDCASE

ENDDO
```

The preceding code sets the environment, opens a loop, and paints a box on-screen. The box is filled with prompts, and the choice is ACCEPTed. A CASE construct then determines the key pressed and takes the appropriate action.

To control this text-based menu, the user types a choice and presses Enter. If the user makes a choice other than those specified, an error message is painted, the bell sounds, and the user is given the opportunity to make another choice.

The text-based menu format is typically used in previous versions of dBASE. Although it is not as flashy as those that can be created with the menu commands available with dBASE IV, the text-based menu format can be useful when you work with old equipment or you must maintain compatibility with previous versions of dBASE.

One advantage of text-based menus is that you can hide secret choices in the `CASE` statements. The programmer can set these choices so that they can only be accessed by selected individuals, such as database administrators. You can, for example, put the following statements inside the `CASE` construct:

```
CASE UPPER(chc) = "FM"
DO fil_maint
```

No prompt is available, and the secret procedure requires a two-keystroke entry. The procedure, however, is available to those who know the secret code. Of course, these types of secret prompts often become common knowledge through word-of-mouth. Truly sensitive procedures should be protected with a password.

Creating BAR Menus

BAR menus are horizontal, light-bar menus whose prompts (called PADs) are usually placed along one line of the screen. The user highlights the chosen prompt with the left- or right-arrow keys and presses Enter to activate the choice.

Placing a BAR menu on-screen involves the following four steps:

1. Define the menu name with the `DEFINE MENU` command.

2. Define the PADs with the `DEFINE PAD` command.

3. Attach actions to the PADs with either the `ON SELECTION PAD` or `ON PAD` commands.

4. Activate the menu with the `ACTIVATE MENU` commands.

These commands are covered in the next sections.

DEFINE MENU

The syntax of the `DEFINE MENU` command is as follows:

```
DEFINE MENU <menu name>
   [MESSAGE <character expression>]
```

The DEFINE MENU command names the menu and optionally attaches a message to be displayed on the bottom line of the screen while the menu is active.

DEFINE PAD

The syntax of the DEFINE PAD command is as follows:

```
DEFINE PAD <pad name> OF <menu name>
   PROMPT <prompt name>
   [AT <row,column>]
   [MESSAGE <character expression>]
```

The DEFINE PAD command initializes and defines the position of each PAD that will appear in the menu. You can attach a MESSAGE to be displayed on the bottom line of the screen when the PAD is highlighted. If you do not include the AT clause of the command, the menu is placed on the top line of the screen with the PADs separated by one space.

ON SELECTION PAD

The syntax of the ON SELECTION PAD command is as follows:

```
ON SELECTION PAD <pad name>
   OF <menu name>
   [<action>]
```

This command specifies the action to be taken when the user chooses the PAD. The action can be a DO statement or another command. If you do not specify an action, the PAD is disabled. The ON SELECTION commands used to DEFINE the menu should be issued before the menu is ACTIVATEd.

ON PAD

The syntax of the ON PAD command is as follows:

```
ON PAD <pad name> OF <menu name>
   [ACTIVATE POPUP <popup name>]
```

This command attaches a POPUP menu to the PAD as a dialog box. When the PAD is chosen by the user, the POPUP is ACTIVATEd. If you do not include the ACTIVATE POPUP clause of the command, the PAD is disabled. ON PAD commands should be issued before the menu is ACTIVATEd or the menu will not work correctly.

ACTIVATE MENU

The syntax of the ACTIVATE MENU command is as follows:

ACTIVATE MENU <*menu name*>

This command calls the menu into action. In some respects, a BAR menu acts like a loop because it remains active until the DEACTIVATE MENU command is issued. When a PAD is chosen by the user, the action attached to the PAD is performed and control is passed back to the menu.

DEACTIVATE MENU

The syntax of the DEACTIVATE MENU command is as follows:

DEACTIVATE MENU

This command clears the menu from the screen. Because the menu remains in memory, however, you can bring it back again with the ACTIVATE MENU command.

RELEASE MENUS

The syntax of the RELEASE MENUS command is as follows:

RELEASE MENUS <*menu list*>

This command clears from memory the BAR menus you listed as an argument to the command. You must redefine these menus to use them again. If you do not specify a list of menus as an argument to the command, all BAR menus are erased from memory. You can also use the CLEAR ALL command to RELEASE menus. The CLEAR ALL command RELEASEs from memory all memory variables, BAR menus, and POPUP menus. CLEAR ALL also closes all files.

Creating POPUP Menus

The second type of light-bar menu available to the dBASE IV programmer is the vertical-POPUP menu. A POPUP menu can serve as the main or highest-level menu for an application, or it can be used as a pull-down dialog box attached to a BAR menu.

Additionally, POPUPs have three specialized uses:

1. Field list   The user chooses a value from a list of field values.

2. Files list   The user can choose files to be used as arguments to commands that use file names as arguments (such as reports and labels).

3. Structure list   The user can pick fields to be used as part of a `LIST/DISPLAY`.

The process of creating these special purpose POPUP menus is discussed later in this chapter. The commands used to create POPUP menus are discussed in the following sections.

DEFINE POPUP

The syntax of the `DEFINE POPUP` command is as follows:

```
DEFINE POPUP <popup name>
    FROM <row,col> TO <row,col>
    [PROMPT FIELD <field name> /PROMPT FILES
    [LIKE <skeleton>]/PROMPT STRUCTURE]
    [MESSAGE <message expression>]
```

You use the `DEFINE POPUP` command to name the POPUP and to place it on-screen. The `FROM` clause of the command positions the top-left corner of the POPUP. The optional `TO` clause specifies the bottom-right corner of the POPUP. If no `TO` clause is included in the command, dBASE IV automatically sizes the POPUP.

The three `PROMPT` clauses turn the POPUP into one of the three special classes of POPUP: a field list, a files list, or a structure list. When one of these `PROMPT` clauses is included in the command, the `DEFINE BAR` command is unnecessary.

The `MESSAGE` clause places an informational message on the bottom line of the screen.

DEFINE BAR

The syntax of the `DEFINE BAR` command is as follows:

```
DEFINE BAR <bar number> OF <popup name>
    PROMPT <character expression>
    [MESSAGE <message expression>]
    [SKIP [FOR <condition>]]
```

You use the `DEFINE BAR` command to create the individual lines of the POPUP menu. The bar numbers are relative to the top of the menu. Bar 1, for example, is the first prompt associated with the menu. The `PROMPT` clause defines the character string displayed when the menu is `ACTIVATE`d. The `MESSAGE` clause specifies a message to be displayed on the bottom line of the screen when the prompt is highlighted by the user.

The `SKIP` clause specifies that the highlight bar will bypass the prompt, making it possible to use prompts as text displays. The `FOR` portion of the `SKIP` clause is used to provide a condition that determines whether the light bar can be positioned on the prompt.

When the POPUP is used as a field list, files list, or structure list, the `DEFINE BAR` command is not used to define the prompts of the POPUP; they will be defined by the conditions that exist at run time.

ON SELECTION POPUP

The syntax of the `ON SELECTION POPUP` command is as follows:

```
ON SELECTION POPUP <popup name>/ALL
    [<command>]
```

This command specifies the action to be taken when any `PROMPT` of the POPUP is chosen. The `ON SELECTION POPUP` command differs from the `ON SELECTION PAD` command. With BAR menus, you assign each PAD an action with the `ON SELECTION PAD` command. With POPUPs, you specify only one action with the `ON SELECTION POPUP` command. Usually this action is a control construct (a `CASE` or `IF` statement) that determines which prompt has been chosen using the `PROMPT()` or `BAR()` functions.

If you specify the `ALL` clause of the command instead of the POPUP's name, the specified action is attached to all POPUPs in memory.

ACTIVATE POPUP

The syntax of the `ACTIVATE POPUP` command is as follows:

```
ACTIVATE POPUP <popup name>
```

This command calls the previously `DEFINE`d POPUP into action.

DEACTIVATE POPUP

The syntax of the `DEACTIVATE POPUP` command is as follows:

```
DEACTIVATE POPUP <popup name>
```

This command clears the POPUP from the screen. The command does not, however, remove the POPUP from memory.

RELEASE POPUPS

The syntax of the `RELEASE POPUPS` command is as follows:

```
RELEASE POPUPS <popup list>
```

This command clears POPUP specifications from memory. If no list of POPUPs is included, all currently DEFINEd POPUPs are erased from memory. You can also use the CLEAR ALL command to RELEASE POPUP menus. The CLEAR ALL command RELEASEs from memory all memory variables, BAR menus, and POPUP menus. CLEAR ALL also closes all files.

POPUP-Related Functions

Two functions provided with dBASE IV, PROMPT() and BAR(), can be used to determine which choice from a POPUP was made by the user. This information can then be used by the program to SEEK a record or to branch off into the proper procedure. The PROMPT() function returns the character string displayed as the last prompt chosen by the user at run time. The BAR() function returns the line number of the last prompt chosen by the user at run time.

Using BAR and POPUP Menus in the Mailing List Application

You can use the menu-creation commands to create the main menu for the Treasure Trove mailing list application introduced in Chapter 4. This section presents the techniques needed to house an application within a structure of BAR and POPUP menus.

Adding BAR Menus

You can take two approaches when creating the menu for the mailing list application. With the first approach, you create a BAR menu with just four PADs: **Edit**, **Import data**, **Print lists**, and **Exit** the application. You can attach POPUP menus to the editing and printing PADs (see the next section on using POPUP menus in the application).

With the second approach, you assign a PAD to the **Add**, **Edit**, **Delete**, and **Import data** functions and attach a POPUP to the **Print lists** PAD. In this case, the second approach works well because there are so few functions to be performed that the menu is not overcrowded. Also, there is only one other menu (a POPUP) to design for the application.

The program MAIN.PRG (see fig. 7.2) produces the main BAR menu of the mailing list application (see fig. 7.3).

Fig. 7.2

*The program
MAIN.PRG.*

```
***** Program: MAIN.PRG *****
* The main menu of the mailing list application
SET TALK OFF
SET SCOREBOARD OFF
SET STATUS OFF
CLEAR

DEFINE MENU main
DEFINE PAD pad1 OF main PROMPT "Add" AT 3,5 ;
        MESSAGE "Add prospects to the file"
DEFINE PAD pad2 OF main PROMPT "Edit" AT 3,10 ;
        MESSAGE "Edit prospects in the file"
DEFINE PAD pad3 OF main PROMPT "Delete" AT 3,16 ;
        MESSAGE "Delete prospects from the file"
DEFINE PAD pad4 OF main PROMPT "Import data" AT 3,24 ;
        MESSAGE "Import data from the new file supplied"
DEFINE PAD pad5 OF main PROMPT "Print lists" AT 3,37 ;
        MESSAGE "Print mailing lists"
DEFINE PAD pad6 OF main PROMPT "Exit" AT 3,50 ;
        MESSAGE "Exit from the application"


ON SELECTION PAD pad1 OF main DO ad_prosp
ON SELECTION PAD pad2 OF main DO ed_prosp
ON SELECTION PAD pad3 OF main DO dl_prosp
ON SELECTION PAD pad4 OF main DO import
ON SELECTION PAD pad5 OF main DO pop_prin
ON SELECTION PAD pad6 OF main DEACTIVATE MENU

@2,2 TO 4,58 DOUBLE
ACTIVATE MENU main

CLEAR
CLEAR ALL
RETURN
***** End of program *****
```

With very few changes, MAIN.PRG can serve as the main menu of the mailing list application. The program opens by SETting the necessary environmentals, and then DEFINEs the menu and the PADs with the ON SELECTION commands. A box is then drawn around the section of the screen where the menu will appear, and the menu is ACTIVATEd. Because all actions attached to the menu return control back to the menu, no `DO WHILE` command is needed to keep the application rolling through a loop. The menu is `DEACTIVATE`d only when the user chooses **Exit**. The final three commands are then issued. These commands clear the screen and memory of all active objects and terminate the program.

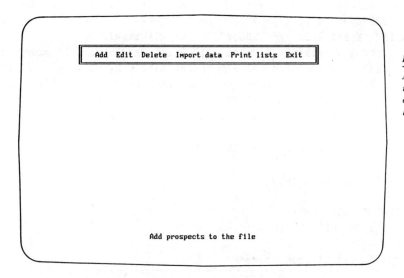

```
Add  Edit  Delete  Import data  Print lists  Exit
```

```
Add prospects to the file
```

Fig. 7.3

A sample of the main BAR menu of the mailing list application.

Adding POPUP Menus

When designing the Treasure Trove mailing list application, you decided that there needed to be several ways of outputting the data. These included the following:

1. A list of all prospects (a report called PROSP.FRM)

2. Labels for all prospects

3. Labels for prospects in certain cities

4. Labels for prospects with a certain income level or higher

Because the main menu of the mailing list application is a horizontal-BAR menu, you want the **Print lists** menu to be a POPUP menu that appears under it as a pull-down dialog box.

The **Print lists** prompt of the horizontal-BAR menu will be placed on row 3, column 37. You want to create the POPUP so that the top-left corner of the window is at line 4, column 37. The program POP_PRIN.PRG (see fig. 7.4) produces a POPUP dialog box for the printing functions of the application. The screen produced as a result of the code is shown in figure 7.5.

Fig. 7.4

The POP_PRIN.PRG program.

```
***** Program: POP_PRIN.PRG *****
* A POPUP menu for printing the mailing list application.
DEFINE POPUP repo FROM 4,37

DEFINE BAR 1 OF repo PROMPT "Print Prospect List" ;
    MESSAGE "This selection will print a list of all prospects."
DEFINE BAR 2 OF repo PROMPT "----------------------------" SKIP
DEFINE BAR 3 OF repo PROMPT "Print all labels" ;
    MESSAGE "This selection will print labels for all prospects."
DEFINE BAR 4 OF repo PROMPT "Print labels by city" ;
    MESSAGE "Print labels for all prospects in a specified city."
DEFINE BAR 5 OF repo PROMPT "Print labels by income code" ;
    MESSAGE "Print labels for a certain income code and higher."

ON SELECTION POPUP repo DO pro_prin

ACTIVATE POPUP repo

DEACTIVATE POPUP
RELEASE POPUPS repo
RETURN
***** End of program *****
```

Fig. 7.5

The POPUP as a dialog box to the Print lists selection.

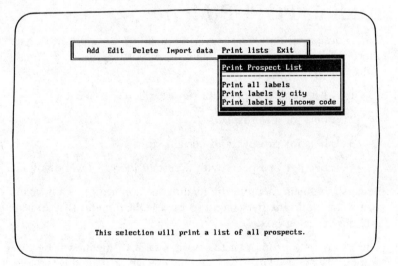

The program PRO_PRIN.PRG (see fig. 7.6) contains the code to DEFINE and ACTIVATE the **Print lists** POPUP.

In the preceding examples, the file POP_PRIN.PRG is called when the user chooses **Print lists** from the main menu. The first command executed is DEFINE. The DEFINE command names the POPUP and positions of the top-left corner of the menu. The bottom-right coordinate is automatically positioned by dBASE IV according to the number of bars DEFINEd and the width of the longest prompt.

```
***** Program: PRO_PRIN.PRG *****
* A routine for printing the mailing list application
DEFINE WINDOW win1 FROM 0,0 TO 24,79
ACTIVATE WINDOW win1


DO CASE
   CASE BAR() = 1
      SET CONSOLE OFF
      CLEAR
      @10,10 SAY "Printing prospect list........"
      USE MAILLIST ORDER ZIP
      REPORT FORM list TO PRINT
      CLOSE DATABASES
      SET CONSOLE ON
   CASE BAR() = 3
      SET CONSOLE OFF
      CLEAR
      @10,10 SAY "Printing labels for all prospects"
      USE MAILLIST ORDER ZIP
      LABEL FORM mail_lbl TO PRINT
      CLOSE DATABASES
      SET CONSOLE ON
   CASE BAR() = 4
      CLEAR
      cit = SPACE(17)
      @10,10 SAY "Print labels for what city? " GET cit
      READ
      CLEAR
      SET CONSOLE OFF
      @10,10 SAY "Printing labels for all prospects from "+ cit
      USE MAILLIST ORDER ZIP
```

Fig. 7.6

*The program
PRO_PRIN.PRG.*

Fig. continues

Fig. continued

```
            LABEL FORM mail_lbl FOR cit = city TO PRINT
            CLOSE DATABASES
            SET CONSOLE ON
        CASE BAR() = 5
            CLEAR
            cod = SPACE(1)
            @10,10 SAY "Print labels for what income code and higher? " ;
                   GET cod
            READ
            CLEAR
            SET CONSOLE OFF
            @10,10 SAY "Printing labels for income codes " + cod + ;
                   " and higher."
            USE MAILLIST ORDER ZIP
            LABEL FORM mail_lbl TO PRINT FOR VAL(cod) <= income_cod
            CLOSE DATABASES
            SET CONSOLE ON
        ENDCASE
        DEACTIVATE WINDOW win1
        RELEASE WINDOWS win1
        ***** End of program *****
```

Each prompt is then DEFINEd and includes a message to display on the bottom line of the screen when the highlight bar is on that prompt. Bar 2 cannot be highlighted because of the SKIP argument. The bar 2 prompt only separates the list from the label portion of the menu.

Once the prompts are DEFINEd, an ON SELECTION command is issued to tell dBASE what to do when one of the prompts is selected by the user.

The PRO_PRIN.PRG program module uses a window to cover the active menus and then opens a CASE construct. The CASE construct uses the BAR() function to determine which prompt was chosen by the user. When the action is performed, the window is deactivated and control is returned to the POPUP. To close the POPUP, the user presses Esc.

NOTE: In most applications, the definition process for the POPUP and the BAR menus is contained in a module which is called at run time by the main (highest-level) program module, or the code is located in the beginning of the main module itself. The POPUP definition is included in the POP_PRIN.PRG file here for ease of reading.

As you can see, defining and using BAR and POPUP menus in dBASE IV is a fairly straightforward process that usually requires fewer commands than text-based menus.

Creating Special-Purpose POPUP Menus

You can use the PROMPT clause of the DEFINE POPUP command to build three special types of POPUP menus: the field list, the files list, and the structure list.

Special purpose POPUPs are limited because only the PROMPT() and BAR() functions can be used to determine which prompt is chosen by the user. Each is helpful, however, in certain situations. For example, a field list can position the record pointer on the record whose value was selected.

Creating Field-List POPUPs

Field-list POPUPs are used to take the values stored in a field and list them as prompts in the POPUP. Of the three special types of POPUPs, the field list is the most limited. Only one field from the data file can be set in the POPUP as a prompt, and the only return values available are the PROMPT() and BAR() functions.

Only the value from a single field can be used to create the prompt for a field-list POPUP. Unfortunately, you cannot specify an expression in the PROMPT portion of the DEFINE command so that both the account number and the customer's name are displayed in the POPUP.

Some programmers, however, try to place an extra field in the data file that is a concatenation of the fields they want displayed. This technique is not a good idea; it wastes disk space and violates the most basic rule of data design: Do not duplicate information in a record rather than assembling it the way it needs to be at run time. Unfortunately, it is often impossible for users to be sure they have the right record when only one field's data is displayed. The users then have the temptation to add a field to the database.

Despite this weakness, you can position the record pointer to the selected field with a little ingenuity. The program VAL.PRG (see fig. 7.7) illustrates the field-list POPUP. The POPUP created by VAL.PRG produces a list of prospects ordered by last name (see fig. 7.8). The user chooses the prospect by highlighting the selection and pressing Enter.

Fig. 7.7

The program VAL.PRG produces a field-list POPUP.

```
***** Program: VAL.PRG *****
* A program to allow users to choose
* a prospect by last name
SET TALK OFF
SET STATUS OFF
SET SCOREBOARD OFF

USE MAILLIST ORDER ZIP

DEFINE POPUP finder FROM 5,20 PROMPT FIELD last_nam

ON SELECTION POPUP finder DEACTIVATE POPUP

ACTIVATE POPUP finder

GO TOP
howmany = BAR() -1
SKIP howmany
var = RECNO()
GOTO var
***** End of program *****
```

Fig. 7.8

Highlighting a prospect on the Print lists POPUP.

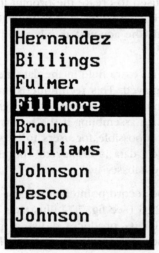

When the POPUP is ACTIVATED, the menu's prompts are the last names of the prospects in the file. When one of the names is selected with the Enter key, the BAR() function creates a variable that tells the program how many records down from the top to SKIP in order to find the same record. Note that the method only works if the ORDER is unchanged and no records are added or deleted.

You must subtract 1 from the value of BAR() because the record pointer is already positioned on the first record in the file. If you press the down-arrow key to highlight the second record in the file, SKIPping the value of BAR() positions the record pointer one record past the one selected because the record pointer doesn't start from BOF(). Once the record number is locked into the variable var, you can let the program do anything to the data file (except DELETE and PACK records) and then reposition the record pointer to the desired location with the GOTO command.

If the prompts of the POPUP menu are the field values of a field used as the index expression, and all the keys have unique values, you can use the following commands:

```
var = PROMPT()SEEK var
```

These commands position the record pointer to the selected record.

Creating Files-List POPUPs

At times, you want users to be able to select a file name from a list of files. For example, you may want the user to select one of several report forms from a list. By using a files-list POPUP, you can add or delete reports used by the application without changing the program code.

The program FILES.PRG (see fig. 7.9) produces a POPUP menu that allows the user to choose any data file (.DBF) on any disk available to the system. When the user chooses the file, the POPUP is terminated, and the value of the PROMPT() function can be used to guide the branching of the program. The program DISP_REC.PRG (see fig. 7.10) displays the selected file.

Because the bottom-right corner of the POPUP is left for dBASE IV to define, the size of the POPUP changes depending on the number of .DBF files found in each subdirectory. Because there are fewer files in the RH subdirectory, the POPUP is smaller because no bottom right corner was specified.

Both screens shown in figures 7.11 and 7.12 are the result of the programs FILES.PRG and DISP_REC.PRG respectively.

Fig. 7.9

The program FILES.PRG program produces a files-list POPUP.

```
***** Program: FILES.PRG *****
* A POPUP menu that offers the user any data file
* available to the system
SET TALK OFF
SET STATUS OFF
SET SCOREBOARD OFF


DEFINE POPUP phile FROM 5,15 PROMPT FILES LIKE *.DBF
ON SELECTION POPUP phile DO disp_rec

ACTIVATE POPUP phile

DEACTIVATE POPUP

CLOSE DATABASES
RETURN
***** End of program *****
```

Fig. 7.10

The program DISP_REC.PRG displays the contents of the selected data file.

```
***** Program: DISP_REC.PRG *****
* A program called by FILES.PRG to display the contents
* of the chosen data file.
DEFINE WINDOW win1 FROM 0,0 TO 24,79
ACTIVATE WINDOW win1

fil = PROMPT()
USE &fil
DISPLAY ALL

WAIT
DEACTIVATE WINDOW win1
RELEASE WINDOWS win1
RETURN
***** End of program *****
```

When FILES.PRG is called, the first command to execute is DEFINE POPUP. The DEFINE BAR command is not used here because the clause FILES LIKE *.DBF determines the prompts of the POPUP. When a choice is made, the subroutine DISP_REC.PRG is called. The subroutine opens a window and DISPLAYs the data in the file. When the DISPLAY is complete, control is passed back to FILES.PRG, and the data file is closed before the program terminates.

Fig. 7.11

A POPUP showing .DBF files in the SAMPLES subdirectory.

Fig. 7.12

The smaller POPUP produced for the RH subdirectory.

Creating Structure-List POPUPs

A structure list is a special POPUP whose prompts are the field names of the currently open data file. If the SET FIELDS command has been issued to restrict the field names available to the LIST/DISPLAY commands, the structure list conforms to the setting.

To create a structure-list POPUP, you set up an action with the ON SELECTION command. The action stores the value of the PROMPT() function to the end of a string which can then be macro-substituted as a field-list argument in the LIST/DISPLAY command.

The program STRU.PRG (see fig. 7.13) and the subroutine ADD_IT.PRG (see fig. 7.14) demonstrate one method of using the structure-list POPUP.

The POPUP produced by STRU.PRG is shown in figure 7.15. The result of the DISPLAY is shown in figure 7.16.

Fig. 7.13

The STRU.PRG program demonstrates the structure-list POPUP.

```
***** Program: STRU.PRG
* A demonstration of the structure-list POPUP
SET TALK OFF
SET STATUS OFF
SET SCOREBOARD OFF

USE MAILLIST
list_it = " "

DEFINE POPUP stru FROM 5,15 PROMPT STRUCTURE ;
    MESSAGE "Choose fields with the ENTER key. End with Ctrl-End."
ON SELECTION POPUP stru DO add_it
ON KEY LABEL CTRL-W DEACTIVATE POPUP

ACTIVATE POPUP stru

list_it = LEFT(list_it,LEN(list_it)-1)
DISPLAY ALL FIELDS &list_it
WAIT
CLEAR
RELEASE POPUPS
CLOSE DATABASES
RETURN
***** End of program *****
```

Fig. 7.14

The program ADD_IT.PRG adds selected files to the list.

```
***** Program: ADD_IT.PRG *****
* A program to add the selection to the list_it variable
add = PROMPT()
list_it = list_it + add + ','
RETURN
***** End of program *****
```

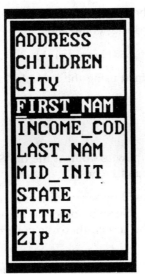

Fig. 7.15

*The appearance of
the structure-list
POPUP.*

```
Record#  FIRST_NAM   LAST_NAM    CHILDREN STATE ZIP
      1  Raoul       Hernandez        2 FL    32345-3444
      2  William     Billings         2 FL    32345-6766
      3  Melinda     Fillmore         3 FL    32354-9874
      4  Sheila      Brown            2 FL    32412-0223
      5  Ralph       Williams         4 AL    32422-5433
      6  Phillip     Johnson          1 AL    32432-3473
      7  Wanda       Pesco            3 AL    32493-3343
      8  Phillip     Johnson          1 AL    37832-3473
      9  Jenny       Fulmer           1 FL    32346-3433
Press any key to continue...
```

Fig. 7.16

*A sample DISPLAY
of data in the
chosen fields.*

Because only the top-left corner of the POPUP is specified, the size of the
POPUP is regulated by the length of the longest field name and the number of
fields in the file. The ON KEY command specifies a command to be executed in
case the user presses Ctrl-W. (Ctrl-W and Ctrl-End are functionally equivalent.)

When the user selects a choice by pressing Enter, the ADD_IT.PRG program is
called and the value of PROMPT() is placed in a variable. The variable list_it
is then given a value equal to itself plus the PROMPT() and a comma (commas
are used to delimit the fields in a field list).

When the POPUP is DEACTIVATEd, the list_it variable is then trimmed of the excess comma with the following command:

```
list_it = LEFT(list_it,LEN(list_it)-1)
```

The DISPLAY is then performed using the variable list_it as a field list.

Summary

In this chapter, you learned how to control the dBASE IV screen-handling environment by using windows and menus.

You saw how windows are used on-screen to cover menus and other structures you do not want disturbed while some other action takes place. When the window is closed, the part of the screen that was covered is again displayed without changes.

You learned how to create a text-based menu compatible with previous versions of dBASE as well as horizontal-BAR menus and POPUP menus. You should now be familiar with the process of DEFINEing and ACTIVATEing both BAR and POPUP menus.

You also saw how to create and use the three special types of POPUP menus: files lists, field lists, and structure lists.

The next chapter will teach you how to write programs that print reports. This information will help you complete the mailing list application.

Modular Programming in dBASE IV

To understand fully how a dBASE IV application is assembled from its individual parts (modules) of program code, you must first understand that all dBASE IV .PRG program files are compiled into .DBO files before the programs are run.

Previous versions of dBASE worked interpretatively. Interpretative processing is similar to dBASE IV's processing of commands entered at the dot prompt. First, the command string is parsed to determine whether errors are in the syntax. If errors exist, an error condition is triggered. If no errors are present, the command string is then converted into machine language—the zeros and ones that a microprocessor can "understand." Then, and only then, is the command executed.

In earlier versions of dBASE, when you typed DO prog_nam at the dot prompt, the program file (.PRG) was opened, and the first command was read into the interpreter. Each line of code was checked for syntax, translated, and executed.

The major drawback to this method is that once the program has become perfected so that it runs free of bugs, the first two steps become redundant. If the program works properly today, you can count on the program working properly tomorrow too. Checking syntax and translating the command into machine language are therefore a waste of time—once those tasks have been done the first time.

dBASE IV, however, compiles your programs before running them. This compilation process first performs syntax checks on each of your command lines and then translates those lines into machine language. The result is an object file, which is written to disk with the extension .DBO. This object code is run when you invoke the program. In practical terms, the compilation process makes the program's execution significantly faster.

Because of the physical structure of a dBASE IV program and the way it is written to disk, you can build into your dBASE IV programs some capabilities not possible in earlier versions. For example, in previous versions of dBASE, you had to place a *subroutine* (a small segment of program code called by dBASE programs to perform a specific task and created with the PROCEDURE command) in a separate program file. Whenever a subroutine was needed, the program file was opened during program execution, reducing by one the number of data and index files that could be opened in an application.

In dBASE IV, this approach is no longer necessary, as you will see in this chapter. You can put procedures anywhere in the program code, but they still are available to any lower-level module that may need to use them.

Another new feature in dBASE IV is the user-defined function. This powerful tool enables you to create functions that can be called from any point in a program, as if they were native dBASE IV functions. Because you create user-defined functions yourself, however, you can make them do more than simply report environment status or transform data.

A user-defined function (UDF for short) can perform commands before returning a value. For example, the native SEEK() function performs a lookup in an indexed database file and also reports whether a matching record was successfully found. You can create a UDF that does the same thing but also CLOSEs the data file if the SEEK is unsuccessful.

You will find these new capabilities of dBASE IV extremely helpful as you design modular programs. This chapter first presents the concept of modular programming and then shows how dBASE IV's new features can help you create modular applications that are faster and more sophisticated than ever before.

Understanding Modular Programming

As you learned in previous chapters, a dBASE IV application begins with a program considered the highest-level module. This module uses the DO command to call other programs, in turn, to perform the various tasks associated with the application. Each lower-level program executes its commands and then passes control back to the higher-level program. Execution in the higher-level module resumes with the command following the DO command that called the lower-level program.

This way, you can construct complex applications by using small, simple pieces of code that can be debugged and maintained more easily. Because each module performs one specific task, finding the section of code that is giving you a problem is also less difficult.

This modular approach has an extra benefit: your applications are much easier to modify later. No application remains static for long. As your users' needs change, they will ask you to modify the application to keep up with new demands on the system.

By far, however, the greatest benefit is that those pieces of code which are common to more than one module are included in the source code (uncompiled program files) only once. This helps to reduce the overall size of the application's code and increase considerably the speed of execution.

Program Files

A dBASE IV program file is a simple ASCII (DOS text) file that contains a list of the dBASE IV commands you want executed in a particular order. By using the `DO WHILE` command, you can create a program that will continue to run until the termination condition is met. In the case of the highest-level program, the termination condition is usually either the `QUIT` command or the `RETURN` command.

When you want the application to execute code not contained in the highest-level module, you include a `DO` statement that tells dBASE IV what code to execute. During the time when this code is executing, the higher-level program "goes to sleep," becoming inactive in favor of the lower-level program that has been called. The length or complexity of the called program is not important in understanding this concept. What is important to know is that all the command lines in the lower-level program will be executed up to the point at which that program is terminated (usually by a `RETURN` command).

When the lower-level program terminates, the higher-level program comes out of its suspension and begins to execute again, with the next command following the `DO` that called the subroutine.

The highest-level module of an application must be a program file. The file's name is the argument of the `DO` command, which gets the application running. This module can then use the `DO` command to call other parts of the program. These other parts of the program code can either be contained in other .PRG files or be procedures.

The sample code in figure 8.1 demonstrates this process. You start the application by typing `DO main` at the dot prompt.

Fig. 8.1

The program module MAIN.PRG.

```
*****  Program: MAIN.PRG  *****
SET TALK OFF
SET STATUS OFF
SET SCOREBOARD OFF

? "This string is printed by MAIN.PRG."
DO SUB1
? "MAIN.PRG is back in control."
WAIT
RETURN
*****  End of program  *****
```

Following is the code for the subroutine SUB1.PRG:

```
*****  Program: SUB1.PRG  *****
? "All this subroutine does is to display"
? "these two lines of screen output."
RETURN
```

Now look at the output of MAIN.PRG:

```
This string is printed by MAIN.PRG.
All this subroutine does is to display
these two lines of screen output.
Main.PRG is back in control.
Press any key to continue...
```

As you can see, the DO command causes the file SUB1.PRG to be opened, and the commands in the file begin executing in the order given. When the RETURN command in SUB1 causes the module to terminate, control is passed back to MAIN.PRG, and MAIN resumes executing with the command below the DO statement.

You also can use control constructs such as IF and CASE to control the branching of a program, depending on how the program evaluates a variable, an environment setting, or a field value. Look at the program module MAIN2.PRG in figure 8.2. This program has three different ways to go. Regardless of the value of the variable, the first line of output is displayed on-screen. The variable's value then determines whether one of two subroutines is run or whether the application is terminated early.

By combining programs and using control constructs in this manner, you can assemble applications that are flexible enough to be contained within one menu system. Therefore, users need to know only one command at the DOS or dot prompt in order to get the application running.

```
*****  Program: MAIN2.PRG  *****
SET TALK OFF
SET STATUS OFF
SET SCOREBOARD OFF

ACCEPT "Choose either A or B" TO var

? "This string is printed by MAIN.PRG."
IF UPPER(var) = "A"
   DO SUB1
ELSEIF UPPER(var) = "B"
   DO SUB2
ELSE
   RETURN
ENDIF
? "MAIN.PRG is back in control."
WAIT
RETURN
*****  End of program  *****
```

Fig. 8.2

The program module MAIN2.PRG.

Procedures

A *procedure* is a special type of program segment that can be executed while an application is running. A procedure can be called by a program or another procedure; you cannot call a procedure from the dot prompt. For this reason, procedures are said to be subroutines. As indicated earlier, a subroutine is a small program that can be called by other programs to perform a specific task (or tasks).

Often these subroutines are pieces of code that can be used over and over by different modules. Instead of having to repeat a section of code several times in an application, you can place that code in a subroutine just once by using the PROCEDURE command, and then have the program modules which need to perform that task call the subroutine. Again, the result is a reduction in the size of the program code, which usually results in faster execution.

The PROCEDURE command is not new in dBASE IV; the command itself has been part of the language of earlier versions of dBASE. However, the implementation of the PROCEDURE command has changed significantly with the release of dBASE IV.

For previous versions of dBASE, procedures had to be stored in a separate program file, with a limit of 32 procedures per file. Before those subroutines could be called, the file in which they were contained had to be opened with the SET PROCEDURE TO command. This meant that a subroutine might not be available at any given moment simply because it was contained in a procedure file that was not open.

dBASE IV, however, enables you to place a procedure in any file in the application. Even though the procedure is initialized in that file, the procedure still will be available to any other lower-level module that needs to use it—without your having to use the SET PROCEDURE TO command to make the procedure available.

Because dBASE IV programs are compiled before they are run, PROCEDURE segments blend right into the object code. Only three limitations apply to procedures: (1) you cannot have more than 963 procedures per file, (2) each procedure must be less than 64K, and (3) each procedure must be placed in a file outside the normal program flow. Usually such procedures are placed at the bottom of the file.

When procedures are called with the DO command, they behave like any other program. Once the application has been compiled, each program file or procedure has an equal status. Both are called with the DO command, and both perform their commands until they are terminated with the RETURN command.

To build a procedure, you issue the PROCEDURE command, using the name of the procedure as the argument. Below the PROCEDURE statement, you place the commands that are to be executed when the DO command is issued. Procedures have the same naming conventions that fields have. Names can contain up to 10 characters, which can include letters, numbers, and the underscore character. The only restriction is that the first character must be a letter.

In the preceding section, the program module MAIN2.PRG illustrated how control is passed between modules. The subroutine SUB1 was called from a .PRG file. The MAIN2.PRG code has been modified in figure 8.3, which shows the subroutines as procedures.

In this example, all three of the modules that make up the program are in the same file. One of the advantages of this arrangement is that only one .DBO file is created by the compiler.

The major advantage to using subroutines as procedures, however, is that the procedures become available to every other module in the application. No matter how large the application gets or what section of code is executing, the command DO SUB1 can find and execute the procedure.

```
*****  Program: MAIN2.PRG  *****
SET TALK OFF
SET STATUS OFF
SET SCOREBOARD OFF

ACCEPT "Choose either A or B" TO var

? "This string is printed by MAIN.PRG."
IF UPPER(var) = "A"
   DO SUB1
ELSEIF UPPER(var) = "B"
   DO SUB2
ELSE
   RETURN
ENDIF
? "MAIN.PRG is back in control."
WAIT
RETURN


PROCEDURE SUB1

? "All this subroutine does is to display"
? "these two lines of screen output."
RETURN


PROCEDURE SUB2

? "This subroutine performs a similar"
? "function to the one above."
RETURN
*****  End of program  *****
```

Fig. 8.3

The modified code for MAIN2.PRG.

Understanding User-Defined Functions

To create user-defined functions, you use the FUNCTION command. Once they are compiled into an application, they can be used in that application as if they were native dBASE IV functions.

Like procedures, user-defined functions have the same naming conventions that fields have. UDFs can contain up to 10 characters, which can include letters, numbers, and the underscore character. Again, the only restriction is that the first character must be a letter.

User-defined functions are useful for many data-manipulation tasks. Such functions can actually be more powerful than their native dBASE IV counterparts because you can include in them command lines to perform tasks, much as the PROCEDURE command enables you to build subroutines. This capability to manipulate data and perform actions gives user-defined functions their power.

A Sample User-Defined Function

The following code creates a user-defined function, named TAX_CALC, that calculates the sales tax on a subtotal:

```
FUNCTION tax_calc

PARAMETERS amt
ret_val = (amt * .05)
RETURN ret_val
```

Here the FUNCTION statement tells dBASE IV that a user-defined function is being created.

The next three lines of code are the working portion of the user-defined function. The line PARAMETERS amt receives a numeric argument and places it in a variable for use. The next line, ret_val = (amt * .05), performs the actual calculation. In this particular case the numeric argument that is supplied when the function is invoked is factored by .05; the value of the variable ret_val is therefore equal to 5 percent of the number that was passed as an argument to the function. The last line, RETURN ret_val, is a special form of the RETURN command. This line passes the computed value back to the calling module so that the result of the calculation is the RETURNed value of the function.

In a program, the following command returns a value of 2.50:

```
var = TAX_CALC(50.00)
```

The variable is of the numeric type. By itself, this user-defined function is useful, if only to avoid repeating the tax formula wherever it is needed in the application. But you can make this function even more useful.

In most cases the return value is used to print an amount on an invoice or in a report of some kind. Before the printing is done, however, the amount probably will have to be converted into a character string, with the leading blanks trimmed away. The amount will then be compatible with other elements being printed on the same line. Remember that the default integer length of a numeric variable is 10 digits. Here is a sample program line containing a user-defined function for output:

```
? "Sales tax: " + LTRIM(STR(TAX_CALC(50.00)))
```

Suppose that you want the UDF to do the transformation before the value is returned. You can use the following code:

```
FUNCTION tax_calc

PARAMETERS amt
ret_val = LTRIM(STR(amt * .05))
RETURN ret_val
```

Using this code simplifies the command in the program, resulting in fewer potential coding errors. The program line might look like this:

```
? "Sales tax: " + TAX_CALC(50.00)
```

Commands Not Supported in User-Defined Functions

Unfortunately you cannot include all the dBASE IV commands in a user-defined function. Table 8.1 lists the commands that cannot be place inside a UDF.

Table 8.1
Commands Not Supported in User-Defined Functions

APPEND	COPY
APPEND FROM	COPY FILE
APPEND FROM ARRAY	COPY INDEXES
APPEND MEMO	COPY MEMO
ASSIST	COPY STRUCTURE
BEGIN TRANSACTION/END	COPY STRUCTURE EXTENDED
TRANSACTION	COPY TAG
BROWSE	COPY TO ARRAY
CANCEL	CREATE or MODIFY STRUCTURE
CHANGE	CREATE FROM
CLEAR ALL /FIELDS	CREATE VIEW FROM ENVIRONMENT
CLOSE ALTERNATE	CREATE/MODIFY APPLICATION
CLOSE FORMAT	CREATE/MODIFY LABEL
CLOSE PROCEDURE	CREATE/MODIFY QUERY/VIEW
COMPILE	CREATE/MODIFY REPORT
CONVERT	CREATE/MODIFY SCREEN

Table 8.1—*Continued*

DEBUG	ON READERROR
DEFINE BAR	ON SELECTION PAD
DEFINE BOX	ON SELECTION POPUP
DEFINE MENU	PACK
DEFINE PAD	PRINTJOB/ENDPRINTJOB
DEFINE POPUP	PROTECT
DEFINE WINDOW	QUIT
DELETE TAG	REINDEX
DIR	REPORT FORM
EDIT	RESTORE
ERASE or DELETE FILE	RESTORE MACROS
EXPORT	RESTORE WINDOW
HELP	RESUME
IMPORT	ROLLBACK
INDEX	SAVE
INSERT	SAVE MACROS
JOIN	SAVE WINDOW
LABEL FORM	SET
LOAD	SORT
LOGOUT	SUSPEND
MODIFY COMMAND/FILE	TOTAL
MOVE WINDOW	TYPE
ON ERROR /ESCAPE/KEY	UPDATE
ON PAD	ZAP
ON PAGE	

Note: **APPEND BLANK** can be used.

Even without these commands, user-defined functions can perform powerful tasks. Some UDFs are described later in this chapter, particularly in the section "Building a Library of Procedures and User-Defined Functions." Other UDFs are presented in later chapters.

User-Defined Functions for Data Validation

One of the most powerful uses of the @...SAY...GET command becomes evident when it is used with a user-defined function. The result is a handy data-validation tool.

The concept of data validation is fairly simple. As a programmer, you construct a user-defined function that will evaluate a user's input and return a logical True if the input is acceptable or a logical False if the input is not acceptable.

The UDF is invoked as part of the `VALID` clause of the `@...SAY...GET` command, as shown in the following example:

```
@10,10 SAY "Enter a part number: " GET prt_no VALID PRT_CHK()
```

In this case the user-defined function `PRT_CHK()` determines whether the entered part number is found in the STOCK.DBF file. If you assume that the STOCK data file is open in the current work area and that the file is `ORDER`ed by an index on the field `part_no`, the code for the UDF might look like this:

```
FUNCTION prt_chk

SEEK prt_no
IF FOUND()
   RETURN .T.
ELSE
   RETURN .F.
ENDIF
```

When the `READ` command activates `GET` and the cursor is in the `GET` area, where the variable `prt_no` is being taken, the user enters a value. When the user presses Enter to terminate `GET`, the UDF is called to determine whether the entry is acceptable.

The UDF then performs a `SEEK` operation, using the value of the entry. If the `FOUND()` function returns a True value, the entry is accepted, and the cursor moves to the next `GET`. Otherwise, an error message is displayed on the bottom line of the screen, telling the user to try again. You can affect the wording of the error message by including an `ERROR` clause in the `@...SAY...GET` command.

Chapter 12, "Ensuring Data Integrity," contains more specific information, along with examples, on how to combine UDFs with the `@...SAY...GET` command.

Universal Procedures and User-Defined Functions

As you become more proficient in writing programs with the dBASE IV language, you will find that most of your applications will contain many of the same tasks. Examples include creating output with the `REPORT FORMAT` command, centering lines of text as on-screen prompts, creating file lists as POPUP menus, creating help screens, and presenting error messages.

Whatever languages programmers work in, they are known for never throwing away code, for it may come in handy later. Although some people may equate this idiosyncrasy with saving gift-wrapping paper for next Christmas, the practice can save much time and effort when the programmer develops a similar application later. You will find that new applications often address the same kinds of problems you have worked on before; only the data structures differ.

As you begin to identify these repetitive tasks, you will want to build them into procedures and user-defined functions that can be included easily in any new applications you build. With a little preplanning, procedures and user-defined functions (even whole programs) can be constructed in such a way that they do not have to be modified whenever you want to use them in a different application.

The key to this process is the writing of code for procedures and user-defined functions so that they are data-independent. When you write code that is generic enough to be included in any application, that code is said to be universal. Furthermore, to write universal modules successfully, you must know that dBASE programs can call subroutines while passing information (data values) as parameters to the subroutine.

Passing Parameters

You can pass information to procedures by using the WITH clause of the DO command. Parameters are passed as arguments to user-defined functions; the arguments are contained within the parentheses of the function. When you pass more than one parameter, you should separate them with commas. Look at the following example:

```
DO sub1 WITH var1,var2,l_nam
ret_val = UDF3(var1,var2,var3)
```

No more than 50 parameters can be passed, and all parameters passed must be collected in the PARAMETERS statement in the procedure or UDF.

To reduce the size of the program code, you can place in procedures and user-defined functions most of the repetitive tasks associated with an application. A good example is code that prints the results of reports created with report form files (.FRM and .FRO). The code for printing such a report might look like the following:

```
USE vendor ORDER ID
CLEAR
```

```
@10,10 SAY 'PRINTING VENDOR REPORT'
SET CONSOLE OFF
REPORT FORM ven_list TO PRINT NOEJECT
EJECT
CLOSE DATABASES
SET CONSOLE ON
CLEAR
```

Although nothing is wrong with this sample code, the problem is that several reports will probably need printing. Repeating in an application the same nine commands for each of the reports will increase the size of the program considerably.

The preceding code contains four varying pieces of information: the name of the data file, the name of the index tag, a screen prompt, and the name of the report form file.

If you make this code a procedure and those four pieces of information variables, you can include the actual working code only once in the application. When a report needs printing, you simply issue a DO command that passes the information as PARAMETERS. For example, you can use the following code:

```
PROCEDURE PRINIT
PARAMETERS nam,t_nam,m_prompt,r_nam

USE &nam ORDER &t_nam
CLEAR
@10,10 SAY m_prompt
SET CONSOLE OFF
REPORT FORM &r_nam TO PRINT NOEJECT
EJECT
CLOSE DATABASES
SET CONSOLE ON
CLEAR
```

Here the procedure is defined with the name PRINIT. The PARAMETERS command accepts the information from the calling program and assigns names to that information.

Using code in this form, you can print any report with just the following line of code in the calling program:

```
DO PRINIT WITH "vendor","id","PRINTING VENDOR REPORT","ven_list"
```

In this example the procedure is called to print the report. The four pieces of information that the procedure needs are passed by the WITH clause. This clause causes the four character strings to be passed as parameters. The PARAMETERS statement in the procedure picks up the parameters and assigns them to four variables. Finally, the values of the variables are then used as arguments for the commands that do the actual work of outputting the report.

In taking this process to its logical conclusion, note that the parameters passed by the WITH clause of the DO command could easily be variable values themselves, such as

```
var1 = "vendor"
var2 = "id"
var3 = "PRINTING THE VENDOR REPORT"
var4 = "ven_list"
```

Then the line of code in the calling program would be

```
DO PRINIT WITH var1,var2,var3,var4
```

How or when the variables are created is a matter for you to decide. They can be created through a PROMPT() function, which will return the character string of the last prompt chosen from a menu. The variables can be the result of user input. Or they can be "hard wired" into the program's code. The only requirement is that the variables be available when they are to be passed as parameters.

Handling Variables with the PARAMETERS Command

The PARAMETERS statement that receives the information passed as parameters to procedures and UDFs creates *private* memory variables automatically. Thus, you can protect any variables by the same name that may have been created in higher-level modules of the application. You do not need to issue a PRIVATE command in the procedure or user-defined function if the variable was passed as a parameter.

The result is that the procedure or user-defined function is prevented from altering the value of any variable that has been passed as a parameter to that procedure or user-defined function. Look at the following example:

```
nam = "Phil"
DO PROC1 WITH nam
? nam

* Elsewhere in the code is a procedure called PROC1.

PROCEDURE proc1
```

```
PARAMETERS nam
? nam
nam = "Lucas"
? nam
RETURN
```

Here the procedure is passed the value of the variable nam, which is received as a parameter in a variable named nam. Even though the procedure assigns a different value to that variable, the original variable remains unchanged.

The result of this program's execution looks like this on-screen:

```
Phil
Lucas
Phil
```

Usually the value passed as a parameter and the variable created by the PARAMETERS statement will not have the same name; but even when they do, the variable in the higher-level module remains protected.

If you want the value of a variable in the higher-level module to be changed by the procedure or user-defined function, do not use the same name in the PARAMETERS statement of the lower-level module. Passing the value as a parameter is not what protects it. The protection is ensured when the name is duplicated by the PARAMETERS statement, as in these lines:

```
nam = "Phil"
DO PROC1 WITH nam
? nam

* Elsewhere in the code is a procedure called PROC1.

PROCEDURE proc1

PARAMETERS other
? other
nam = "Lucas"
? nam
RETURN
```

Because the variable nam is available to the lower-level module and the name nam is not assigned as a result of the PARAMETERS statement, the output looks like this:

```
Phil
Lucas
Lucas
```

Because the variable is created in the higher-level module and the PARAMETERS command does not create a duplicate name, the procedure or user-defined function, like any lower-level module, is allowed to change the variable's value.

Remember, too, that any variable created in a procedure or user-defined function will be released when that procedure or function terminates—just as the variable would be released if it were in a module in a .PRG file. If you want the procedure or user-defined function to leave a variable in memory, declare the variable PUBLIC, as you would in any other program module.

Building a Library of Procedures and User-Defined Functions

Although you do not have to place procedures and user-defined functions in a separate file (as in previous versions of dBASE), you still retain that option in dBASE IV. When a call is made to a procedure or user-defined function, dBASE IV checks its internal tables to see whether the name of the procedure or UDF has been made known to the compiler and whether the file that contains the module is in the chain of modules, from highest to lowest levels.

In the case of a procedure, if no such name exists, dBASE IV then tries to open a .PRG or .DBO file by that name. That is why you must use the SET PROCEDURE TO command to declare procedures and user-defined functions when they are not contained in a program file that exists in the chain from the highest-level module to the currently executing module. By using the SET PROCEDURE TO command to identify in the highest-level module a file that contains procedures and user-defined functions, you make them available to any module in the application.

As mentioned previously, a procedure file can contain as many as 963 procedures and user-defined functions; you are not likely, therefore, to exceed the capacity allowed in a normal application. Each entry in the procedure file must begin with either the PROCEDURE or the FUNCTION command and be terminated with a RETURN.

Several procedure files can be maintained in an application, but only one such file can be active at a time. A second SET PROCEDURE TO command will CLOSE the previously cited procedure file when the command opens the new procedure file. To remove access to any opened procedure file, you use the CLOSE PROCEDURE command.

For practical purposes, you can use procedure files to contain any universal procedures and user-defined functions you want to include in almost all the applications you write. You can place any procedures and user-defined functions that are specific to the application (that is, they need modification for use in another application) in one of the program files of the application.

A Starter Set for Your Procedure File

This section presents a starter set of three user-defined functions and one procedure. The set can become the nucleus of a library of procedure files for use with any application.

Centering Text

dBASE IV does not provide a function that enables you to center text across a given number of spaces. The user-defined function in figure 8.4 is handy for any centering job you may have. The function, named PAD(), is especially useful for centering text in a POPUP menu.

```
FUNCTION PADC
PARAMETERS string, stlen      && Accepts the string to be padded
                              && and the width of the the area
                              && where the string is to be painted
lpad = INT((stlen - LEN(TRIM(LTRIM(string))))/2) && Leading pad
tpad = stlen - lpad - LEN(TRIM(LTRIM(string)))    && Trailing pad
* Assembles the return value
ret_val = SPACE(lpad) + TRIM(LTRIM(string)) + SPACE(tpad)
RETURN ret_val   && Sends it back to the calling module
```

Fig. 8.4

The user-defined function for centering text.

This function accepts as parameters the string and the length of the area where the string is to be painted. Then, to determine the "true length" of the string, the function trims all the leading and trailing blank spaces from the string that has been passed. The leading pad (the number of character spaces to precede the RETURNed string) is calculated as half the difference between the needed length of the returned string minus the "true length." The trailing pad is calculated as the number of character spaces that are left. Finally, the RETURN value is assembled as a variable called ret_val and then returned.

Now look at the following sample code containing the user-defined function PADC():

```
    DEFINE POPUP jazz FROM 10,10 TO 13,30

    DEFINE BAR 1 OF jazz PROMPT PADC("First",18)
    DEFINE BAR 2 OF jazz PROMPT PADC("Second",18)
```

Note that the string length is 18, for the strings should be centered from column 11 to column 29 of the screen (29 − 11 = 18).

Trimming Blank Spaces

In the preceding example the form TRIM(LTRIM(string)) was used to remove trailing and leading blank spaces. The user-defined function in figure 8.5 accomplishes the same thing with the form BTRIM(string).

Fig. 8.5

The user-defined function for trimming blank spaces.

```
FUNCTION btrim
PARAMETERS char_val

ret_val = TRIM(LTRIM(char_val))
RETURN ret_val
```

This user-defined function, named BTRIM(), is a keystroke saver. The function merely limits the number of keystrokes you must type when you want the action taken. Because the function eliminates potential errors, such as placing parentheses incorrectly, it is worth including in your library of procedure files.

Printing Currency Amounts

You can create a user-defined function to change a numeric value into a string, with commas in the right places and a dollar sign in front of the string. You can specify in the UDF a length of up to 23 characters. One of the advantages of using such a function is that the decimal places will be aligned in the output. Figure 8.6 contains the code for the user-defined function DOLLAR().

Fig. 8.6

The user-defined function for printing currency amounts.

```
FUNCTION dollar
PARAMETERS val,length

string = ("$"+ LTRIM(TRANSFORM(val,"999,999,999,999,999.99")))
pad = INT(length - LEN(TRIM(LTRIM(string))))
ret_val = SPACE(pad) + TRIM(LTRIM(string))
RETURN ret_val
```

The following sample code illustrates the use of DOLLAR():

```
num = 1234567.99
dnum = 12345.999
? DOLLAR(num,15)
? DOLLAR(dnum,15)
```

The output of DOLLAR() looks like this:

```
$1,234,567.99
    $12,346.00
```

Notice the rounding effect.

Presenting Error Messages in a Standard Format

This procedure, named E_WIN, presents error messages in a standard format in any application (see fig. 8.7). Whenever an error condition is detected, an appropriate message is placed in a variable and passed as a parameter to this procedure. The procedure then pops a window onto the screen and displays the error message until the user presses a key.

```
PROCEDURE e_win
PARAMETERS mess

DEFINE WINDOW err_win FROM 8,20 TO 16,60
ACTIVATE WINDOW err_win
@2,0 SAY PADC(mess,38)
@4,0 SAY PADC("Press any key to continue.",38)
var = INKEY(0)
DEACTIVATE WINDOW err_win
RELEASE WINDOW err_win
RETURN
```

Fig. 8.7

The procedure for presenting error messages.

Notice that this procedure includes the user-defined function PADC(), which positions the message laterally in the window. The PADC() function therefore must be available whenever the E_WIN procedure is called.

Look at the following sample code containing the E_WIN procedure:

```
SEEK lk
IF EOF()
   mes = "There is no such account number on file."
   DO e_win WITH mes
   CLOSE DATABASES
   CLEAR
   RETURN
ENDIF
```

Because the procedure for displaying an error message is one level down from the calling module, the procedure cannot abort the module in which the error occurred. The procedure's sole purpose is to alert the user that an error has taken place. The calling module must terminate and RETURN to the menu, or to whatever module called it.

A Program File for Putting the Library Together

Once you have developed a group of procedures and user-defined functions you want to include in a standard library, you simply place them in an ASCII file with the extension .PRG, as if the file were a program file in an application. The starter set of procedures and user-defined functions is included here in a program file named STANDARD.PRG (see fig. 8.8), just as you might prepare it for use in your applications.

Fig. 8.8

The program file STANDARD.PRG.

```
*****  Program: STANDARD.PRG  *****
* Functions and procedures to be included in all applications

FUNCTION PADC
PARAMETERS string, stlen        && Accepts the string to be padded
                                && and the width of the area where
                                && the string is to be painted
lpad = INT((stlen - LEN(TRIM(LTRIM(string))))/2)   && Leading pad
tpad = stlen - lpad - LEN(TRIM(LTRIM(string)))      && Trailing pad
* Assembles the return value
ret_val = SPACE(lpad) + TRIM(LTRIM(string)) + SPACE(tpad)
RETURN ret_val     && Sends it back to the calling module


FUNCTION btrim
PARAMETERS char_val

ret_val = TRIM(LTRIM(char_val))
RETURN ret_val


FUNCTION dollar
PARAMETERS val,length

string = ("$"+ LTRIM(TRANSFORM(val,"999,999,999,999,999.99")))
pad = INT(length - LEN(TRIM(LTRIM(string))))
```

Fig. continues

Fig. continued

```
ret_val = SPACE(pad) + TRIM(LTRIM(string))
RETURN ret_val


PROCEDURE e_win
PARAMETERS mess

DEFINE WINDOW err_win FROM 8,20 TO 16,60
ACTIVATE WINDOW err_win
@2,0 SAY PADC(mess,38)
@4,0 SAY PADC("Press any key to continue.",38)
var = INKEY(0)
DEACTIVATE WINDOW err_win
RELEASE WINDOW err_win
RETURN
*****  End of program  *****
```

To include these procedures and functions in your application, you issue the following command as early as possible in your highest-level module:

```
SET PROCEDURE TO standard
```

Because you include the name of the program globally in the highest-level module, the functions and procedures will be available throughout the entire application to any module that needs to call them.

Finishing the Mailing List Application in Modular Format

The code that appears in figure 8.9 demonstrates how the entire mailing list application can be placed into one program file when it is written in modular format. This application contains essentially the same snippets of code presented as individual programs in the last several chapters. None of that code has been altered significantly here.

Summary

This chapter introduced important concepts for understanding and writing modular code. You saw how the flow of applications is affected when control is passed from the highest-level module to a lower-level module and then back. You can create small modules of code to perform individual tasks, and then combine those modules into complex applications. By passing parameters to these small modules, you can use them in more than one application.

You learned also how to create procedures and user-defined functions and how to make them universally applicable. Although user-defined functions are somewhat limited because they exclude many commands, such functions are still quite useful in transforming data values and verifying user input.

Finally, you saw how to build a library of procedures and user-defined functions for use in your applications. Included were UDFs for centering text, trimming blank spaces, and printing currency amounts, and a procedure for presenting error messages.

In the next chapter, you will learn six steps to writing successful modular applications.

Fig. 8.9

The finished mailing list application.

```
*****  Program: MAIN.PRG  *****
* The mailing list application in modular format
* This contains all the pieces of the application as they
* appeared in Chapters 4, 5, 6, and 7. The pieces are put
* together here as modules in a single .PRG file.

SET TALK OFF
SET SCOREBOARD OFF
SET STATUS OFF
CLEAR

* Menu-creation code

DEFINE MENU main
DEFINE PAD pad1 OF main PROMPT "Add" AT 3,5 ;
   MESSAGE "Add prospects to the file"
DEFINE PAD pad2 OF main PROMPT "Edit" AT 3,10 ;
   MESSAGE "Edit prospects in the file"
DEFINE PAD pad3 OF main PROMPT "Delete" AT 3,16 ;
   MESSAGE "Delete prospects from the file"
DEFINE PAD pad4 OF main PROMPT "Import data" AT 3,24 ;
   MESSAGE "Import data from the new file supplied."
DEFINE PAD pad5 OF main PROMPT "Print lists" AT 3,37 ;
   MESSAGE "Print mailing lists"
```

Fig. continues

Fig. continued

```
DEFINE PAD pad6 OF main PROMPT "Exit" AT 3,50 ;
    MESSAGE "Exit from the application"


DEFINE POPUP repo FROM 4,37

DEFINE BAR 1 OF repo PROMPT "Print Prospect List" ;
    MESSAGE "This selection will print a list of all prospects."
DEFINE BAR 2 OF repo PROMPT "----------------------------" SKIP
DEFINE BAR 3 OF repo PROMPT "Print all labels" ;
    MESSAGE "This selection will print labels for all prospects."
DEFINE BAR 4 OF repo PROMPT "Print labels by city" ;
    MESSAGE "Print labels for all prospects in a specified city."
DEFINE BAR 5 OF repo PROMPT "Print labels by income code" ;
    MESSAGE "Print labels for a certain income code and higher."

ON SELECTION PAD pad1 OF main DO ad_prosp
ON SELECTION PAD pad2 OF main DO ed_prosp
ON SELECTION PAD pad3 OF main DO dl_prosp
ON SELECTION PAD pad4 OF main DO import
ON SELECTION PAD pad5 OF main ACTIVATE POPUP repo
ON SELECTION PAD pad6 OF main DEACTIVATE MENU

ON SELECTION POPUP repo DO pro_prin

DEFINE WINDOW win1 FROM 0,0 TO 24,79

@ 2,2 TO 4,58 DOUBLE
ACTIVATE MENU main

CLEAR
CLEAR ALL
RETURN
***** End of MAIN.PRG


* Everything below is a PROCEDURE.

PROCEDURE ad_prosp
```

Fig. continues

Fig. continued

```
* Formerly AD_PROSP.PRG
* A module that adds prospects to the mailing list

ACTIVATE WINDOW win1
USE maillist ORDER zip
APPEND BLANK
DO WHILE .T.

   @ 4,22 SAY "Treasure Trove Mailing List Program"
   @ 5,10 TO 17,70 DOUBLE
   @ 7,15 SAY "Title & Name: "
   @ 7,29 GET title PICTURE "XXXX"
   @ 7,34 GET first_nam PICTURE "XXXXXXXXXXX"
   @ 7,47 GET mid_init PICTURE "X"
   @ 7,48 SAY ". "
   @ 7,50 GET last_nam PICTURE "XXXXXXXXXXX"
   @ 9,16 SAY "    Address:"
   @ 9,29 GET address PICTURE "XXXXXXXXXXXXXXXXXXXXXXXXXXXXXX"
   @ 11,29 GET city PICTURE "XXXXXXXXXXXXXXXX"
   @ 11,47 GET state PICTURE "@! AA"
   @ 11,50 GET zip PICTURE "99999-9999"
   @ 13,33 SAY "Income Code: "
   @ 13,46 GET income_cod PICTURE "9"
   @ 15,22 SAY "Number of Children in the Family:"
   @ 15,56 GET children PICTURE "99"
   READ
   STORE ' ' TO confirm
   @ 19,22 SAY "Add another prospect? (Y/N) ---> " GET confirm
   READ
   IF UPPER(confirm) = 'Y'
      CLEAR
      APPEND BLANK
      LOOP
   ELSE
      EXIT
   ENDIF
ENDDO
CLEAR
CLOSE DATABASES
```

Fig. continues

Fig. continued

```
DEACTIVATE WINDOW win1
RETURN


PROCEDURE ed_fnd

* Formerly ED_FND.PRG
* This module takes user entry of a last name and positions the
* record pointer at the closest match. The module also tests to
* make sure that the record pointer is not at the end of the
* file. This procedure is used by both the edit and delete
* modules.

ACTIVATE WINDOW win1
STORE SPACE(12) TO l_name
@ 4,22 SAY "Treasure Trove Mailing List Program"
@ 5,10 TO 7,70 DOUBLE
@ 6,15 SAY "Enter the last name of the prospect: " GET l_name
READ
SET NEAR ON
SEEK l_name
SET NEAR OFF
IF EOF()
   @ 6,11 CLEAR TO 6,69
   @ 6,11 SAY "Error. No records found. Press any key to return to menu."
   WAIT ""
   CLEAR
   RETURN
ENDIF
RETURN


PROCEDURE ed_prosp

* Formerly ED_PROSP.PRG
* A program to edit prospects on the mailing list
```

Fig. continues

Fig. continued

```
USE maillist ORDER last_name
DO ed_fnd
IF EOF()
   CLEAR
   CLOSE DATABASES
   DEACTIVATE WINDOW win1
   RETURN
ENDIF

DO WHILE .T.
CLEAR
   @ 4,22 SAY "Treasure Trove Mailing List Program"
   @ 5,10 TO 17,70 DOUBLE
   @ 7,15 SAY "Title & Name: "
   @ 7,29 GET title PICTURE "XXXX"
   @ 7,34 GET first_nam PICTURE "XXXXXXXXXXX"
   @ 7,47 GET mid_init PICTURE "X"
   @ 7,48 SAY ". "
   @ 7,50 GET last_nam PICTURE "XXXXXXXXXXX"
   @ 9,16 SAY "    Address:"
   @ 9,29 GET address PICTURE "XXXXXXXXXXXXXXXXXXXXXXXXXXXXX"
   @ 11,29 GET city PICTURE "XXXXXXXXXXXXXXX"
   @ 11,47 GET state PICTURE "@! AA"
   @ 11,50 GET zip PICTURE "99999-9999"
   @ 13,33 SAY "Income Code: "
   @ 13,46 GET income_cod PICTURE "9"
   @ 15,22 SAY "Number of Children in the Family:"
   @ 15,56 GET children PICTURE "99"
   @ 17,12 SAY " Press PgUp for previous record   PgDn for next record "
READ
   IF LASTKEY() = 18
      SKIP -1
      IF BOF()
         @ 18,18 SAY "Top of file. Press any key to return to menu."
         WAIT ''
         EXIT
      ENDIF
      LOOP
   ENDIF
```

Fig. continues

Fig. continued

```
      IF LASTKEY() = 3
         SKIP
         IF EOF()
            @ 18,18 SAY "End of file. Press any key to return to menu."
            WAIT ''
            EXIT
         ENDIF
         LOOP
      ENDIF
      STORE ' ' TO confirm
      @ 19,22 SAY "Edit another prospect? (Y/N) ---> " GET confirm
      READ
      IF UPPER(confirm) = 'Y'
         CLEAR
         DO ed_fnd
         IF EOF()
            EXIT
         ENDIF
         LOOP
      ELSE
         EXIT
      ENDIF
ENDDO
CLEAR
CLOSE DATABASES
DEACTIVATE WINDOW win1
RETURN


PROCEDURE dl_prosp
* Formerly DL_PROSP.PRG
* A program to delete prospects from the mailing list
* This module is a slightly altered version of ed_prosp.

USE maillist ORDER last_name

DO ed_fnd
IF EOF()
   CLEAR
```

Fig. continues

Fig. continued

```
      CLOSE DATABASES
      RETURN
   ENDIF
   DO WHILE .T.
      CLEAR
      @ 4,22 SAY "Treasure Trove Mailing List Program"
      @ 5,10 TO 17,70 DOUBLE
      @ 7,15 SAY "Title & Name: "
      @ 7,29 GET title PICTURE "XXXX"
      @ 7,34 GET first_nam PICTURE "XXXXXXXXXXX"
      @ 7,47 GET mid_init PICTURE "X"
      @ 7,48 SAY ". "
      @ 7,50 GET last_nam PICTURE "XXXXXXXXXXX"
      @ 9,16 SAY "    Address:"
      @ 9,29 GET address PICTURE "XXXXXXXXXXXXXXXXXXXXXXXXXXXXX"
      @ 11,29 GET city PICTURE "XXXXXXXXXXXXXXX"
      @ 11,47 GET state PICTURE "@! AA"
      @ 11,50 GET zip PICTURE "99999-9999"
      @ 13,33 SAY "Income Code: "
      @ 13,46 GET income_cod PICTURE "9"
      @ 15,22 SAY "Number of Children in the Family:"
      @ 15,56 GET children PICTURE "99"
      @ 17,12 SAY "  Press PgUp for previous record   PgDn for next record "
      CLEAR GETS
      STORE ' ' TO confirm
      @ 21,22 SAY "Delete this prospect? (Y/N) ---> " GET confirm
      READ
      IF LASTKEY() = 18
         SKIP -1
         IF BOF()
            @ 18,18 SAY "Top of file. Press any key to return to menu."
            WAIT ''
            EXIT
         ENDIF
         LOOP
      ENDIF
      IF LASTKEY() = 3
         SKIP
```

Fig. continues

Fig. continued

```
        IF EOF()
            @ 18,18 SAY "End of file. Press any key to return to menu."
            WAIT ''
            EXIT
        ENDIF
        LOOP
    ENDIF
    IF UPPER(confirm) = 'Y'
        DELETE
        PACK
        EXIT
    ELSE
        EXIT
    ENDIF
ENDDO
CLEAR
CLOSE DATABASES
DEACTIVATE WINDOW win1
RETURN


PROCEDURE import
* Formerly NEW DATA.PRG
* Appends information from a file specified by the user and
* purges any duplicate records

ACTIVATE WINDOW win1
@ 10,1 SAY PADC("Import new prospects into the mailing list",77)
?
ACCEPT SPACE(10)+"Enter the name of the file with new records: " TO new_fil
USE maillist ORDER dup_find
?
? SPACE(10)+ "Stand by.  Working..........."
APPEND FROM &new_fil DELIMITED
SET SAFETY OFF
COPY TO temp
ZAP
SET SAFETY ON
APPEND FROM TEMP
```

Fig. continues

Fig. continued

```
ERASE temp.dbf
CLOSE DATABASES
DEACTIVATE WINDOW winl
RETURN


PROCEDURE pro_prin
* Formerly PRO_PRIN.PRG
* A routine for printing from the mailing list application

ACTIVATE WINDOW winl

DO CASE
   CASE BAR() = 1
      SET CONSOLE OFF
      CLEAR
      @ 10,10 SAY "Printing prospect list........"
      USE MAILLIST ORDER ZIP
      REPORT FORM list TO PRINT
      CLOSE DATABASES
      SET CONSOLE ON
   CASE BAR() = 3
      SET CONSOLE OFF
      CLEAR
      @ 10,10 SAY "Printing labels for all prospects"
      USE MAILLIST ORDER ZIP
      LABEL FORM mail_lbl TO PRINT
      CLOSE DATABASES
      SET CONSOLE ON
   CASE BAR() = 4
      CLEAR
      cit = SPACE(17)
      @ 10,10 SAY "Print labels for what city? " GET cit
      READ
      CLEAR
      SET CONSOLE OFF
      @ 10,10 SAY "Printing labels for all prospects from "+ cit
      USE MAILLIST ORDER ZIP
```

Fig. continues

Fig. continued

```
        LABEL FORM mail_lbl FOR cit = city TO PRINT
        CLOSE DATABASES
        SET CONSOLE ON
    CASE BAR() = 5
        CLEAR
        cod = SPACE(1)
        @ 10,10 SAY "Print labels for what income code and higher? " ;
                GET cod
        READ
        CLEAR
        SET CONSOLE OFF
        @ 10,10 SAY "Printing labels for income codes " + cod + ;
                " and higher."
        USE MAILLIST ORDER ZIP
        LABEL FORM mail_lbl TO PRINT FOR VAL(cod) <= income_cod
        CLOSE DATABASES
        SET CONSOLE ON
ENDCASE
DEACTIVATE WINDOW win1


FUNCTION padc
PARAMETERS string, stlen   && Accepts the string to be padded
                           && and the width of the area where
                           && the string is to be painted
lpad = INT((stlen - LEN(TRIM(LTRIM(string))))/2) && Leading pad
tpad = stlen - lpad - LEN(TRIM(LTRIM(string)))   && Trailing pad
* Assembles the return value
ret_val = SPACE(lpad) + TRIM(LTRIM(string)) + SPACE(tpad)
RETURN ret_val           && Sends it back to the calling module
*****  End of program file: MAIN.PRG  *****
```

Six Steps to
Good Programming

Although the creation of a dBASE IV program involves making decisions about many details, most of your programming tasks will fall into six main categories:

1. Controlling the environment
2. Using data files and indexes
3. Processing data
4. Creating output
5. Restoring the environment
6. Documenting your program

These activities provide a systematic approach to programming—six steps you can follow in designing a dBASE IV program whose main benefit is consistency. If you follow these steps in roughly the same order and manner in all your applications, you will soon learn that you can borrow code from previous applications with ease and efficiency. You also will discover that the tasks of debugging and maintaining your code are less difficult when the code has been written systematically.

Being systematic, however, does not mean stagnation. As your skill increases, you will find new methods to apply in your programming. Remember that programming is an evolutionary skill. The more you program, the better you get.

Being systematic does mean that as you develop new ways of doing things, you can easily include any improvements in the applications you are modifying. The new applications you develop will be more consistent as well.

Obviously no two applications are exactly alike. You will never be able to adapt Henry Ford's assembly-line approach to the writing of dBASE IV programs. Nevertheless, a consistent approach to providing solutions to database management problems will reduce the time you spend in developing and testing.

This chapter covers each of the six steps to good programming. Included are techniques and suggestions for using various forms of the SET command to control the environment, using indexes to speed program execution, positioning the record pointer, and adding help screens to your applications.

Controlling the Environment

The flexibility of dBASE IV programming is evident in the control you have over the environment in which your programs and applications run. Typical actions include turning the bell on and off, turning the status bar on and off, changing screen colors, echoing commands to the printer, and displaying a help screen.

You assert control over the environment by using variations of the SET command. Two methods of control are available: placing control lines in the CONFIG.DB configuration file and placing SET commands in your programs.

Using the CONFIG.DB File

The CONFIG.DB configuration file is created in the same subdirectory as that of the dBASE IV executable file (.EXE or .COM, depending on whether that file is installed for multiusers). You use the CONFIG.DB file to create the environment in effect when dBASE IV is invoked.

If you are absolutely certain that the application you are writing will always be run on the same computer and that the user will never modify the CONFIG.DB file, you can use the control lines in the CONFIG.DB file to control the initial settings of the environment in which your application will run.

Using the CONFIG.DB file, however, is not a good method to rely on for controlling the environment. The addition of the DBSETUP utility to dBASE IV makes changing the contents of the CONFIG.DB file easier than ever. Thus, you can never be certain that a user won't attempt to modify the file.

How you terminate your application will help you determine whether to use the CONFIG.DB file for controlling the environment. If your application contains the RETURN command for exiting from the highest-level module (returning control to either the dot prompt or the Control Center), you will need to restore the environment settings to whatever they were before the application ends. If, however, your application ends with the QUIT command (aborting dBASE IV altogether and returning to DOS), you do not need to worry about restoring the environment.

In short, you will be much better off not to rely totally on the CONFIG.DB file for controlling the environment.

Using the SET Commands

As a programmer, you must make certain decisions about the environment in which your applications will run. Does the user have to confirm entries by pressing the Enter key, or will a field that is filled in automatically advance the cursor to the next GET? Do you want the Caps and Ins indicators to show on line 0 of the screen? Do you want the usual dBASE IV non-error messages to be displayed? These are questions you need to answer even before the first line of code is executed in your highest-level module.

In previous chapters, you were advised to include the following lines in each of the applications you write:

```
SET TALK OFF
SET STATUS OFF
SET SCOREBOARD OFF
```

You also should consider including some other SET commands at the beginning of the highest-level module of your application:

```
SET TALK OFF
SET STATUS OFF
SET SCOREBOARD OFF
SET BELL OFF
SET ESCAPE OFF   && Leaves ESCAPE on until you distribute the
                 && application so that you can abort during
                 && testing
```

Optionally you may want to include the following commands:

```
SET CONFIRM OFF
SET EXACT ON
SET DEFAULT TO <drive>
SET PATH TO <directory>
SET DELETED ON
SET COLOR TO <color string>
```

These and other variations of the SET command are described in the following sections. Unless otherwise noted, all the commands have the arguments ON and OFF.

SET AUTOSAVE

When changes are made to data files, the information is not always written immediately to disk. For a speedier performance, data modifications are usually held in a memory buffer and committed to disk in batches. If your application will be run on a system plagued by frequent power outages or if other factors are present that might cause buffered information to be lost, you can SET AUTOSAVE ON. This command causes any data changes to be written to file whenever the record pointer is moved.

SET BELL

When a user fills in a GET area, the default of SET BELL ON causes the system to sound a tone, warning that the cursor has moved to another GET area. This intrusion may be annoying to experienced data-entry personnel. If you SET BELL OFF, the tone will not sound.

SET CENTURY

As the year 2000 approaches, the SET CENTURY command will gain significance. Usually the year of any date-oriented data is displayed as two digits. If your application tracks historical or future events (such as archaeological records or 30-year bond maturities) across one or more century marks, you will need to SET CENTURY ON. The year will be displayed as four digits instead of two.

SET COLOR TO

You can use the ISCOLOR() function to determine whether the video card in a system is capable of displaying the screen in different colors. If they are possible, you use the SET COLOR TO command to specify the colors for your screen displays. Note that many of the new computers (PS/2s and COMPAQs as well as some laptops) have color cards as standard equipment but may have monochrome monitors that display colors as shades of gray. In those cases, you should test your color selections carefully. Although these computers will accept the color settings, the screen may be hard to read for lack of contrast.

SET CONFIRM

The SET CONFIRM command determines whether a user can terminate a GET by filling in the GET area completely, or whether the user must terminate the GET by pressing the Enter key.

SET DATE

SET DATE provides a number of choices for formatting date-type fields and variables. If your application will be used outside the U.S., or if the data will be transferred to places outside the U.S., you may want to SET DATE to AMERICAN, ANSI, BRITISH, FRENCH, GERMAN, ITALIAN, JAPAN, USA, MDY, DMY, or YMD.

SET DECIMALS

The SET DECIMALS command determines the default precision with which numeric data is displayed. This command does not affect the computation of numeric data, only its display and rounding characteristics.

SET DEFAULT TO

The SET DEFAULT TO command determines the disk drive to be used when a program tries to open a file. If you SET DEFAULT TO A:, the application will look for files on the diskette in drive A.

SET DELETED

The SET DELETED command determines how the application will react to records marked for deletion. If you use SET DELETED ON, the application ignores them. Note that this setting has no effect on indexing. All records in the file are indexed, regardless of the setting for this command.

SET ESCAPE

SET ESCAPE determines whether the user can terminate the application by pressing the Esc key. Usually you will want to SET ESCAPE OFF to deny the user this option. Letting users terminate with the Esc key can leave files open and vulnerable.

SET EXACT

SET EXACT is one of the most misunderstood of the SET commands. When a string comparison is performed by dBASE IV, the string on the left side of the = operator is compared, character by character, with the string on the right side of the = operator, until no characters remain for comparison in the string on the left side. If each of those characters matches a character on the right side of the = operator and EXACT is OFF, the result of the comparison is True. For example, "ABC" = "ABCD" will be True. If EXACT is ON, however, the result will be False because the strings are of different lengths.

SET MARGIN

The SET MARGIN command determines the page offset of printed matter. The default is 0. If your application requires that reports be printed with a wider left margin, you will want to use this command to specify how many columns to the right the printing should be offset.

SET PATH TO

The SET PATH TO command is independent of the DOS PATH command. SET PATH TO specifies the directory to be searched for any files the application attempts to open that are not found in the current subdirectory. If a file is not found, dBASE IV will then search the current directory.

SET SCOREBOARD

When the command SET STATUS OFF is issued, the indicators for Caps, Ins, Num, and so on, are shifted to the top of the screen. SET SCOREBOARD OFF suppresses this display.

SET STATUS

The SET STATUS command determines whether the status bar will be displayed at the bottom of the screen. Usually you will want to SET STATUS OFF so that you can take complete control of the application's screen display.

SET TALK

SET TALK suppresses the non-error messages and variable value messages that dBASE IV normally displays. Again, you will want to SET TALK OFF so that you can have complete control of the screen display.

SET TYPEAHEAD

The type-ahead buffer is used to store keystrokes before they are read by an application. If you are using memo fields and your user is an extremely fast typist, you will want to use the SET TYPEAHEAD command to expand the buffer from its normal size of 20 characters to a larger size (up to 32,000 characters). That way, the possibility of losing input is reduced.

Once you have used the appropriate SET commands to take control of the environment in which your application will run, you are ready to set up your user interface.

Selecting a User Interface

As far as your users are concerned, the most noticeable evidence of the programmer's control of the computer environment is the user interface built into the application.

A user interface is not limited to menu structures, although they represent a large portion of the interface. Other factors help determine how a user perceives and interacts with your application. How and where are error messages and user prompts displayed? What are the settings for SET BELL and SET CONFIRM? Are windows necessary? How should the entry screens be designed? These are the kinds of questions you must ask yourself in determining what kind of user interface to provide your users.

Once you get comfortable with the everyday functions of data handling and reporting, you will find that you spend an increasing amount of time on user interface issues. Generally you will want to assume that your users are beginners. Your goal is to create complex applications that beginning users could learn to use—even without the documentation to the application. The extra time you take to design a simple yet "bulletproof" user interface is time well spent toward achieving this goal (see fig. 9.1).

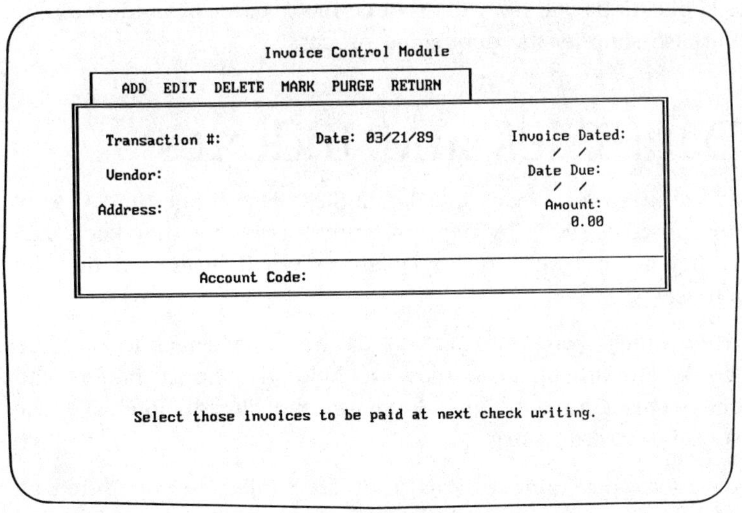

Fig. 9.1

A well-designed user interface.

In designing your user interface, make liberal use of the MESSAGE and ERROR clauses of the @...SAY...GET command. Put borders around data-entry areas; at the bottom of the borders place messages telling users of unusual keystrokes, such as Press F7 to abort or Press PgDn to end entry. Remember to make sure that the user is always informed of the options available.

Remember, too, that the issue of designing a user interface is aesthetic as well as technical. Strive for an uncluttered, professional appearance in your screens. Avoid the overuse of color. Screens that change colors at every keystroke or use garish color combinations are fine for games, but such screens are seldom appreciated by business users. Watch color combinations; use nondistracting colors with plenty of contrast. One of the most readable, though perhaps unexciting, color combinations is bright yellow on blue, with GETs in black on cyan. This combination shows up well also on monochrome screens if a color card is built into the system.

One way of finding a user interface that works for you is to emulate, as much as possible, the user interface of one of your favorite programs. Analyze the transitions from menus to data-entry screens. How is the menu structure designed? Is it flexible enough to work with most applications, or will it be useful only for certain types of operations?

Once you find a comfortable interface, use it. If you are designing multiple applications for the same organization, use the same interface and thus reduce the training time. If the interface is consistent, your users will pick up on new applications faster. You also will be able to lift code from other applications more often. Why redesign a pop-up menu when you can take the code from an old one and simply modify the menu size and prompts? Lifting tested, proven code from older applications will not only reduce the time spent on developing an application but also simplify the debugging process.

Using Data Files and Indexes

dBASE IV enables you to have as many as 10 data files open at one time. One of the most common mistakes made by new programmers is that they keep data files open when they are not needed. Data files are not delicate, but they do have some weaknesses.

As indicated earlier, unless you SET AUTOSAVE ON, not all changes to data are immediately recorded to disk. Instead they are held in memory buffers and written as batches. This approach cuts down on the already intensive use dBASE IV makes of the hard disk drive.

When data files are left open unnecessarily, they are subject to corruption by power failures, voltage surges, accidental reboots, and the like. As a precautionary measure, you should have data files open only when they are needed. Once a data file becomes corrupted, you will have a hard time getting the file right again, for the data is written in fixed-field lengths.

A dBASE IV data file has a header at the beginning of the file that contains information about the structure of the data. The way dBASE IV extracts the ZIP code, for example, is to determine from the header how many bytes from the beginning of the record the ZIP code is offset and how many bytes should be in the field. If even one byte is dropped out of the data file, all the following records will be shifted one byte. As a result, the information extracted will be in error.

The best advice is to open data files as late as possible and close them as soon as possible in your modules. Never leave a data file open when a menu is on-screen. (The exception to this rule is in creating a pop-up menu that allows users to pick the fields to be included in a LIST/DISPLAY.)

Opening and Closing Data Files

You can use the USE command to open and close data files in the current work area as well as in other work areas. For example, consider this segment of code:

```
USE vendors        && Opens the vendor data file in the current
                   && area
USE                && Without an argument, closes the file in
                   && the current work area
USE employee IN 2  && Opens the employee data file in work
                   && area 2
USE vendor IN 2    && Closes the employee file and opens
                   && vendor
USE IN 2           && Closes the current file in work area 2
CLOSE DATABASES    && Closes all data files in all work areas
```

The USE command also opens indexes at the same time that the data file is opened. Note that an .MDX production file is opened automatically when you USE the data file. (A production file is created at the same time that the underlying data file is created—when you mark any field as an index key.) Unless you specify an index TAG to control the order of the file, however, the database acts as if it is unindexed.

Look at the following sample lines of code:

```
USE vendor INDEX id,company,zip  && dBASE III compatible indexes

USE vendor ORDER id  && Data file with .MDX TAG as master index
```

To change the index order without having to close the data file, you SET ORDER TO the following:

```
SET ORDER TO 3     && In the list of indexes in the USE
                   && command, this makes the third .NDX file
                   && the master index.
```

```
SET ORDER TO TAG id   && Specifies which TAG of the .MDX
                      && file to use as the master index
```

Getting the Most from Indexes

Unless you need to retain compatibility with dBASE III Plus, you should not use the old-style .NDX index files. Because each .NDX file requires its own file handle, you will be able to keep fewer files open.

When DOS opens files, they are kept track of in a file-handling table. The term *file handle*, which derives from the DOS table name, means that a handle is attached to each open file. With this "handle," the file can be manipulated. Depending on your DOS version, dBASE IV can have as many as 99 files open at one time. Because dBASE IV uses 5 file handles for its internal workings, the limit on user-generated files (such as data, index, format, and program files) is actually 94. Check your DOS manual to see how many files your version of DOS can have open. You also will need to set the number in your CONFIG.SYS file.

To avoid running out of file handles, use the .MDX form of the index file. An .MDX file requires only one file handle but can provide as many as 47 different indexing options (TAGs).

Of course, each index TAG has some amount of overhead. Having a large number of TAGs in an .MDX file will therefore affect performance. You will probably never approach the limit of 47 TAGs per .MDX file, however.

Using Indexes To Speed Program Execution

One of the most significant factors affecting the execution speed of your application is how you use indexing to position the record pointer. An application that takes maximum advantage of indexing on an XT-class computer can actually get more work done in less time than a poorly designed application running on a 386-class computer.

You learned in Chapter 1 that a search through a large database is considerably faster when an index is used. Each test of the search key effectively eliminates half the remaining records from the search. For this reason, you should avoid using LOCATE commands in your applications whenever possible, for the LOCATE command searches the data file sequentially. If you issue the command

```
LOCATE FOR acct = "912345"
```

the record pointer will be positioned at the top of the file, and each record will be evaluated in turn until either the search expression is satisfied or the record pointer reaches the end of the file. The execution of this process takes considerably longer than a SEEK or FIND that makes use of an index to determine which record contains the specific account number.

Because dBASE IV enables you to create complex index keys (for example, INDEX on ZIP + 1_name + f_nam), you can make sophisticated multilevel searches in seconds. Using indexing and the SEEK command, you should be able to position the record pointer on any individual record in a 10,000-record data file in less than two seconds.

A word of caution is in order, however. Often new programmers will try to create index keys on TRIM()ed fields. This approach does not speed up indexed searches. The length of an index key is related directly to the length of the field in the data file. If 1_nam is 12 characters long and f_nam is 12 characters long, the key length of the combination of those two fields will be 24 characters. Issuing the command

```
INDEX on TRIM(1_nam) + TRIM(f_nam)
```

will do nothing to shorten the resulting key expression and will actually make the SEEK take fractionally more time. More time is needed because the SEEK expression will have to TRIM() the variables in order to make the SEEK key compatible with the index key. If you forget to process the SEEK expression, you will run the risk that the SEEK will fail to find a matching record which actually exists.

Processing Data

Data processing can be defined as the manipulation of stored data into a form needed for output. If you have been working at the dot prompt and following the programming examples presented in this book, you already have an understanding of most of the data processing techniques used in dBASE IV. Ordering the data with indexes, using functions to convert data for display, SEEKing records in the data file, storing information in variables, using report formats to output data, making comparisons of pieces of data—all these operations fall into the broad category of data processing.

In a dBASE IV program, you can think of data processing as the assembling of data so that it is easier to output. Two of the programmer's primary tasks in writing a dBASE IV program are to position the record pointer at the proper place in a file and to manipulate the data contained in the record in the file. The first task is discussed in this section. The second task is usually accomplished in dBASE IV programs concurrently with the actual output and is therefore discussed in the next section.

When new records are added to the data file, the APPEND BLANK command creates a new record at the end of that file and positions the record pointer at the new record. This process is automatic, requiring no interference from the user or the programmer.

When records must be found for editing, outputting, and deleting, the task of positioning the record pointer is raised to the level of an art. In many ways the art of positioning the record pointer is also the art of creating indexes.

Understanding two points is important in positioning the record pointer. First, all the records with the same key will be grouped together. Second, if the key expression is compared with the next record's key each time you SKIP to the next record, you can identify the break between groups. You can use this break to control the processing of data; that is why the break is sometimes called a *control break*.

A good example that illustrates these two points is found in the inventory data file INV_TORY.DBF, which was created in the Applications Generator in Chapter 3. This file has a many-to-one relationship with VENDOR.DBF; the relationship is defined by the vendor identification number common to both files.

When indexed by the vendor ID number, all the items in inventory that are supplied by a particular vendor are grouped together. A listing of the data file's records, when indexed by the vendor ID number, shows clearly the effects of the grouping and the control break (see fig. 9.2).

Fig. 9.2

A listing of the indexed items in INV_TORY.DBF.

PART #	VENDOR ID	DESCRIPTION
454F2	11111	Chemistry Set
341F3	11111	Telescope
259J	12345	The Little Encyclopedia
543HG34	22222	Rabbit Fur Hand Muff
298H	22222	Baseball Glove
153S	22222	Basketball Set
863L1	33123	Little Jobber Printing Press
303L3	33333	Girl's Bookbag
303M3	33333	Boy's Bookbag

Notice that all three of the items offered by vendor 22222 are grouped together. All the items offered by vendor 33333 are similarly grouped. To extract all the items offered by either vendor, you simply position the record pointer on the first item with the correct vendor ID (the key value) and then output the information. To get to the next item, you issue the SKIP command. The program then determines whether a control break has occurred. One of two things will happen in a control break: the vendor ID of the new record will be different, or the record pointer will reach the end of the file.

At the end of the file is a blank phantom record. Its record number is one greater than the number of records in the file—a number indicated by the DISPLAY STRUCTURE command. No error condition will occur if the record pointer is placed on this phantom record. Likewise, no error will occur if the value of a field is placed in this phantom record. You can even go so far as to use the REPLACE command to put a value in one of the fields without triggering an error message from dBASE IV. Of course, when you issue the APPEND BLANK command and the phantom record is turned into a real record, it will be blank.

The only way you will know that you have moved the record pointer onto the phantom record is that the EOF() function will return a value of .T. The error is not triggered until you try to SKIP past the phantom record. Your job as programmer is to keep error messages from being triggered. To extract vendor 2222's items, you should therefore structure the code something like this:

```
look = "22222"
SEEK look

DO WHILE .T.
    DO output  && Where output is a subroutine to do printing
    SKIP
    IF vendor_id <> look .OR. EOF()
        EXIT
    ENDIF
ENDDO
```

The line that tests for the control break is

```
IF vendor_id <> look .OR. EOF()
```

Whenever the next record has a different ID number or whenever this record is the end-of-file phantom record, the loop is aborted with the EXIT command. With just seven lines of code, you can process all the records with the same key expression regardless of their positions in the file or how many records need to be processed.

Creating Output

Once you have the record pointer in the correct position, you need to select a destination for the output, convert the data, and then send it. You usually convert and send data in one step with various dBASE IV functions, including STR(), VAL(), and SUBSTR(); or with mathematical expressions, such as qty * unit_cost. You also can combine functions and expressions, as in the following examples:

```
? "Part #: " + TRIM(part_no) + "Retail Price: " + STR(cost * .37)

@1,0 SAY "Part #: " + TRIM(part_no) + "Retail Price: " + STR(cost * .37)
```

Choosing the Destination for Output

Two commands will direct your output to the intended destination: `SET PRINTER` and `SET DEVICE`. The `SET PRINTER` command directs to the printer or a file all output not sent with the `@...SAY` command. `SET PRINTER` is used mostly with the `?/??` commands and has several forms.

1. `SET PRINTER on/OFF`

   This command begins and ends the direction of output to the printer. The default is `OFF`.

2. `SET PRINTER TO <device>`

   With this command, you can specify that the output be directed to any of the DOS logical devices (LPT1, LPT2, LPT3, COM1, or COM2) that can receive output. The default value is the DOS device PRN; however, you cannot redirect to PRN once you have changed it. Because most systems use LPT1 as the PRN device, the following command usually redirects output to the normal printer port:

   `SET PRINTER TO LPT1`

3. `SET PRINTER TO FILE <filename>`

   This command establishes an ASCII file to receive the output so that it can be edited or stored for later printing. For example, the following command causes the output to be captured in a file named REPORT.TXT:

   `SET PRINTER TO FILE report.txt`

You can use the `SET DEVICE` command to direct the output of the `@...SAY` command. The advantage to using `SET DEVICE` and `@...SAY` together is that you can then use the `?/??` commands to paint screen messages without having to redirect output. The `SET DEVICE` command can select any of the following destinations as a device to receive output:

The screen
The printer
  (as selected with the `SET PRINTER TO <device>` command)
An ASCII file

Look at the following examples:

```
SET DEVICE TO PRINTER
SET DEVICE TO SCREEN
SET DEVICE TO FILE text.txt
```

Two cautions apply to the SET DEVICE command. First, some printers will not print the last @...SAY, holding it instead in a buffer. To flush the buffer, you must issue an EJECT command at the end of the printing commands. The EJECT advances the paper to the next page after the last line is printed. Second, if you issue an @...SAY command that will print on a previous line of the page, a page eject is issued automatically. Consider these sample lines of code:

```
SET DEVICE TO PRINT
@10,10 SAY "This will print on line 10 of the page."
@ 9,10 SAY "This will print on line 9 of the next page."
```

You can, however, print an item on the same line closer to the left margin without ejecting a page, as in the following code:

```
SET DEVICE TO PRINT
@1,50 SAY "This will begin at column 50."
@1,10 SAY "This will be on the same line."
```

Controlling the Printer

Chapter 11 discusses some of dBASE IV's advanced features for taking full control of the printing environment. These features, including the new system memory variables, enable you to take advantage of the enhanced printing capabilities of modern printers, including font changes, line printing, and boxing. Refer to Chapter 11 for more information on controlling the printing environment.

Restoring the Environment

Before your program module or application terminates, you will want to assess the need to restore the environment to its previous condition, before the application or module took control. This technique is especially handy when your highest-level module is a menu enabling the user to choose from several different applications, or when a module in an application needs to alter the environment's condition radically.

As indicated previously, if your application ends with the QUIT command, you will not have to restore the environment. The QUIT command exits dBASE IV and returns to DOS.

Whenever you need to restore the environment settings, you can use the SET() function. This function determines the conditions of the various SET commands whose arguments are ON or OFF. By storing the results of the SET() function to variables, you can later restore those SET conditions to their former settings. Look at the following example:

```
talk = SET("TALK")
confirm = SET("CONFIRM")
```

When the application ends, you simply issue these commands:

```
SET TALK &talk
SET CONFIRM &confirm
```

The previous conditions of the SET TALK and SET CONFIRM commands will be restored.

Obviously you will want to put the commands that store information about the environment at the top of the program, before any SET commands are issued. The commands to restore the environment settings will be placed just before the RETURN command, which passes control back to the calling module or the dot prompt.

Documenting Your Programs

When you design an application in the dBASE IV programming language, you must provide support to your users. As indicated at the beginning of the chapter, the customer support staff at Ashton-Tate cannot possibly answer questions about the thousands of applications that are written each month. Part of the support you must provide is documentation for each of your applications. Three kinds of documentation are important for your users (clients):

1. Documentation in the program code
2. A user's manual
3. Context-sensitive help within the application

First, the code itself should be documented so that another programmer can pick up easily on the application's operations, especially if you are unavailable for later modifications. This kind of documentation is helpful to you as well, for after three months you may forget the details of a particular application.

Second, you should provide a user's manual to accompany your application. This manual does not have to be elaborately printed and bound. In fact, it can be as simple as an ASCII file that the user can print. What is important is that the manual clearly explain the goals of the application and the processes a user must follow to implement those goals with the software provided.

Third, you should embed context-sensitive help within the application itself so that the user can get immediate answers about any procedure. This help system usually takes the form of a help screen invoked by a designated key.

Documenting the Code

dBASE IV provides three ways to include nonexecuting statements in your code: the NOTE command, the asterisk (*), and double ampersands (&&).

Any line that you begin with the word NOTE or an asterisk signals to the dBASE IV compiler that the line is not a command to be executed. You also can include short comments on executing lines by following the code with double ampersands (&&). Look at these examples:

```
NOTE This line will not execute and can contain information
NOTE you will need later.
* Likewise, this line will not be compiled or executed
USE vendor    && Anything after the ampersands will be ignored
              && by the compiler. You also can use the
              && ampersands to offset longer comments so that
              && they are easier to read.
```

The advantage to adding comments to your code is fairly obvious. As time passes, you will not remember the details of complex algorithms or the logic behind some of the choices you made for doing things in the application. Commenting will save you from having to rediscover the problems that caused you to make some of the programming decisions for the application.

Commenting is also indispensable if you work on a team that produces code. Good, solid commenting makes it easier for the other programmers on the team to follow your thought processes. Thus, the code they write can mesh more completely with yours.

Writing the User's Manual

Even if you work in the same building with the users of your applications, you should produce a written manual for every application. The manual should contain at least the following elements:

1. A table of contents

2. Installation and start-up instructions

3. A tutorial

4. An explanation of each module and how it should be used

5. A table showing the editing keystrokes and any function-key assignments the application makes

6. Detailed explanations of error messages

These elements are the minimum requirements for a good manual. You also may decide to include pictures of menus and data-entry screens. These can be prepared with commercially available software such as HotShot or InSet, or a frieze utility that is part of a program like Microsoft Paintbrush or PC Paintbrush. Using screen shots will enliven the look of the manual and make it easier for the user to follow the examples.

One of the most overlooked features of a manual for a dBASE IV application is a table showing the editing keystrokes for use during data entry. Chapter 7 of the *Quick Reference* supplied with dBASE IV provides a list of all the cursor-control keystrokes. Be sure to include any function-key assignments that are a part of your application's user interface.

In addition, you should make sure that a section of the user's manual explains in detail the error messages you have included in the application. Include the text of the error message as well as instructions on how to correct the problem.

Remember, too, that your users are not technically oriented. Keep your text free of jargon and explain processes in simple terms. It is often helpful to think of someone you know who is completely afraid of computers, and then write the text as if you were trying to explain the procedures to that person. The manual is not a vehicle for impressing users with your programming prowess. Let the simplicity of the user interface and the power of the application demonstrate you programming skills. The application itself will do a much better job of letting people know how good you are than you ever could.

Providing Help Screens

In addition to using the MESSAGE clauses of the DEFINE PAD, DEFINE BAR, and @...SAY...GET commands, you can deliver extra information to your users. Whenever your application is paused for data entry into a variable or a field, you can provide a context-sensitive help system in the form of a help screen that the user can activate with a "hot key."

Unfortunately this technique will not work when a menu is active on-screen. You will therefore have to turn the help screen on and off by using the ON KEY command before and after issuing GETs.

The dBASE IV VARREAD() function returns the name of the current variable or field when a GET is active. Thus, you can build a program or procedure that will display text in a window whenever the user presses the hot key. If you include the help module as a procedure, you will have to either place it in the highest-level module or use several procedures in the modules in which entry takes place. An alternative is to create a program that can be called with a DO statement from anywhere in the application. The code segment shown in figure 9.3 illustrates this alternative.

```
* This section of code is an excerpt from a program that accepts
* entry. You can assume that the file has already been opened and
* that everything is set up for the @...SAY...GETs.

DEFINE WINDOW help_em  FROM 2,10 TO 9,70  && This command would
                                          && actually be in the
                                          && menu-creation
                                          && module.
ON KEY LABEL F1 DO help_sub    && Specifies the hot key and the
                               && action to be done

@ 5,10 SAY "Enter name: " GET nam        && Takes the entry
@ 6,10 SAY "Enter account #: " GET acct   PICTURE "A9999"
READ

ON KEY LABEL F1    && Cancels the hot key assignment
RELEASE WINDOW help_em


***** HELP_SUB.PRG
* The help system for the application
PRIVATE ln1,ln2,ln3,ln4,ln5
DO CASE
   CASE VARREAD() = "NAM"  && VARREAD() will return the name as
                          && uppercase.
      ln1 = "Enter the first name, middle initial and last name"
      ln2 = "of the customer into this box. Do not type the"
      ln3 = "information in all capital letters. Be sure to"
      ln4 = "include a period after the initial."
      ln5 = ""
   CASE VARREAD() = "ACCT"
      ln1 = "Enter the customer's account number in this box."
      ln2 = "Valid account numbers begin with a capital letter"
      ln3 = "followed by four numbers."
      ln4 = ""
      ln5 = ""
```

Fig. 9.3

Using the ON KEY command to set a hot key for activating a help screen.

Fig. continues

Fig. continued

```
     OTHERWISE
        ln1 = "Sorry there is no information available about"
        ln2 = "this item."
        ln3 = ""
        ln4 = ""
        ln5 = ""
  ENDCASE

  ACTIVATE WINDOW help_em
  ? ln1
  ? ln2
  ? ln3
  ? ln4
  ? ln5
  WAIT "Press any key to resume entry."
  DEACTIVATE WINDOW help_em
  RETURN
```

Here the hot key is set with the ON KEY command just before the GETs are issued, and the hot key is terminated after the READ. You must open and close the access to the help module, for a user who presses the hot key at a menu will trigger an error.

Summary

This chapter presented six steps to good programming, including many useful coding techniques. You learned ways to control the environment by using the CONFIG.DB file and the SET commands. You saw how to speed program execution by using indexes to process data files. And you learned how to control the destination for output by directing it to a particular printer port or file. In addition, you learned how to restore the environment and how to document your applications so that they can be understood easily by users as well as other programmers.

By incorporating these techniques into your applications, you will achieve a more consistent coding style, which will make it easier to move code segments from one application to another.

In Chapter 10, you will learn how to put these coding techniques into practice with programs that use multiple data files.

10

Handling Multiple
Data Files

Writing programs that use multiple data files is not nearly as difficult as many new programmers may think. You already have a foundation in the techniques required to handle multiple files efficiently.

All you have to remember is that each opened file has its own record pointer. When you move from one work area to another, the record pointers do not reposition themselves. Therefore, through your code, you must open the files you need, position the record pointers wherever you want in each of the files, and perform the actions of the module. The information you obtain is the data being pointed to with the individual record pointers.

As you move from one work area to another, you can easily access data in a data file located in another work area by using the alias of that data file. An *alias* is simply the name of that file or its work area, or a name you give to the file.

Let's assume, for example, that two files are opened in the following manner:

```
USE vendor ORDER id
SELECT 2
USE inv_tory ORDER vendor_id
```

The current work area in this example is work area 2. Ten work areas are available. Each of these work areas can be identified by a letter—work area 1 is identified by A, work area 2 is identified by B, and so on.

To extract the company name of the vendor, you can use either of these forms:

```
? A->company
```

```
? VENDOR->company
```

The `A->` and `VENDOR->` are the default forms of the alias for VENDOR.DBF.

Alternatively, you can specify an alias when the file is opened:

```
USE vendor ORDER id ALIAS vend
```

In this case, you use the form `VEND->company` to extract the company name.

You can read field values in the current work area by simply naming the field, as in

```
? company
```

Using the alias, however, is sometimes clearer if you are making many references to field values when several files are open. Look at this example:

```
? VENDOR->company
```

This way, the alias serves as documentation, telling you at a glance from which file the value is coming.

Whenever you have a variable with the same name as that of a field, the field takes precedence. For example, if you have in the current work area a variable called `vendor_id` and a field named `vendor_id`, the command

```
? vendor_id
```

will return the value of the field. To specify that the return value should be that of the variable, use the alias for memory variables (`M->`). The following example will return the value of the variable rather than the field of the same name:

```
? M->vendor_id
```

Adding Records to Files

Often you will need to design a program enabling the user to add records to two or more files in the same operation. Such a transaction may be necessary during the creation of invoices, packing slips, and bank deposit slips. In these examples, a record in one file will relate to several records in a second file through a field common to both files. That field might be an invoice number or a transaction code.

The logic behind this kind of transaction is fairly direct. In most cases, you will have a one-to-many relationship between a parent file and a child file. For an invoice, for instance, the parent file contains the base information about the invoice, and the child file contains the different items that appear on the invoice.

In figure 10.1, you can see that one record in the parent file tracks the information about an invoice related to several records in the child file. The child file contains detailed information about all the individual items purchased for that particular invoice.

```
Parent Invoice File
INV#      DATE        ACCT     SALES REP
30127     01/01/88    33275    DJ
30128     01/01/88    14382    RS
★30129    01/02/88    12375    BL
30130     01/02/88    12781    RS
```

Fig. 10.1

Invoice records showing the relationship between a parent file and a child file.

```
Child File of Items Purchased
INV#      QTY   STOCK#      COST
30127     4     47329       1.00
30127     1     40127       2.39
30128     1     83745       4.55
★30129    2     40127      19.95
★30129    7     21735        .99
★30129    3     11732       1.47
★30129    1     74351       2.17
30130     2     17329       3.95
30131     1     40127       2.57
30132     5     47329        .72
30132     3     40111      19.95
30132     2     27125      25.01
```

To create an invoice, you open the files and then APPEND to the parent file a record (the main record that will have many records related to it). After the information is written to that record, the individual items need to be APPENDed to the child file.

You may want to add other features to an invoice-creation module. Many such modules require the user to enter a valid customer account number before the invoice is created. This addition ensures that the invoice will be correctly billed. The user enters the account number, and the account information is displayed on-screen.

Another common feature is a self-generating account number. The program will read a .MEM file from the disk to determine the last invoice number assigned. Then the program increments the number by one and uses the SAVE command to write the value of the variable back to disk.

Other features you may want to consider adding to an invoice-creation module are the lookup and verification of items by part number, and the automatic printing of the invoice. How complex the module becomes is determined by your level of expertise and the needs of your users.

The invoice-creation module shown in figure 10.2 uses three files (CUSTOMER.DBF, INVOICE.DBF, and INV_ITEM.DBF) whose structures were listed in Chapter 1. In this module, the user first is prompted for a customer number for verification and then fills in the invoice. The module's data-entry screen is shown in figure 10.3.

Fig. 10.2

The invoice-creation module INV.PRG.

```
*****  Program: INV.PRG  *****
* A sample invoice program
SET TALK OFF
SET STATUS OFF
SET SCOREBOARD OFF
DEFINE WINDOW cover FROM 0,0 TO 23,79   && A window to hide menus
* Note that the window does not cover line 24, for if an entry
* error is triggered, the error message blasts the bottom line of
* the border, and it is not restored when the error message is
* cleared.

ACTIVATE WINDOW cover    && Takes over the screen

USE customer ORDER acct_no        && Opens the data files
USE invoice IN 2 ORDER invoice_no
USE inv_item IN 3 ORDER inv_no

v_acct = SPACE(5)     && Inits a variable for the account #
flag = ' '            && A variable to let the main module
                      && determine whether a lower-level module
                      && says to abort
@ 1,0 SAY PADC("Rock Bottom Discounters   Invoice Module",77)
@ 2,0 TO  2,77

DO cust_fnd      && Performs the PROCEDURE to find a customer
IF flag = '*'
   CLOSE DATABASES          && If no customer is found in the
   DEACTIVATE WINDOW cover   && subroutine, this section will
   RELEASE WINDOW cover      && detect the flag and abort.
   RETURN
ENDIF
```

Fig. continues

Fig. continued

```
RESTORE FROM invno.mem ADDITIVE  && ADDITIVE keeps the current
                                 && variable from being RELEASEd.
v_inv = v_inv + 1      && Increments the number,
SET SAFETY OFF         && avoids the overwrite confirmation,
SAVE ALL LIKE v_inv TO invno.mem   && and writes the file back
SET SAFETY ON                      && to disk
v_inv = STR(v_inv,7,0) && Converts the variable to character
                       && type

REPLACE acct_no WITH v_acct           && Stuffs the invoice
REPLACE invoice_no WITH v_inv         && driver record with the
REPLACE ship_name  WITH A->company    && default values so that
REPLACE ship_addr  WITH A->address    && the user can edit them
REPLACE ship_city  WITH A->city       && for special shipping
REPLACE ship_state WITH A->state      && instructions
REPLACE ship_zip   WITH A->zip
REPLACE pur_date   WITH DATE()

@11,0 TO 11,77 DOUBLE
@ 4, 5 SAY "Account: " + v_acct
@ 5, 5 SAY "Company:" GET ship_name
@ 7, 5 SAY "Ship to:" GET ship_addr   && Finalizes the contents
@ 9,14 GET ship_city                  && of the driver record
@ 9,32 GET ship_state
@ 9,35 GET ship_zip
@ 4,45 SAY "   Invoice #: " + v_inv
@ 7,45 SAY "   Sale date:" GET  pur_date
@ 9,45 SAY " Salesperson:" GET sal_per
READ

DO items    && Calls the PROCEDURE that takes the items

* Here is where the invoice-printing routine will be added (refer
* to the next chapter).

CLOSE DATABASES
DEACTIVATE WINDOW cover
RELEASE WINDOWS cover
RETURN
```

Fig. continues

Fig. continued

```
* This function would normally be included in the highest-level
* module or a PROCEDURE file. The function is included here so
* that the code will work for this example.

FUNCTION PADC
PARAMETERS string, stlen        && Accepts the string to be padded
                                && and the width of the area where
                                && the string is to be painted
lpad = INT((stlen - LEN(TRIM(LTRIM(string))))/2)   && Leading pad
tpad = stlen - lpad - LEN(TRIM(LTRIM(string)))     && Trailing pad
* Assembles the return value
ret_val = SPACE(lpad) + TRIM(LTRIM(string)) + SPACE(tpad)
RETURN ret_val    && Sends the return value back to the calling
                  && module


* This is the section of code that locates the proper customer
* record. Because this code is one level under the calling module,
* it cannot just say RETURN and have the program abort to the menu.
* That is why the variable flag exists. If there is a problem in
* finding the customer, the lower-level module will set the flag
* so that the calling module can do the abort.



PROCEDURE cust_fnd

DO WHILE .T.

    @ 6,10 SAY "Enter customer account number: " GET v_acct
    READ
    SEEK v_acct
    IF FOUND()
        @ 3,0 CLEAR
        SELECT 2
        APPEND BLANK
        RETURN
    ELSE
        @ 8,10 SAY "Sorry no customer found with that account number."
        conf = ' '
        @10,10 SAY "Try again (Y/N)-----> " GET conf
        READ
        IF UPPER(conf) = 'Y' && Any key but Y will answer no.
```

Fig. continues

Fig. continued

```
            v_acct = SPACE(5)
            @ 3,0 CLEAR && Erases all but the first 3 lines of screen
            LOOP
         ELSE
            flag = '*'  && Sets the abort flag variable. Because this
                        && module is one level too low to abort to the
                        && menu, you need a way to tell the calling
                        && module to abort.

            CLEAR
            RETURN
         ENDIF
      ENDIF
ENDDO


PROCEDURE items       && This module takes user entry for the
                      && individual items on the invoice.
SELECT 3
DO WHILE .T.

   conf = ' '
   APPEND BLANK              && Creates the record, stuffs the
   REPLACE inv_no WITH v_inv && invoice # into the field, and
                            && takes the entry
   @12, 0 SAY PADC("Enter the information about items purchased",77)
   @13, 0 SAY PADC("in this area.",77)
   @15, 5 SAY "Item number:" GET item_no
   @15,29 SAY "Quantity:" GET qty RANGE 1,999
   @15,45 SAY "Unit price:" GET price PICTURE '99999.99'
   @17, 5 SAY "Is this item backordered? (Y/N)----->" GET b_ordered ;
                PICTURE 'Y'
   READ
* Keeping the confirmation with its own READ prevents it from
* appearing until entry is made into the record.
   @20, 5 SAY "Enter another item? (Y/N)----->" GET conf
   READ
   IF UPPER(conf) = 'Y'
      @12,0 CLEAR
      LOOP     && Does it again
   ELSE
```

Fig. continues

Fig. continued

```
        EXIT      && Drops out of the loop and goes back to calling
                  && module
      ENDIF
   ENDDO
   RETURN
   *****  End of program  *****
```

Fig. 10.3

The data-entry screen prompting the user for an account number.

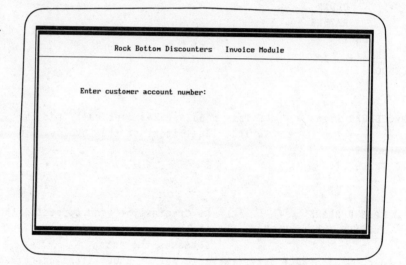

```
                Rock Bottom Discounters    Invoice Module


      Enter customer account number:
```

The code in this program contains several major operations in three modules. The module INV.PRG sets the environment, defines and opens a window, opens the data files, and initializes variables to hold entry for an account number and to act as a flag. The flag variable is used by lower-level modules to tell INV.PRG when an abort is called for. Before calling the CUST_FND procedure, INV also paints a screen header and a line.

The CUST_FND procedure then takes the user's entry and performs a SEEK in an attempt to locate the account. If the SEEK is successful, a new record is APPENDed in the invoice file, and control is RETURNed to INV.PRG. If the SEEK is not successful, the user is queried about another attempt. The CUST_FND procedure will cycle through its loop until the proper account is found or until the user indicates that another attempt is unnecessary. If the user doesn't want to make another attempt, the flag variable is set to tell the higher-level module to abort.

When `CUST_FND` terminates, INV.PRG checks whether the abort variable has been set. If it has, the module closes the data files and terminates. Otherwise, the module will read a .MEM file to acquire the next invoice number.

Because the record pointer in the customer file is set at the proper account's record, the next operation is simple. The invoice record created by `CUST_FND` is stuffed with the invoice number and the customer's address information for shipping. INV.PRG then lets the user edit the shipping information before passing control to the `ITEMS` procedure.

The `ITEMS` procedure opens a loop that allows the user to enter in the invoice as many different items as necessary, prompting after each item to see whether the user wants to add another item. `ITEMS` will roll through its loop until the user declines to add another item. Once the user declines, the procedure terminates, and control is passed back to INV.PRG. At this point, INV simply closes the files and restores the environment before terminating.

Editing Records in Two Files Simultaneously

As long as the record pointer is correctly positioned before editing begins, a program can accept data entry into two data files at the same time with no problem. Look, for example, at the following code:

```
@ 5,10 SAY "Enter Payment Date:" GET pay_day
@ 7,10 SAY "Enter Payment Amt.:" GET pay_amt
@ 9,10 SAY "Enter Bank Account for Deposit:" GET B->acct
READ
REPLACE B->pmt WITH pay_amt
```

Here the same set of `GETs` is used to accept keyboard entry in two files at the same time. Because the fields `pay_day` and `pay_amt` are in the file in the current work area, they do not need to be identified by aliases.

The `REPLACE` statement is typically used in most programs that alter data in two files at the same time. Generally if your application requires that the user enter data from the keyboard into two files at the same time, you should take a close look at the data structures of the application. Because a one-to-one relationship probably exists between the files, you may want to consider combining them into one larger file. At times, however, you should keep the files separate (for instance, if a combined file exceeds 255 fields, which is the maximum number allowed in a data file). In that case, you can commingle the files in the same entry screen.

More commonly, you will need to change data in one file to reflect data that exists in another file. For example, in an accounts-receivable module, in which payments are credited to a customer account, typical inquiries are "What was the date of the last payment?" and "What was the amount?" To answer these questions easily, you can arrange to have two fields in the customer file hold this information, and to have the information displayed whenever the customer record is edited.

The following code represents two excerpts from the payment-acceptance module of a membership-tracking application. Once the payment is accepted, the amount of the last payment and the date it was received are entered into the membership file with the REPLACE command. Here is the code for accepting payments:

```
@  7, 16  SAY "MEMBERSHIP NUMBER:"
@  7, 35  GET   memno  VALID PMTACC()
@  7, 42  SAY "PAYMENT DATE:"
@  7, 56  GET   pamentdat
@  9, 20  SAY "DUE DATE:"
@  9, 30  GET   duedat
@  9, 41  SAY "RECEIVED:"
@  9, 51  GET   pmtamt  PICTURE "99999.99"
@ 11, 17  SAY "PAYMENT DUE:"
@ 11, 30  GET   pmt  PICTURE "99999.99"
@ 11, 40  SAY "MEMBER DUES:"
@ 11, 53  GET   dues  PICTURE "99999.99"
@ 13, 27  SAY "LATE FEES:"
@ 13, 38  GET   late  PICTURE "99999.99"
READ
REPLACE MEMB->curbal WITH MEMB->curbal - RFP->pmtamt
REPLACE MEMB->lastpay WITH RFP->pamentdat
REPLACE MEMB->lastpayamt WITH RFP->pmtamt
```

Now look at the code for editing membership records:

```
@  2,  5  SAY PADC("BLOUNTSTOWN MEMBERSHIP MANAGEMENT PROGRAM",75)
@  4, 53  SAY "LAST PAYMENT: "
@  4, 68  GET lastpay
@  5, 53  SAY " AMOUNT PAID: "
@  5, 68  GET lastpayamt  PICTURE "99999.99"
@  6, 53  SAY " CURRENT BAL: "
@  6, 68  GET curbal  PICTURE "99999.99"
CLEAR GETS
```

```
@  6,  6  SAY "MEMBERSHIP #:"
@  6, 20  GET   memno
@  6, 30  SAY "MEMB. TYPE:"
@  6, 43  GET   memtype PICTURE "@!!!"
@  8, 59  SAY "SALES REP:"
@  9, 54  GET   salsrep
@  8,  7  SAY "FIRST NAME:"
@  8, 20  GET   memfir
@ 10, 57  SAY "CONTRACT DATE:"
@ 11, 60  GET   contdat
@ 10,  8  SAY "LAST NAME:"
@ 10, 20  GET   memlas
@ 12, 11  SAY "ADDRESS:"
@ 12, 20  GET   memadd
@ 12, 60  SAY "SOURCE:"
@ 12, 68  GET   source
@ 13, 20  GET   memcit
@ 13, 40  GET   memst  PICTURE "!!"
@ 13, 45  GET   memzip  PICTURE "99999"
@ 13, 55  SAY "MEMB. PRICE:"
@ 13, 68  GET   memprice  PICTURE "99999.99"
READ
```

In the first module the payment is accepted, and the values in the relevant fields in the MEMB.DBF file are REPLACEd with the values entered in comparable fields in the file RFP.DBF. Knowing the structures of the files is not important. You need to know only that the balance is maintained in the membership record and that the date of the last payment and its amount are repeated in that file (MEMB.DBF). When a request is made to edit the membership record, the upper right corner of the screen displays the date of the last payment, the amount paid, and the current balance (see fig. 10.4). None of these three fields can be edited.

This arrangement may seem to contradict the general principle of not repeating in one file the information contained in another file. The reason for designing the module this way, however, is evident: a member inquiring about a bill can get a much faster answer if only one file—the membership record file (MEMB.DBF)—must be opened and checked. That way, no search needs to be made of the payments file (RFP.DBF) for the most recent payment to that account. Furthermore, in this application the payment records are purged from the system once the end-of-month audit is completed. If a member falls behind, the information is therefore not available from any other source.

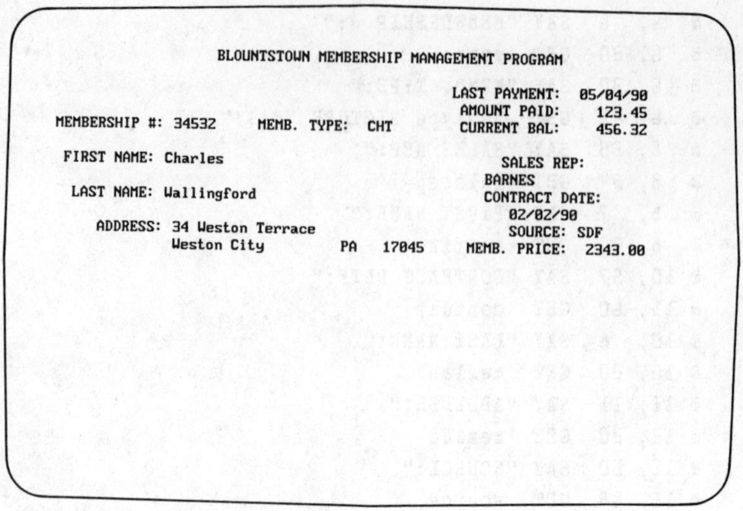

Fig. 10.4

*The customer file,
showing three
fields that
cannot be edited.*

```
            BLOUNTSTOWN MEMBERSHIP MANAGEMENT PROGRAM

                                           LAST PAYMENT:  05/04/90
                                           AMOUNT PAID:     123.45
        MEMBERSHIP #: 34532   MEMB. TYPE: CHT   CURRENT BAL:     456.32

         FIRST NAME: Charles                    SALES REP:
                                               BARNES
          LAST NAME: Wallingford             CONTRACT DATE:
                                                02/02/90
           ADDRESS: 34 Weston Terrace           SOURCE: SDF
                    Weston City      PA   17045  MEMB. PRICE:  2343.00
```

Accepting Data Entry in Memory Variables instead of Fields

One of the shortcomings of the invoice-creation module presented in figure 10.2 is that until the user makes entries for the individual items sold, the bottom half of the screen is left blank. Although this flaw is not fatal, a new user may wonder what is coming next. At the very least, the screen is a bit unsightly.

One solution is to create a set of memory variables of the same types and lengths as the memory variables in the entry screen. You can paint these variables on-screen and then issue a CLEAR GETS command to abort the entry process. The result will be an attractive screen that lets the user know what is coming next. This technique offers some interesting side benefits, including that of flexibility.

For years most experienced dBASE programmers have used memory variables to accept data entry from users (instead of accepting entry directly into fields). Several advantages are evident, besides the improved appearance of the screen. For example, when a user is APPENDing records to the data file, the APPENDed record will remain blank if a power loss occurs or if the computer is accidentally rebooted during the entry process. If, however, an accident happens when a user is making entries directly into the fields of a record, that record will be incomplete. Furthermore, the condition may go unnoticed for a while. Worse yet, the data written to the record could be so badly corrupted that the data file is unrecognizable to dBASE IV.

Another advantage to using memory variables for data entry becomes evident during the editing of records. The user is given the chance to abort the edit, even if changes have already been made. The method is simple. Before the edit begins, the variables are stuffed with the values from the fields in the record, and the GETs are issued. After the READ command is issued, a section of code placed before the REPLACE commands determines what key was used to terminate the READ.

Because any changes that the user has typed are stored in variables and not in the fields themselves, it is a simple matter to CLOSE the file and abort if the READ has been terminated by the trigger key, which is often the Esc key.

If the user terminates the READ with any other keystroke, the field values are then REPLACEd with the variable values, and the program moves to the next step.

The invoice-editing module presented in figure 10.5 is long, but don't let that discourage you. There is little in the program module ED_INV.PRG that you have not seen before, and most of the length is taken up with the handling of memory variables and the data-entry screen. The code also is heavily documented with comments to help you follow the process as it occurs.

```
*****  Program: ED_INV.PRG  *****
* A sample invoice-editing program that paints the screen before
* editing and lets the user abort any changes to data

* You can see by the beginning of this program that the sample
* program INV.PRG was used as the basis. In fact, much of that
* code remains in this module but with some alterations. Some of
* the code has been retained as comment material so that you can
* see the differences between APPENDing and EDITing.

SET TALK OFF
SET STATUS OFF
SET SCOREBOARD OFF
DEFINE WINDOW cover FROM 0,0 TO 23,79    && A window to hide menus
* Note that the window does not cover line 24, for if an entry
* error is triggered, the error message blasts the bottom line
* of the border, and it is not restored when the error message
* is cleared.

ACTIVATE WINDOW cover   && Takes over the screen
```

Fig. 10.5

The program module ED_INV.PRG.

Fig. continues

Fig. continued

```
* USE customer ORDER acct_no      && This file is not needed for
                                  && this module and is commented
                                  && out so that the command will
                                  && not execute.


USE invoice ORDER invoice_no
USE inv_item IN 2 ORDER inv_no

flag = ' '        && Sees whether lower-level module has problems

DO scr_set        && Paints the screen; this PROCEDURE will init
                  && variables and paint the screen with them.
                  && Look ahead in the printout for the code for
                  && this PROCEDURE to see what it does.


* DO cust_fnd     && This PROCEDURE is not needed in this module
                  && unless you want to print the information in
                  && the customer record. Since the shipping
                  && information is in the invoice record already,
                  && CUST_FND has been commented out for this
                  && module.


DO inv_fnd        && CUST_FND is replaced with a PROCEDURE to
                  && locate the driver record for the invoice.


IF flag = '*'
    CLOSE DATABASES           && If no invoice is found in the
    DEACTIVATE WINDOW cover   && subroutine, this section
    RELEASE WINDOW cover      && detects the flag and aborts.
    RELEASE ALL LIKE v_*      && Because the editing variables
                             && were declared PUBLIC, this
                             && RELEASEs them manually before
    RETURN                    && terminating.
ENDIF


v_acct       = acct_no       && Gives the variables the field
v_ship_name  = ship_name     && values so that they can be edited
v_ship_addr  = ship_addr
v_ship_city  = ship_city
v_ship_state = ship_state
```

Fig. continues

Fig. continued

```
    v_ship_zip   =   ship_zip
    v_pur_date   =   pur_date
    v_sal_per    =   sal_per

    * Now edits the variables
    @ 3,0 SAY PADC("Press ESCAPE to abort edit without changes being made.",77)
    @ 4, 5 SAY "Account: " + v_acct
    @ 5, 5 SAY "Company:" GET v_ship_name
    @ 7, 5 SAY "Ship to:" GET v_ship_addr
    @ 9,14 GET v_ship_city
    @ 9,32 GET v_ship_state
    @ 9,35 GET v_ship_zip
    @ 7,45 SAY "   Sale date:" GET  v_pur_date
    @ 9,45 SAY " Salesperson:" GET v_sal_per
    READ

    IF LASTKEY() = 27           && Tests to see whether the READ was
       CLOSE DATABASES          && terminated with the Esc key
       DEACTIVATE WINDOW cover  && If so, cleans up and aborts
       RELEASE WINDOW cover
       RELEASE ALL LIKE v_*
       RETURN
    ENDIF
    @3,0 CLEAR TO 3,77    && As Esc will no longer abort, this takes
                          && the advertisement off the screen

    REPLACE ship_name    WITH  v_ship_name    && Stuffs the fields
    REPLACE ship_addr    WITH  v_ship_addr     && with the new values
    REPLACE ship_city    WITH  v_ship_city
    REPLACE ship_state   WITH  v_ship_state
    REPLACE ship_zip     WITH  v_ship_zip
    REPLACE pur_date     WITH  v_pur_date
    REPLACE sal_per      WITH  v_sal_per

    DO ed_items    && Calls the PROCEDURE that edits the items

    IF flag = '*'
       CLOSE DATABASES           && If no item is found in the
       DEACTIVATE WINDOW cover   && subroutine, this section detects
       RELEASE WINDOW cover      && the flag and aborts.
       RELEASE ALL LIKE v_*
       RETURN
    ENDIF
```

Fig. continues

Fig. continued

```
* Here is where the duplicate-invoice printing routine will be
* added (refer to the next chapter).

CLOSE DATABASES
DEACTIVATE WINDOW cover
RELEASE WINDOWS cover
RELEASE ALL LIKE v_*
RETURN


PROCEDURE scr_set

* Because this is one level down from the module that does the
* work, the variables have to be made PUBLIC or else they will
* release just as soon as the PROCEDURE terminates.

PUBLIC v_ship_state, v_acct, v_ship_zip, v_inv, v_sal_per, v_item_no, ;
       v_ship_city, v_ship_name, v_ship_addr, v_pur_date, v_qty, ;
       v_price, v_b_ordered

STORE SPACE(2)  TO v_ship_state          && Gives them values of
STORE SPACE(5)  TO v_acct,v_ship_zip     && the same type and
                                         && length
STORE SPACE(7)  TO v_inv
STORE SPACE(10) TO v_sal_per, v_item_no
STORE SPACE(17) TO v_ship_city
STORE SPACE(30) TO v_ship_name, v_ship_addr
STORE CTOD(' / / ') TO v_pur_date
STORE 0 TO v_qty, v_price       && Controls the length of these two
                               && with PICTURE clauses in the GET
                               && statement
STORE .F. TO v_b_ordered

* Paints the screen, including the lines drawn and messages

@ 1,0 SAY PADC("Rock Bottom Discounters   Invoice Editing Module",77)
@ 2,0 TO  2,77
@11,0 TO 11,77 DOUBLE
@ 4, 5 SAY "Account: " + v_acct
@ 5, 5 SAY "Company:" GET v_ship_name
@ 7, 5 SAY "Ship to:" GET v_ship_addr  && Finalizes the contents
@ 9,14 GET v_ship_city                 && of the driver record
```

Fig. continues

Fig. continued

```
@ 9,32 GET v_ship_state
@ 9,35 GET v_ship_zip
@ 4,45 SAY "   Invoice #: " + v_inv
@ 7,45 SAY "   Sale date:" GET  v_pur_date
@ 9,45 SAY " Salesperson:" GET v_sal_per
@12, 0 SAY PADC("Edit items purchased. Press PgDn to see next item,",77)
@13, 0 SAY PADC("ESCAPE to abort current item without saving.",77)
@15, 5 SAY "Item number:" GET v_item_no
@15,29 SAY "Quantity:" GET v_qty PICTURE '999' RANGE 1,999
@15,45 SAY "Unit price:" GET v_price PICTURE '99999.99'
@17, 5 SAY "Is this item backordered? (Y/N)----->" GET v_b_ordered
CLEAR GETS
RETURN


* This function would normally be included in the highest-level
* module or a PROCEDURE file. The function is included here so
* that the code will work for this example.

FUNCTION PADC
PARAMETERS string, stlen        && Accepts the string to be padded
                                && and the width of the area where
                                && the string is to be painted
lpad = INT((stlen - LEN(TRIM(LTRIM(string))))/2)  && Leading pad
tpad = stlen - lpad - LEN(TRIM(LTRIM(string)))    && Trailing pad
* Assembles the return value
ret_val = SPACE(lpad) + TRIM(LTRIM(string)) + SPACE(tpad)
RETURN ret_val    && Sends the return value back to the calling
                  && module


PROCEDURE inv_fnd    && Finds the proper invoice driver record

@ 4,45 SAY "   Invoice #:" GET v_inv VALID SEEK(v_inv) ;
        MESSAGE "Enter the invoice number to edit." ;
        ERROR  "No such invoice number found on file."
READ
IF LASTKEY() = 27
   flag = '*'
   RETURN
ENDIF
RETURN
```

Fig. continues

Fig. continued

```
PROCEDURE ed_items        && This module takes user entry for the
                          && individual items in the invoice.
SELECT 2
SEEK v_inv
IF EOF()
   ? CHR(7)
   @20,0 SAY PADC("ERROR. No items are attached to this invoice",77)
   @21,0 SAY PADC("Press any key to return to menu.",77)
   null = INKEY(0)
   flag = '*'
ENDIF

DO WHILE .T.

   v_item_no = item_no
   v_qty = qty
   v_price = price
   v_b_ordered = b_ordered

   @15, 5 SAY "Item number:" GET v_item_no
   @15,29 SAY "Quantity:" GET v_qty PICTURE '999' RANGE 1,999
   @15,45 SAY "Unit price:" GET v_price PICTURE '99999.99'
   @17, 5 SAY "Is this item backordered? (Y/N)----->" GET v_b_ordered ;
               PICTURE 'Y'
   READ
   IF LASTKEY() = 27
      flag = '*'      && If the user wants to abort, you are one
      RETURN          && level too low. This sets the flag and
   ENDIF              && terminates.
   REPLACE item_no WITH v_item_no    && If the READ is terminated
   REPLACE qty WITH v_qty            && normally, this stuffs the
   REPLACE price WITH v_price        && fields with the edited
   REPLACE b_ordered WITH v_b_ordered  && values.
   SKIP
   IF EOF() .OR. inv_no <> v_inv    && Tests to make sure that
      RETURN                        && the next item is from the
   ENDIF                            && same invoice; if not, this
                                    && terminates.
ENDDO
*****  End of program  *****
```

The program module ED_INV.PRG is one step higher on the evolutionary scale than the invoice-creation module presented earlier in this chapter. Even though ED_INV.PRG performs a different task, the primary difference is noticeable in the user interfaces.

ED_INV starts out in almost the same way as the invoice-creation module (INV.PRG). The only difference in the first few lines of code in ED_INV is that the customer file is not opened. This invoice-editing module does not need the information in that file.

The user interfaces for these two modules are not alike. In the invoice-editing module, all the data-entry areas are painted on-screen before the user is asked to enter the first piece of information. As you can see in figure 10.6, the data-entry screen not only is more attractive but also enables the user to see what entries will be required before any entry is made. Compare this screen with the data-entry screen for the invoice-creation module, shown earlier in figure 10.3.

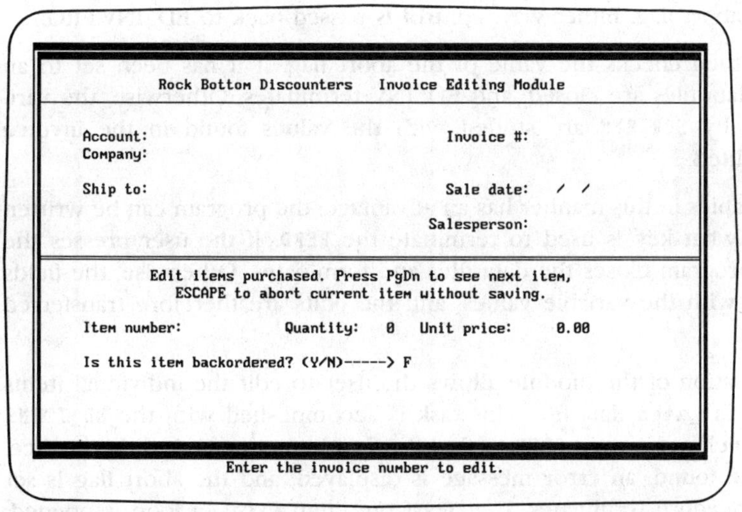

Fig. 10.6

The data-entry screen for the invoice-editing module.

```
          Rock Bottom Discounters    Invoice Editing Module

   Account:                              Invoice #:
   Company:

   Ship to:                              Sale date:    /  /

                                         Salesperson:

             Edit items purchased. Press PgDn to see next item,
             ESCAPE to abort current item without saving.

   Item number:          Quantity:  0  Unit price:    0.00

   Is this item backordered? (Y/N)-----> F


                 Enter the invoice number to edit.
```

Many times, the screen image will alert a user that the wrong choice was made at the menu, allowing the user to back out of the module before doing any damage. The invoice-editing module paints this screen image by creating a group of variables that are given values with the same type and length of the fields those variables represent. Character fields are replaced with character variables whose contents are spaces. If the character field is 10 characters in length, the variable is given the value SPACE(10). Date fields are replaced with date variables that are given the value CTOD(' / / ') or DATE(). Numeric variables are given the value 0, and the length of their display is controlled with PICTURE clauses.

The SCR_SET procedure is called by ED_INV.PRG to create these variables. Before the procedure terminates, @...SAY...GETs are issued, painting on-screen the image of the data-entry areas and their associated prompts. The SCR_SET procedure then issues a CLEAR GETS command, which has the effect of terminating the GETs. This way, the screen is painted without offering the user a chance to edit the variables. Because the variables are declared PUBLIC, they are not released when the procedure terminates. Thus, the variables remain active so that they can be used to take data entry later in the process.

Once the screen is set up for the user, the INV_FND procedure is called. This procedure prompts the user to enter an invoice number and then tries to find a corresponding record in the INVOICE.DBF file. The VALID clause of the @...SAY...GET verifies that the invoice number entered by the user actually exists. The VALID clause will require the user either to enter a valid invoice number or to terminate the search by pressing the Esc key. If the READ is terminated with the Esc key, the abort flag is set, and the procedure terminates. If the user enters a valid invoice number, the procedure terminates without changing the abort flag. Either way, control is passed back to ED_INV.PRG.

ED_INV.PRG then checks the value of the abort flag. If it has been set to an asterisk, the data files are closed, and ED_INV terminates. Otherwise, the variables created by SCR_SET are stuffed with the values found in the invoice record and edited.

Using the variables in this manner has an advantage: the program can be written to determine what key is used to terminate the READ. If the user presses the Esc key, the program closes the data files and terminates. Otherwise, the fields are REPLACEd with the variable values, and the edits are therefore transferred into the file.

The next operation of the module allows the user to edit the individual items stored in the inv_item data file. This task is accomplished with the ED_ITEMS procedure, which performs a SEEK to find the first item attached to the invoice. If no items are found, an error message is displayed, and the abort flag is set before the procedure terminates. If at least one item exists, a loop is opened, and the appropriate variables are given the field values of the record. The user can then edit the data.

As long as the READ is not terminated with the Esc key, the procedure will REPLACE the field values with the variable values and move to the next record in the data file. This new record is tested to make sure that it belongs to the current invoice. If the record belongs to the invoice, the editing portion of the procedure is repeated. Otherwise, the procedure terminates.

Once the ED_ITEMS procedure ends and control is returned to ED_INV, the data files are closed, the environment is restored, and the entire process is terminated.

In many ways the code for the invoice-editing module is quite similar to the code for the invoice-creation module. This similarity is not an accident. As you begin to create your own programs, you will find that a slight twist of logic can turn a record-creation module into a record-editing module. Another small step can turn a record-editing module into a record-deletion module. In most cases each of these three types of modules will share the same data-entry screens. The real differences in the modules are fairly slight. (For examples of these types of modules, refer to Chapter 13.)

Suppose that you must write three modules to add, edit, and delete customer records. The add module prompts the user to enter an account number into a variable. A SEEK is performed to test whether the account number previously exists. In this case the EOF() function is used right after the SEEK to make sure that the record pointer falls to the end of the file. If the end of the file is reached, the account number is not a duplicate, and the module can APPEND a new record and take data entry. If the record pointer does not fall to the end of the file, the account number is already in use.

The edit module uses almost the same code, but the record pointer should not fall to the end of the file when the SEEK is performed on the user's entry. If the pointer falls to the end of the file, the user has entered an account number that does not exist. Otherwise, the entry is valid, which means that the record pointer is on the proper record, and the edit can proceed.

To delete an account, you need to change the edit module only a little. The code is the same right up to the READ command. But instead of issuing a READ to let the user edit the information, you issue a CLEAR GETS to terminate the @...SAY...GETs after they have been displayed on-screen. Then you issue a prompt asking whether the user wants to delete the record. If the user responds with Yes, the DELETE command is issued; otherwise, the menu is returned to the screen.

Using Caution in Assigning Variable Names

A note of caution is necessary about the method used to name the variables in the ED_INV module (refer to fig. 10.5). The entry variables are the names of the fields with the addition of the prefix v_. In this case the letter *v* stands for virtual.

Because a variable name is limited to 10 characters, the addition of a prefix (such as v_ or mem_) may truncate the last few characters of the variable name. Figure 10.7 shows how the entry variable names used in ED_INV are actually stored in memory after the prefix v_ is added to each name. Notice that v_b_ordered and v_ship_state are truncated to just the first 10 characters. In figure 10.7 the variable names that get truncated are dissimilar. With variable names whose first eight characters are alike, however, the truncation can cause a problem.

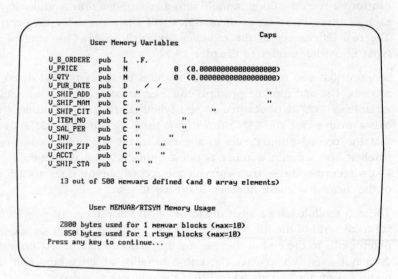

Fig. 10.7

Storing variable names in memory.

```
                                                      Caps
                 User Memory Variables

     V_B_ORDERE  pub  L   .F.
     V_PRICE     pub  N          0  (0.000000000000000000)
     V_QTY       pub  N          0  (0.000000000000000000)
     V_PUR_DATE  pub  D    /  /
     V_SHIP_ADD  pub  C   "                        "
     V_SHIP_NAM  pub  C   "                        "
     V_SHIP_CIT  pub  C   "                 "
     V_ITEM_NO   pub  C   "          "
     V_SAL_PER   pub  C   "          "
     V_INV       pub  C   "      "
     V_SHIP_ZIP  pub  C   "    "
     V_ACCT      pub  C   "    "
     V_SHIP_STA  pub  C   " "

         13 out of 500 memvars defined (and 0 array elements)


                 User MEMVAR/RTSYM Memory Usage

         2800 bytes used for 1 memvar blocks (max=10)
          850 bytes used for 1 rtsym blocks (max=10)
     Press any key to continue...
```

Assume, for example, that you have variables named v_payment_1 and v_payment_2. Both will be read as v_payment_. If two variable names are truncated so that they are indistinguishable, dBASE IV accepts data entries for payment_1 and payment_2 into the same variable, and the value of that variable will be written to both fields. No error message will be triggered if you use the names v_payment_1 and v_payment_2 in assigning variable names or in issuing the GETs.

Theoretically you can use more than 10 characters to name your variables, but only the first 10 characters are significant. The only way to avoid the problem of truncation is to be aware of the lengths of variables with similar names.

Remember, too, that because the entry variables are created by a subroutine, they must be declared PUBLIC. If they are not, they will be RELEASEd from memory when the SCR_SET procedure terminates. Because the entry variables are PUBLIC, you will have to issue the RELEASE ALL LIKE command to get rid of them before the program terminates and returns to the menu. Otherwise, these variables will still be taking up memory when the program terminates.

Handling the Record Pointer

A number of experienced programmers would argue that when the record pointer is positioned on the parent invoice record, the ED_INV.PRG module should test for the items that are attached to the invoice. The rationale is that the program should keep the user from editing base information when no items are attached to the invoice. An invoice may have no items attached if a power failure or an accidental reboot occurs, or if an index becomes corrupted. To prevent an invoice from having no items attached, the invoice-creation module creates the first item automatically. An interruption of the program's execution would have to be timed precisely for this record *not* to be created automatically.

There are two methods for handling an invoice with no items attached. The first method is to consider the condition to be an error and to disallow any editing of the invoice. In this case, the user must delete the invoice and re-create it from scratch. The second method is to allow the user to add items to the invoice during the editing process.

In either case, you must make a design decision. How do you handle situations in which items need to be added to the invoice? Again, two possible solutions are available. First, you can force the user to create a new invoice (which may not be practical if purchase orders are involved). Second, you can provide a way for the invoice-editing module to call the item-creation procedure (ITEMS) used in the invoice-creation module.

Remember that for the item-creation procedure to be available, it must either be in the same .PRG file as the calling module or be part of a PROCEDURE file that is open.

The code presented in figure 10.8 is a rewrite of the ED_ITEMS procedure from ED_INV.PRG, with the ITEMS procedure included. This modified ED_ITEMS procedure allows the user to add items to the invoice if no items are attached to it. The procedure also asks the user whether additional items are needed after all the existing items have been edited.

```
PROCEDURE ed_items      && This module takes user entry for the
                        && individual items on the invoice.
SELECT 2
SEEK v_inv
IF EOF()
   STORE " " TO conf     && Inits a confirmation variable
   @20,10 SAY "No items are attached to this invoice. Add them?" ;
          GET conf
```

Fig. 10.8

The modified ED_ITEMS procedure.

Fig. continues

Fig. continued

```
   READ
   IF UPPER(conf) = "Y"
      DO items     && This is the item-creation module from
                   && INV.PRG.
   ELSE
      flag = '*'  && Sets the abort flag
      RETURN       && and terminates
   ENDIF
ENDIF
RETURN


DO WHILE .T.

   v_item_no = item_no
   v_qty = qty
   v_price = price
   v_b_ordered = b_ordered

   @15, 5 SAY "Item number:" GET v_item_no
   @15,29 SAY "Quantity:" GET v_qty PICTURE '999' RANGE 1,999
   @15,45 SAY "Unit price:" GET v_price PICTURE '99999.99'
   @17, 5 SAY "Is this item backordered? (Y/N)----->" GET v_b_ordered ;
               PICTURE 'Y'
   READ
   IF LASTKEY() = 27
      flag = '*'      && If the user wants to abort, you are one
      RETURN          && level too low; sets the flag and
                      && terminates
   ENDIF
   REPLACE item_no WITH v_item_no   && If the READ is terminated
   REPLACE qty WITH v_qty           && normally, this stuffs the
   REPLACE price WITH v_price       && fields with the edited
   REPLACE b_ordered WITH v_b_ordered  && values.
   SKIP
   IF EOF() .OR. inv_no <> v_inv    && Tests to make sure that
                                    && the next item is from the
                                    && same invoice. If not, this
                                    && asks about adding more.
      STORE " " TO conf     && Inits a confirmation variable
      @20,10 SAY "Add additional items to the invoice?" GET conf
```

Fig. continues

Fig. continued

```
          READ
          IF UPPER(conf) = "Y"
             DO items     && This is the item-creation module from
                          && INV.PRG.
                EXIT
          ELSE
                EXIT
          ENDIF
       ENDIF
    ENDDO
 ENDDO
 RETURN
```

Summary

In this chapter, you saw how modular programming techniques can be applied to modules using more than one data file at a time. Whenever possible, you should use subroutines to deal with each file. If you need to take entry into two files simultaneously, be sure that the record pointers are properly positioned, and specify a field by its alias.

You also learned a method for storing sequential variable values to disk so that they can be used from one session to the next. And you saw the advantage of taking entry into memory variables instead of fields. Under certain conditions, these variables can be thrown away with much less difficulty than restoring a record to its former values.

The chapter advised caution when you create memory variables with names longer than 10 characters. Although dBASE IV will accept such variables, their names will be truncated. To avoid this problem, you must be sure that the first 10 characters are unique.

Finally, you saw that design decisions can have a great effect on the flexibility your application provides to the user. As programmer, you are the arbiter of what constitutes an error condition, as long as the basic dBASE IV rules are not broken.

In the next chapter, you will learn how to create and print reports.

11

Writing Programs
That Produce Reports

O f the three major functions of a database management system—inputting data, manipulating data, and outputting data—the last function generally receives the most attention. Many people who have no other contact with the database system often see its printed output. For this reason, you should pay as much attention to the look and accuracy of your reports as you do to the look and accuracy of the user interface.

Two methods are available for controlling output from your applications. The first method is to use streaming output. This type of output is produced through report and label form files, the LIST and DISPLAY commands, and the ?/?? commands. Using streaming output has two major advantages. First, you can direct such output to the screen, the printer, or a file. Second, you can use the system memory variables, introduced with the current release of dBASE IV, to format streaming output. These system memory variables enable you to take advantage of more features of the printer attached to your user's system.

The second method for controlling output is to use the @...SAY command to write programs. The advantage of using @...SAY is that compatibility with previous versions of dBASE is retained.

Streaming Output

All but a few dBASE IV commands produce streaming output. These commands include the LIST/DISPLAY, TEXT...ENDTEXT, REPORT FORM, REPORT LABEL, EJECT PAGE, and ?/?? commands. Reports and labels created with the CREATE REPORT and CREATE LABEL commands produce streaming output because the code gen-erated by these commands formats output with the ?/?? commands. Neither the @ command forms nor the EJECT command creates streaming output.

Streaming output is just what it sounds like—a stream of characters. Streaming output is also device-independent. In other words, such output will be sent to whatever output devices are active at the time the output occurs. For example, if you SET PRINTER ON, SET CONSOLE ON, and SET ALTERNATE ON, the output will be picked up by the printer and the screen, and also sent simultaneously to the ALTERNATE file.

Unlike streaming output, the output from the @...SAY command is device-dependent. The output device is determined by the SET DEVICE status at the time the @...SAY command is issued. Although you can SET DEVICE to the screen, the printer, or a file, you cannot direct the output from @...SAYs to more than one of these devices at a time.

As indicated earlier, both methods of controlling output have advantages. If you create streaming output by using the ?/?? commands and the system memory variables in your report programs, you can use many of the new features offered in dBASE IV. These include the automatic page break, automatic page numbering, word wrapping of text between margins, font changes, and special effects (such as bold, italic, and underlined printing). With @...SAYs, you can control the exact placement of output items.

On the whole, however, the introduction of the dBASE IV system memory vari-ables and the enhancements made to the ?/?? commands tip the balance in favor of writing programs that produce streaming output. Using streaming out-put is the only way to take full advantage of the new system memory variables.

The System Memory Variables

dBASE IV provides a number of system memory variables that enable you to control your printed output more easily. They are called *system memory variables* because dBASE IV automatically creates and maintains them. All these memory variables begin with the underscore character. This convention sets them apart from any other variables you might use in your programs. To avoid any possible confusion, you should never initialize variables that begin with the underscore character.

Twenty-five system memory variables are available. In the following sections, each variable is described, including its syntax, function, and one or more examples of the variable's use in program code.

_alignment

Syntax: _alignment = "LEFT"/"right"/"center"

The _alignment variable positions output from the ?/?? commands so that the output is centered, flush against the left margin, or flush against the right margin. To use the _alignment variable, you must be sure that the _wrap variable is set to .T. The _wrap variable determines how text will appear on a line produced by the ?/?? commands (see also _wrap).

```
_wrap = .T.
SET PRINTER ON
_alignment = "right"
? "Page # " + TRIM(STR(_pageno,3,0))
SET PRINTER OFF
_alignment = "left"
```

_box

Syntax: _box = ⟨condition⟩

The _box variable prints boxes that are specified with the DEFINE BOX command. When the condition in the _box statement evaluates to .T., the box specified with DEFINE BOX will print; otherwise, the box will not. Boxes specified with the @...TO command will print regardless of the setting of the _box variable.

```
CLEAR
_box  = .T.
?
?
?
?
DEFINE BOX FROM 5 TO 75 HEIGHT 10 DOUBLE
?
?
"This line will print inside the box." AT 10
?
?
? "So will this line." AT 10
```

Figure 11.1 shows the boxed output created by the preceding lines of code.

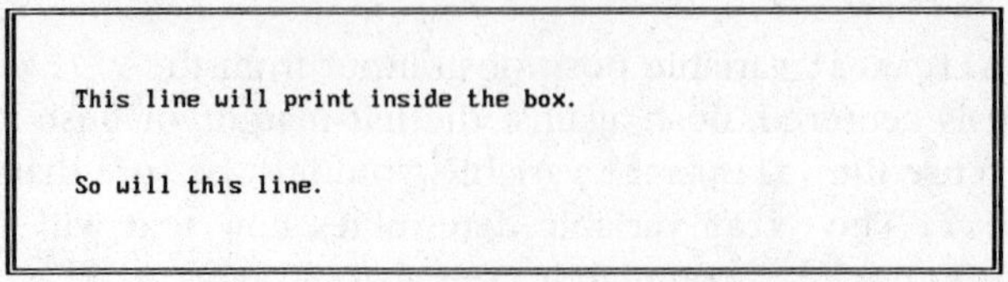

Fig. 11.1

*Output created
with the _ box
variable.*

```
This line will print inside the box.

So will this line.
```

_indent

Syntax: _indent = ‹*expN*›

This variable is effective only when _wrap is set to .T. The _indent variable
specifies the indentation of the first line of each new paragraph. For purposes of
a dBASE IV report, a new paragraph is begun whenever the single ? command is
issued. Values assigned to the _indent variable can be in the range

     - (_lmargin) to (_rmargin - _lmargin - 1)

In other words, if the value of the _lmargin variable is 5 and the _rmargin
variable is set to 75, the _indent variable can be as low as − 5 or as high as 74.

```
_indent = 2            && All new paragraphs will be
                       && indented 2 spaces to the right
                       && of the left margins.
```

_lmargin

Syntax: _lmargin = ‹*expN*›

This variable is active only when _wrap is set to .T. The _lmargin variable
determines the left margin of printed output produced by the ?/?? commands.

Actually two system variables, _lmargin and _ploffset, determine the amount
of space between the left edge of the paper and the beginning of the printed line. The _ploffset variable sets the absolute left edge allowed for any
printed matter on the page. The _lmargin variable determines how many
spaces from the _ploffset setting that printing may occur. If your report must
have at least a 1-inch left margin, you will want to set _ploffset to 10 (assuming that you are using 10 pitch). The _lmargin variable sets the left margin
relative to this page offset.

```
SET PRINTER ON
_lmargin = 0
? "This line will print at the left edge of the printing area."
_lmargin = 5
? "This will print 5 spaces to the right of the previous line."
? "So will this line."
SET PRINTER OFF
```

_padvance

Syntax: _padvance = "FORMFEED"/"linefeeds"

You use the _padvance variable to determine the method for advancing to the top of the next sheet of paper. If _padvance is set to "FORMFEED", the FORM-FEED character is sent to the printer, and the printer will then determine where the next page begins. When you are using short forms (such as checks, packing slips, or index cards), you can set _padvance to "LINEFEEDS". dBASE IV will then use the _plength variable to determine how many lines remain before the top of the next page. This technique is quite handy when you do not know the individual printer code needed to set the page length internally in the printer.

```
* This example prints address labels that are on a
* continuous roll, with 4 inches between the top of one
* label and the top of the next label. The standard setting
* for printers is to print b lines per inch.
_plength = 24
_padvance = "LINEFEEDS"
SET PRINTER ON
@13,10 SAY name
? Address
? TRIM (City)+", "+State+" "+ Zip
EJECT
```

_pageno

Syntax: _pageno = <expN>

You use this variable to determine what the current page number is or to set the page number if a new number is needed.

```
* To print the current page number
? STR(_pageno,3,0)

* To set the page number so that a report might be included
```

```
* in a document that is prepared with a word processor
_pageno = 52
* The first page will now bear the page number 52, which can
* then be inserted into a preprinted document.
```

_pbpage

Syntax: _pbpage = ‹*expN*›

The _pbpage variable prints only a portion of the report. For instance, if you printed a report 50 pages in length and the last three pages had coffee spilled on them, you can use _pbpage to print only the last three pages instead of having to print the entire report again.

The variables _pbpage, _pepage, and _pageno are interrelated. If, for example, you set _pbpage to 3 and then set _pageno to 15, no printing will occur because the beginning page specified by _pbpage is less than any of the page numbers being produced by the report.

```
_pbpage = 48
REPORT FORM coffee TO PRINT

_pbpage = 3
_pepage = 7
DO tax_rpt
* This configuration causes only pages 3, 4, 5, 6, and 7 of
* the report to be printed.
```

_pcolno

Syntax: _pcolno = ‹*expN*›

This variable determines the present value of the current column number of streaming output or gives a new value to that current column number. As mentioned previously, streaming output is the output produced by any dBASE IV commands except the @, @...SAY, @...TO, and EJECT commands. In practice, using the _pcolno variable is nearly the same as using the AT clause in the ?/?? commands.

The _pcolno variable and the PCOL() function, though similar, are distinguishable. If you SET PRINTER ON, _pcolno and PCOL() work in tandem. However, the PCOL() function determines the current position of the printer's printhead. If you SET PRINTER OFF, the PCOL() function will remain unaffected by the _pcolno setting.

In the example provided here, the printed output of the commands will be the digits 1 through 0, with the digits 3, 4, and 5 overprinted with a hyphen so that they are struck out.

```
SET PRINTER ON
? "1234567890"
_pcolno = 3
??"---"
SET PRINTER OFF
```

_pcopies

Syntax: _pcopies = <expN>

The _pcopies variable specifies the number of report copies to be printed by a
PRINTJOB...ENDPRINTJOB construct. The value of _pcopies can range from 1 to
32,767. The _pcopies setting is honored by only those reports that use the
PRINTJOB...ENDPRINTJOB construct. If you need multiple copies of a report,
use _pcopies to set the number. The lines in the example provided here cause
two copies of the report to be printed.

```
_pcopies = 2
PRINTJOB
... && Commands contained within the PRINTJOB construct
ENDPRINTJOB
```

_pdriver

Syntax: _pdriver = "<name of printer driver>"

The _pdriver variable returns the name of the current dBASE IV printer driver
or SETs a new printer driver as current. During the installation process of
dBASE IV, you can specify as many as four printer drivers to be used by a copy
of dBASE IV. You can include the _pdriver variable within your program to
switch from one driver to the other. This technique is handy with a system that
has one type of printer attached to the parallel port (LPT1) and a second
printer attached to either a COM port or another LPT port.

The printer driver determines which port is used for the output. For example, if
a computer system has a dot-matrix printer attached to LPT2 and a laser printer
attached to LPT1, you can use the _pdriver variable to switch back and forth,
sending reports that require high-quality presentation to the laser printer, and
reports that need a wide carriage to the dot-matrix printer.

```
* This example assumes that the installation routine of the
* DBSETUP utility has been used to install both an HP
* LaserJet and an Epson FX series dot-matrix printer.
_pdriver = "hplas2id.pr2"   && This command causes output to
                            && be sent to the HP.
```

```
_pdriver = "fx85_1.pr2"      && This command sends output to
                             && an Epson FX 85 dot-matrix
                             && printer.
```

_pecode

Syntax: _pecode = <*expC*>

You use the _pecode variable only with the PRINTJOB...ENDPRINTJOB construct. The variable is appropriate when the printer needs some sort of reset code at the end of a PRINTJOB. In the example provided here, the line sends a printer reset code to the HP LaserJet.

```
_pecode = "{27}{69}"       && This is equivalent to sending
                           && the code ESC E.
```

_peject

Syntax: _peject = "BEFORE"/"after"/"both"/"none"

The _peject variable determines whether (and when) a page eject is to be sent to the printer when printing is controlled with the PRINTJOB...ENDPRINTJOB construct. You must set this variable before the PRINTJOB command is issued.

Because of the setting in this example, no page eject occurs before the first line of the report is printed, but a page eject is issued after the printing is completed.

```
_peject = "after"
```

_pepage

Syntax: _pepage = <*expN*>

The _pepage variable, which is a complement to _pbpage, specifies the last page to be printed. If, for example, you have printed a 100-page report but pages 49, 50, and 51 are illegible because of a ribbon problem, you can specify that the _pbpage begin printing at page 49 and the _pepage variable end printing with page 51. In the example provided here, only pages 3, 4, and 5 of the report will be printed.

```
_pbpage = 3
_pepage = 5
DO tax_rpt
```

_pform

Syntax: _pform = "⟨*print form filename*⟩"

You use the _pform variable to identify or set the current print form file (.PRF). A print form file is one you can create as an option from the work surface of either the CREATE/MODIFY LABEL or CREATE/MODIFY REPORT commands. The file can contain settings for the system memory variables _padvance, _pageno, _pbpage, _pcopies, _pdriver, _pecode, _peject, _pepage, _plength, _ploffset, _ppitch, _pquality, _pscode, _pspacing, and _pwait, as well as a file name that is used to receive the report's output. Because .PRF files are interchangeable, you can have multiple versions that cause the report to act differently.

```
_pform = "set_b.prf"
SET CONSOLE OFF
REPORT FORM tax_rpt TO PRINT
SET CONSOLE ON
```

_plength

Syntax: _plength = ⟨*expN*⟩

The _plength variable sets the physical length of the page. The default setting, for example, is 66 lines at 6 lines per inch. Thus, the default is set to a sheet of paper 11 inches long. When you are printing forms, checks, or any other material shorter than 11 inches, you can use _plength with _padvance to control ejects from one page to the next.

If your printer prints 6 lines per inch and you are printing information onto continuous-form, perforated 3″ x 5″ index cards, use the command

```
_plength = 30
```

_plineno

Syntax: _plineno = ⟨*expN*⟩

The _plineno system variable determines or sets the line number for streaming output. This variable tracks the current line number of your output. As each new line is sent to the printer, the variable is incremented by 1. You can use _plineno to determine when page breaks will occur.

```
_plineno = _plineno +5   && Adds five to the value; skips
                         && five lines
```

_ploffset

Syntax: _ploffset = <expN>

The _ploffset variable establishes a page offset for the left margin that cannot be violated by the setting of the _lmargin variable. The _ploffset and _lmargin variables act independently. If you have a _ploffset of 10 and a _lmargin of 5, printing will begin at the 15th column. If you set the _lmargin to 0, printing will begin at column 10.

```
_ploffset = 10     && This command provides a 1-inch left
                   && margin that cannot be violated by any
                   && other margin-setting commands.
```

_ppitch

Syntax: _ppitch = "pica"/"elite"/"condensed"/"DEFAULT"

With the _ppitch variable, you can specify the pitch setting at which a report will be printed. The **"DEFAULT"** setting is equivalent to whatever pitch setting your printer is normally set to when turned on. Following are the values associated with the four possible arguments:

Pica	10 pitch
Elite	12 pitch
Condensed	17.16 pitch (approximate)
DEFAULT	The setting defined by your printer's dip switches or setup code

To print your report in 17.16 pitch, use the command

```
_ppitch = "condensed"
```

_pquality

Syntax: _pquality = <condition>

The _pquality variable determines whether the printer is to use draft mode or letter-quality mode. If the _pquality variable is set to .T., letter-quality or near-letter-quality mode (whichever is supported by your dot-matrix printer) is used. If the condition returns a value of .F., draft mode is used.

```
_pquality = .T.          && Selects letter-quality or
                         && near-letter-quality printing
```

_pscode

Syntax: _pscode = ‹*expC*›

You use the _pscode variable within a PRINTJOB...ENDPRINTJOB construct to send a start-up string to the printer before a PRINTJOB begins. To send a report in landscape mode to an HP LaserJet printer, issue the command

```
_pscode = "{27}{38}{108}{49}{79}"    && ESC &l00
```

_pspacing

Syntax: _pspacing = 1/2/3

The _pspacing variable presents printed output in single-, double-, or triple-spaced lines. To print a report that is double-spaced, use the command

```
_pspacing = 2
```

_pwait

Syntax: _pwait = ‹*condition*›

The _pwait variable determines whether the printer will pause between pages of output so that the user can manually insert paper into the printer. If _pwait is set to .F. (the default condition), dBASE IV assumes that the user has continuous-feed paper or a laser printer with automatic feed. If _pwait is set to .T., the printer pauses between each page of output so that the user can insert a new sheet of paper.

```
_pwait = .T.
```

_rmargin

Syntax: _rmargin = ‹*expN*›

The _rmargin variable determines the right margin for output from the ?/?? commands. This variable's setting is ignored unless _wrap is set to true (.T.). The setting of _rmargin must be at least one greater than _lmargin plus _indent. To create a right margin that is 75 spaces from the left margin, use the command

```
_rmargin = 75
```

_tabs

Syntax: _tabs = ‹*expC*›

The _tabs variable sets one or more tab stops for output printed with the ?/??
commands or through the word-wrap editor.

By default, the _tabs setting is a null string, but by default, the tabs are set
every 8 columns (8, 16, 24, 32, and so on). You can use the _tabs variable to
determine the tabs to be used inside the word-wrap editor or when output
is created by the ?/?? commands.

In the output processed by the ?/?? commands, whenever CHR(9) is encountered, it will be expanded to equal the number of spaces required to reach the
next tab stop.

```
_tabs = "5,10,15,20,25"   && Sets tab stops at column 5, 10,
                          && 15, and so on
```

_wrap

Syntax: _wrap = ‹*condition*›

When the _wrap variable is set to .T., output created by the ?/?? commands
will be word-wrapped between the left and right margins. If, for example, you
send output that is 70 characters long and the difference between the left and
right margins is 40, the output created by the ? command will be wrapped onto
two lines.

```
_lmargin = 40
_rmargin = 60
_wrap = .T.
SET PRINTER ON
? "This line, because of its length, will not fit between the "
?? "left and right margins. The _wrap variable will cause the "
?? "printed output to be broken onto multiple lines."
SET PRINTER OFF
```

The PRINTJOB...ENDPRINTJOB
Construct

To make full use of the system memory variables provided in dBASE IV, you
will need to use the PRINTJOB...ENDPRINTJOB construct to control the flow of
your output. This construct can be used only in programs; it is not available for

use from the dot prompt. PRINTJOBs cannot be nested, and only one PRINTJOB can be active at a time.

When issued, the PRINTJOB part of the construct sends any starting codes that have been assigned to the _pscode variable, sends a page eject if the _peject variable has been set to "before" or "both", and initializes the _plineno variable to zero.

ENDPRINTJOB, when issued, sends any end-of-job codes that are assigned to the _pecode variable, issues a page eject if the _peject variable has been set to "after" or "both", and loops back to the PRINTJOB statement as many times as necessary to satisfy the setting of _pcopies.

The ON PAGE Command

Another new dBASE IV command you can use for controlling streaming output is the ON PAGE command. As a cousin of the ON KEY and ON ERROR commands, ON PAGE determines what is to be done if a page break occurs in a report. As for other forms of the ON command, the routine called by the ON PAGE command is not allowed to use any of the commands that cannot be used in user-defined functions. The syntax of the ON PAGE command is

ON PAGE AT LINE <expN> <command>

The AT LINE clause determines the exact line where the page break will occur (taking into account headers, footers, and top and bottom margins). Generally you will want to use the formula

<expN> = _plength − # of lines in header − # of lines in footer

Any blank lines that provide the top and bottom margins should be included in the count of lines for the header and footer.

The command that is invoked when the ON PAGE is triggered is called the *page handler*. Usually, it is included in the program as a procedure or group of procedures. The page handler can invoke other procedures for handling headers and footers. Look at the example in figure 11.2.

As the contents of each record is printed, the _plineno variable is incremented by one. When the line number reaches 58, the page handler will trigger the footer and header procedures to print a page number at the bottom right of the page and to eject the page. A new header is then printed on the next page, and the page handler is terminated.

Fig. 11.2

Using the ON PAGE command to handle headers and footers.

```
_plength = 66
ON PAGE AT LINE 58 DO pager
SET PRINTER ON
?
? "     Name                              Title              Phone #" AT 0
? REPLICATE("-",70) AT 5
?
SCAN
    ? name AT 5
    ?? title AT 35
    ?? phone_no AT 55
ENDSCAN
DO foot
SET PRINTER OFF
ON PAGE            && Cancels previous setting


PROCEDURE pager

DO foot
DO head
RETURN


PROCEDURE head

?
? "     Name                              Title              Phone #" AT 0
? REPLICATE("-",70) AT 5
?
RETURN


PROCEDURE foot

?
? REPLICATE("-",60) AT 5, "Page: " + TRIM(STR(_pageno,3,0))
EJECT PAGE
RETURN
```

Using REPORT and LABEL Form Files

You can use the REPORT FORM and LABEL FORM commands to create output from report form files (.FRM and .FMO) and label form files (.LBL and .LBO), which have been created with the CREATE/MODIFY REPORT and CREATE/MODIFY LABEL commands. Using these form files is the easiest way to produce output contained in a single file or in a view created with a query file (.QBE).

Typically the commands to print a report will look like either of these two segments of code:

```
USE datafile ORDER index_tag
@10,10 SAY "Printing the report you wanted......"
SET CONSOLE OFF          && Keeps output off the screen
REPORT FORM frm_file NOEJECT FOR ship_st = "Ca" TO PRINT
SET CONSOLE ON           && Reactivates the screen
CLOSE DATABASES

USE datafile ORDER index_tag
@10,10 SAY "Printing the labels you wanted......"
SET CONSOLE OFF          && Keeps output off the screen
LABEL FORM lbl_file SAMPLE FOR ship_st = "Ca" TO PRINT
SET CONSOLE ON           && Reactivates the screen
CLOSE DATABASES
```

The only difference between these code segments occurs in the commands to initiate the output.

In addition to the .FRM or .LBL (uncompiled) files created with the CREATE/MODIFY REPORT and CREATE/MODIFY LABEL commands, a file with an .FRG or .LRG extension is written to disk. (The extension is determined by which CREATE/MODIFY command you use.) This file is a program written in the dBASE IV command language. The file cannot be executed directly, for dBASE IV does not recognize an .FRG or .LRG extension as a program. To run such a file, you will need to change its extension to the program extension of .PRG.

In Chapter 3 you were asked to create a report form file for the VENDOR application. The code listed in figure 11.3 is the .FRG file that was created when that report was saved to disk. Keep in mind that the code is generated by a template that has been written to be absolutely generic; the code therefore turns some flips that you may not feel are necessary in hand-coded reports. However, the code does show effectively how you can use the system memory variables to control streaming output.

Many comments have been added to guide you through this code. To distinguish these comments from those included in the output from the template, the added comments are marked with three asterisks or three ampersands, depending on the position of the comment.

Although this example deals with only one file, you can easily construct a program that uses the same techniques to create output from more than one database. You can apply the same basic techniques for positioning the record pointer used in the invoice-editing module presented in Chapter 10, or in the procedure that uses the @...SAY command to produce output (see the later section "Using the @...SAY Command To Produce Reports"). Using the PRINTJOB...ENDPRINTJOB construct does not prevent you from changing work areas and positioning the record pointer to find the records you need.

Fig. 11.3

VEN_LIST.FRG.

```
* Program............: VEN_LIST.FRG
* Date...............: 1-1-89
* Versions...........: dBASE IV, Report 1
*
* Notes:
* ------
* Prior to running this procedure with the DO command
* it is necessary to use LOCATE because the CONTINUE
* statement is in the main loop.
*** In other words, you will have to issue a LOCATE command before
*** this program is called (or add a LOCATE to this code) so that
*** the record pointer is properly positioned and the CONTINUE
*** does not trigger an error in the absence of a matching LOCATE.


*-- Parameters
PARAMETERS gl_noeject, gl_plain, gl_summary, gc_heading, gc_extra
** The first three parameters are of type Logical.
** The fourth parameter is a string.  The fifth is extra.
*** If you look at the syntax of the REPORT FORM command, these
*** first four parameters are among the authorized arguments to
*** the command. This selection of variables provides a small
*** insight into the dBASE IV internals.


PRIVATE _peject, _wrap    &&& You can declare system variables
                          &&& PRIVATE so that they remain
                          &&& unchanged at termination. The vars
```

Fig. continues

Fig. continued

```
                              &&& cited as PARAMETERS will
                              &&& automatically be PRIVATEd.


*-- Test for no records found
IF EOF() .OR. .NOT. FOUND()    &&& Did the LOCATE find a record
   RETURN                      &&& to match the condition?
ENDIF


*-- turn word wrap mode off
_wrap=.F.


IF _plength < 7    &&& Does the number of bands specified in the
                   &&& report exceed the page length?
   SET DEVICE TO SCREEN
   DEFINE WINDOW gw_report FROM 7,17 TO 11,62 DOUBLE
   ACTIVATE WINDOW gw_report
   @ 0,1 SAY "Increase the page length for this report."
   @ 2,1 SAY "Press any key ..."
   x=INKEY(0)
   DEACTIVATE WINDOW gw_report
   RELEASE WINDOW gw_report
   RETURN
ENDIF


_plineno=0         && Set lines to zero
*-- NOEJECT parameter
IF gl_noeject
   IF _peject="BEFORE"
      _peject="NONE"
   ENDIF
   IF _peject="BOTH"
      _peject="AFTER"
   ENDIF
ENDIF


*-- Set-up environment
ON ESCAPE DO prnabort    &&& If the user presses Esc, this does
                         &&& an abort routine. Therefore, you
                         &&& don't have to include a clause in the
```

Fig. continues

Fig. continued

```
                            &&& REPORT FORM command similar to
                            &&& WHILE INKEY() <> 27. This method is
                            &&& much more orderly.

   IF SET("TALK")="ON"    &&& This form is found in most of the code
      SET TALK OFF        &&& generated with Ashton-Tate templates.
      gc_talk="ON"        &&& It is a way of setting the environment
   ELSE                   &&& and leaving a record so that the
      gc_talk="OFF"       &&& environment can be restored before
                          &&& termination.

   ENDIF


   *** More environmental and memory-handling statements
   gc_space=SET("SPACE")
   SET SPACE OFF
   gc_time=TIME()         && system time for predefined field
   gd_date=DATE()         && system date  "    "    "      "
   gl_fandl=.F.           && first and last page flag
   gl_prntflg=.T.         && continue printing flag
   gl_widow=.T.           && flag for checking widow bands
   gn_length=LEN(gc_heading)  && store length of the HEADING
   gn_level=2             && current band being processed
   gn_page=_pageno        && grab current page number


   *-- Set up procedure for page break
   IF _pspacing > 1                        &&& This figures out
      gn_atline=_plength - (_pspacing + 1) &&& whether the report
   ELSE                                    &&& is double-spaced
      gn_atline=_plength - 1               &&& and sets the line #
                                           &&& page breaks.

   ENDIF
   ON PAGE AT LINE gn_atline EJECT PAGE    &&& This establishes a
                                           &&& page handler.


   *-- Print Report

   PRINTJOB       &&& Starts the engine
```

Fig. continues

Fig. continued

```
IF gl_plain     &&& Depending on the value of the variable, this
                &&& specifies a new page handler. Why the other
                &&& was established three lines ago must have
                &&& something to do with the vagaries of the
                &&& template used to produce this code.
   ON PAGE AT LINE gn_atline DO Pgplain
ELSE
   ON PAGE AT LINE gn_atline DO Pgfoot
ENDIF

DO Pghead       &&& Ink on paper at last

gl_fandl=.T.         && first physical page started

*-- File Loop
DO WHILE FOUND() .AND. .NOT. EOF() .AND. gl_prntflg
   DO Upd_Vars
   *-- Detail lines
   IF .NOT. gl_summary
      DO Detail          &&& Detail bands are put in a PROCEDURE.
   ENDIF
   CONTINUE     &&& If you do not issue a LOCATE, this command
                &&& will trigger an error.
ENDDO

IF gl_prntflg   &&& You do not have to include lines to execute if
                &&& the result is True. If the flag is True, this
                &&& does nothing!
ELSE
   DO Reset     &&& Otherwise, this resets the process.
   RETURN
ENDIF

ON PAGE         &&& This cancels the page handler.

ENDPRINTJOB

DO Reset
RETURN
* EOP: VEN_LIST.FRG  &&& From here on are procedures.
```

Fig. continues

Fig. continued

```
*-- Update summary fields and/or calculated fields in the detail band.
PROCEDURE Upd_Vars    &&& None were included in the report, so this
RETURN                &&& procedure does nothing.
* EOP: Upd_Vars


*-- Set flag to get out of DO WHILE loop when escape is pressed.
PROCEDURE prnabort
gl_prntflg=.F.
RETURN
* EOP: prnabort


PROCEDURE Pghead
?? "Treasure Trove Children's Gift Shop" AT 23
?
?? "Current Vendors List" AT 30
?
*-- Print HEADING parameter ie. REPORT FORM <name> HEADING <expC>
IF .NOT. gl_plain .AND. gn_length > 0
   ?? gc_heading FUNCTION "I;V"+LTRIM(STR(_rmargin - _lmargin))
   ?
ENDIF
?? "As of " AT 33,
?? IIF(gl_plain,'',gd_date)
?
?? "-----------------------------------------------------------------" AT 8
?
?
RETURN
* EOP: Pghead



PROCEDURE Detail
IF 8 < _plength      &&& This determines whether enough lines
                     &&& are left on the page for the detail
                     &&& lines. If not, this forces a page
                     &&& break.
   IF gl_widow .AND. _plineno+7 > gn_atline
      EJECT PAGE
```

Fig. continues

Fig. continued

```
    ENDIF
ENDIF
?? "Vendor ID: " AT 0,
?? ID FUNCTION "T"       &&& FUNCTION "T" causes a TRIM().
?
?
?? "Company Name: " AT 0,
?? COMPANY FUNCTION "T"
?
?? "Sales Rep:    " AT 0,
?? REP_NAME FUNCTION "T"
?
?? "Address:      " AT 0,
?? ADDRESS FUNCTION "T"
?
?? CITY FUNCTION "T" AT 14,
?? ", " ,
?? STATE FUNCTION "T" ,
?? " " ,
?? ZIP FUNCTION "T"
?
?? "Telephone #:  " AT 0,
?? PHONE FUNCTION "T"
?
?? ;
"===================================================";
+ "======================";
AT 0
?
RETURN
* EOP: Detail



PROCEDURE Pgfoot
PRIVATE _box

*** A widow is a typesetting/word processing term that means a
*** single word at the end of a paragraph which will not fit on
```

Fig. continues

Fig. continued

```
*** the page and thus will be printed on a line by itself at the
*** top of the next page.
gl_widow=.F.            && disable widow checking
EJECT PAGE
*-- is the page number greater than the ending page
IF _pageno > _pepage
   GOTO BOTTOM        &&& These two lines will force EOF() = .T.,
   SKIP               &&& thus ending the DO WHILE.
   gn_level=0
ENDIF
IF .NOT. gl_plain .AND. gl_fandl
   DO Pghead
ENDIF
gl_widow=.T.            && enable widow checking
RETURN
* EOP: Pgfoot

*-- Process page break when PLAIN option is used.
PROCEDURE Pgplain
PRIVATE _box
EJECT PAGE
RETURN
* EOP: Pgplain

*-- Reset dBASE environment prior to calling report
PROCEDURE Reset
SET SPACE &gc_space.
SET TALK &gc_talk.
ON ESCAPE
ON PAGE
RETURN
* EOP: Reset
```

Offering a Choice of Destinations

Even though the code shown in figure 11.3 is rather elaborate, it presents some interesting methods of outputting a report. Because the output is streamed, you can offer the user a POPUP menu for determining where the output will be sent. Look at the example shown in figure 11.4.

```
DEFINE POPUP choos_out FROM 5,5
DEFINE BAR 1 OF POPUP choos_out PROMPT "Select destination" SKIP
DEFINE BAR 2 OF POPUP choos_out PROMPT "Send to PRINTER"
DEFINE BAR 4 OF POPUP choos_out PROMPT "Send to SCREEN"
DEFINE BAR 5 OF POPUP choos_out PROMPT "Send to FILE"


ON SELECTION POPUP choos_it DO sub_1


PROCEDURE sub_1

DO CASE
   CASE BAR() = 2
      SET PRINTER ON
      SET CONSOLE OFF
      DO a_report
      SET PRINTER OFF
      SET CONSOLE ON
   CASE BAR() = 3
      _plength = 25
      _pwait = .T.
      DO a_report
      _plength = 66
      _pwait = .F.
   CASE BAR() = 4
      SET DEVICE TO FILE report.txt
      SET CONSOLE OFF
      DO a_report
      SET DEVICE TO SCREEN
      SET CONSOLE ON
ENDCASE
DEACTIVATE POPUP choos_it
```

Fig. 11.4

Using a POPUP menu to determine where output is sent.

Using the @...SAY Command To Produce Reports

If you want to maintain compatibility with earlier versions of dBASE (which do not have the system memory variables), or if you are more comfortable with the @...SAY command than you are with the ?/?? commands, you can use the

SET DEVICE command and the @...SAY command to write your reports. Be aware, however, that you forfeit the dBASE IV enhancements to the ?/?? commands, particularly the STYLE and AT clauses.

You still can access the printer directly with the ??? command and thus select font and style (such as bold, condensed, and underlined characters). The ??? statements need to be specific escape sequences in code that the individual printer "understands," rather than generic codes that are interpreted by the dBASE IV printer driver. For more details, see the section "Using dBASE IV Printer Drivers To Format Printed Output" later in the chapter.

Positioning Output

In dBASE IV, four functions are available that can help you position output from the @...SAY command:

ROW( )	Returns the line number where the cursor is currently positioned on-screen
COL( )	Returns the column number where the cursor is currently positioned on-screen
PROW( )	Returns the row where the printhead of the printer is currently positioned
PCOL( )	Returns the column number where the printhead is currently positioned

With these functions, you can establish the relative positions of the output produced with @...SAYs. Look at these two examples:

```
@PROW()+2,10 SAY l_nam
@PROW(),PCOL()+5 SAY "This will print five spaces to the right."

CLEAR          && Resets the ROW() and COL() functions to zero
@ROW()+5,0 SAY "This will print on line five."
@ROW(),COL()+3 SAY "This will go three spaces to the right."
```

In addition, you can create variables to be used as substitutes for the dBASE IV functions. Consider the following example:

```
line = 1
@line+1,10 SAY "This will go on line two of the screen or page."
line = line +1
```

Writing a Report Program Using @...SAYs

In the previous chapter, an invoice-creation program was presented without the routine necessary to print the invoice. If you like, you can include in that program the code presented here (see fig. 11.5) for printing the invoice.

In the invoice-creation module, the customer record pointer was positioned with a SEEK, and the invoice driver record was APPENDed, leaving the pointer positioned at the appended record. Repositioning those two record pointers is therefore not necessary. Only the items file record pointer needs to be repositioned, for that record pointer is positioned at the last of the items to be entered into the invoice. You could easily print the items in reverse order, but that might prove confusing to a user who expects the items to print in the same order in which they were entered.

If you prefer to use this code to begin the printing process from scratch (for example, to print a duplicate invoice), you need to include additional code to open the files, take user input to find out the invoice number, and then position the record pointer in all three files.

Because such code is usually included in a program like the invoice-creation module, the code presented in figure 11.5 is built as a procedure rather than a free-standing program.

As you can see by comparing streaming output with the output from hand-coded @...SAYs, you can use either method of generating output to get the information onto paper. Which method you choose will depend on your need to maintain compatibility with older versions of dBASE, and on the extent to which you want to use the system memory variables to format your output (for word wrapping, setting text margins, and so on).

```
PROCEDURE prin_in

line = 1    && Inits variables to hold the line and page numbers
page = 1


CLEAR    && Blanks the screen and tells the user what's happening
@10,10 SAY "Printing the invoice......."


SET DEVICE TO PRINTER    && Turns on the printer

@line,5 SAY PADC("Rock Bottom Discounters    INVOICE",75)
@line+1,5 SAY PADC("123 Ez St.  Walla Walla, WA 97663",75)
```

Fig. 11.5

A procedure for printing an invoice.

Fig. continues

Fig. continued

```
@line+2,5 SAY PADC("(800) 555-4324",75)
@line+3,5 SAY PADC("--------------------------------",75)
line = line +4     && Manually increments the line number


@line+1,5  SAY "Account #: " + v_acct
@line+1,45 SAY "Ship To:"
@line+2,5  SAY A->company
@line+2,45 SAY B->ship_name
@line+3,5  SAY A->address
@line+3,45 SAY B->ship_addr
@line+4,5  SAY TRIM(A->city) + ', ' + A->state + ' ' + A->zip
@line+4,45 SAY TRIM(B->ship_city) + ', ' + B->ship_state + ;
                 ' ' + B->ship_zip
@line+6,5  SAY "Invoice number: " + v_inv
@line+7,5  SAY "    Sale Date: " + DTOC(B->pur_date)
@LINE+8,5  SAY "   Salesperson: " + B->sal_per

@line+9,5 SAY REPLICATE("-",75)
line = line + 10
   .
@line+1,5 SAY "Item            Back       Item"
@line+2,5 SAY "Number    Qty.  Order      Price        Subtotal"
@line+3,5 SAY REPLICATE("-",75)
line = line + 4
   .
SELECT 3
SEEK v_inv     && Positions the record pointer at the first item
IF EOF()       && Tests for an error condition. Because the
               && invoice module appends a blank record before
               && taking the entry, this error message should
               && never happen unless the index tag is corrupted.

   @line+1,5 SAY "There is an error. No items are found for invoice."
   SET DEVICE TO SCREEN
   RETURN
ENDIF
v_total = 0    && Inits a variable to hold the final total
```

Fig. continues

Fig. continued

```
DO WHILE .T.   && Opens a loop to process all the items

    IF line > 57   && An old-style page handler
        EJECT        && Pushes the page out of the printer
        line = 0     && and resets the page and line numbers
        page = page + 1
        @line+1,5  SAY "Account #: " + v_acct  && Prints a header
        @line+2,5  SAY A->company              && for the next page
        @line+3,5  SAY "Invoice number: " + v_inv
        @line+4,5  SAY "    Sale Date: " + DTOC(B->pur_date)
        @line+6,5  SAY "Item              Back      Item"
        @line+7,5  SAY "Number    Qty.   Order      Price        Subtotal"
        @line+8,5  SAY REPLICATE("-",60) + "Page #: " + TRIM(STR(page,2,0))
        line = line + 9
    ENDIF
    @line+1,5  SAY item_no        && Prints the information for
    @line+1,16 SAY STR(qty,3,0)   && the item
    @line+1,24 SAY IIF(b_ordered,'YES','NO')
    @line+1,32 SAY STR(price,8,2)
    @line+1,45 SAY STR(price * qty,9,2)
    v_total = v_total + (price * qty)   && Makes the total current
    line = line + 2
    SKIP                        && Moves to the next record and
    IF EOF() .OR. v_inv <> inv_no && tests to make sure that it
                                && belongs to this invoice
* If not, this prints the total and terminates.
        @line+1,5 SAY REPLICATE("-",75)
        @line+2,35 SAY "  Total: " + STR(v_total,10,2)
        EJECT
        SET DEVICE TO SCREEN
        RETURN
    ENDIF
ENDDO          && If the record does belong, the loop will be
               && automatic.
```

Using dBASE IV Printer Drivers To Format Printed Output

When dBASE IV is installed, the user can select printer drivers from a menu offering most of the popular printers on the market today. These drivers contain the escape sequences used by the printers to perform formatting tasks that can improve the look of printed output. These formatting tasks include printing the output in bold, italic, or underlined characters (or a combination of these), as well as changing fonts and type styles.

Printer drivers are made available to dBASE IV in the CONFIG.DB file and can be used with the STYLE clause of the ?/?? commands. Look at the following sample code:

```
? "This will print normally", "This will be bold." STYLE "B"
```

The following formatting codes are recognized in the STYLE clause:

- B - Bold
- I - Italic
- U - Underline
- R - Raised (Superscript)
- L - Lowered (Subscript)

These codes can be used together to produce Italic Bold, Bold Italic Underlined, Underlined Italic, and so on. Consider the following example:

```
? "This will print in Bold Italic" STYLE "BI"
? "Underlined characters" STYLE "U", "Bold Underlined" STYLE "BU"
```

The setting does not remain in effect until canceled. Instead, each separate piece of information must be formatted individually.

Font changes are accomplished just as easily if the fonts available have been installed through the **Output** dialog box of the DBSETUP program. At the **PRINTER** prompt of that dialog box, you can tell dBASE IV how to access the fonts that your printer (or your user's printer) is capable of producing. Each of the installed fonts will have a number. To print in a certain font, use that font's number in the STYLE clause of the ?/?? commands. Here is an example:

```
? "Change Fonts " STYLE "2", "two times." STYLE "3"
```

With a little extra work, you can obtain the same effects with the @...SAY command. The ??? command sends escape sequences directly to the printer. If the code to change to bold printing is ESC Q, you can bold the output of an @...SAY in the following manner:

```
??? "{ESC}Q"
@1,10 SAY "This will print bold."
```

You also will have to issue the escape sequence to return the printer to normal print once all the lines you want in bold have been printed. Check your printer's manual for the proper escape sequences for that printer.

Summary

In this chapter, you learned how to format the output of your reports by using the system memory variables, the ?/?? commands, and the @...SAY command. You saw that using the PRINTJOB...ENDPRINTJOB construct enabled you to take advantage of the system memory variables.

In addition, you learned how to produce reports with either the ?/?? commands or the @...SAY command. And you saw how to direct output to the screen, the printer, or a file.

Finally, you learned how to change font and type styles in your reports with the STYLE clause of the ?/?? commands and with the ??? command.

In the next chapter, you will see how to provide maximum data integrity for your applications.

12

Ensuring Data Integrity

The ultimate purpose of a database management system is to answer questions. How much does a customer owe us? How many slingshots were sold in Detroit in December? How many cases of polio were reported in the U.S. during the first quarter of 1984? What percent of an organization's members are members of another fraternal organization also?

If the data collected by dBASE IV is erroneous, the answers to these and other queries will be erroneous as well. Your job as a programmer is to construct the database management system in such a way that errors are not introduced into the data and that data reported is processed correctly. The overall correctness of the information stored by the database management system is known as data integrity. Obviously the best way to ensure data integrity is to make certain that bad data does not get into the files in the first place.

Of course, some data-entry errors are simply beyond your control. For instance, you cannot possibly prevent a user from typing a wrong ZIP code in a field even though your GET area restricts the entry to five characters, all of which must be digits. You can, however, pass the ZIP code entry through a data-validation process that compares the entry with a list of valid ZIP codes for the city and state. This step will reduce the possibility of an error but will not completely prevent it.

Unfortunately you cannot provide this level of error checking for every entry your application accepts; the execution would be too slow. The solution is a compromise. You must choose in an application those spots where bad data can do the most harm, and then apply validation techniques judiciously.

This chapter covers a number of data-validation tools, most of which are used with the @...SAY...GET command. You will learn how to validate data, keep bad data out of the files, and find corrupt data once it gets into the files.

Validating Data with the @...SAY...GET Command

dBASE IV provides several data-validation tools you can use with the `@...SAY...GET` command. These include the `RANGE` clause, which lets you specify upper and lower limits for both numeric and character data; and the `VALID` clause, which lets you specify a condition or call a user-defined function.

In addition, you can use the `PICTURE` and `FUNCTION` clauses to generate edit masks. These enable you to control, character by character, the entry taken into variables and fields. For a discussion of edit masks, see the section "Using Edit Masks" later in the chapter.

You should make liberal use of the `RANGE`, `PICTURE`, and `FUNCTION` clauses in the `@...SAY...GET` command, for these clauses do 90 percent of the data validation needed with little, if any, performance degradation.

Other traditional methods of data validation are also available, including the retype and lookup verifications. With a little clever programming, you can ensure data integrity by incorporating the appropriate data-validation tools in all your applications.

Using the RANGE Clause

The `RANGE` clause, along with the `PICTURE` and `FUNCTION` clauses, provides most of the data-validation routines you will need for ensuring data integrity. Whenever your application requires that the user's entry must fall between two values, you can use the `RANGE` clause of the `@...SAY...GET` command to evaluate the entry and decide whether it is acceptable.

You should be aware of one quirk in the `RANGE` evaluation. If *no* entry is made (that is, if the user presses the Enter key without entering data), the `RANGE` check is not performed. You can use this quirk to your advantage, however, for dBASE IV lets you provide a default value outside the range. If the user presses Enter to accept this default value, it is accepted because the range check is not performed.

The syntax of the `RANGE` clause is

RANGE *lower,upper*

Both limits are inclusive. Thus, the clause

RANGE 1,5

limits the entry to a number greater than or equal to 1, and less than or equal to 5.

You can specify only an upper limit with the form

```
RANGE ,100
```

Here the entry is limited to a number less than or equal to 100.

If you do not specify an error message with the `ERROR` clause of the `@...SAY...GET` command, dBASE IV will present a default error message informing the user that the entry must fall within the range specified in the `RANGE` clause. Providing an `ERROR` clause will override the default message prepared by dBASE IV.

Numeric Ranges

The most common range-checking task is to ensure that a number is within a certain range. Look at the following example:

```
@10,10 SAY "Pick a number from 1 to 10: " GET num RANGE 1,10
```

In this case the entry is limited to a value from 1 through 10.

If the edit mask generated with the `PICTURE` clause of the `@...SAY...GET` command allows for decimal entry, the entry is not limited to integers. For more information about the `PICTURE` clause, see the later sections "Character Ranges" and "Using Edit Masks."

Date Ranges

If the variable is a date or if the field where the range to be evaluated is a date field, each argument of the `RANGE` clause must be a date expression also. The argument can be either a `CTOD()` conversion (date expressed as a character string) or a date variable. Consider the following example:

```
a_dat = CTOD("  /  /  ")  && A null date that will appear empty
@10,10 GET a_dat RANGE CTOD("12/25/67"),DATE()
```

Here the entry must be a date from Christmas Day of 1967 through the current date as set by the system clock.

Character Ranges

The most complex, and perhaps most interesting, range comparison involves character data. For a character `RANGE` clause, the test is whether the entry falls between the upper and lower limits (or is equal to either limit) in an ASCII sort. An index is an example of an ASCII sort. Look at the following sample code:

```
char = SPACE(1)
@10,10 SAY "Enter a letter:" GET char RANGE "A","F"
READ
```

Here the user is allowed to enter an uppercase letter from A through F. Remember that the ASCII values for upper- and lowercase letters are different. This command excludes lowercase letters entirely and is functionally equivalent to `VALID $ "ABCDEF"`.

The character `RANGE` clause becomes more interesting when you create a form that accepts multiple characters:

```
strg = SPACE(3)
@10,10 GET strg RANGE "bcc","gbz"
READ
```

In this example only those entries in the character progression bcc, bcd, bce...gbx, gby, gbz are acceptable.

When digits are a part of the character string, the comparison becomes more complex. Consider an example in which product codes or account numbers consist of a single alpha character followed by numbers:

```
strg = SPACE(3)
@10,10 GET strg RANGE "A11","B99"
READ
```

At first glance, you might think that this `RANGE` clause limits entries to the character progression A11, A12, A13...B98, B99. That's not the case, however. If you look at the ASCII table, you will see that the digits come before the capital letters. In fact the `RANGE` clause accepts the following characters:

```
; : < = > ? @
```

This range of acceptance is probably not what you want.

To rectify the problem, you need to include a `PICTURE` clause, which restricts the characters allowed in the GET:

```
@10,10 GET strg RANGE "A11","B99" PICTURE "!99"
READ
```

By adding the `PICTURE` clause, you can restrict any entry that does not have a letter in the first position, or a digit in the second and third positions. Such possibilities as A:@ or B:? are therefore unacceptable.

Using the VALID Clause

You can use the `VALID` clause of the `@...SAY...GET` command in two different ways: for making a direct comparison or for returning a logical value. The condition presented in the `VALID` clause can be explicit (for example, `VALID $ "ABCabc"`), or the condition can be either a native dBASE IV function or a user-defined function that returns a logical value. For the `@...SAY...GET` command to accept the entry, the condition stated in the `VALID` clause must return a True or False value. If the evaluation is True, the entry is accepted; otherwise, an error message is displayed. If you specify an `ERROR` clause, it will supersede the default error message displayed by dBASE IV.

Making Direct Comparisons

If you want to make a direct comparison, the argument of the `VALID` clause can be a direct logical expression, such as

```
VALID var > 100.43
```

If the expression is True, the entry is accepted; otherwise, the entry is refused. Note that you control whether this check is inclusive by your choice of comparison operators.

This method is appropriate for checking any data type. Here are some examples that use direct comparison:

```
@10,10 GET memvar VALID memvar > 10 .AND. memvar < 20

@10,10 GET memvar VALID memvar > CTOD("07/19/91")

@10,10 GET memvar VALID memvar <> "consolidated"
```

Using Functions To Return a Logical Value

You may want to include in the `VALID` clause a function (either a native dBASE IV function or a user-defined function) that returns a logical value. This technique offers some powerful opportunities. For example, you may want to check the entry of an account number so that a duplicate number will not be issued to two customers. In that case, you can use the `SEEK()` function to do the work (assuming that the master index has as its key the account number).

Using the `SEEK()` expression is equivalent in many ways to issuing a `SEEK` or `FIND` followed by the `EOF()` function to test for the end of the file. To reject duplicate account numbers, you can include a command similar to the following:

```
@10,10 SAY "Enter account number:" GET acct ;
   VALID .NOT. SEEK(acct) ;
   ERROR "Sorry that account number is already used."
READ
```

Because the SEEK() function returns a True value if a match is found, you can invert the value with the .NOT. operator. This check gives you a True value if the record pointer falls to the end of the file. If the SEEK() function returns a True value, a matching record has been found, in which case you want the entry to be refused. This simple technique keeps duplicate account numbers out of a data file.

You also can place in the VALID clause a user-defined function that returns a logical value. Look at the following example:

```
@10,10 SAY "Enter account number:" GET acct VALID ACCT_CHK()
READ

FUNCTION acct_chk

ret_val = SEEK(acct)
RETURN ret_val
```

This code does exactly what the preceding code does and nothing more. If you are just trying to deflect duplicate account numbers, the VALID SEEK(acct) form of the @...SAY...GET is a better choice for its brevity.

You can make the user-defined function do more, however. Despite the limited number of commands that can be included in a UDF, such a function can extend the power of associated commands—in this case, the VALID clause of the @...SAY...GET command.

For instance, you can take the code that validates account numbers one step further. If the entry is acceptable, the application must APPEND a blank record to the database and put the account number in the field. Both these tasks must be done before entry can be accepted in the other fields. You can include a user-defined function to do both operations. Consider the following sample code:

```
@10,10 SAY "Enter account number:" GET acct VALID ACCT_CHK()
READ

FUNCTION acct_chk

IF SEEK(acct)
   RETURN .F.
ELSE
```

```
      APPEND BLANK
      REPLACE acct_no WITH acct
      RETURN .T.
   ENDIF
```

This arrangement solves a problem of design philosophy as well. If the program APPENDs the new record before accepting data entry and the user cannot enter a valid account number, the user will be left with a blank record in the data file. (For this example, let's assume that only the accounting department can issue account numbers and that, in case of a problem, your user must send the paper-work back to that department.) At the very least, the newly appended record will need to be deleted.

By having the user-defined function append the new record only after the account number has been validated, you will never end up with a blank record in the file. As you will see in Chapter 15, sometimes a network application will refuse the APPEND BLANK command. If you accept all data entry and then find that the request to create a new record cannot be honored at the present time, you will have some upset users. After a user makes an entry, the new record will be refused, and the user will then have to retype the entire entry when the logjam is finally cleared.

Using Other Types of Verifications

You are, of course, free to program other types of validation techniques to pro-tect the integrity of the data collected by your application. Two of the most helpful routines are the retype verification and the lookup verification.

The retype verification requires a user to type the information twice. If the sec-ond entry differs from the first, the process is repeated until the user types the information the same way twice.

In a data lookup, the entry from your user is checked against either a set of variables or a data file. This technique is useful in bringing valid information into the module in which the user is working. A good example of a lookup verification is included in the invoice-creation module presented in Chapter 10. In that module the user was asked for an account number; only when the account number was verified as existing did the module continue.

Retype Verifications

One of the most common uses of the retype verification is in changing pass-words. Because no written record of a password is available, you must be sure that the user knows exactly what the new password will be. The best way to make certain that the user can repeat the entry is to require it twice. This ensures, as much as possible, that the user will not be locked out of the application for making a typing mistake while changing the password. The code shown in figure 12.1 is typical of this type of verification.

Fig. 12.1

Using a retype verification in changing a password.

```
* The variable old_pw contains the old password.
* For this code, the assumption is that the password is stored
* in a data file which is encrypted.

old_pw = "SECRET"
CLEAR
STORE SPACE(20) TO WORD
SET COLOR TO GR+/B,X
SET COLOR OF BOX TO W+/B
DEFINE WINDOW pw FROM 8,14 TO 12,65
ACTIVATE WINDOW pw
@ 1,2 SAY "Enter OLD password: "
SET CONFIRM ON
@ 1,22 GET word
READ
SET CONFIRM OFF
SET EXACT ON
IF old_pw <> word
   CLEAR
   @ 1,2 SAY "ACCESS DENIED.................."
   * Make some noise; someone is hacking!!
   ? CHR(7)+CHR(7)+CHR(7)+CHR(7)+CHR(7)+CHR(7)+CHR(7)+CHR(7)
   DEACTIVATE WINDOW pw
   RELEASE WINDOW pw
   CLOSE DATABASES
   RETURN
ENDIF
CLEAR

DO WHILE .T.
   STORE SPACE(20) TO WORD,WORD2
   CLEAR
   @ 1,2 SAY "Enter NEW password: "
   SET CONFIRM ON
   SET ESCAPE ON
   @ 1,22 GET word
```

Fig. continues

Fig. continued

```
      READ
      IF LASTKEY() = 27
         EXIT
      ENDIF
      SET ESCAPE OFF
      CLEAR
      @ 1,1 SAY "Type password again: "
      @ 1,22 GET word2
      READ
      IF WORD <> WORD2
         CLEAR
         @ 1,1 SAY "Password not changed. Press any key."
         null = INKEY(0)
         LOOP
      ENDIF
      EXIT
ENDDO
SET CONFIRM OFF
SET EXACT OFF
* REPLACE passw with word   && Writes the password to the file
CLOSE DATABASES
SET COLOR TO GR+/B,N/BG
SET COLOR OF BOX TO GR+/B
DEACTIVATE WINDOW pw
RELEASE WINDOW pw
RETURN
```

This code requires a certain amount of overhead in that the window is generated and released within the code segment. The result is a slight delay, which many users may find annoying. For this reason, you probably will want to use a retype verification for only the most sensitive data. For instance, you might use the technique in making adjustments to customer balances, so that you can override an amount being stored by the database.

You can make this overhead less noticeable in two ways. First, you can use the DEFINE command to define the window in the start-up code at the beginning of the application. Second, you can construct the retype verification so that it does not require a window.

Lookup Verifications

Occasionally you will want to restrict entry in a record so that a user can include only information contained in another data file. For an example of a lookup verification, refer to the customer lookup routine in the invoice-creation module in Chapter 10. The user was prompted to enter an account number, and the program performed a SEEK to make sure that the entered account number existed. If the account number did not exist, the program stopped.

You may want also to force a lookup verification for other types of information. Another good example of this technique is found in invoicing activities. A common practice is to prompt the user for a stock or part number and then have the program verify the existence of the item. If it exists, you will want the program to fill in the information to make sure that it is exactly correct. Acquiring the information this way requires less typing; the user can therefore complete the invoice in less time.

dBASE IV provides a LOOKUP() function for use in lookup verifications. You can use this function to locate a record in another file and position the file's record pointer on the located record so that information can be drawn from the record—all without having to change work areas. The syntax of the LOOKUP() function is

LOOKUP(<*return field*>,<*search expression*>,<*search field*>)

The *return field* provides the function with its return value, which will be the value stored in the *search field* of a found record. The *search expression* is a value being sought in the database. And the *search field* specifies the field to be matched in the database being searched. Usually this database will be in another work area, and you will have to specify the alias of that data file (for instance, stock->part_no) in order to keep the LOOKUP() from triggering an error message.

If the search field corresponds to the key expression of the current index, the LOOKUP() will work like a FIND or SEEK. If the database is not indexed or if the search field is not the object of the current index, the database will be processed sequentially, as with a LOCATE. Having a proper index will, in effect, enhance the performance of the LOOKUP() function.

You can use the LOOKUP() function to position the record pointer in response to a user's entry, thus enabling the program to stuff fields of the current record with information in the data file being searched.

This approach presents a problem for the programmer, however. Once a READ is issued, dBASE IV will not redisplay the contents of the GET area even if the value of the field or variable changes. Look at the sample code in figure 12.2.

```
PUBLIC var,var2,var3 && Makes them PUBLIC so that they won't
                      && be released when the routine
                      && terminates. This way, you can see them
                      && with the DISPLAY MEMORY command.
var = "    "
var2 = "BBB"
var3 = "CCC"

@10,10 SAY " Enter a value:" GET var VALID CHG_IT()
@11,10 SAY " Enter another:" GET var2
@12,10 SAY "Enter one more:" GET var3
READ

RETURN


FUNCTION chg_it

var2 = "DDD"
var3 = "EEE"
RETURN .T.
```

Fig. 12.2

Sample code containing the user-defined function CHG_IT.

Here the UDF called in the VALID clause of the first GET simply alters the contents of the next two variables to be processed. When the function terminates, those variables will still display the values they had, but in fact the values will be different from those displayed. To test this process, you can press the Esc key to terminate the READ from the second GET area, and then DISPLAY MEMORY. You will find that the values are different from the values displayed.

The lookup verification routine in figure 12.3 deals with this same quirk in an unusual way. When the values are changed, the color setting is changed so that a SAY will paint information in the same colors that would normally be used for the GET. The new information is then painted over the GET areas, and the colors are reset to their former status. When the cursor moves into the GET, the user will see the true contents of the variable or field.

In the routine shown in figure 12.3, the user is prompted to enter the part number. The description and cost fields are supplied automatically from the information in the INV_TORY database. Thus, you prevent the user from including an inaccurate description or, worse, an inaccurate or dishonest price.

If a user enters a valid part number but for an item other than the one intended, the user can make the change simply by pressing the up-arrow key. This action returns the user to the part_no field, where the entry can then be altered. The UDF in the VALID clause is reinvoked when the user presses Enter the second time. This way, a user can try until the entry is correct.

```
*****  Program: TRIAL.PRG  *****
* A test of a lookup verification
* ITEM.DBF has five fields with the following structure:
*
*  inv_no    character  5
*  part_no   character  5
*  dscr      character  30
*  unit_cst  numeric    7  2
*  qty       numeric    3  0
*
* INV_TORY.DBF is unchanged from previous use.
*


USE item ORDER inv_no
USE inv_tory in 2 ORDER part_no

v_part = SPACE(5)       && Inits variables to be used to paint
v_dscr = SPACE(30)      && fake GETs
v_unit_cst = "    .  "
v_qty =   SPACE(3)


@5,5    SAY "Part #   Description                       Cost    Qty."
@6,5    GET v_part
@6,15   GET v_dscr
@6,47   GET v_unit_cst PICTURE '9999.99'
@6,56   GET v_qty
CLEAR GETS            && Paints the fake GETs and then CLEARs them
                      && The screen will look right, because you
                      && are not actually going to let the user
                      && enter the description or cost information.


APPEND BLANK

@6,5    GET v_part VALID CHK_IT()    && Here are the "real" GETs.
@6,56   GET qty
READ
```

Fig. continues

Fig. continued

```
WAIT                && Pauses so that you can see the results
CLOSE DATABASES
RETURN


* The real work is done here.
FUNCTION chk_it

PRIVATE hold,ret_val

* You use hold to take the return value from the LOOKUP()
* function. If the search expression is not found in the file,
* the return value will be a null string.
hold = LOOKUP(inv_tory->part_no,v_part,inv_tory->part_no)

SET EXACT ON
IF hold = ""        && If hold is a null string (LEN() = 0),
   RETURN .F.       && the entry is refused.
ENDIF
SET EXACT OFF
SET COLOR TO N/BG   && This assumes that the color setting for
                    && this application is GR+/B, N/BG.
                    && Sets the color so that the SAY will look
                    && like a GET area
@6,15 SAY inv_tory->descript    && Paints the two pieces of
                                && information in the right
                                && place
@6,47 SAY inv_tory->cost PICTURE '9999.99'
SET COLOR TO GR+/B  && Resets the normal color

REPLACE part_no WITH v_part
REPLACE dscr WITH inv_tory->descript
REPLACE unit_cst WITH inv_tory->cost
RETURN .T.      && The work is done.
*****  End of program  *****
```

Keeping Bad Data Out of the Files

Once corrupt data gets into your application's data files, getting rid of it is not an easy task. The problem is that some time may pass before anyone notices the erroneous entry. During that time, the effects of the bad data may become compounded.

A bad part number, for example, can get into a catalog and be used in hundreds of invoices before the mistake is noticed. Even worse, an incorrect price may show up. If the price is too low, the company loses money on sales. If the price is too high, the company loses money in processing refunds. Either way, the mistake can be a public relations nightmare. Either way, you get part of the blame.

To some extent, you are fighting a losing battle. You cannot possibly provide data validations that will ensure 100-percent accuracy. Even if you could, performance would suffer. You can, however, follow several guidelines that will provide the maximum in data validation with a minimum loss in performance.

Using Edit Masks

As mentioned at the beginning of the chapter, you should make liberal use of the PICTURE and FUNCTION clauses of the ⓐ...SAY...GET command to create edit masks that restrict the user to certain forms of acceptable entries. A PICTURE clause allows you to write a mask that accepts or rejects individual keystrokes, but a FUNCTION clause applies a condition to the entire entry. Remember that a PICTURE clause can contain a combination of FUNCTION and PICTURE template characters; such a clause can act as both a PICTURE clause and a FUNCTION clause. The PICTURE and FUNCTION clauses cost almost nothing in performance, yet they help to ensure that the information entered at least fits the format.

Look at the following code containing a PICTURE clause:

```
@10,10 GET fone PICTURE '(999) 999-9999'
```

In this example, the user will have to type the numbers only. There is no need for the user to fumble with, say, the Shift key or even the space bar. Thus, the possibility that you will get a phone number entered as 5(55) 4443-333 is eliminated.

Avoiding Duplicate Index Keys

Whenever possible, you should require (as part of the program) that duplicate index keys be refused, especially for items like part numbers, account numbers, and employee numbers.

Often programmers will use telephone numbers as substitutes for membership or employee numbers, thinking that phone numbers are always unique. Consider, for example, an application for a neighborhood health spa or a video rental store. What do you use as an index key when two roommates or members of the same family want to open separate accounts?

Even when using a Social Security number as an index key, you should include a routine to check for duplicates, for the government has been known to issue duplicate numbers mistakenly.

By refusing duplicate index keys, you will catch many clerical errors that are accepted during data entry.

Designing for Error Reduction

Throughout the book, a number of recommendations have been made for designing data-entry screens efficiently. If you follow the suggestions, you will cut down automatically on the number of errors. Keep in mind that well-balanced, attractive screens with unabbreviated prompts will keep your users fresher longer. Tired users make more mistakes. It's just that simple.

In creating new records, hold off on the `APPEND BLANK` command until all the error checking is done. If you do, you will reduce the likelihood that blank records will be left in the data file should a problem cause the module to abort. You can weigh this approach against that of taking data entry before the record is created and then finding that the record cannot be created—which is a real possibility on a multiuser network. Let the `APPEND` be the last thing done before entry is taken.

Finally, make sure that all prompts, error messages, and message strings associated with `@...SAY...GET`s are unabbreviated and clearly stated. Users will make fewer mistakes if they know what is expected of them.

Including User-Defined Functions

In most cases, including user-defined functions in your `@...SAY...GET`s causes little degradation in performance. The extra second or two required for the UDFs is time well spent, especially if they help to ensure data integrity.

Don't get caught up in the race for speed at the expense of data integrity. If a piece of wrong information can do harm, you need to provide whatever means you can (such as including UDFs) to make sure that the information is correct. Everyone wants a speedy application, but managers want accuracy more.

Finding Bad Data in the Files

Once bad data gets into the files, the corrupted information is difficult to identify. Ordinarily a user will see an error and be able to correct it. For example, if a user creates an invoice and the system tries to charge the customer a hundred dollars for a box of paper clips, the user probably will spot the error easily and do something about it.

More likely, a file will contain misspellings, small discrepancies in price amounts, or blank fields. You can write a report for the data file that can help to point out some of the possible problem areas. The sample code in figure 12.4 examines a name and address file and applies some tests to the values in the fields.

Fig. 12.4

Reporting on blank fields in a data file.

```
USE LIST     && Does not include an order statement, so the file
             && will be in natural order (the order in which
             && records are added to the file)

SET DEVICE TO PRINT
line = 0
@line+1,0 SAY "VERIFICATION REPORT FOR THE LIST.DBF DATA FILE"

DO WHILE .NOT. EOF()

IF name = SPACE(30) .AND. company = SPACE(30)    && If both are
                                                 && blank
   @line+1,0 SAY "Name and company are blank in record: "+ RECNO()
   STORE line +1 TO line
ENDIF
IF address = SPACE(30)
   @line+1,0 SAY "The address field is blank in record: "+ RECNO()
   STORE line +1 TO line
ENDIF
```

Fig. continues

Fig. continued

```
IF city = SPACE(17)
   @line+1,0 SAY "The city field is blank in record: "+ RECNO()
   STORE line +1 TO line
ENDIF
IF state = SPACE(2)
   @line+1,0 SAY "The state field is blank in record: "+ RECNO()
   STORE line +1 TO line
ENDIF
IF ZIP = SPACE(5)
   @line+1,0 SAY "The ZIP field is blank in record: "+ RECNO()
   STORE line +1 TO line
ENDIF
SKIP
IF line > 60 .AND. .NOT. EOF()
   EJECT
   line = 0
   @line+1,0 SAY "VERIFICATION REPORT FOR THE LIST.DBF DATA FILE"
ENDDO

SET DEVICE TO SCREEN
CLOSE DATABASES
RETURN
```

This code simply checks the existence of blank fields in the data file. You can easily provide other comparisons that depend on the data structure. Following are some examples:

1. Is the markup of an item more than a certain percent?

2. Does the number of items on hand exceed the normal stocking levels by more than a certain percent?

3. Is the number of items on hand a negative number?

4. Are invoices that were entered more than *x* days ago contained in the file?

5. Are there transactions (invoices) pending for a nonexistent client?

The types of comparisons you will want to make depend greatly on the structure and purpose of the data.

In the report, each comparison should be placed inside a separate IF structure so that all the comparisons which fail are reported. Placing them inside a CASE structure will result in the report of only one true comparison.

Of course, this kind of report will not pinpoint misspellings or similar mistakes. The only way to deal with such errors is to print the data periodically and go over each record by hand. Although this method requires a great deal of time and work, it is the only way to correct certain types of bad data.

Handling Corrupted Index Files

The .MDX index file structure introduced with dBASE IV seems to be much more robust that the previous version's .NDX file. Even a power failure during a REINDEX does not seem to bother .MDX files.

The one condition almost guaranteed to create problems with an index, however, is a power failure or reboot *while* the key field is being REPLACEd. Several negative results are possible. For example, multiple records may end up with the same record number, or dBASE IV may fail to recognize that any records are even in the file.

You can use the REINDEX command to rebuild damaged indexes. It uses the current .NDX or .MDX file and rebuilds the indexes by writing the index keys into the existing nodes. Ordinarily the use of REINDEX is enough to restore the index to working order. At times, however, dead nodes may be left in the file.

An alternative is to use the INDEX ON command, which rebuilds indexes from scratch. With INDEX ON, any dead nodes are eliminated from the file because those nodes are not rebuilt when the index file is re-created. This command is preferred in providing file maintenance for your applications, if only for safety's sake. In most cases the REINDEX command will work nicely. But in those rare circumstances in which dead nodes will interfere with the index's operation, the INDEX ON command is the better choice. Look at the following examples of code:

```
USE stock
INDEX ON st_no TO TAG st OF stock
INDEX ON cost TO TAG stcost OF stock

USE stock
REINDEX
```

Here the first example is preferable to the second example.

If an .MDX file is erased or destroyed, you can use the INDEX ON command to create the new .MDX file. Another option is to use the MODIFY STRUCTURE command to gain access to the work surface. For this second method, you place a Y in the appropriate index columns. When you press Ctrl-End to save the structure, the new .MDX file is created automatically.

Summary

In this chapter, you learned how to validate user entry in the `@...SAY...GET` command with the `RANGE` and `VALID` clauses, as well as with the `PICTURE` and `FUNCTION` clauses.

You learned also how to keep bad data out of the files by testing for duplicate index keys and by including user-defined functions to test data validity. A small program was presented that tests existing data and checks for conditions indicating incorrect data. Some suggestions also were included for dealing with corrupted index files.

The next chapter presents a full application you can use as a model in designing your own dBASE IV programs.

13

Using Sample Programs as Models

This chapter presents a short application for Belinda's Bike Boutique. Included in the application are the main module, the inventory module, the sales module, the reports module, and two sections of code for generating reports. The model illustrates how an application is put together from its individual pieces of program code. Studying the program modules as well as the full application will help you design and write programs of your own. If you like, you can use the sample programs as models for your program code, applying many of the techniques presented here and in other chapters.

The application's user interface and error-trapping routines offer techniques you can adapt and combine to fit your own application needs. Many of the techniques have appeared in previous chapters but are refined in this application. In addition, the sales module includes two techniques for using the `@...SAY` command to control printing. The reports module focuses on getting the most from report form files created with the `CREATE REPORT` command.

Each program module is accompanied by a brief description of the module's operation. Comments are sprinkled liberally throughout the code as well, focusing on the details of each module.

Each of the modules that has a menu presents a slightly different twist to the user interface. The combination of menu placement and the painting of blank data forms on-screen gives a different look to each of the menu screens without changing the underlying fundamentals of error trapping.

Throughout these programs, locations in which the wrong user keystroke can cause harm or trigger a dBASE IV error message are guarded by an error-trapping routine.

In some of the sample code, error conditions cannot be detected except by a lower-level module. The practice of setting a flag variable that can be modified by a lower-level module when an error is discovered is used extensively. Because a lower-level module cannot by itself cause the calling module to terminate execution (except in the case of the RETURN TO MASTER command), using the value of a variable to determine whether the program should continue after a subroutine terminates is a way to avoid the problem.

The Main Module

The main module of this application DEFINEs the menu structure, which is based on POPUPs. This approach is different from that used in previous examples in which the main menu was a horizontal bar with pop-up menus attached. In two of the modules in this application, the main POPUP menu calls BARs for submenus.

All the menus are DEFINEd in the beginning of the application. The reason is that the programs will execute faster this way. If you put the menu definitions for the submodules in the lower-level program files, the menus must be defined each time the submodules are called. Because of the delay in execution while a menu is being created and stored in memory, the menu does not appear as quickly when it is created on-the-fly. As a result, the application is slowed down considerably. If, however, you place all the menu definitions up front, they can be made ready and called as needed, with an apparent boost in speed. The same amount of time is required to produce the menus, but each menu needs to be created only once. The resulting delay at load time is less annoying to users than a similar delay between menu screens.

Figure 13.1 shows the application's main menu, which is a POPUP. The program code for the main module appears in figure 13.2.

The Inventory Module

The inventory module appears second on the menu, after the sales module. Here the inventory module is presented first, however, because the sales module uses the information entered into the system with the inventory module. This arrangement also represents a new twist to menu making.

As indicated previously, other sample applications have used the BAR menu to open POPUPs. In this application the main menu is a POPUP that will call another POPUP or BAR menu as a subroutine.

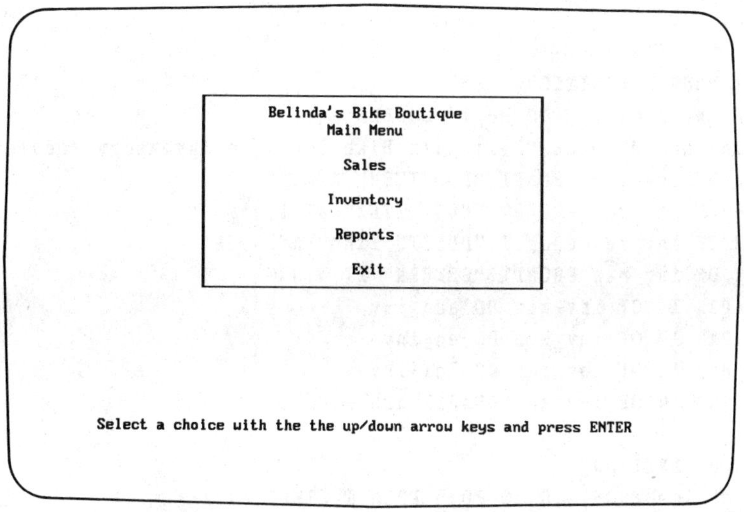

Fig. 13.1

*The main menu
for the application.*

```
***** Program: MAIN.PRG  *****
* Main module for Belinda's Bike Boutique
SET TALK OFF             && Takes control of the environment
SET STATUS OFF
SET SCOREBOARD OFF
SET BELL OFF
SET COLOR TO 'W+/B,N/BG,B,B'


* SYSTEM-WIDE MENU DEFINITIONS

*** MAIN MENU DEFINITION
DEFINE POPUP main FROM 5,20 TO 16,60 ;
   MESSAGE "Select a choice with the up/down arrow keys and press Enter"
DEFINE BAR  1 OF main PROMPT PADC("Belinda's Bike Boutique",38) SKIP
DEFINE BAR  2 OF main PROMPT PADC("Main Menu",38) SKIP
DEFINE BAR  4 OF main PROMPT PADC("Sales",38)
DEFINE BAR  6 OF main PROMPT PADC("Inventory",38)
DEFINE BAR  8 OF main PROMPT PADC("Reports",38)
DEFINE BAR 10 OF main PROMPT PADC("Exit",38)
ON SELECTION POPUP main DO branch

*** WORK SURFACE WINDOW DEFINITION
DEFINE WINDOW work FROM 1,0 TO 23,79 DOUBLE
```

Fig. 13.2

*The program
module MAIN.PRG.*

Fig. continues

Fig. continued

```
*** INVENTORY MENU DEFINITION
DEFINE WINDOW inv FROM 3,0 TO 22,79 DOUBLE
DEFINE MENU inv_men MESSAGE "Belinda's Bike Boutique Inventory Module"
DEFINE PAD I1 OF inv_men PROMPT "ADD ITEM" AT 1,5
DEFINE PAD I2 OF inv_men PROMPT "EDIT ITEM" AT 1,15
DEFINE PAD I3 OF inv_men PROMPT "DELETE ITEM" AT 1,26
DEFINE PAD I4 OF inv_men PROMPT "RETURN" AT 1,39
ON SELECTION PAD I1 OF inv_men DO add_inv
ON SELECTION PAD I2 OF inv_men DO ed_inv
ON SELECTION PAD I3 OF inv_men DO del_inv
ON SELECTION PAD I4 OF inv_men DEACTIVATE MENU

*** SELL MENU DEFINITION
DEFINE POPUP choice FROM 1,0 TO 20,9 PROMPT FIELD part ;
    MESSAGE "Choose a part number and press ENTER"
ON SELECTION POPUP choice DO register
DEFINE MENU regis MESSAGE ' '
DEFINE PAD r1 OF regis PROMPT "Make Sale" AT 1,15
DEFINE PAD r2 OF regis PROMPT "Take Return" AT 1,26
DEFINE PAD r3 OF regis PROMPT "Main Menu" AT 1,39
ON SELECTION PAD r1 OF regis DO ring
ON SELECTION PAD r2 OF regis DO mer_ret
ON SELECTION PAD r3 OF regis DEACTIVATE MENU

*** REPORT POPUP MENU DEFINITION
DEFINE POPUP rep FROM 7,42 TO 14,68
DEFINE BAR 2 OF rep PROMPT PADC("Inventory Status",24)
DEFINE BAR 4 OF rep PROMPT PADC("Sales Report",24)
DEFINE BAR 6 OF rep PROMPT PADC("Return to Main",24)
ON SELECTION POPUP rep DO repo

ACTIVATE POPUP main  && This command is for all practical
                     && purposes the entire main module,
                     && providing the "loop" that keeps the
                     && application running.

SET TALK ON          && Once the main menu is deactivated,
SET STATUS ON        && this cleans up and terminates.
SET SCOREBOARD ON
SET BELL ON
RELEASE ALL
```

Fig. continues

Fig. continued

```
CLEAR ALL
RETURN      && If you want the application to terminate to DOS,
            && put a QUIT here instead of a RETURN.


PROCEDURE branch      && This PROCEDURE provides the directions
                      && for branching out from the main menu.

DO CASE
   CASE BAR() = 4
      DO sell        && A pseudo-cash-register routine
   CASE BAR() = 6
      DO inven       && A typical add, edit, and delete module
   CASE BAR() = 8
      ACTIVATE POPUP rep   && Calls another POPUP to layer over
                           && the main menu for reports
   CASE BAR() = 10
      DEACTIVATE POPUP   && This choice terminates the application
                         && by DEACTIVATEing the main menu.
ENDCASE
RETURN


* Placing the UDF in the main module makes it available to
* all the lower-level modules.
* This is the same function seen in earlier applications.


FUNCTION padc
PARAMETERS string, stlen   && Accepts the string to be padded
                           && and the width of the area where
                           && the string is to be painted
lpad = INT((stlen - LEN(TRIM(LTRIM(string))))/2)   && Leading pad
tpad = stlen - lpad - LEN(TRIM(LTRIM(string)))      && Trailing pad
* Assembles the return value
ret_val = SPACE(lpad) + TRIM(LTRIM(string)) + SPACE(tpad)
RETURN ret_val    && Sends it back to the calling module
*****  End of program  *****
```

In the inventory module, a horizontal BAR menu is placed inside the box (see fig. 13.3) used to hold data entry. In some ways this placement of the menu and its box resembles a printed form that must be filled in.

Fig. 13.3

The BAR menu for the inventory module.

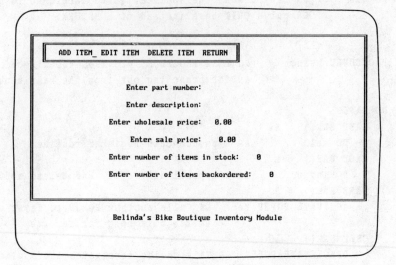

```
      ADD ITEM_ EDIT ITEM  DELETE ITEM  RETURN

                Enter part number:

                Enter description:

          Enter wholesale price:    0.00

             Enter sale price:      0.00

      Enter number of items in stock:       0

      Enter number of items backordered:       0



         Belinda's Bike Boutique Inventory Module
```

An image of the information that will be needed is painted inside the "body of the form." In this way, the user can see what information is needed for the task before choosing a menu item. Informal tests suggest that users like this type of interface better than a blind menu showing only the blanks to be filled in after the choice is made.

All the operations of the inventory module (represented by the menu options) take place within the screen as it appears when the menu becomes active. Because none of the operations performed will cover or obliterate that part of the screen where the menu is painted, the user always can determine the currently executing operation by looking to see which menu item is highlighted. The image of the information is placed on the screen through a group of variables that are created to have the same type and length as those of the fields in the data file. These variables are declared PUBLIC by the IN_SCR procedure; otherwise, the variables would no longer exist when IN_SCR terminated. Because these variables are of no use to a higher-level module, they have a common pattern in their names: each begins with the characters v_. When it is time for the inventory module to terminate, all these variables can be cleared from memory with the command

```
RELEASE ALL LIKE v_*
```

As you build and test this code, you will find that most of the programming work is done by the time the screen-painting and add-inventory modules are completed. To create the edit and delete modules, you will mostly just copy the add code, making changes in logic to suit the situation. Each of the modules builds on the one written before it.

For the inventory module, the inventory data file is simple and straightforward. The structure of this file is shown in figure 13.4. The program code for the inventory module appears in figure 13.5.

Layout Organize Append Go To Exit 4:41:57 pm

Bytes remaining: 3957

Num	Field Name	Field Type	Width	Dec	Index
1	PART	Character	7		Y
2	DESC	Character	15		N
3	COST	Numeric	6	2	N
4	SALE_PR	Numeric	7	2	N
5	IN_STOCK	Numeric	4	0	N
6	B_ORDER	Numeric	4	0	N

Database D:\pdb\bui\INVENT Field 1/6
Enter the field name. Insert/Delete field:Ctrl-N/Ctrl-U
Field names begin with a letter and may contain letters, digits and underscores

Fig. 13.4
The structure of the inventory file INVENT.DBF.

```
*****  Program: INVEN.PRG  *****
ACTIVATE WINDOW inv  && Puts the inventory window on-screen
@0,2 TO 2,48 DOUBLE  && Adds a box for the menu to the box around
DO in_scr            && the window and paints a picture of the
ACTIVATE MENU inv_men   && data on-screen; then turns on the menu
DEACTIVATE WINDOW inv
RELEASE ALL LIKE v_*    && Terminates the screen and entry
                        && variables
RETURN


PROCEDURE in_scr  && Here is the procedure to paint the data
                  && picture on-screen. Remember that unless the
                  && variables are PUBLIC, they will be RELEASEd
```

Fig. 13.5
The program module INVEN.PRG.

Fig. continues

Fig. continued

```
                          && when the procedure terminates. This would
                          && make them unavailable for use as
                          && data-entry variables in other modules.

PUBLIC v_part, v_desc, v_cost, v_sale_pr, v_in_stock, v_b_order

* Gives to the variables values that will make them paint
* on-screen just as the values would appear in a GET. Numeric
* GETs will need a PICTURE clause to format them.

STORE 0 TO v_cost, v_sale_pr, v_in_stock, v_b_order
STORE SPACE(7) TO v_part
STORE SPACE(15) TO v_desc

@ 5, 18 SAY "    Enter part number:" GET v_part
@ 7, 18 SAY "    Enter description:" GET v_desc
@ 9, 18 SAY "Enter wholesale price:" GET v_cost PICTURE '999.99'
@11, 18 SAY "     Enter sale price:" GET v_sale_pr PICTURE '9999.99'
@13, 18 SAY "Enter number of items in stock:" GET v_in_stock ;
                                            PICTURE '9999'
2@15, 18 SAY "Enter number of items backordered:" GET v_b_order ;
                                            PICTURE '9999'
CLEAR GETS  && CLEARs the GETS to disallow a read and terminates
RETURN


PROCEDURE add_inv    && The code to add inventory items

USE invent ORDER part   && Opens the data file

DO WHILE .T.   && Puts program control into a loop so that the
               && user can enter more than one inventory item
               && without having to go back to the menu

* The NO_DUP() function is a UDF that eliminates duplicate
* part numbers. When an unused number is entered, the UDF
* APPENDs a blank record.
   @ 5, 18 SAY "    Enter part number:" GET v_part VALID NO_DUP() ;
             ERROR "Sorry that part number is already on file."
   @ 7, 18 SAY "    Enter description:" GET v_desc
   @ 9, 18 SAY "Enter wholesale price:" GET v_cost PICTURE '999.99'
```

Fig. continues

Fig. continued

```
    @11, 18 SAY "    Enter sale price:" GET v_sale_pr PICTURE '9999.99'
    @13, 18 SAY "Enter number of items in stock:" GET v_in_stock ;
                                        PICTURE '9999'
    @15, 18 SAY "Enter number of items backordered:" GET v_b_order ;
                                        PICTURE '9999'
    READ
    IF LASTKEY() = 27    && If the READ is terminated with an
                         && ESCAPE, the UDF isn't called. This
                         && construct aborts back to the menu.
        EXIT
    ENDIF
    REPLACE PART WITH v_part, ;    && A way of doing REPLACEs you
            DESC WITH v_desc, ;    && may not have seen before
            COST WITH v_cost, ;
            SALE_PR WITH v_sale_pr, ;
            IN_STOCK WITH v_in_stock, ;
            B_ORDER WITH v_b_order

* Sees whether the user wants to add another item to the database
    STORE ' ' TO conf
    @17,14 SAY "Do you want to add another item?  (Y/N)-->" GET conf
    READ
    IF UPPER(conf) = 'Y' && If so, this clears the messages,
        @16,0 CLEAR      && repaints the blank screen, and rolls
                         && it over.
        DO in_scr
        LOOP
    ELSE
        @16,0 CLEAR      && Otherwise, program control drops out
        EXIT             && of the loop.
    ENDIF
ENDDO
CLOSE DATABASES    && Closes the database and paints the screen
DO in_scr
RETURN



FUNCTION no_dup   && This is a simple UDF to check the file for
                  && duplicate part numbers.
```

Fig. continues

Fig. continued

```
    SEEK v_part        && Seeks the variable just entered
    IF EOF()           && If not found, this creates a new record and
       APPEND BLANK    && accepts the entry.
       RETURN .T.
    ELSE
       RETURN .F.      && Refuses the entry if the part number exists
    ENDIF


    PROCEDURE ed_inv      && A procedure to edit invoices. This
                          && code is based on the add module. Look
                          && to see how similar the code is. This
                          && is true of almost all add, edit, and
                          && delete modules. Once you have the add
                          && module perfected, you can adapt it to
USE invent ORDER part     && fit the other two. Opens the data file.

DO WHILE .T.    && Opens a loop so that the user can edit more
                && than one invoice without having to go back to
                && the menu

 * This VALID does not use a UDF. Instead, VALID uses the SEEK()
 * function to position the record pointer. If the SEEK() fails,
 * it will return a value of False, which refuses the entry.
    @ 5, 18 SAY "   Enter part number:" GET v_part VALID SEEK(v_part) ;
             ERROR "Sorry that part number is not on file."
    READ
    v_desc = desc        && Stuffs the entry variables with the
    v_cost = cost        && field values. This makes it easy to
    v_sale_pr = sale_pr  && let the user abort without changes
    v_in_stock = in_stock    && to the data.
    v_b_order = b_order


 * Now takes the entry. The prompt on line 17 tells the user how
 * to abort. If you build in the feature, advertise it.

    @ 7, 18 SAY "   Enter description:" GET v_desc
    @ 9, 18 SAY "Enter wholesale price:" GET v_cost PICTURE '999.99'
    @11, 18 SAY "    Enter sale price:" GET v_sale_pr PICTURE '9999.99'
```

Fig. continues

Fig. continued

```
    @13, 18 SAY "Enter number of items in stock:" GET v_in_stock ;
                                    PICTURE '9999'
    @15, 18 SAY "Enter number of items backordered:" GET v_b_order ;
                                    PICTURE '9999'
    @17,0 SAY PADC("To abort without saving, press ESCAPE.",77)
    READ
    IF LASTKEY() = 27     && If the READ is terminated by the
       @16,0 CLEAR        && ESCAPE, clears the prompt on 17 and
       EXIT               && aborts past the REPLACEs. No change
    ENDIF                 && to the data!
    REPLACE PART WITH v_part, ;   && With the entry terminated
            DESC WITH v_desc, ;   && normally, this stuffs the new
            COST WITH v_cost, ;   && values into the record.
            SALE_PR WITH v_sale_pr, ;
            IN_STOCK WITH v_in_stock, ;
            B_ORDER WITH v_b_order

 * Sees whether the user wants to edit another record
    STORE ' ' TO conf
    @16,0 CLEAR
    @17,14 SAY "Do you want to edit another item?  (Y/N)-->" GET conf
    READ
    IF UPPER(conf) = 'Y' && If so, this paints the screen, CLEARs
       @16,0 CLEAR       && the prompts, and loops back up.
       DO in_scr
       LOOP
    ELSE
       @16,0 CLEAR    && Otherwise, clears the prompts and aborts
       EXIT
    ENDIF
ENDDO
CLOSE DATABASES     && Closes the files and paints the screen
DO in_scr           && before going back to the menu
RETURN


PROCEDURE del_inv    && This is a variation of the edit module.

USE invent ORDER part

DO WHILE .T.
```

Fig. continues

Fig. continued

```
@ 5, 18 SAY "    Enter part number:" GET v_part VALID SEEK(v_part) ;
             ERROR "Sorry that part number is not on file."
READ
IF LASTKEY() = 27
   @16,0 CLEAR
   EXIT
ENDIF
v_desc = desc
v_cost = cost
v_sale_pr = sale_pr
v_in_stock = in_stock
v_b_order = b_order
@ 7, 18 SAY "    Enter description:" GET v_desc
@ 9, 18 SAY "Enter wholesale price:" GET v_cost PICTURE '999.99'
@11, 18 SAY "     Enter sale price:" GET v_sale_pr PICTURE '9999.99'
@13, 18 SAY "Enter number of items in stock:" GET v_in_stock ;
                                        PICTURE '9999'
@15, 18 SAY "Enter number of items backordered:" GET v_b_order ;
                                        PICTURE '9999'



CLEAR GETS       && The code is the same as the edit module
                 && right up to this point. The CLEAR GETS
                 && displays the found record without taking
                 && keyboard entry. Notice that the code is
                 && in a DO WHILE loop, but it will only go
                 && through once. It is simply easier to
                 && modify the edit module to fit the
                 && purpose than it is to take out the loop.


STORE ' ' TO conf    && Asks whether the item should be deleted
@16,0 CLEAR
@17,14 SAY "Do you want to delete this item?  (Y/N)-->" GET conf
READ
IF UPPER(conf) = 'Y'
   @16,0 CLEAR       && If so, this does the operation and
                     && packs the file right away.
   @16,5 SAY "Stand by for file maintenance..."
   DELETE
   PACK
```

Fig. continues

Fig. continued

```
        EXIT  && You could add another confirmation here to ask the
              && user whether to delete another item. If you add
              && the feature, put above the DO WHILE a flag
              && variable that is used to determine whether any
              && records have been deleted. Here's an example:
              && pakit = .F.
              && Replace the PACK command here with a statement
              && that sets the variable to .T. Then when the loop
              && is exited, you can put something like this:
              && IF pakit
              &&    PACK
              && ENDIF
              && This will cause the module to pack the file only
              && one time instead of packing the file after every
              && deletion. This will enhance execution speed.
    ELSE
        @16,0 CLEAR
        EXIT
    ENDIF
ENDDO
CLOSE DATABASES
DO in_scr
RETURN
*****  End of program  *****
```

The Sales Module

The sales module, which contains a number of procedures and functions, simulates a simple cash register. The user interface for this module adds a pick list to the screen whenever an item is being sold. The user simply highlights the part number for that item. Then the program automatically fills in all the needed information, except the quantity. With this technique, you can avoid many errors commonly made during typing. The sales module's BAR menu shows the different parts of the invoice (see fig. 13.6).

Two techniques are used for printing. The sales module saves all the printing tasks until the end, but the returns module (the procedure mer_ret) prints as it goes.

Besides the inventory file, two other files are used in this module. Figure 13.7 shows the structure of the INV database, and figure 13.8 shows the structure of the SAL_ITEM database. The program code for the sales module appears in figure 13.9.

Fig. 13.6

The BAR menu for the sales module.

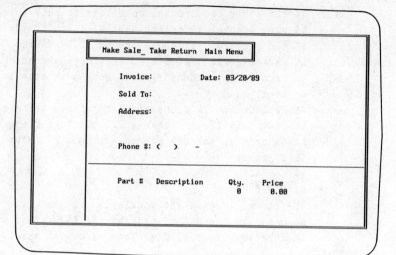

Fig. 13.7

The structure of the INV database.

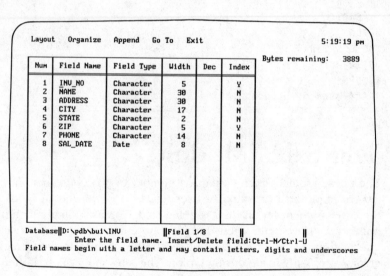

```
 Layout   Organize   Append   Go To   Exit              5:28:13 pm
                                              Bytes remaining:   3964
  ┌─────┬──────────────┬──────────────┬───────┬─────┬───────┐
  │ Num │ Field Name   │ Field Type   │ Width │ Dec │ Index │
  ├─────┼──────────────┼──────────────┼───────┼─────┼───────┤
  │  1  │ INO          │ Character    │   5   │     │   Y   │
  │  2  │ PART         │ Character    │   7   │     │   Y   │
  │  3  │ DESCRIPT     │ Character    │  15   │     │   N   │
  │  4  │ QUANT        │ Numeric      │   2   │  0  │   N   │
  │  5  │ PRICE        │ Numeric      │   7   │  2  │   N   │
  └─────┴──────────────┴──────────────┴───────┴─────┴───────┘




 Database║D:\pdb\bui\SAL_ITEM     ║Field 1/5      ║        ║
              Enter the field name. Insert/Delete field:Ctrl-N/Ctrl-U
 Field names begin with a letter and may contain letters, digits and underscores
```

Fig. 13.8

The structure of the SAL _ ITEM database.

```
*****  Program: SELL.PRG  *****
* A simplified cash-register simulation
ACTIVATE WINDOW work && Pops open a window to cover the menu and
@0,12 TO 20,12       && paints lines and a box for the menus
@14,13 TO 14,77
@0,12 TO 2,51 DOUBLE
DO r_scr             && Paints the data picture on-screen and
ACTIVATE MENU regis  && turns on the menu. Once the menu is
DEACTIVATE WINDOW work  && turned off, this closes the window and
RELEASE ALL LIKE v_*    && RELEASEs the temporary variables.


PROCEDURE r_scr   && A screen-painting module for this set of
                  && procedures
PUBLIC v_name, v_address, v_city, v_state, v_zip, ;
      v_phone, v_sal_date, v_inv_no
PUBLIC v_part, v_quant, v_price, v_desc

STORE SPACE(2) TO v_state
STORE SPACE(5) TO v_zip, v_inv_no
STORE SPACE(7) TO v_part
STORE SPACE(15) TO v_desc
STORE SPACE(17) TO v_city
STORE SPACE(30) TO v_name,v_address
STORE 0 TO v_quant, v_price
```

Fig. 13.9

The program module SELL.PRG.

Fig. continues

Fig. continued

```
    STORE '(   )    -   ' TO v_phone
    STORE DATE() TO v_sal_date

    @ 4,20 SAY "Invoice:" GET v_inv_no
    @ 4,36 SAY "   Date:" GET v_sal_date
    @ 6,20 SAY "Sold To:" GET v_name
    @ 8,20 SAY "Address:" GET v_address
    @10,20 SAY "         " GET v_city
    @10,47 GET v_state
    @10,51 GET v_zip
    @12,20 SAY "Phone #:" GET v_phone
    @16,20 SAY "Part #   Description     Qty.    Price"
    @17,20 GET v_part
    @17,29 GET v_desc
    @17,47 GET v_quant PICTURE '99'
    @17,53 GET v_price PICTURE '9999.99'
    CLEAR GETS
    RETURN



    PROCEDURE ring    && Here is the code to ring up a sale.

    * This section takes the next invoice number from a .MEM file on
    * the disk.
    RESTORE FROM invno.mem ADDITIVE  && ADDITIVE keeps the current
                                     && variable from being RELEASEd.
    v_inv = v_inv + 1      && Increments the number,
    SET SAFETY OFF         && avoids the overwrite confirmation,
    SAVE ALL LIKE v_inv TO invno.mem   && and writes the file back
    SET SAFETY ON                      && to disk
    v_inv_no = STR(v_inv,5,0)  && Converts the variable to character
                               && type



    USE inv ORDER inv_no       && Opens the data files
    USE sal_item IN 2 ORDER ino
    USE invent IN 3 ORDER part

    APPEND BLANK   && In this module there is no variable value to
                   && look up, so the APPEND is just done outside
                   && the VALID.
```

Fig. continues

Fig. continued

```
@ 4,20 SAY "Invoice:" GET v_inv_no      && Because these two are
@ 4,36 SAY "   Date:" GET v_sal_date    && automatic, this just
CLEAR GETS                              && paints them and
                                        && doesn't take entry.


@ 6,20 SAY "Sold To:" GET v_name        && Takes entry for the
@ 8,20 SAY "Address:" GET v_address     && customer information
@10,20 SAY "        " GET v_city
@10,47 GET v_state PICTURE '@! AA'
@10,51 GET v_zip PICTURE '99999'
@12,20 SAY "Phone #:" GET v_phone PICTURE '(999) 999-9999'
READ
IF LASTKEY() = 27      && If the user terminates the READ with an
    DELETE             && ESCAPE, this doesn't leave a blank record
    PACK               && in the file but kills it now!
    CLOSE DATABASES
    DO r_scr
    RETURN
ENDIF
REPLACE name WITH v_name       && Stuffs the record with the
REPLACE address WITH v_address && entered values
REPLACE city WITH v_city
REPLACE state WITH v_state
REPLACE zip WITH v_zip
REPLACE phone WITH v_phone
REPLACE sal_date WITH v_sal_date
REPLACE inv_no WITH v_inv_no
REPLACE phone WITH v_phone


its = 0  && A flag variable to determine whether items are
         && actually sold. If this variable is still equal to 0
         && at termination, the record added above is deleted.

DO WHILE .T.

    SELECT 3               && Makes the inventory file active and
    ACTIVATE POPUP choice  && turns on the POPUP that lets the
                           && user pick the item to be sold. If
    IF BAR() = 0           && the menu is ended with an ESCAPE,
                           && the value of the BAR() will be 0.
        IF its = 0         && If no other items are part of the
                           && sale, this kills the driver record.
```

Fig. continues

Fig. continued

```
        SELECT 1
        DELETE
        PACK
     ENDIF
     EXIT                   && Either way, drops out of the loop
  ENDIF
  its = 1                   && If an item is chosen from the menu,
                            && this sets the flag so that the driver
                            && record will be retained even if the
                            && user wants to add another item, then
                            && decides against it, and ESCAPES from
                            && the pick menu.
  GO TOP                    && Uses the value of BAR() to position
  SKIP (BAR() -1)           && the record pointer and stuffs the
  v_desc = desc             && variables with the values from that
  v_price = sale_pr         && record
  SELECT 2                  && Goes to the items file, creates a
  APPEND BLANK              && record, and then displays the info
  @17,20 GET v_part
  @17,29 GET v_desc
  @17,53 GET v_price PICTURE '9999.99'
  CLEAR GETS
  @17,47 GET v_quant PICTURE '99'   && The only information
                                    && needed from the user is
                                    && the quantity.
  READ
  REPLACE ino WITH v_inv_no   && Stuffs the record with the
  REPLACE part WITH v_part    && values
  REPLACE descript WITH v_desc
  REPLACE quant WITH v_quant
  REPLACE price WITH v_price
* The next line reduces the inventory by the number of items
* sold. The line does not check to see whether the file says that
* the item is in stock; an assumption is that the customer has
* placed the item on the counter. In this case you certainly
* can't refuse to sell it. If the physical inventory differs from
* the file, the inventory file could be reduced to negative
* numbers, thus indicating to the user that the inventory count
* was wrong to begin with.
  REPLACE C->in_stock WITH (C->in_stock - v_quant)
```

Fig. continues

Fig. continued

```
* Offers the user another roll through the loop
   STORE " " TO conf
   @19,20 SAY "Do you want to add another item? (Y/N)-->" GET conf
   READ
   IF UPPER(conf) = 'Y'              && If so, this just
      STORE SPACE(7) TO v_part       && refreshes the bottom
      STORE SPACE(15) TO v_desc      && half of the screen;
      STORE 0 TO v_quant, v_price    && otherwise, the customer
      @17,20 GET v_part              && info would be erased.
      @17,29 GET v_desc
      @17,47 GET v_quant PICTURE '99'
      @17,53 GET v_price PICTURE '9999.99'
      CLEAR GETS
      @19,20 CLEAR TO 19,77
      LOOP
   ELSE
      @19,20 CLEAR TO 19,77    && If not, clears the prompts
      EXIT                     && and drops out of the loop
   ENDIF
ENDDO
DO receipt          && Prints the receipt
CLOSE DATABASES     && Cleans up and aborts
DO r_scr
RETURN


PROCEDURE register   && This little routine returns the part
                     && number from the pick POPUP that is used
v_part = PROMPT()    && to determine which item is being sold.
DEACTIVATE POPUP     && The routine turns off the POPUP.
RETURN


PROCEDURE receipt    && This routine prints the receipt.

line = 0
SET DEVICE TO PRINT
@line+1,5 SAY PADC("Belinda's Bike Boutique",75)
@line+2,5 SAY PADC("234 Easy Rider Road  Wheeling, WV 21211",75)
@line+3,5 SAY PADC("(555) 555-4354",75)
@line+4,5 SAY REPLICATE("-",75)
```

Fig. continues

Fig. continued

```
@line+6,5 SAY "Invoice:" + v_inv_no
@line+6,50 SAY "INVOICE"
@line+7,5 SAY "   Date:" + DTOC(v_sal_date)
@line+9,5 SAY "Sold To: " + v_name
@line+10,5 SAY "Address:" + v_address
@line+11,14 SAY TRIM(v_city)+ " " + v_state + " " + v_zip
@line+12,5  SAY "Phone #:" + v_phone
@line+13,5 SAY REPLICATE("-",75)
       @line+15,5 SAY "Part #   Description      Qty.      Price      Subtotal"
line = line + 16


SELECT 2         && Makes the items file active and
SEEK v_inv_no    && searches for the first item

IF EOF()    && Theoretically this error message should never
            && appear, for the sales module should delete any
            && driver records without items attached. You will
            && find, however, that you need to expect the
            && unexpected. If something is wrong with the index,
            && this error condition will give you an indication.
            && In fact, you could include the code to REINDEX the
            && file and try the SEEK again.
   @line+1,5 SAY "ERROR. THERE ARE NO ITEMS ON THIS INVOICE!!!!!!!"
   EJECT
   SET DEVICE TO SCREEN
   RETURN
ENDIF
page = 1
v_tot = 0   && Stores the subtotal

DO WHILE .T.

   IF line > 60   && If the sale is big, you will need a second
      EJECT       && page, so this prints a new header.
      line = 0
      @line+1,5 SAY PADC("Belinda's Bike Boutique",75)
      @line+2,5 SAY PADC("234 Easy Rider Road  Wheeling, WV 21211",75)
      @line+3,5 SAY PADC("(555) 555-4354",75)
      @line+4,5 SAY REPLICATE("-",65) + "Page: " + STR(page,2,0)
      @line+6,5 SAY "Invoice:" + v_inv_no
```

Fig. continues

Fig. continued

```
            @line+6,50 SAY "INVOICE"
            @line+7,5 SAY "   Date:" + DTOC(v_sal_date)
            @line+9,5 SAY "Sold To: " + v_name
            @line+10,5 SAY "Address:" + v_address
            @line+11,14 SAY TRIM(v_city)+ " " + v_state + " " + v_zip
            @line+12,5  SAY "Phone #:" + v_phone
            @line+13,5 SAY REPLICATE("-",75)
            @line+15,5 SAY "Part #  Description        Qty.       Price      Subtotal"
            line = line + 16
        ENDIF

        @line+1,5  SAY part              && Prints the information about
        @line+1,14 SAY descript          && the item
        @line+1,32 SAY STR(quant,2,0)
        @line+1,40 SAY STR(price,7,2)
        @line+1,51 SAY STR((price*quant),8,2)
        v_tot = v_tot + (price*quant)         && Increments the subtotal
        line = line + 1

        SKIP     && Moves to the next record and tests to see whether
                 && it belongs to the invoice. If so, the loop will be
                 && automatic.
        IF EOF() .OR. v_inv_no <> ino     && If not, prints the total
            @line + 2,45 SAY "TOTAL: " + STR(v_tot,8,2)
            EXIT
        ENDIF
    ENDDO
    SET DEVICE TO SCREEN     && Cleans up and terminates
    EJECT
    RETURN



    PROCEDURE mer_ret    && This is the module that lets the user
                         && take returns. Because returned items are
                         && deleted from the file, this receipt is
                         && printed piecemeal as the code goes along.


    USE inv ORDER inv_no       && Opens the files
    USE sal_item IN 2 ORDER ino
    USE invent IN 3 ORDER part

    line = 0
```

Fig. continues

Fig. continued

```
* This next statement points out an interesting fact. The
* original invoice number started as a numeric data type, so it
* is padded with leading blanks rather that trailing blanks, as
* for a normal character field. Since the number was converted to
* a character type with the STR() function, you have to replicate
* the process with the entry in order to get a search string that
* is properly padded the way field values are. You take the entry
* as a numeric and then convert it to character type for the
* SEEK() function.
v_inv_no = 0
@ 4,20 SAY "Invoice:" GET v_inv_no PICTURE '@Z 99999' ;
   VALID SEEK(STR(v_inv_no,5,0)) ;
   ERROR "There is no invoice on file by that number."
READ
IF LASTKEY() = 27     && IF the user presses ESCAPE, this closes it
   CLOSE DATABASES    && all down.
   DO r_scr
   RETURN
ENDIF
@ 4,20 SAY "Invoice:" GET inv_no
@ 4,36 SAY "  Date:" GET sal_date
@ 6,20 SAY "Sold To:" GET name       && Shows the customer info
@ 8,20 SAY "Address:" GET address    && but takes no entry
@10,20 SAY "         " GET city
@10,47 GET state PICTURE '@! AA'
@10,51 GET zip PICTURE '99999'
@12,20 SAY "Phone #:" GET phone PICTURE '(999) 999-9999'
CLEAR GETS
STORE " " TO conf     && Confirms that this is the proper invoice
@13,20 SAY "Is this the invoice to modify? (Y/N)-->" GET conf
READ
IF UPPER(conf) = 'Y'       && If so, prints the header for the
   @13,20 CLEAR TO 13,77    && return receipt
   SET DEVICE TO PRINT
   @line+1,5 SAY PADC("Belinda's Bike Boutique",75)
   @line+2,5 SAY PADC("234 Easy Rider Road  Wheeling, WV 21211",75)
   @line+3,5 SAY PADC("(555) 555-4354",75)
   @line+4,5 SAY REPLICATE("-",75)
   @line+6,5 SAY "Invoice:" + inv_no
   @line+6,50 SAY "RETURNS"
   @line+7,5 SAY "  Date:" + DTOC(v_sal_date)
   @line+9,5 SAY "Sold To: " + name
```

Fig. continues

Fig. continued

```
    @line+10,5 SAY "Address:" + address
    @line+11,14 SAY TRIM(city)+ " " + state + " " + zip
    @line+12,5  SAY "Phone #:" + phone
    @line+13,5 SAY REPLICATE("-",75)
    @line+15,5 SAY "Part #   Description      Qty.       Price     Subtotal"
    line = line + 16
    SET DEVICE TO SCREEN
ELSE
    @13,20 CLEAR TO 13,77      && If not, closes down the module
    CLOSE DATABASES
    DO r_scr
    RETURN
ENDIF


SELECT 2       && Makes the items active and searches for the
               && first item belonging to the invoice

IF .NOT. SEEK(STR(v_inv_no,5,0)) ;
    SET DEVICE TO PRINT      && Since you have already printed the
                            && header, this prints the error
                            && message. Again, in theory this
                            && error should never occur unless the
                            && index is corrupted.

    @line+3,5 SAY "ERROR. There are no items on file."
    SET DEVICE TO SCREEN
    CLOSE DATABASES
    DO r_scr
    EJECT
    RETURN
ENDIF
v_tot = 0      && A running total

pakit = .F.    && A flag to tell the program that at least one of
               && the items has been deleted and the file needs
               && packing
allout = .T.   && This flag determines whether all the items have
               && been deleted. If so, the driver record needs to
               && be deleted as well.

DO WHILE .T.
```

Fig. continues

Fig. continued

```
            @17,20 GET part              && Paints the information
            @17,29 GET descript          && about the item
            @17,47 GET quant PICTURE '99'
            @17,53 GET price PICTURE '9999.99'
            CLEAR GETS
            STORE " " TO conf             && Asks the user if the item
                                          && should be deleted
            @19,20 SAY "Do you want to return this item? (Y/N)-->" GET conf
            READ
            @19,20 CLEAR TO 19,77
            IF UPPER(conf) = 'Y'    && If the answer is yes, this stores
               look = PART          && the part number to the variable and
               SELECT 3             && finds the inventory record so that
               SEEK look            && the item can be accounted for.

   * This next section is needed just in case the item has been
   * dropped from inventory since the sale was made. This section
   * makes the notation and lets the program continue.
               IF EOF()
                   SET DEVICE TO PRINT
                   @line+1,5 SAY "Part # " + look + " not replaced in inventory."
                   line = line + 1
                   SET DEVICE TO SCREEN
               ENDIF
               REPLACE C->in_stock WITH C->in_stock + B->quant && Adjusts
                                                               && inventory
               SELECT 2             && Prints the information about the
               SET DEVICE TO PRINT  && returned item
               @line+1,5  SAY part
               @line+1,14 SAY descript
               @line+1,32 SAY STR(quant,2,0)
               @line+1,40 SAY STR(price,7,2)
               @line+1,51 SAY STR((price*quant),8,2)
               v_tot = v_tot + (price*quant)    && Updates the total
               line = line + 1
               DELETE          && Deletes the record and marks the flag
               pakit = .T.      && so that the file will be packed at the
                                && end of the process
               SET DEVICE TO SCREEN
```

Fig. continues

Fig. continued

```
    ELSE
        allout = .F.    && If the user says not to delete the item,
                        && then at least one item remains on the
                        && invoice, and the driver record should be
                        && retained in the file.
    ENDIF
    SKIP  && Moves to the next item and tests to see whether it
          && belongs to this invoice. If not, this prints the
          && totals and aborts. If the item does belong, the loop
          && will be automatic.
    IF EOF() .OR. ino <> STR(v_inv_no,5,0)
        SET DEVICE TO PRINT
        @line + 2,43 SAY "REFUND: " + STR(v_tot,8,2)
        SET DEVICE TO SCREEN
        EXIT
    ENDIF
ENDDO
EJECT
IF pakit    && If items have been returned/deleted, this packs
    PACK    && the file.
ENDIF
IF allout     && If all the items have been returned, this
    SELECT 1  && kills the driver record as well.
    DELETE
    PACK
ENDIF
CLOSE DATABASES     && Closes up and goes back to the menu
DO r_scr
RETURN
*****  End of program  *****
```

The Reports Module

The reports module contains a POPUP menu (see fig. 13.10) offering the user a choice of two report forms. A CASE construct is used to determine which report the user wants to run.

Fig. 13.10

The POPUP menu for the reports module.

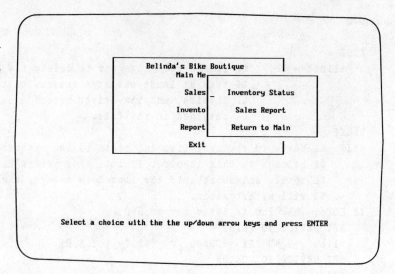

The second report, dealing with the invoicing, is produced by combining the INV.DBF and SAL_ITEM.DBF files through a query file (.QBE). Because the content of a .QBE file is written in dBASE, the code is simply imported into the module itself, and the original .QBE file is discarded altogether.

Do not erase the original .QBE file prematurely, however, as it is handy for creating the report. To make the fields from both files available on the reports work surface, you simply SET VIEW TO *<query file name>*. You can then use the work surface to write the report program for your users, and all the fields from both files will be available for placement.

Figure 13.11 shows the CREATE REPORT work surface with the sales report opened. The field on the second line of the Detail Band is actually a *hidden* calculated field, used for totaling the sales to be printed at the bottom of the report. This field is shown in the figure just so that you will be aware of its existence.

Figure 13.12 shows the work surface of the CREATE QUERY command. Notice that a link is forged between the files, with the invoice number used as the field that sets up the relationship. All the records in both files (except the invoice number field of the items file) have been included in the view. Figure 13.13 shows the CREATE REPORT work surface for the inventory report.

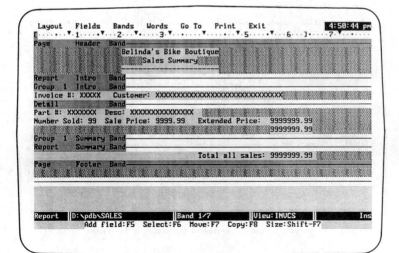

Fig. 13.11

The CREATE REPORT work surface for the sales report.

Fig. 13.12

The CREATE QUERY work surface.

Fig. 13.13

The CREATE REPORT work surface for the inventory report.

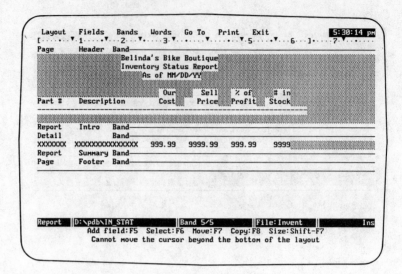

The program code for the reports module appears in figure 13.14. Following that program code is the generated code for both reports.

Fig. 13.14

The program module REPO.PRG.

```
***** Program: REPO.PRG *****
* A POPUP to offer reports
* This module consists of a single DO CASE construct used to
* determine which prompt on the POPUP was chosen.

DO CASE
    CASE BAR() = 2          && The inventory report

    ACTIVATE WINDOW work    && Opens the window and tells the
                            && user what is happening
    @10,10 SAY "Printing inventory report......."
    USE invent ORDER part   && Opens the data file with index
    SET CONSOLE OFF         && Doesn't let the report echo
                            && on-screen
    REPORT FORM in_stat TO PRINT
    SET CONSOLE ON          && Turns the screen back on
    CLOSE DATABASES         && Cleans up and terminates
    DEACTIVATE WINDOW work
    RETURN

    CASE BAR() = 4
```

Fig. continues

Fig. continued

```
* This code is pulled into this file from the .QBE file created
* with the CREATE VIEW command.

    SET FIELDS TO
    SELECT 1
        USE INV.DBF AGAIN NOUPDATE
    USE SAL_ITEM.DBF AGAIN NOUPDATE IN 2 ORDER INO
    SET EXACT ON
    SET FILTER TO FOUND(2)
    SET RELATION TO A->INV_NO INTO B
    SET SKIP TO B
    GO TOP
    SET FIELDS TO A->INV_NO,A->NAME,A->ADDRESS,A->CITY,A->STATE,A->ZIP,A->;
    PHONE,A->SAL_DATE,B->PART,B->DESCRIPT,B->QUANT,B->PRICE

    ACTIVATE WINDOW work    && Opens the window and takes entry
                            && from the user, specifying the
                            && beginning and ending dates for the
                            && report

    STORE CTOD(' / / ') TO hi,lo  && Variable to hold the
                                  && dates
* Takes the entry
    @10,10 SAY "Enter the beginning and ending dates for this report."
    @11,10 SAY "All sales between these dates (inclusive) will print."
    @13,10 SAY "Beginning date:        Ending date: "
    @13,26 GET lo
    @13,50 GET hi
    READ

    SET CONSOLE OFF         && Uses the date variables as
                            && arguments to the REPORT command
    REPORT FORM sales TO PRINT FOR A->sal_date >= lo .AND. ;
        A->sal_date <= hi
    SET CONSOLE ON
    CLOSE DATABASES         && Closes up and terminates
    DEACTIVATE WINDOW work
    RETURN
    CASE BAR() = 6
        DEACTIVATE POPUP    && Turns off the reports menu
ENDCASE
***** End of program *****
```

The Inventory Report Code

dBASE IV generates the inventory report code for the inventory report. No comments have been added to this code. The listing, which appears exactly as it was produced by dBASE IV, is presented in figure 13.15.

Fig. 13.15

The program module IN_STAT.FRG.

```
* Program.............: IN_STAT.FRG
* Date................: 1-1-89
* Versions............: dBASE IV, Report 1
*
* Notes:
* ------
* Prior to running this procedure with the DO command
* it is necessary to use LOCATE because the CONTINUE
* statement is in the main loop.
*
*-- Parameters
PARAMETERS gl_noeject, gl_plain, gl_summary, gc_heading, gc_extra
** The first three parameters are of type Logical.
** The fourth parameter is a string.  The fifth is extra.
PRIVATE _peject, _wrap

*-- Test for no records found
IF EOF() .OR. .NOT. FOUND()
   RETURN
ENDIF

*-- turn word wrap mode off
_wrap=.F.

IF _plength < 10
   SET DEVICE TO SCREEN
   DEFINE WINDOW gw_report FROM 7,17 TO 11,62 DOUBLE
   ACTIVATE WINDOW gw_report
   @ 0,1 SAY "Increase the page length for this report."
   @ 2,1 SAY "Press any key ..."
   x=INKEY(0)
   DEACTIVATE WINDOW gw_report
   RELEASE WINDOW gw_report
   RETURN
ENDIF
```

Fig. continues

Fig. continued

```
   _plineno=0              && set lines to zero
*-- NOEJECT parameter
IF gl_noeject
   IF _peject="BEFORE"
      _peject="NONE"
   ENDIF
   IF _peject="BOTH"
      _peject="AFTER"
   ENDIF
ENDIF


*-- Set-up environment
ON ESCAPE DO prnabort
IF SET("TALK")="ON"
   SET TALK OFF
   gc_talk="ON"
ELSE
   gc_talk="OFF"
ENDIF
gc_space=SET("SPACE")
SET SPACE OFF
gc_time=TIME()         && system time for predefined field
gd_date=DATE()         && system date  "    "    "     "
gl_fandl=.F.           && first and last page flag
gl_prntflg=.T.         && Continue printing flag
gl_widow=.T.           && flag for checking widow bands
gn_length=LEN(gc_heading)  && store length of the HEADING
gn_level=2             && current band being processed
gn_page=_pageno        && grab current page number


*-- Initialize calculated variables.
MARGIN=0

*-- Set up procedure for page break
IF _pspacing > 1
   gn_atline=_plength - (_pspacing + 1)
ELSE
   gn_atline=_plength - 1
ENDIF
```

Fig. continues

Fig. continued

```
ON PAGE AT LINE gn_atline EJECT PAGE

*-- Print Report

PRINTJOB

*-- Assign initial values to calculated variables.
MARGIN=COST/SALE_PR*100

IF gl_plain
   ON PAGE AT LINE gn_atline DO Pgplain
ELSE
   ON PAGE AT LINE gn_atline DO Pgfoot
ENDIF

DO Pghead

gl_fandl=.T.          && first physical page started

*-- File Loop
DO WHILE FOUND() .AND. .NOT. EOF() .AND. gl_prntflg
   DO Upd_Vars
   *--Detail lines
   IF .NOT. gl_summary
      DO Detail
   ENDIF
   CONTINUE
ENDDO

IF gl_prntflg
ELSE
   DO Reset
   RETURN
ENDIF

ON PAGE

ENDPRINTJOB

DO Reset
RETURN
* EOP: D:\PDB\IN_STAT.FRG
```

Fig. continues

Fig. continued

```
*-- Update summary fields and/or calculated fields in the detail band.
PROCEDURE Upd_Vars
MARGIN=COST/SALE_PR*100
RETURN
* EOP: Upd_Vars

*-- Set flag to get out of DO WHILE loop when escape is pressed.
PROCEDURE prnabort
gl_prntflg=.F.
RETURN
* EOP: prnabort


PROCEDURE Pghead
?? "Belinda's Bike Boutique" AT 20
?
?? "Inventory Status Report" AT 20
?
*-- Print HEADING parameter ie. REPORT FORM <name> HEADING <expC>
IF .NOT. gl_plain .AND. gn_length > 0
   ?? gc_heading FUNCTION "I;V"+LTRIM(STR(_rmargin - lmargin))
   ?
ENDIF
?? "As of " AT 25,
?? IIF(gl_plain,'',gd_date)
?
?
?? " Our" AT 29,
?? "  Sell" AT 37,
?? " % of" AT 46,
?? "# in" AT 56
?
?? "Part #    Description       Cost" AT 0,
?? "   Price" AT 35,
?? "Profit" AT 46,
?? " Stock" AT 54
?
?? "----------------------------------------------------------------" AT 0
?
?
RETURN
* EOP: Pghead
```

Fig. continues

Fig. continued

```
PROCEDURE Detail
?? PART FUNCTION "T" AT 0,
?? " " ,
?? DESC FUNCTION "T" ,
?? COST PICTURE "999.99" AT 27,
?? SALE_PR PICTURE "9999.99" AT 36,
?? MARGIN PICTURE "999.99" AT 46,
?? IN_STOCK PICTURE "9999" AT 56
?
RETURN
* EOP: Detail


PROCEDURE Pgfoot
PRIVATE _box
gl_widow=.F.          && disable widow checking
EJECT PAGE
*-- is the page number greater than the ending page
IF _pageno > _pepage
   GOTO BOTTOM
   SKIP
   gn_level=0
ENDIF
IF .NOT. gl_plain .AND. gl_fandl
   DO Pghead
ENDIF
gl_widow=.T.          && enable widow checking
RETURN
* EOP: Pgfoot


*-- Process page break when PLAIN option is used.
PROCEDURE Pgplain
PRIVATE _box
EJECT PAGE
RETURN
* EOP: Pgplain


*-- Reset dBASE environment prior to calling report
PROCEDURE Reset
SET SPACE &gc_space.
```

Fig. continues

Fig. continued

```
SET TALK &gc_talk.
ON ESCAPE
ON PAGE
RETURN
* EOP: Reset
```

The Sales Report Code

The code for the sales report is generated by dBASE IV also. Again, no comments have been added to this code. It is presented in figure 13.16 just as it was created by dBASE IV.

```
* Program............: SALES.FRG
* Date...............: 1-1-89
* Versions...........: dBASE IV, Report 1
*
* Notes:
* ------
* Prior to running this procedure with the DO command
* it is necessary to use LOCATE because the CONTINUE
* statement is in the main loop.
*
*-- Parameters
PARAMETERS gl_noeject, gl_plain, gl_summary, gc_heading, gc_extra
** The first three parameters are of type Logical.
** The fourth parameter is a string.  The fifth is extra.
PRIVATE _peject, _wrap

*-- Test for no records found
IF EOF() .OR. .NOT. FOUND()
   RETURN
ENDIF

*-- turn word wrap mode off
_wrap=.F.

IF _plength < 6
   SET DEVICE TO SCREEN
   DEFINE WINDOW gw_report FROM 7,17 TO 11,62 DOUBLE
   ACTIVATE WINDOW gw_report
```

Fig. 13.16

The program module SALES.FRG.

Fig. continues

Fig. continued

```
        @ 0,1 SAY "Increase the page length for this report."
        @ 2,1 SAY "Press any key ..."
        x=INKEY(0)
        DEACTIVATE WINDOW gw_report
        RELEASE WINDOW gw_report
        RETURN
ENDIF


_plineno=0              && set lines to zero
*-- NOEJECT parameter
IF gl_noeject
   IF _peject="BEFORE"
      _peject="NONE"
   ENDIF
   IF _peject="BOTH"
      _peject="AFTER"
   ENDIF
ENDIF


*-- Set-up environment
ON ESCAPE DO prnabort
IF SET("TALK")="ON"
   SET TALK OFF
   gc_talk="ON"
ELSE
   gc_talk="OFF"
ENDIF
gc_space=SET("SPACE")
SET SPACE OFF
gc_time=TIME()         && system time for predefined field
gd_date=DATE()         && system date  "    "    "     "
gl_fandl=.F.           && first and last page flag
gl_prntflg=.T.         && Continue printing flag
gl_widow=.T.           && flag for checking widow bands
gn_length=LEN(gc_heading)  && store length of the HEADING
gn_level=2             && current band being processed
gn_page=_pageno        && grab current page number


*-- Initialize calculated variables.
TOT=0
```

Fig. continues

Fig. continued

```
EXT=0

*-- Set up procedure for page break
IF _pspacing > 1
   gn_atline=_plength - (_pspacing + 1)
ELSE
   gn_atline=_plength - 2
ENDIF
ON PAGE AT LINE gn_atline EJECT PAGE

*-- Print Report

PRINTJOB

*-- Initialize group break vars.
r_mvar4=INV_NO

*-- Assign initial values to calculated variables.
TOT=ext+tot
EXT=QUANT*PRICE

IF gl_plain
   ON PAGE AT LINE gn_atline DO Pgplain
ELSE
   ON PAGE AT LINE gn_atline DO Pgfoot
ENDIF

DO Pghead

gl_fandl=.T.          && first physical page started

DO Grphead

*-- File Loop
DO WHILE FOUND() .AND. .NOT. EOF() .AND. gl_prntflg
   DO CASE
   CASE .NOT. (INV_NO = r_mvar4)
      gn_level=4
   OTHERWISE
      gn_level=0
   ENDCASE
```

Fig. continues

Fig. continued

```
       *-- test whether an expression didn't match
       IF gn_level <> 0
          DO Grpinit
       ENDIF
       *-- Repeat group intros
       IF gn_level <> 0
          DO Grphead
       ENDIF
       DO Upd_Vars
       *-- Detail lines
       IF .NOT. gl_summary
          DO Detail
       ENDIF
       CONTINUE
    ENDDO

    IF gl_prntflg
       gn_level=3
       DO Rsumm
       IF _plineno <= gn_atline
          EJECT PAGE
       ENDIF
    ELSE
       gn_level=3
       DO Rsumm
       DO Reset
       RETURN
    ENDIF

    ON PAGE

    ENDPRINTJOB

    DO Reset
    RETURN
    * EOP: D:\PDB\SALES.FRG

    *-- Update summary fields and/or calculated fields in the detail band.
    PROCEDURE Upd_Vars
    TOT=ext+tot
```

Fig. continues

Fig. continued

```
EXT=QUANT*PRICE
RETURN
* EOP: Upd_Vars

*-- Set flag to get out of DO WHILE loop when escape is pressed.
PROCEDURE prnabort
gl_prntflg=.F.
RETURN
* EOP: prnabort

*-- Reset group break variables.  Reinit summary
*-- fields with reset set to a particular group band.
PROCEDURE Grpinit
IF gn_level <= 4
   r_mvar4=INV_NO
ENDIF
RETURN
* EOP: Grpinit

*-- Process Group Intro bands during group breaks
PROCEDURE Grphead
IF EOF()
   RETURN
ENDIF
gl_widow=.T.           && enable widow checking
IF gn_level <= 4
   DO Head4
ENDIF
gn_level=0
RETURN
* EOP: Grphead.PRG

PROCEDURE Pghead
?? "Belinda's Bike Boutique" AT 21
?
?? "Sales Summary" AT 26
?
*-- Print HEADING parameter ie. REPORT FORM <name> HEADING <expC>
IF .NOT. gl_plain .AND. gn_length > 0
   ?? gc_heading FUNCTION "I;V"+LTRIM(STR(_rmargin - _lmargin))
   ?
ENDIF
```

Fig. continues

Fig. continued

```
    ?? "-----------------------" AT 21
    ?
    RETURN
    * EOP: Pghead


    PROCEDURE Head4
    IF gn_level=1
       RETURN
    ENDIF
    IF 1 < _plength
       IF (gl_widow .AND. _plineno+3 > gn_atline)
          EJECT PAGE
       ENDIF
    ENDIF
    ?? "Invoice #: " AT 0,
    ?? INV_NO FUNCTION "T" ,
    ?? "   Customer: " ,
    ?? NAME FUNCTION "T"
    ?
    RETURN

    PROCEDURE Detail
    IF 3 < _plength
       IF gl_widow .AND. _plineno+2 > gn_atline
          EJECT PAGE
       ENDIF
    ENDIF
    ?? "Part #: " AT 0,
    ?? PART FUNCTION "T" ,
    ?? "  Desc: " ,
    ?? DESCRIPT FUNCTION "T" ,
    ?? " "
    ?
    ?? "Number Sold: " AT 0,
    ?? QUANT PICTURE "99" ,
    ?? "  Sale Price: " ,
    ?? PRICE PICTURE "9999.99" ,
    ?? "   Extended Price:  " ,
    ?? EXT PICTURE "9999999.99"
    ?
    ?
```

Fig. continues

Fig. continued

```
RETURN
* EOP: Detail


PROCEDURE Rsumm
??  "                                    Total all sales: " AT 0,
?? ext+tot PICTURE "9999999.99" ,
?? " "
gl_fandl=.F.          && last page finished
?
RETURN
* EOP: Rsumm

PROCEDURE Pgfoot
PRIVATE _box
gl_widow=.F.          && disable widow checking
?
IF .NOT. gl_plain
ENDIF
EJECT PAGE
*-- is the page number greater than the ending page
IF _pageno > _pepage
   GOTO BOTTOM
   SKIP
   gn_level=0
ENDIF
IF .NOT. gl_plain .AND. gl_fandl
   DO Pghead
ENDIF
IF gn_level = 0 .AND. gl_fandl
   gn_level=1
   DO Grphead
ENDIF
gl_widow=.T.          && enable widow checking
RETURN
* EOP: Pgfoot


*-- Process page break when PLAIN option is used.
PROCEDURE Pgplain
PRIVATE _box
```

Fig. continues

Fig. continued

```
EJECT PAGE
IF gn_level = 0 .AND. gl_fandl
   gn_level=1
   DO Grphead
ENDIF
RETURN
* EOP: Pgplain

*-- Reset dBASE environment prior to calling report
PROCEDURE Reset
SET SPACE &gc_space.
SET TALK &gc_talk.
ON ESCAPE
ON PAGE
RETURN
* EOP: Reset
```

Summary

This chapter presented a sample application demonstrating most of the concepts introduced in previous chapters. Included in the modules were techniques for handling multiple files, presenting user interfaces, and programming error-trapping routines.

The main module showed you how to set up the menu structures for the entire application before activating the main menu, as well as how to set up your applications in memory. The inventory module demonstrated how to take information into one file while rejecting duplicate key values. In addition, this module showed you how to edit and delete data files.

The sales module contained a group of functions allowing a user to sell items from inventory, take items being returned by customers, and print the invoices on paper. Finally, the reports module showed you how to include report forms created with the report-creation work surface.

The next chapter shows you how to use dBASE IV's debugger and other debugging methods to find and correct errors in your program code.

Part III

Exploring
Advanced Topics

Includes

Debugging dBASE IV Programs

Networking with dBASE IV

Distributing Programs with the RunTime Module

Using the dBASE IV Template Language

14

Debugging
dBASE IV Programs

No matter how careful you are or how good a programmer you become, you will always make mistakes. Mistakes or unforeseen complications in programs are known as bugs.

The term *bug* is nearly as old as the computer. Legend has it that during early experiments conducted on vacuum tube computers by Navy Commander Grace Hopper, an insect came into contact with electrically charged wires and caused a malfunction. One of the technicians, after removing the charred remains of the insect, made an entry in the logbook to the effect that a bug had been removed from the computer. The term stuck.

Debugging has become a bit less gruesome in recent years, but it is still one of the most annoying tasks a programmer has to perform. Fortunately, well over 90 percent of all bugs are simple and easy to fix. In dBASE IV, the most common bugs are misspellings of commands, functions, and variable names. Other bugs caused by programmers or users include forgetting to move to the proper work area, issuing a CLOSE PROCEDURE command and then calling a procedure listed in the file that was closed, and trying to use a variable that has been RELEASEd.

Usually when a program acts differently than expected, you have made a mistake in the code. Occasionally, though, bugs are in the underlying software. Software vendors like to refer to these bugs euphemistically as "anomalies." If you have an account with CompuServe, for instance, you can download an anomaly report by accessing the Ashton-Tate special-interest group. Any software as large and powerful as dBASE IV is bound to have a few small problems. The anomaly report will tell you what the problems are and give you "workarounds," which are different approaches you can use to achieve an intended result. Be assured, however, that 999 of 1,000 bugs will be in your implementation of the program code, not as an anomaly in dBASE IV.

dBASE IV provides a wide selection of tools you can use in finding and eradicating problems in your programs. These tools include commands that can be used either at the dot prompt or in your programs. An interactive debugger is available as well.

Knowing the Debugging Commands

Several commands for finding simple bugs in your programs are available. You issue some of these commands at the dot prompt, before you call the program to be debugged. Others you place inside the program code. The commands for debugging are SET ECHO, SET DEBUG, SET STEP, SUSPEND, and CANCEL. The functions of these commands are described briefly in table 14.1. These commands are included in dBASE IV mostly to be compatible with earlier versions that did not include the interactive debugger.

Table 14.1
Debugging Commands

SET ECHO on/OFF	Displays the lines of code on-screen or on a printed page as the lines are executed.
SET DEBUG on/OFF	Routes the results of the SET ECHO command to the printer when it is on. If you SET DEBUG OFF (its default condition), the result of SET ECHO will go to the screen.
SET STEP on/OFF	Pauses the execution of the program after every line in the program code. A message is then displayed that reads Press SPACE to Step, S to Suspend, or Esc to Cancel...
SUSPEND	Pauses the execution of the program, returning you to the dot prompt. While the program is in suspension, you can test the values of fields and the values of variables, and you can check the positioning of the record pointer. To begin executing the code from the point where it was suspended, you issue the RESUME command.

Table 14.1—*Continued*

CANCEL	Terminates the program and returns you to the dot prompt. Because the program is terminated, variables are also released. You cannot RESUME a canceled program.

Finding Errors in Your Programs

Most of the bugs in your applications will trigger a dBASE IV error message. In fact, triggering such a message is how most bugs will announce themselves.

Typically you will find most bugs when you issue the DO command and dBASE IV compiles your program code. Syntax errors (the most common type of bug) will be pointed out to you through error messages. Those bugs that remain will usually be errors in assignments of variables, work areas, and so on. You can find most of these bugs by using the SET ECHO and SET STEP commands.

You will soon discover, however, that the interactive debugger included in dBASE IV will be your tool of choice in all but the simplest situations.

Using the dBASE IV Debugger

The dBASE IV debugger is made up of four windows tiled together to present you with all the options available. Figure 14.1 shows how the debugger is displayed on-screen.

The Edit window takes up the top half of the screen and shows the program code (with line numbers) as it is being executed. The next line of code to be executed is highlighted. From this window, you can also choose to edit the program code. Changes you make will not be incorporated into the program until it is recompiled, however. You can access the Edit window by pressing E at the ACTION prompt of the Debugger window.

Just below the Edit window, on the left half of the screen, is the Display window. In this window, you can enter any valid dBASE expression and watch what happens to its value as the program executes. The expression must be valid, but it does not have to be part of a valid command. For example, if you want to see the value of LASTKEY(), you do not have to enter ? LASTKEY(). You can also display a variable that is not yet initialized. Instead of triggering an error message, the Display window will simply inform you that the variable is not

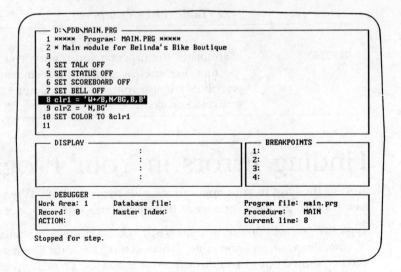

Fig. 14.1

The dBASE IV debugger shown on-screen.

```
 ┌── D:\PDB\MAIN.PRG ──
 1 ××××× Program: MAIN.PRG ×××××
 2 × Main module for Belinda's Bike Boutique
 3
 4 SET TALK OFF
 5 SET STATUS OFF
 6 SET SCOREBOARD OFF
 7 SET BELL OFF
 8 clr1 = 'W+/B,N/BG,B,B'
 9 clr2 = 'N,BG'
10 SET COLOR TO &clr1
11

 ┌── DISPLAY ──                          ┌── BREAKPOINTS ──
                         :               1:
                         :               2:
                         :               3:
                         :               4:

 ┌── DEBUGGER ──
 Work Area: 1      Database file:         Program file: main.prg
 Record:   0       Master Index:          Procedure:    MAIN
 ACTION:                                  Current line: 8

 Stopped for step.
```

defined. When the program initializes the variable, its value is then displayed. You can access the Display window by pressing D at the `ACTION` prompt of the Debugger window.

To the right of the Display window is the Breakpoint window. Here you can enter any logical expression. All breakpoints are evaluated after each command in the program is executed. If the value of one of the breakpoint expressions is True, the program halts execution, and the debugger is invoked. To enter a breakpoint, press B at the `ACTION` prompt of the Debugger window.

The Debugger window displays current information about the program that is executing, including the program file name, the procedure that is executing, the line number of the next command to be executed, the current work area, the current database and index files, and the current record number. If the debugger is activated by an error condition, the error message is displayed as well.

You use the `ACTION` prompt of the Debugger window to access the various features of the debugger. You can access this prompt from any of the other windows by pressing the Esc key.

If you press the F1 key, a help screen pops up listing the various options available with the debugger (see fig. 14.2). Table 14.2 explains the use of each of the debugger command keys.

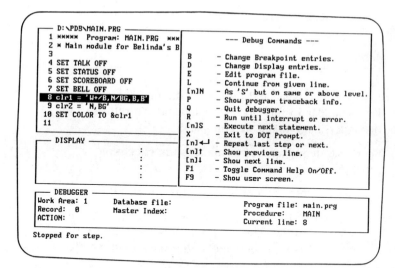

Fig. 14.2

The debugger help screen displayed.

Table 14.2
Debugger Command Keys

Command Key	Action
B	Activates the Breakpoint window.
D	Activates the Display window.
E	Activates the Edit window.
R	Causes the program to execute until an error occurs or a breakpoint is triggered.
L	Begins execution of the program at a specific line. When you press L, the debugger prompts you to enter the line number.
[n]S	Steps through the execution of the program [n] lines at a time.
[n]N	Steps through the execution of the program [n] lines at a time. If, however, another lower-level module is called, that module will execute independently of the debugger.
P	Displays a trace of program execution back to the highest-level module.

Table 14.2—*Continued*

Command Key	Action
X	Exits the debugger and returns to the dot prompt; the X key is similar to the SUSPEND command. To return to the debugger, issue a RESUME command.
Q	Quits the debugger and terminates the executing program.
Enter	Repeats the most recent [n]S or [n]N command.
↑	Lets you move the highlight bar one line toward the top of the program file. The up arrow only lets you see the contents of the file; you cannot step through the code again.
↓	Lets you see the code closer to the bottom of the file (the down arrow is a complement to the up arrow).
F1	Displays a window of debugger command keys.
F9	Clears the debugger from the screen and shows the screen as created by the application. To return to the debugger, press F9 again.

Invoking the Debugger

You can use two commands to invoke the debugger: SET TRAP and DEBUG. The SET TRAP command tells dBASE IV to invoke the debugger whenever an error condition is triggered. If you do a great deal of development, you will want to place the line TRAP = ON in your CONFIG.DB file. Otherwise, you will have to issue the command SET TRAP ON whenever you want the debugger to be automatically invoked when an error condition exists.

With SET TRAP ON, you run your programs just as you normally would with the DO command. If an error condition is not caught in the compile stage, the debugger will be triggered when dBASE IV encounters the error.

Sometimes you will want to see the program running from the Debugger window. Just substitute the DEBUG command for the DO command. Instead of issuing the command DO prog (in which prog is the name of the program), issue the command DEBUG prog.

One other method of invoking the debugger is available: using the Esc key. Whenever you press Esc (ON ESCAPE must not be active, and you must not SET ESCAPE OFF), the debugger is activated.

One small problem is associated with using the Esc key as a "hot" key to invoke the debugger. If you press the Esc key during a READ, the GETs are terminated, but the debugger is not invoked.

The solution to this problem is to create your own hot key as a breakpoint. For example, the INKEY() value of the Alt-X key combination is the number -412. Invoke the program with the DEBUG command. Before the program runs, the debugger will appear. Type INKEY() = -412 in the Breakpoint window. You can then run the program normally by pressing R at the ACTION prompt. The debugger will retain the INKEY()-driven breakpoint for the rest of your dBASE IV session or until you clear the breakpoint. From that point on, you can invoke the debugger by pressing Alt-X. For a list of the INKEY() values, see INKEY() in your dBASE IV *Language Reference* manual, which comes with dBASE IV.

Trying the Debugger

To see the debugger in action, get a copy of the application presented in the last chapter and edit the file INVEN.PRG.

Make the PUBLIC statement on line 16 of that file a comment by putting an asterisk in front of the statement. Commenting out the PUBLIC statement will cause the variables to be RELEASEd when the screen-painting procedure terminates. Make sure that you have SET DEVELOPMENT ON so that the module will be recompiled before it is executed.

To begin the debugging process, issue the command DEBUG main. Press B at the ACTION prompt and then enter the breakpoints shown. Once your screen looks exactly like that shown in figure 14.3, press the Esc key to return to the ACTION prompt.

Next, press D to move to the Display window, and then type the variable name tpad, which is part of the user-defined function PADC(). The message Variable not found will be displayed. Press the Esc key to return to the ACTION prompt, and then press S to step through the lines of code until the first line of the main menu is prepared for display. When the program pointer passes through the PAD() function, the variable tpad is initialized briefly. Note how its value is displayed until the function terminates. The Variable not found message is again shown in the Display window.

If you like, you can step through the entire menu-definition process and watch the variable tpad being created and released as each of the menus is DEFINEd.

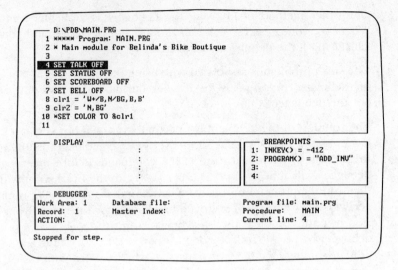

Fig. 14.3

The debugger loaded with breakpoints before the program runs.

When you have seen this process, press R at the ACTION prompt and let the program run. The debugger will be cleared from the screen, and the program will execute normally. Once the main menu is displayed, choose **Inventory** and press the Enter key. The **Inventory** menu will then be displayed (see fig. 14.4), and you will be at the same point in the program as that shown in figure 14.3.

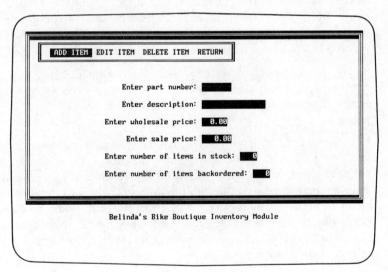

Fig. 14.4

The inventory screen just before the debugger is invoked.

When you choose to add an item to the inventory, the debugger will again be invoked because of the breakpoint PROGRAM() = "ADD_INV". Notice in figure 14.5 that the message on the bottom line of the screen (just under the Debugger window) tells you that the trigger was breakpoint 2. Because the breakpoint remains True the entire time you are in the procedure ADD_INV, you will need to press S twice to step through one line of code.

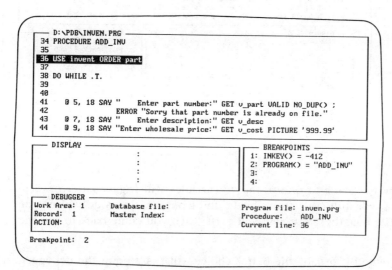

Fig. 14.5

The second breakpoint returning a True value.

Figure 14.6 shows the error message that is displayed on the bottom line of the Debugger screen when the program tries to accept data entry in the variable v_part. Because the PUBLIC command was effectively removed from the screen-painting routine, the variable no longer exists, having been RELEASEd when the screen-painting routine terminated.

At this point, you have identified a bug. You have not actually isolated the offending program line or the absence of a program statement; you have isolated only the place where the problem is manifested. You may have to step through the code again with the variable entered into the Display window in order to find out why the variable does not exist.

You can use one of two methods to correct any bugs you may find with the debugger. You can either edit the code or quit the debugger, edit the code, and run it again.

If other places in the program need testing, you can press E at the ACTION prompt and edit the code. Watch out for two problems with this method, however. First, the bug may have wide-reaching effects. In the current example, for

Fig. 14.6

The error condition detected.

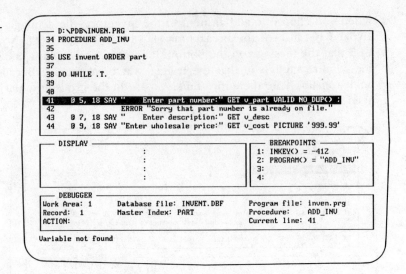

```
┌─ D:\PDB\INVEN.PRG ──────────────────────────────────────────────┐
│ 34 PROCEDURE ADD_INV                                             │
│ 35                                                               │
│ 36 USE invent ORDER part                                        │
│ 37                                                               │
│ 38 DO WHILE .T.                                                  │
│ 39                                                               │
│ 40                                                               │
│ 41    @ 5, 18 SAY "    Enter part number:" GET v_part VALID NO_DUP() ; │
│ 42            ERROR "Sorry that part number is already on file." │
│ 43    @ 7, 18 SAY "   Enter description:" GET v_desc             │
│ 44    @ 9, 18 SAY "Enter wholesale price:" GET v_cost PICTURE '999.99' │
└──────────────────────────────────────────────────────────────────┘
┌─ DISPLAY ──────────────────┐  ┌─ BREAKPOINTS ──────────────────┐
│                      :     │  │ 1: INKEY() = -412              │
│                      :     │  │ 2: PROGRAM() = "ADD_INV"       │
│                      :     │  │ 3:                             │
│                      :     │  │ 4:                             │
└────────────────────────────┘  └────────────────────────────────┘
┌─ DEBUGGER ────────────────────────────────────────────────────────┐
│ Work Area: 1     Database file: INVENT.DBF   Program file: inven.prg│
│ Record:  1       Master Index: PART          Procedure:    ADD_INV  │
│ ACTION:                                      Current line: 41       │
└────────────────────────────────────────────────────────────────────┘
Variable not found
```

instance, every reference to one of the v_ variables will trigger an error. Second, when you edit the code from inside the debugger, the code will not be recompiled. The bug, therefore, will still exist when you come back to run the program.

The second method is usually the better choice—that is, to quit the debugger, edit the code, and run the program again. This way, the program is recompiled, and the bug is out of your way. You are free to go on to other things.

Applying Some Debugging Tips

Finding an elusive bug in a program can be maddening, especially when the program being debugged has structural problems. To make debugging simpler, write your applications as small modules, each performing a single task. You will find these smaller programs to be much easier to follow through the debugger.

Unless you are sharing a computer with users who do not program in dBASE, put a statement in your CONFIG.DB file that SETs TRAP ON. Then, as you test your code during development, most of the bugs will work themselves out.

Remember that some types of bugs will never trigger an error message or the debugger. A good example is the use of a REPLACE command that references the wrong field. If the field is of the same type and length as the intended field, dBASE IV will never tell you of the bug. How could it? All that will happen is that you will get bad data.

For this reason, always test the program extensively and then pass it along for further testing to another programmer and to a trusted user also. Usually a programmer is so close to the code that problems will not become evident.

When using the debugger, stop the program frequently to test variable values and record-pointer positions, which are responsible for the most common problems found in programs.

Finally, don't beat your head against a brick wall. If you spend more than fifteen minutes or so looking for a problem and it is eluding you, get up and walk outside or do something else for a few minutes. Sometimes a programmer can get so wound up looking for an error that an obvious situation is overlooked. If you are involved in any type of user support, you probably have seen users get so frustrated that they overlook simple things. Consequently, the original error is compounded many times over.

If you are unable to focus your attention on the problem, take a walk. When you come back, that simple solution will probably come right to you.

Summary

In this chapter, you learned how to use the dBASE IV debugging commands. Remember that most of these commands remain in dBASE IV solely to be compatible with earlier versions of the language.

You learned how to use dBASE IV's interactive debugger also. If you have TRAP set ON, the debugger will automatically be invoked whenever an error condition is triggered. Some general debugging tips were provided as well.

The next chapter covers networking in dBASE IV.

15

Networking
with dBASE IV

T he number of local area networks used in business has increased dramatically over the last few years. The advantage of networking is that expensive peripherals can be shared by users at different workstations. Additionally networks enable users to communicate with one another, share data files, receive electronic mail, and exchange messages.

In its simplest form, a local area network (LAN) is a group of computers (workstations) connected by wire or fiber optic cables to one or more central file servers that handle requests for data and system resources (printers, modems, scanners, and so on). The advantage of a LAN in database management is that multiple users can access the same information simultaneously. Moreover, data-security measures can be taken to prevent unauthorized access to sensitive or proprietary information.

dBASE IV supports a full range of features that make multiuser applications possible on a LAN. In this chapter, you will learn how to take advantage of those features so that you can create applications which can be used at several workstations at one time. The topics covered include dBASE IV locking procedures, commands and functions used in networking, data security on networks, and transaction processing.

Handling Multiple Users

Whenever you have more than one user accessing a data file at the same time, you must take precautions to preserve data integrity. Simultaneous writes to the data file can corrupt the data.

385

Let's assume that both user A and user B are using an inventory data file at the same time and that both call up the same record for editing at the same time. User A plans to edit the number of units in stock to reflect a shipment just received. User B calls up the same information with the idea of changing the description of the item. Both users get exactly the same information about the record at the same time.

After user A edits the number of items in stock, she writes the information back to the file. User B takes a little longer to change the description field and then writes the data back as well. The contents of the record, as edited by user B, will then become what is written in the file. Because user B made no changes to the quantity field, the old quantity will be written back to the file. The final version of the file will not contain user A's edited record because user B's update contained the old information.

A worse situation can occur when the updates from both users are sent to the file server simultaneously. The resulting collision can corrupt the entire data file structure, not just the one record.

The way to avoid these kinds of problems is to prevent simultaneous writes to the data file through a system of record- and file-locking procedures. A *lock* signals to other users on the network that a file or record is unavailable during the time that a particular user needs access.

In the preceding example, the application should have granted access to user A to edit the record, while telling user B to wait for the lock to be released. In that case, user A accesses the record and begins to make the adjustment to the quantity field. User B attempts to access the same record, but the system informs him that the record is unavailable for a few minutes. User B tells the application to keep trying. As soon as user A writes her changes to the file, the lock is released, and user B is given the record with a lock of his own. Because user B is prevented from accessing the record until user A's changes are incorporated into the file, user B's copy of the record will contain the changes made by user A.

As a programmer, you can arrange for a data file to be opened for the exclusive use of a single user in one of two ways. You can either include in the application the SET EXCLUSIVE ON command or add the EXCLUSIVE clause to the USE command.

If a data file is opened EXCLUSIVEly, you have no need to include a locking procedure, for other users are prevented from accessing the file in any way. If a data file is opened in shared mode (that is, if SET EXCLUSIVE is off), you can apply two types of locks: file locks and record locks.

A *file lock* provides temporary EXCLUSIVE use of the file. Usually this type of lock is applied when more than one record in the data file is likely to be modified by the operation of the program. A *record lock* provides temporary EXCLUSIVE use of a single record in the data file. Usually such a lock is applied when the contents of that record might be modified by the program.

No locking is needed to provide read-only access to a data file opened in a non-EXCLUSIVE mode. In that case, it is not necessary to open a file EXCLUSIVEly, or to apply a file lock in order to run a report or provide a simple lookup function within an application.

Using dBASE IV Locking Procedures

In dBASE IV, users can create and manipulate data files in either an interactive mode (working from the Control Center or the dot prompt) or a batch-processing mode (under program control). Four different levels of locking are therefore available to the programmer: automatic file locking, automatic record locking, explicit file locking, and explicit record locking.

Automatic File Locking

Certain dBASE IV commands cause a data file to be locked automatically when the file has been opened in a non-EXCLUSIVE mode during interactive operations. The commands that lock files automatically are the following:

```
APPEND FROM†
AVERAGE†
CALCULATE†
COPY†
COPY STRUCTURE†
COUNT†
DELETE*
INDEX†
JOIN†
LABEL†
PROTECT
RECALL*
REPLACE*
REPORT†
SORT†
SUM†
TOTAL†
UPDATE
```

The asterisk (*) indicates a command that will apply a file lock when the scope of the command is likely to contain more than one record. The dagger (†) indicates a command for which automatic locking can be disabled with the SET LOCK OFF command.

Automatic file locks are applied without intervention from the user. In other words, they are transparent. If an attempt to lock the file fails, a prompt box is presented, enabling the user to decide whether to retry the locking attempt or to abandon the operation. Automatic file locks are canceled automatically when the operation is completed.

Automatic Record Locking

dBASE IV tries to apply a record lock automatically whenever an attempt is made to alter data in a file opened in a non-EXCLUSIVE mode. The commands that apply an automatic record lock include the following:

```
APPEND [BLANK]
CHANGE
DELETE*
EDIT
RECALL*
REPLACE*
```

Again, the asterisk (*) indicates a command that applies a file lock when the scope of the command is likely to affect more than one record. If the scope of the command affects only one record, a record lock is placed.

Explicit File Locking

The FLOCK() function is used in an application to place explicit file locks. You can arrange for an explicit file lock if you want your application to generate a lock-failure message instead of displaying the default prompt box presented by dBASE IV. If the FLOCK() function is rejected (when another user has a lock currently in place or has opened the data file EXCLUSIVEly), the return value of the function will be False. You can use this value to trigger whatever error message you want displayed. For example, you can include a procedure, called NO_LOCK, that displays a lock-failure message:

```
IF .NOT. FLOCK()
    DO no_lock WITH "There is already a lock on that file."
ENDIF
```

Explicit file locking is also handy when you want to make sure that several files are available before the application begins an operation requiring that two or more files be locked. Finally, you can explicitly lock a file in another work area by including the file's alias as an argument of the FLOCK() function.

To avoid deadlocks, you must release explicit file locks by using the UNLOCK command or closing the file. A deadlock is created when two users attempt to lock one another's files. For example, user A has a file lock on A.DBF, and user B has a file lock on B.DBF. Unless the locks are released before an attempt is made to lock the next file, neither user will be able to place the new lock. It is important, therefore, to release locks as soon as they are no longer needed.

Explicit Record Locking

You can use the RLOCK()/LOCK() function to place explicit record locks in an application. Both forms of the function perform exactly the same way.

The major reason for placing an explicit record lock is to prevent the user from wasting time entering data for a record that cannot be locked. The inventory module of the bicycle shop application presented in Chapter 13 is a good example of code that needs explicit record locks. That code positions the record pointer, stuffs variables with the field values, and then REPLACEs the fields with the edited variables.

Although dBASE IV will place an automatic record lock when the REPLACE statement is encountered, the user's time may be wasted if another user has the record locked already, or if a file lock is already in place on the whole file. In that case, the user would have little choice except to wait for the lock to be cleared, or to abandon the editing that has already taken place.

Included later in this chapter is a portion of the application presented in Chapter 13. The code includes the explicit locking routines necessary to adapt the program for multiusers.

When programming explicit locking routines, you should always lock the record before allowing entry. That way, data integrity is ensured. A limit of 50 locks (file and/or record) are available for each workstation. An attempt to place the 51st lock will trigger an error message.

You can clear explicit record locks by using the UNLOCK command or closing the file.

Using Commands and Functions in Networking

Some commands and functions are to be used only in multiuser applications, or act somewhat differently in a multiuser environment. These commands and functions provide the framework for building applications that lock records and files so that they can be used simultaneously at more than one workstation. The following sections describe each of the commands and functions useful in networking with dBASE IV. Commands and functions used only for networking are marked by an asterisk (*).

BEGIN TRANSACTION...END TRANSACTION

This command creates on disk a transaction log that records all changes made to data files during an operation in which multiple changes are made to one or more records and files. If the transaction cannot be completed because of power failure, file/record unavailability, or some other unforeseen circumstance, the data can be restored to its former condition with the ROLLBACK command.

For more details on the BEGIN TRANSACTION...END TRANSACTION command, refer to the section "Handling Transaction Processing" later in this chapter.

CHANGE/EDIT

The CHANGE and EDIT commands are identical. They provide a full-screen editing window in which the contents of data files can be modified. In a multiuser environment, either command will display one of the following messages in the status bar:

Exclusive use	Means that the file is opened in EXCLUSIVE mode
File locked	Shows that the file has a file lock in place
Read only	Means that the file cannot be written to
Record locked	Shows the record lock status
Record unlocked	Shows the record lock status

To issue an explicit record lock in the editing window, just press Ctrl-O. Pressing Ctrl-O again will release the lock.

If the record's contents change while the record is displayed on-screen (when a record lock is applied), the screen is refreshed to show the new contents of the record.

CONVERT*

The CONVERT command alters the structure of a data file so that it can be used with the CHANGE() function, the LKSYS() function, or the SET REFRESH command.

CONVERT adds to the data structure an extra field ranging from 8 to 24 characters in length. Although this field cannot be read directly, it contains information about the date and time any current locks were placed, as well as the name of the user at the workstation where the lock was placed.

The command syntax is

CONVERT [TO <*expN*>]

The default length of the created field is 16. If you set the length to 8, you can then use the SET REFRESH command, check whether the record has been altered with the CHANGE() function, and retrieve the lock times and dates with the LKSYS() function. By specifying a value of 16 or greater, you also will be able to use the LKSYS() function to return the name of the user placing the lock.

DISPLAY/LIST STATUS

In a LAN environment the DISPLAY/LIST STATUS command displays lock information about file and record locks in addition to the normal file and environment information.

DISPLAY/LIST USERS*

The DISPLAY/LIST USERS command displays a list of all the workstations currently logged into dBASE IV in a multiuser environment.

LOGOUT*

The LOGOUT command logs out of the current dBASE IV session. If PROTECT has not been used to initiate log-in procedures, the LOGOUT command returns the user to the dot prompt.

PROTECT

PROTECT is a system administrator's tool for setting data-security parameters. It is used to establish user accounts that include the passwords and group names necessary to log into a multiuser installation of dBASE IV. The PROTECT command is used also to establish user-access levels so that sensitive data cannot be viewed or edited by unauthorized persons. PROTECT must be used before data can be written to disk in an encrypted form.

RESET

The RESET command restores the integrity tag in a data file when a transaction has not been completed. Like the PROTECT command, RESET is a tool of the system administrator or network supervisor and should not be included in an application.

The integrity tag is used to determine whether a transaction failed or whether a ROLLBACK command was unsuccessful.

RETRY

The RETRY command is similar to the RETURN command. The only difference is that RETRY executes again the same command in the calling module, whereas RETURN executes the next line in the module.

Although RETRY is not strictly limited to networking, the command is often handy when an application needs to keep trying to place a lock.

ROLLBACK

ROLLBACK restores data to the condition it was in before a transaction was declared with the BEGIN TRANSACTION command. ROLLBACK can restore only those data files that were changed by a transaction that failed to complete. Two factors can cause a ROLLBACK to be unsuccessful: discrepancies in the contents of a record between its pre-transaction status and its post-transaction status, and a log file that cannot be read.

SET ENCRYPTION

In a network environment the SET ENCRYPTION command determines whether encrypted data can be copied in an unencrypted form. For more information on creating encrypted data files, see the section "Entering File and Field Information" later in the chapter.

SET EXCLUSIVE*

The SET EXCLUSIVE command determines whether files can be opened in a shared mode. If you SET EXCLUSIVE ON, any file opened will be reserved for the EXCLUSIVE use of the person who opened the file. Other users cannot open the file while it is open EXCLUSIVEly.

As mentioned earlier, you can open a file EXCLUSIVEly (regardless of the SET EXCLUSIVE condition) with the EXCLUSIVE clause of the USE command.

SET LOCK ON/off

The SET LOCK ON/off command enables or disables automatic file locking when one of the following commands is issued:

```
APPEND FROM
CALCULATE
COPY
COPY STRUCTURE
COUNT
INDEX
JOIN
LABEL
REPORT
SORT
SUM
TOTAL
```

SET PRINTER

The SET PRINTER command redirects output to a network or local printer. See the entry in your *Language Reference* manual, supplied with dBASE IV, for the exact syntax you should use for your particular network software.

SET REFRESH

SET REFRESH determines the number of seconds between screen updates (which show changes made to data) when the user views data on the BROWSE or EDIT work surfaces. The default value is 0, which disables screen refreshment entirely. Acceptable values range from 0 to 3,600.

SET REPROCESS*

The SET REPROCESS command specifies the number of times that a command which triggers a network error is retried before an error message is displayed. You can intercept the triggered error condition with the ON ERROR command.

The default value is 0. Acceptable values range from -1 to 32,000. Setting the value to -1 causes dBASE IV to retry until the command is executed. If the value is set to 0 and no ON ERROR command is active, dBASE IV displays an error message and then retries the operation an infinite number of times. The only way to back out of that situation is for the user to press the Esc key.

UNLOCK*

UNLOCK terminates record and file locks so that other users can gain control of records and files that have been locked. The command syntax is

    UNLOCK [ALL/IN <alias>]

A lock remains in place until released by the user/workstation originating the lock. Locks can be released only when the UNLOCK command is used or when the file is closed.

USE

In a network environment you can add the EXCLUSIVE clause to the USE command to open a file in EXCLUSIVE mode regardless of the SET EXCLUSIVE condition. Six commands require that you have EXCLUSIVE use of the data file before those commands can be executed:

    INSERT [BLANK]
    MODIFY (all forms)
    PACK
    REINDEX
    RESET
    ZAP

ACCESS()*

The ACCESS() function determines the user's access level, which is specified with the PROTECT command. You can use this function to limit a user's rights so that only authorized persons can perform sensitive operations. Consider the following example:

    IF ACCESS() > 4
       @10,10 SAY "This routine is not available to you. Press any key."
       null = INKEY(0)
       RETURN
    ENDIF

CHANGE()*

To use the CHANGE() function, you must first CONVERT the data file. The field added to the data structure by the CONVERT command can be used to learn whether another user has altered the record's contents since the last time the record was displayed. If the record has been altered, the CHANGE() function will read the alteration and return a value of True.

COMPLETED()

The COMPLETED() function determines (by returning a logical True) whether a transaction begun with the BEGIN TRANSACTION command has finished. This function returns a True value also if ROLLBACK has been successfully completed.

ERROR()

The ERROR() function can be used by the active ON ERROR command to determine what error condition exists so that corrective action can be taken. Appendix A of the *Language Reference* manual, supplied with dBASE IV, contains a complete listing of the error numbers associated with triggered error conditions.

FLOCK()

The FLOCK() function, with its companion locking functions RLOCK() and LOCK(), is unusual because it is a native dBASE IV function that performs an action and returns a value.

When executed, FLOCK() attempts to apply a file lock to the data file located in the current work area. (To apply a lock in another work area, you specify an alias as the argument between the parentheses.) If the locking attempt is successful, the FLOCK() function returns a value of True. Look at the following example:

```
IF FLOCK()
    @10,10 SAY "The file is locked."
ELSE
    @10,10 SAY "There is no file lock placed."
ENDIF
```

ISMARKED()*

The ISMARKED() function returns a True value if the file is currently being processed by a BEGIN TRANSACTION construct. If the operation of the application might cause a transaction being processed to fail, you should test to make sure that a transaction on the file is not in progress (initiated by another user) before allowing the program to proceed.

LKSYS()*

The LKSYS() function returns one of three available pieces of information (time, date, and log-in name) about a record or file lock stored in the _dbaselock field. This field is added to a data file by the CONVERT command. The syntax of this function is

    LKSYS(<*expN*>)

For the function's argument, the acceptable range is from 1 to 3, in which

   1 returns the time the lock was placed.
   2 returns the date the lock was placed.
   3 returns the log-in name of the user who placed the lock.

If the length of the _dbaselock field is 8, the name is returned as a null string.

MESSAGE()

A companion to the ERROR() function, MESSAGE() returns a character string containing an error message associated with the error condition that has been triggered.

NETWORK()*

The NETWORK() function returns a logical value indicating whether the application is being run in a copy of dBASE IV installed for a multiuser environment. If the copy has been installed for a multiuser environment, this function returns a value of True; otherwise, the return value is False.

RLOCK()/LOCK()*

Both forms of this function are identical and share the same syntax:

    RLOCK([<*expC*>,<*alias*>]/[<*alias*>])

    LOCK([<*expC*>,<*alias*>]/[<*alias*>])

The argument *expC* can be a list of record numbers to be locked. With a maximum of 50 allowed, the record numbers are separated by commas. The *alias* argument is used to apply the lock in another work area. If no argument is given, the function attempts to lock the current record in the current work area.

Locks placed with this function are not released by subsequent RLOCK()s. These locks can be released only when the UNLOCK command or FLOCK() function is used, or when the file is closed.

Consider the following example:

```
IF RLOCK()
   @10,10 SAY "The record is locked."
```

```
ELSE
    @10,10 SAY "There is no record lock placed."
```

ROLLBACK()

If the last ROLLBACK command was successful, the ROLLBACK() function returns a value of True; otherwise, the function returns a False.

USER()*

The USER() function determines the user name of a workstation logged onto a dBASE IV system that has been PROTECTed. If PROTECT has not been run, the USER() function returns a null string.

Programming Explicit Locks

The RLOCK() and FLOCK() locking functions are an unusual hybrid of command and function. RLOCK() and FLOCK() are used syntactically just like functions, and each returns a value. Yet RLOCK() and FLOCK() both resemble commands, for each function performs an action. They also are the tools used to place explicit locks. Remember that you can substitute LOCK() for RLOCK(); both functions are identical.

Because functions cannot be placed on a command line by themselves, the locking functions are usually placed in an IF statement. Look at this example in which a file is locked:

```
IF FLOCK()
    @10,10 SAY "The file is locked."
ELSE
    @10,10 SAY "There is no file lock placed. Press any key to abort."
    null = INKEY(0)
    CLOSE DATABASES
    RETURN
ENDIF
```

Locking a record is just as simple. You simply substitute the RLOCK() function and the word *record*.

Programming explicit locking routines for multiuser applications is similar to writing code for trapping errors. Essentially the locking process is just another form of error trapping. You make a request for a lock and then take appropriate actions if the lock is refused.

When an attempt to place locks on files or records fails, a dBASE IV error is triggered. Such errors can be identified by the `ERROR()` function and trapped with an `ON ERROR` statement in the program. The most common errors you will encounter are these:

1. ERROR 108 `File in use by another`

   This error occurs if you attempt to place a file lock when another user has a current file or record lock in place.

2. ERROR 109 `Record in use by another`

   This error occurs if you attempt to place a record lock when another user has a current file lock or a lock on that same record in place.

3. ERROR 110 `File must be opened in exclusive mode`

   This error occurs when a command is issued that requires EXCLUSIVE use of a data file. The condition is considered a bug in the program.

4. ERROR 217 `Lock table is full`

   This error is triggered when more than 50 locks are attempted to be placed. Again, the condition is considered a bug in the program.

Of these four error conditions, you must trap errors 108 and 109, for they are situational. In other words, you have no control over who tries to lock what records and files once the application is installed on the network. You can only trap the condition and then allow the user to back out gracefully without affecting data integrity.

To write good multiuser code, you must have a sense of timing. In other words, you need to know when to apply the lock. When you are writing code that needs to lock a file or a record, you should place and confirm the lock before painting the information on-screen.

Suppose, for example, that you are writing a routine which allows a user to edit customer records. You will want to place the record lock before you allow the user to make any editing keystrokes. That way, any changes the user makes are not lost because of the failure of the locking procedure. The programming steps you should follow are these:

1. Take entry for a customer account number.

2. SEEK the file to make sure that such a record exists.

3. If the record is found, attempt the lock before taking entry into the fields.

Otherwise, a user will be understandably annoyed after typing a large chunk of information and then being told either to wait for a lock to clear, or to lose the information just typed.

If a user has to wait for a lock to clear, the user will be wasting valuable time, and the application's overall productivity will suffer. In your programming, be sure to let the user know that the lock cannot be placed so that the user can go to another record that needs editing.

Remember that the APPEND BLANK command will automatically lock the record that is created; you do not have to issue an explicit record lock. The only potential problem arises when another user has a file lock applied. In that case, the APPEND BLANK will trigger error 108 as read by ERROR().

Besides having a sense of timing, a programmer needs to have a sense of persistence. That is, you need to know how long to let a user wait before a locking request is either granted or refused. If you make the wait too long, the user may think that the system has hanged and thus do something stupid, like rebooting the computer. Of course, the results can be disastrous—scrambled data and index files, corrupted current record, and so on. A good rule of thumb is to allow the user to try for the lock for 5 to 10 seconds. If the persistence factor needs to be longer than 10 seconds, you will want to paint a message telling the user to wait.

You set the rate of persistence with the SET REPROCESS command, as in the following command line:

```
SET REPROCESS TO 15
```

This command tells dBASE IV to try the lock 15 times before triggering the error condition.

Modifying the Inventory Module for Multiusers

The code at the end of this section (see fig. 15.1) is the inventory module from the bicycle shop application presented in Chapter 13. Here the code has been modified to run in a multiuser environment. All the locking is done explicitly.

The first line (a window definition) creates the window named err, which is used to put file- and record-locking error messages on-screen. Although the DEFINE WINDOW command is included here, it would normally be found in the menu-creation module.

SET REPROCESS is included so that the example will work properly. This command would usually be found in a higher-level module.

No changes are needed in the section of code that paints the screen.

The ADD_INV procedure for adding records is essentially the same as the original. An ON ERROR command has been added for calling an error-trapping routine and for passing a parameter to that routine, telling it that an APPEND has failed. The only other change to the code is the addition of the UNLOCK command before the LOOP command. This UNLOCK clears any record locks already in place, freeing the records for use by other users, as well as eliminating the possibility of a too-many-locks error.

The ED_INV procedure for editing records is essentially unchanged also, the modifications being additive in nature. In this case ON ERROR has been added to tell the error trap that the failure was in locking a record. The code to find the needed record is unchanged.

Notice that the added IF RLOCK() statement is the key to networking this code. A record lock is attempted at this point. If the lock fails, the code terminates the module and returns to the menu. The values are not even placed in the entry variables until the lock is confirmed. This way, you assure the user that an entry will not be wasted for lack of a lock.

The rest of the code in the ED_INV procedure is unchanged until the UNLOCK command. This UNLOCK serves exactly the same purpose as in the ADD_INV module.

The necessary changes to the DEL_INV procedure for deleting records are similar to the changes in the ED_INV procedure. The difference is that DEL_INV needs two commands with different locking requirements. Because the scope of the DELETE command is just one record, DELETE needs only a record lock in order to mark the record for deletion. The PACK command, however, requires a full file lock.

At this point, you need to make a design decision. You can include the PACK in the module and lock the file; or you can make the PACK part of a separate application that is run at the end of each day, and lock just the affected record. If you choose the second method, you will want to SET DELETED ON, which will cause most of the dBASE IV commands to ignore records marked but not yet actually deleted.

The questions you need to consider are the following:

How big is the file?
How often is data deleted?
How many workstations use this same application/data file?

If your respective answers are a small file, seldom deleted, and just a few users, you will want to keep the PACK in the module. If, however, your answers are a file with many records, data often deleted, and five or more users, you will want to put the PACK in a housekeeping routine for the database administrator to run once a day.

The next section of code is primarily a DO CASE construct that passes the messages to the error-trapping routine based on the number of the error, as read by ERROR(), and the parameter passed by the ON ERROR statement.

```
*****  Program: INVEN.PRG  *****
* Modified for network use

DEFINE WINDOW err FROM 5,10 TO 10,70     && A window for displaying
                                         && messages due to lock
                                         && failure

ACTIVATE WINDOW inv
@0,2 TO 2,48 DOUBLE
DO in_scr
SET REPROCESS TO 20  && Sets the number of lock requests to be
                     && executed before an error is triggered
ACTIVATE MENU inv_men
DEACTIVATE WINDOW inv


* There are no changes to the screen-painting module.
PROCEDURE in_scr

PUBLIC v_part, v_desc, v_cost, v_sale_pr, v_in_stock, v_b_order

STORE 0 TO v_cost, v_sale_pr, v_in_stock, v_b_order
STORE SPACE(7) TO v_part
STORE SPACE(15) TO v_desc

@ 5, 18 SAY "    Enter part number:" GET v_part
@ 7, 18 SAY "    Enter description:" GET v_desc
@ 9, 18 SAY "Enter wholesale price:" GET v_cost PICTURE '999.99'
@11, 18 SAY "      Enter sale price:" GET v_sale_pr PICTURE '9999.99'
@13, 18 SAY "Enter number of items in stock:" GET v_in_stock ;
                                         PICTURE '9999'
@15, 18 SAY "Enter number of items backordered:" GET v_b_order ;
                                         PICTURE '9999'
```

Fig. 15.1

The modified code for INVEN.PRG.

Fig. continues

Fig. continued

```
CLEAR GETS
RETURN


PROCEDURE add_inv

USE invent ORDER part

flag = ' '      && A variable to determine whether the append is
DO WHILE .T.    && rejected

ON ERROR DO lok_err WITH "append"    && Lets the error module know
                                     && that the error was in
                                     && APPENDing
   @ 5, 18 SAY "   Enter part number:" GET v_part VALID NO_DUP() ;
              ERROR "Sorry that part number is already on file."
   READ
   ON ERROR
   IF flag = '*'
      EXIT
   ENDIF
   @ 7, 18 SAY "   Enter description:" GET v_desc
   @ 9, 18 SAY "Enter wholesale price:" GET v_cost PICTURE '999.99'
   @11, 18 SAY "     Enter sale price:" GET v_sale_pr PICTURE '9999.99'
   @13, 18 SAY "Enter number of items in stock:" GET v_in_stock ;
                                           PICTURE '9999'
   @15, 18 SAY "Enter number of items backordered:" GET v_b_order ;
                                           PICTURE '9999'
   READ
   IF LASTKEY() = 27
      DELETE       && Since the record exists, it will have to
                   && be deleted.
      EXIT
   ENDIF
   REPLACE PART WITH v_part, ;
           DESC WITH v_desc, ;
           COST WITH v_cost, ;
           SALE_PR WITH v_sale_pr, ;
```

Fig. continues

Fig. continued

```
          IN_STOCK WITH v_in_stock, ;
          B_ORDER WITH v_b_order
    STORE ' ' TO conf
    UNLOCK
    @17,14 SAY "Do you want to add another item?  (Y/N)-->" GET conf
    READ
    IF UPPER(conf) = 'Y'
       UNLOCK            && This releases the lock so that another
                         && user can have the record and eliminates
                         && a "too many locks" error.

       @16,0 CLEAR
       DO in_scr
       LOOP
    ELSE
       @16,0 CLEAR
       EXIT
    ENDIF
ENDDO
CLOSE DATABASES
DO in_scr
RETURN


FUNCTION no_dup

SEEK v_part
IF EOF()
   APPEND BLANK
   RETURN .T.
ELSE
   RETURN .F.
ENDIF


PROCEDURE ed_inv

USE invent ORDER part

DO WHILE .T.
```

Fig. continues

Fig. continued

```
ON ERROR DO lok_err WITH "record"     && Lets the error module know
                                       && that the error occurred
                                       && while locking a record
    @ 5, 18 SAY "   Enter part number:" GET v_part VALID SEEK(v_part) ;
              ERROR "Sorry that part number is not on file."
    READ
    ON ERROR
    IF LASTKEY() = 27
       EXIT
    ENDIF
    IF RLOCK()
       v_desc = desc
       v_cost = cost
       v_sale_pr = sale_pr
       v_in_stock = in_stock
       v_b_order = b_order
    ELSE
       EXIT
    ENDIF
    @ 7, 18 SAY "   Enter description:" GET v_desc
    @ 9, 18 SAY "Enter wholesale price:" GET v_cost PICTURE '999.99'
    @11, 18 SAY "    Enter sale price:" GET v_sale_pr PICTURE '9999.99'
    @13, 18 SAY "Enter number of items in stock:" GET v_in_stock ;
                                         PICTURE '9999'
    @15, 18 SAY "Enter number of items backordered:" GET v_b_order ;
                                         PICTURE '9999'
    @17,0 SAY PADC("To abort without saving press ESCAPE.",77)
    READ
    IF LASTKEY() = 27
       @16,0 CLEAR
       EXIT
    ENDIF
    REPLACE PART WITH v_part, ;
            DESC WITH v_desc, ;
            COST WITH v_cost, ;
            SALE_PR WITH v_sale_pr, ;
            IN_STOCK WITH v_in_stock, ;
            B_ORDER WITH v_b_order
```

Fig. continues

Fig. continued

```
      STORE ' ' TO conf
      @16,0 CLEAR
      @17,14 SAY "Do you want to edit another item?  (Y/N)-->" GET conf
      READ
      IF UPPER(conf) = 'Y'
         UNLOCK
         @16,0 CLEAR
         DO in_scr
         LOOP
      ELSE
         @16,0 CLEAR
         EXIT
      ENDIF
   ENDDO
   CLOSE DATABASES
   DO in_scr
   RETURN


   PROCEDURE del_inv

   USE invent ORDER part

   DO WHILE .T.

   ON ERROR DO lok_err WITH "file"  && Lets the error module know
                                    && that the error occurred while
                                    && locking a file
      @ 5, 18 SAY "    Enter part number:" GET v_part VALID SEEK(v_part) ;
               ERROR "Sorry that part number is not on file."
      READ
      ON ERROR
      IF LASTKEY() = 27
      @16,0 CLEAR
         EXIT
      ENDIF
      IF FLOCK()
         v_desc = desc
         v_cost = cost
```

Fig. continues

Fig. continued

```
        v_sale_pr = sale_pr
        v_in_stock = in_stock
        v_b_order = b_order
    ELSE
        EXIT
    ENDIF
    @ 7, 18 SAY "    Enter description:" GET v_desc
    @ 9, 18 SAY "Enter wholesale price:" GET v_cost PICTURE '999.99'
    @11, 18 SAY "     Enter sale price:" GET v_sale_pr PICTURE '9999.99'
    @13, 18 SAY "Enter number of items in stock:" GET v_in_stock ;
                                          PICTURE '9999'
    @15, 18 SAY "Enter number of items backordered:" GET v_b_order ;
                                          PICTURE '9999'
    CLEAR GETS
    STORE ' ' TO conf
    @16,0 CLEAR
    @17,14 SAY "Do you want to delete this item?  (Y/N)-->" GET conf
    READ
    IF UPPER(conf) = 'Y'
        @16,0 CLEAR
        DELETE
* The PACK command requires the file lock instead of just a
* record lock. You may want to SET DELETED ON so that marked
* records are ignored and leave the PACK to a separate utility
* that is run daily by the system administrator. By arranging
* things that way, you could just get a record lock, which would
* be easier to get because the file lock will be refused if any
* other user has a record locked at the time. In other words, the
* system would have to be almost deserted in order to get the
* lock.
        PACK
        EXIT
    ELSE
        @16,0 CLEAR
        EXIT
    ENDIF
ENDDO
CLOSE DATABASES
DO in_scr
RETURN
```

Fig. continues

Fig. continued

```
* This procedure provides the user interface and code necessary
* to handle rejected locking requests.
PROCEDURE lok_err

ACTIVATE WINDOW err
PARAMETERS specific

DO CASE

   CASE ERROR() = 108 .AND. specific = "append"
      @2,5 SAY "Another user has the file locked. You cannot"
      @3,5 SAY "APPEND a new record at this time."
      @4,5 SAY "Press R to retry, any other key to abort."
      WAIT TO which
      IF UPPER(which) = 'R'
         DEACTIVATE WINDOW err
         RETRY
      ELSE
         flag = '*'
         DEACTIVATE WINDOW err
         RETURN
      ENDIF

   CASE ERROR() = 108 .AND. specific = "record"
      @2,5 SAY "Another user has the file locked. You cannot"
      @3,5 SAY "lock a record at this time."
      @4,5 SAY "Press R to retry, any other key to abort."
      WAIT TO which
      IF UPPER(which) = 'R'
         DEACTIVATE WINDOW err
         RETRY
      ELSE
         DEACTIVATE WINDOW err
         RETURN
      ENDIF

   CASE ERROR() = 108 .AND. specific = "file"
      @2,5 SAY "Another user has the file locked. You cannot"
      @3,5 SAY "lock the file at this time."
```

Fig. continues

Fig. continued

```
      @4,5 SAY "Press R to retry, any other key to abort."
      WAIT TO which
      IF UPPER(which) = 'R'
         DEACTIVATE WINDOW err
         RETRY
      ELSE
         DEACTIVATE WINDOW err
         RETURN
      ENDIF
   CASE ERROR() = 109 .AND. specific = "record"
      @2,5 SAY "Another user has this record locked. You cannot"
      @3,5 SAY "lock this record at this time."
      @4,5 SAY "Press R to retry, any other key to abort."
      WAIT TO which
      IF UPPER(which) = 'R'
         DEACTIVATE WINDOW err
         RETRY
      ELSE
         DEACTIVATE WINDOW err
         RETURN
      ENDIF

   CASE ERROR() = 109 .AND. specific = "file"
      @2,5 SAY "Another user has the file locked. You cannot"
      @3,5 SAY "lock a record at this time."
      @4,5 SAY "Press R to retry, any other key to abort."
      WAIT TO which
      IF UPPER(which) = 'R'
         DEACTIVATE WINDOW err
         RETRY
      ELSE
         DEACTIVATE WINDOW err
         RETURN
      ENDIF

   OTHERWISE
      @2,5 SAY MESSAGE()   && Generic dBASE IV error message
      @3,5 SAY "See your network administrator for instructions."
      @4,5 SAY "Press any key to abort."
      WAIT TO which
      DEACTIVATE WINDOW err
      RETURN
ENDCASE
```

Handling Multiple Data Files on a Network

Handling multiple data files on a network does not pose any great problems. The procedures are exactly the same as those presented in the modified inventory module shown in figure 15.1. A problem may arise, however, during the editing of multiple-record sets. Consider, for example, an invoice with a parent file and one or more records in the child file.

Suppose that a user is editing the item records in an invoice. When he gets to the third item and finds that it is locked for some reason, he cannot complete his editing task. One programming solution to such a problem is to have the edit done as a transaction and perform a ROLLBACK in case of an error. The problem with this approach, however, is that editing time can be potentially wasted because all the editing will have to be redone. Imagine how frustrated a user may become if three or four tries are required to finish the editing.

A much better solution is available to the programmer. You simply insist that all actions on child records require that the parent record be locked beforehand. If in every module in the application the parent record is locked before attempts to lock any of the child records are granted, then requests for record locks in the child file will never be refused—unless a record lock is slipped in between the time that one record is UNLOCKed and the next record is locked.

To eliminate that possibility, you can insist that in every module of the application the parent file be locked before the child record can be locked. If a user has a parent file locked while editing the child records, another user's request for a file lock of the parent file will be refused. Because the lock on the parent file is denied, the application will not even try to lock the child file.

Using Semaphore Locks

The dBASE IV file- and record-locking procedures apply only to data files and their associated indexes. Other types of files are therefore vulnerable to multiuser collisions. Some examples are memory variable files, window files, macro libraries, and text files created with the SET PRINTER TO FILE command.

To avoid multiuser collisions with such files, you can create a small data file, called a semaphore database, that contains one record for each of the files you need to protect. This file is called a *semaphore* because you use it to flag any potential collisions over nondatabase files.

To access a .MEM file, for example, an application must first open the semaphore database and then lock the record you have created to correspond with that .MEM file. These steps are necessary before the application can perform the commands needed to access the .MEM file. Look at the following example:

```
USE semi_4
LOCATE FOR flag = "invno.mem"   && As there are only a few
                                && records, LOCATE is plenty
                                && fast.
IF RLOCK()
   RESTORE FROM invno.mem ADDITIVE
   v_inv = v_inv + 1
   SET SAFETY OFF
   SAVE ALL LIKE v_inv TO invno.mem
   SET SAFETY ON
   v_inv_no = STR(v_inv,5,0)
   UNLOCK
ELSE
   DO no_lock WITH "invno.mem"
   CLOSE DATABASES
   RETURN
ENDIF
```

In this example, the application attempts to lock the semaphore record before accessing the .MEM file. The lock is rejected if another user is accessing the same .MEM file, and the application is aborted. In actual practice (assuming that the SET REPROCESS level is high enough), the lock is seldom rejected because reading and writing the .MEM file take only a few seconds. That should be enough time to let the other user's lock clear before the error condition is triggered. The important thing is that both users do not hit the file at the same moment.

Using PROTECT To Provide Data Security on Networks

The PROTECT command is intended solely for the use of the network supervisor. PROTECT invokes a menu-driven work surface in which the supervisor can set up three levels of data security within the dBASE IV system: log-in security, file and field access, and data encryption. These types of data security are discussed in greater detail in later sections of this chapter.

Log-In Security

Log-in security restricts access to the system by unauthorized users. Anyone wanting to use the system must enter a log-in name, a password, and a group name. The log-in name identifies the user. The password verifies that the user is authorized. And the group name identifies which data files are available to that user.

In addition, a user is given an access level, which is a number from 1 to 8. This number determines which features of dBASE IV or what portions of an application are accessible to that user. The highest level of access is 1; the lowest level is 8.

File and Field Access

Data files are arranged in groups, and a particular group of data files is available to users whose log-in procedures include that group. Fields within data files can be restricted to three access levels: full access (FULL), read-only access (R/O), and no access (NONE). If you specify log-in names without specifying any files, all files in any subdirectory that the user can access will be available.

Data Encryption

Because dBASE IV data files are, by default, written in ASCII on the disk, any sufficiently educated person can open a data file outside the control of dBASE IV and read the information in that file. The PROTECT command enables you to encrypt data files so that they can be read by authorized users only. Someone opening an encrypted file outside dBASE IV will see only gibberish.

Knowing When To PROTECT

Often the job of administering a network operating system falls to the person or department responsible for the programming in an organization. Let's assume for the moment that you will be in charge of the network, or that you will be supervising the person in charge. Several issues require careful consideration before you assign security measures to the dBASE IV installation.

A number of network operating systems, such as Novell's NetWare or 3Com +, have security systems with some of the same features offered by PROTECT in dBASE IV. For example, NetWare provides an elaborate set of security measures that restrict access to files. The security system determines whether files can be opened by more than one user at a time, and also decides which users can write in the files as well as erase them. These levels of security may work fine for your installation; in fact, they may even supersede any settings you establish with the PROTECT command. A file that has been made unavailable to certain users will not become accessible simply because you set the file to be available through PROTECT. The network used by your organization, then, will help you determine whether to PROTECT your applications.

Network software also provides log-in procedures. On a network operating system level, you can thus provide users with log-in scripts that automatically call dBASE IV and begin to run an application. You simply include in the log-in procedure the command

> DBASE *app_name*

If the application terminates with the QUIT command (which does not return the user to the dot prompt), the network log-in process can effectively restrict the user to performing only those tasks included in the application.

In that case your programming becomes a data-security measure, for an application gives access to only those files and fields explicitly included in the application. If the application does not allow the user to get to the dot prompt, and if error conditions are trapped well enough so that the user cannot slip out somehow to the dot prompt, your system will be fairly secure.

The issue of data encryption is a little thornier on a network operating system. Network security measures allow the network supervisor to restrict file access for individual users. You need to decide whether such protection will sufficiently thwart mischief and vandalism. The essential question you must ask is, How secure is the network itself? If the network is secure and users are not operating in an ad hoc manner at the dot prompt, you may decide not to use the PROTECT command in dBASE IV.

Keep in mind, however, that lax network security (especially if control of the network rests with another department) can open your dBASE IV system to abuse. Disgruntled or just plain nosy users can wreak havoc on an unprotected database management system. Unfortunately, office politics and the questionable business ethics of a few unscrupulous users may require that you provide additional safeguards, especially where sensitive data is concerned.

Using the PROTECT command to set up database security has several advantages. For one thing, the command provides the only complete protection for the system when users are performing tasks at either the Control Center or the dot prompt.

Although most programmers prefer to restrict users to running applications, many users (especially those with some dBASE background) will want to work on a less restrained basis. The solution is usually a compromise. Low-level users who have little or no background are restricted to running applications, whereas experienced users are given the freedom to operate from the Control Center and the dot prompt—but only on the files they own. In this kind of multiuser environment, the PROTECT command is certainly recommended.

Another advantage to using PROTECT is that data encryption is available only through this command. Encrypting data can be your only effective safeguard when network security is inadequate, or when users have the bad habit of sharing their passwords with other users.

If an unauthorized person gets hold of a supervisor's password, data is available to that person for the taking. dBASE IV is widely used in business and government to keep track of a host of sensitive information ranging from employee records and pricing information to bank examiner records, medical records, and information relating to the national defense. To leave this information unguarded when data-security tools are handy and easy to use is inexcusable.

Properly PROTECTing a database management system also can reduce your workload. Instead of having to maintain several different versions of an application in order to deny important routines to unauthorized users, you can use the ACCESS() function to determine whether a particular user is authorized to perform certain actions. Unless the PROTECT command is used, the ACCESS() function will always return a value of 0. Suppose that you have written a personnel application in which only certain users have the authority to make changes to salary fields. Instead of having to compile a separate application for this process (or including another level of passwords in the application), you can have the application check the ACCESS() level of the user before allowing the procedure to run. Look at the following example:

```
CASE BAR() = 3

   IF ACCESS() > 2
      @10,10 SAY ;
         "This routine is not available to you. Press any key."
      null = INKEY(0)
   ELSE
      DO sal_chg
   ENDIF
```

This sample code, which is extracted from a DO CASE construct, effectively rejects a request for access by any user who does not have an ACCESS() level of 1 or 2. This way, you can rely on the log-in process to identify unauthorized persons and thus avoid bogging down an application with internal passwords. Remember that users are only human; if they are required to keep too many passwords in their heads, they will either write down the passwords where they can be stolen, or start using the same password for everything. The latter case is especially dangerous, for anyone who obtains that password will be able to get into all areas accessible to the password holder.

Installing Data Security with PROTECT

To install data security with PROTECT, you will need to access the dot prompt and issue the command PROTECT. If you have not previously installed protection, you will be prompted first to enter a password and then to enter the password a second time just to confirm that you can repeat it. After that, you will be presented with a log-in setup screen in which you can make and save your security assignments.

Once you have saved security assignments to disk, any user who tries to start dBASE IV will be presented with a log-in screen in which that user must enter a log-in name, a password, and a group name before starting the program.

Keep in mind that you can use PROTECT on a single-user system to enhance security; PROTECT is not limited to network installations.

Entering User Information

Figure 15.2 shows the **Users** dialog box of the PROTECT work surface in which you make security assignments. In this first menu, you provide the log-in name for a user, assign the user a password, and include the user in a group.

Because log-in names can access only the files in a particular group, you may have to assign two or more log-in names to the same user. Keep this in mind as you assign names.

If SQL commands will be processed on the system, you need to create for the supervisory user a log-in name of SQLDBA (SQL database administrator). Only that log-in name can invoke the GRANT and REVOKE commands, which control access to SQL.

When you assign passwords, be arbitrary. Don't let users pick their own passwords, for they will invariably choose something familiar (family names, street names, and so on). Unfortunately, such passwords are easily guessed by co-workers. You should assign passwords that are entirely random and that also include non-alpha characters (such as &, %, #, +, and =). One of the best password schemes is used by CompuServe, which requires that each password be two words separated by a non-alpha character. For example, "fish*carpet" is acceptable. You have 16 spaces for each password; try to use most of them.

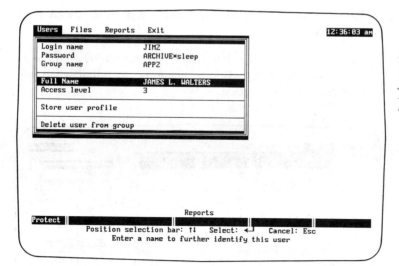

Fig. 15.2

The work surface for making security assignments.

The third line of the menu lets you assign the user to a group. Groups are used to control access to sets of files. A data file can be assigned to just one group, which usually includes the files needed for a particular application. Again, you may need to assign more than one log-in name to someone who needs to access several groups of files.

In the next section of the menu, you enter the user's full name and access level. If you need to give more than one log-in name to a user, this prompt can be handy for keeping several log-in names straight. The **Full Name** prompt is the only optional one on the menu.

The access level you assign to a user will determine what permissions are granted to that user if you assign file and field protections through the **Files** dialog box. The assigned access level also will become the return value of the ACCESS() function whenever that user is logged into the system.

To save the user information to disk, you highlight **Store user profile** and press Enter. To delete a user from your security assignments, just enter the user's log-in name, highlight **Delete user from group**, and press Enter.

Entering File and Field Information

When you highlight the **Files** option at the top of the setup screen, a pull-down dialog box appears. In this box, you can provide information about the files you want to make available to users of the system.

To begin entering information about a file, just highlight **New file** and press Enter. Then you can choose a data file from a POPUP menu of file names. Once you have highlighted your selection, press Enter. The screen should look similar to the one shown in figure 15.3.

The second line of the **Files** dialog box lets you assign the file to a group. As indicated earlier, a file can belong to only one group. Be sure that when you assign files, you group them by application.

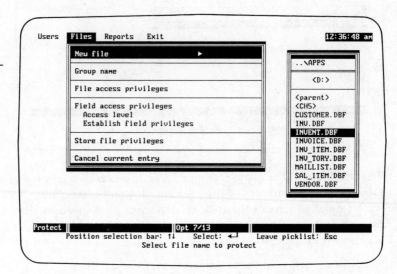

Fig. 15.3

*The POPUP menu
listing file names.*

The next step is to assign file-access privileges. When you highlight **File access privileges**, you will be presented with a POPUP menu similar to that shown in figure 15.4. In this POPUP, you can set the access levels required for the following types of privileges:

Read privilege	The ability to look at data
Update privilege	The ability to modify data
Extend privilege	The ability to add new records to the file
Delete privilege	The ability to remove records from the file

By default, each of these privileges is set to 8, allowing all users each type of access to the data file. If you set the access level of one type of privilege to 4, only those users whose access level is 1, 2, 3, or 4 will be able to perform that particular action on the file. Because 8 valid access levels are available, you can establish 8 categories of users, depending on your specific security needs. Figure 15.4 shows some sample assignments for these file-access privileges.

Next in the dialog box is the **Field access privileges** prompt. As soon as the process for assigning file-access privileges is completed, you will be positioned

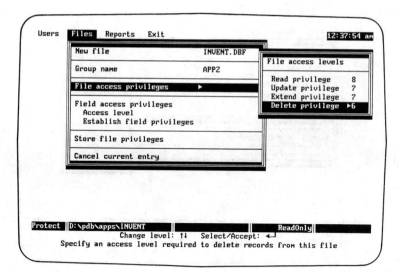

Fig. 15.4

Assigning file-access privileges.

at the **Access level** prompt. Here you enter each of the field-access levels, in turn, and you set the individual field privileges for each of the access levels by pressing the space bar to rotate through the settings. Figure 15.5 shows the type of display you can expect, with some sample assignments indicated. Three settings for field-access privileges are available:

FULL   The user may read and write to the field.
R/O   The user may read but not edit the contents of the field.
NONE   The user may not access the field in any manner.

If an application is written so that a user is able to access a field for which that user does not have the proper ACCESS() level, an error message will be triggered. For example, if a user's ACCESS() level causes a field's privilege level to be NONE and the application tries to address this field, a Variable not found error will result. If this condition occurs, you should consider it a bug, for your responsibility is to make sure that the access levels are properly assigned for the application.

After you have entered the privilege settings for each of the eight field-access levels, just highlight **Store** and press Enter.

Note that you can establish field-access levels for only nine files at a time, for dBASE IV can handle the information necessary to encrypt the data for only nine files at once. If you need to establish settings for more than nine files, move to the **Exit** dialog box and choose **Save**. The files you have specified thus far will be processed. You can then move back to the **Files** dialog box and continue adding files to the protection scheme.

Fig. 15.5

*Assigning field-
access privileges.*

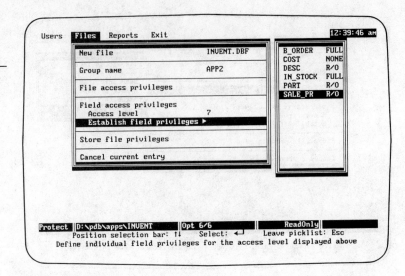

To remove a file from the security assignments, call up the file name at the
New file prompt and answer Yes to **Overwrite**. Then highlight **Cancel** and
press Enter.

Once you have saved your file and field specifications to disk, an encrypted
form of each data file is created with the extension .CRP. To put a file into use,
you follow these steps:

1. Make a backup of the unencrypted .DBF file so that you can later
   modify the structure if needed. Encrypted files cannot be accessed
   with the `MODIFY STRUCTURE` command.

2. At the DOS prompt, copy the .CRP file over the .DBF file. For
   example, type

   ```
   COPY ACCTS.CRP ACCTS.DBF
   ```

3. Delete the .CRP file.

4. Encrypt the index files by opening the data file and all associated
   indexes and then issue the `REINDEX` command.

The data will now be encrypted.

Please understand that the data encryption techniques used in dBASE IV do *not*
reflect the Department of Defense's state-of-the-art technology. Data encryption
depends on an algorithm that takes a semirandom key (in the case of dBASE IV,
the key is the group name installed with `PROTECT`) and uses that key to
scramble the data into seemingly random ASCII characters. To unscramble the
file, a vandal would need only the file and the group name (the key) in order to

unencrypt the file. Moreover, anyone who has the ability—for example, through a stolen password—to access the file from the dot prompt can SET ENCRYPTION OFF and copy the file into an unencrypted state.

To ensure the safety of your data, passwords and other security measures for network operating systems are needed in addition to encryption. Remember that any *one* security measure can be defeated by a dedicated vandal. You must provide several levels of security so that stealing sensitive data will not be worth the effort.

Reporting on PROTECT

Two reports are available for double-checking any assignments you have made. When you access the **Reports** dialog box, two options appear: **User information** and **File information**.

If you select **User information**, a report will be printed providing detailed information about all the users that have been given log-in scripts. If you select **File information**, a report will be printed providing detailed information about the assignments made for each of the different file- and field-access privileges. These reports can be directed to either the printer or the screen.

Exiting PROTECT

The **Exit** menu provides you with three choices: **Save**, **Abandon**, and **Exit**. **Save** writes protections to the disk and then remains in PROTECT. You use this prompt if you have more than nine files that need processing. **Abandon** aborts any changes you have made since the last save. Finally, **Exit** writes protections to the disk and then returns you to the dot prompt.

Protecting PROTECT

In the subdirectory from which dBASE IV is started, security assignments made with PROTECT are written to two files: DBSYSTEM.DB and DBSYSTEM.SQL. You must take precautions with these two files, for they are written to disk simply with the DOS attribute ARCHIVE. Anyone wanting to defeat your security measures needs only to delete these files in order to bypass the log-in routine and obtain full access to the system.

Consequently, you need to use the network operating system security to set the attributes of these files so that only the highest-level supervisor can delete or modify them. You will have to make the files readable by dBASE IV, however, at the lowest authorized level. In other words, the attributes of these files must be set so that the lowest-level user who has a log-in script to start dBASE IV has read-only privileges to the two files. Because these files are encrypted and protected by a supervisory password, you shouldn't have any problems.

Handling Transaction Processing

The term *transaction processing* simply means that an application has a task or set of tasks to perform involving modifications to multiple records in one or more data files. To be considered successful, all the modifications must be completed without an error. Although transaction processing is not limited to network operation, some special considerations must be taken into account when transactions are processed in a multiuser environment.

The simplest example of transaction processing is the use of a REPLACE command issued to alter two or more records in a data file. Look at the following sample code:

```
USE inv_tory ORDER inv_no
REPLACE ALL unit_price WITH unit_price * 1.05
CLOSE DATABASES
```

These lines of code will put a five percent price increase on each of the items in inventory. If the power fails halfway through the transaction, the data file will become corrupted. You will not know which of the items have been processed and which have not. In previous versions of dBASE, the only remedies available to correct an aborted transaction were to edit the data by hand or to restore the file from a backup.

dBASE IV introduces two new commands designed to make transaction processing as simple and as trouble-free as possible. These commands are BEGIN TRANSACTION...END TRANSACTION and ROLLBACK.

Whenever a BEGIN TRANSACTION command is issued, dBASE IV creates a log file (a summary of transactions) that keeps track of all changes made to the file. If a problem occurs that prevents the transaction from being completed, the ROLLBACK command acts as an "undo" command.

You also can use the following functions to test the success of a transaction or to check whether a transaction is currently being performed on a file:

COMPLETED()	Determines whether a transaction has been successfully terminated
ROLLBACK()	Determines whether an aborted transaction has been successfully rolled back

```
ISMARKED()            Determines whether a file is currently involved in a
                      transaction controlled by the BEGIN
                      TRANSACTION...END TRANSACTION construct
```

The following sample code represents a simple transaction controlled by the BEGIN TRANSACTION...END TRANSACTION construct:

```
ON ERROR ROLLBACK     && Specifies the action to be taken if
                      && an error condition is triggered

USE cust ORDER cust_no EXCLUSIVE

BEGIN TRANSACTION     && Opens the transaction
     DELETE ALL FOR last_purch < CTOD('01/01/88')
   PACK
END TRANSACTION
ON ERROR
CLOSE DATABASES
RETURN
```

Here the transaction is started by the BEGIN TRANSACTION command. If an error develops (for instance, if a record that is needed is locked, the power goes out, or the workstation is rebooted), the ON ERROR command will take over and cause a ROLLBACK to be issued.

Rules for Transaction Processing

You should be aware of several rules for writing code that performs transaction processing. First, all data files involved in a transaction must be in separate work areas. This is true whether the USE commands occur before or after the BEGIN TRANSACTION statement. If you close a data file during a transaction, you may not open another data file in that work area during the transaction processing.

Second, when transaction processing is performed on a network, each user must be logged in with a unique user name. In single-user mode, the log file is named TRANSLOG.LOG; on a network, though, the log file is the first eight characters of the user name followed by the extension .LOG.

Third, all file and record locks that are placed (explicitly or automatically) should be maintained until the transaction is completed. This rule can make it difficult for other users to do their work, however. For this reason, you will want to break a transaction into two or more smaller transactions if possible. Remember that once a transaction is completed—that is, once COMPLETED() returns a .T.—a ROLLBACK cannot be accomplished. Therefore, each of the smaller transactions must be able to stand on its own. In other words, if the first transaction depends on the second transaction to maintain data integrity, you should keep them together as one transaction. You can schedule large transactions to be run at times when few users are on the network.

Remember, too, that a transaction is limited to 50 file/record locks. Be sure to write your transaction so that no more than 50 locks are placed.

Finally, commands that create new files are allowed in transactions, but files that overwrite existing files are not allowed because such changes cannot be rolled back. Similarly, commands that close opened files are not allowed in a transaction.

The following commands cannot be used inside a transaction:

```
CLEAR ALL
CLOSE ALL/DATABASES/INDEX
CREATE [FROM]
DELETE FILE
ERASE
INDEX ON
INSERT
MODIFY STRUCTURE
PACK
RENAME
SET CATALOG
SET INDEX
UNLOCK
USE (without an argument)
ZAP
```

Note that you may use USE to open a file. Without an argument, however, USE closes the file in the current work area.

A Sample Network Transaction

The code shown in figure 15.6 comes in two sections: the transaction itself and an error-trapping routine. The first section contains the setup code that gets things rolling. The procedure TRANS is then called to open the files and start the processing. Note that the argument to the BEGIN TRANSACTION statement sends the transaction log to a specific subdirectory where the log can be found easily in case of a system-wide failure.

Because of the ON ERROR statement in the setup code, any circumstance that would trigger a dBASE IV error will cause the TRANS_ERR procedure to kick in and attempt the ROLLBACK. The procedure attempts to tell the user why the transaction failed, as well as whether the ROLLBACK failed.

```
SET REPROCESS TO 20   && Attempts to get a lock 20 times before
                      && triggering an error

DEFINE WINDOW err_win FROM 10,10 TO 15,70
ON ERROR DO trans_err
DO trans
ON ERROR
RELEASE WINDOW err_win

PROCEDURE trans

BEGIN TRANSACTION F:\DB4\LOGS      && Writes the transaction log
                                   && to a specific directory
    USE stock ORDER part_no
    SELECT 2
    USE returns ORDER part
    DO WHILE .T.
       look = part
       SELECT 1
       SEEK look
       IF .NOT. FOUND()
          DO trans_err WITH "nofind"
          RETURN
       ENDIF
* This next command can present a danger! Because the scope of
* the REPLACE is only one record, the lock will be a record lock.
* If there are more than 50 returns, the error code will be
* called and a ROLLBACK issued.
       REPLACE qty WITH qty + B->rtn_qty
       SELECT 2
       IF EOF()
          EXIT
       ENDIF
    ENDDO
END TRANSACTION


PROCEDURE trans_err
PARAMETERS er_cond
```

Fig. 15.6

A sample transaction.

Fig. continues

Fig. continued

```
DO CASE
    CASE er_cond = "nofind"
        ACTIVATE WINDOW err_win
        @2, 5 SAY "An item has been returned with the part #: "+ look
        @3, 5 SAY "Number not in stock file. Press any key to ROLLBACK."
        null = INKEY()
        ROLLBACK
        CLEAR
        IF ROLLBACK()
            @3, 5 SAY "ROLLBACK SUCCESSFUL. Press any key."
            null = INKEY()
        ELSE
            @2, 5 SAY "ROLLBACK NOT SUCCESSFUL. Restore from backup."
            @3, 5 SAY "Press any key."
            null = INKEY()
        ENDIF
        DEACTIVATE WINDOW err_win
        RETURN TO MASTER
    CASE ERROR() = 108
        @2, 5 SAY "Another user has a file locked that is needed"
        @3, 5 SAY "to complete transaction. Press any key to ROLLBACK."
        null = INKEY()
        ROLLBACK
        CLEAR
        IF ROLLBACK()
            @3, 5 SAY "ROLLBACK SUCCESSFUL. Press any key."
            null = INKEY()
        ELSE
            @2, 5 SAY "ROLLBACK NOT SUCCESSFUL. Restore from backup."
            @3, 5 SAY "Press any key."
            null = INKEY()
        ENDIF
        DEACTIVATE WINDOW err_win
        RETURN TO MASTER
    ...        && Other CASE statements to cover other errors
ENDCASE
```

System-Wide Failures

If the entire network operating system goes down—say, from a power failure—more than one transaction may be in progress at the time. If you have specified a particular subdirectory where all transaction logs are written, you can easily determine whether a transaction was in progress at the time of the failure.

To recover from a system-wide failure, check the log subdirectory and user names to see what users were processing transactions. Log onto the system under each of the user names found in the log subdirectory, and in each case issue the ROLLBACK command at the dot prompt.

Summary

This chapter presented a number of techniques for writing applications that can be run in a multiuser environment. You learned how to lock files and records, both automatically and explicitly. You also reviewed the commands and functions used in programs in a multiuser environment.

One recommendation was that you include explicit locks in your multiuser programs to make sure that your user's entry is never wasted in case of a locking failure. The point also was made that controlling multiple files is not much different from using file- and record-locking procedures when only one file is open.

The chapter introduced the PROTECT command, which is used to control log-in procedures in a dBASE IV multiuser environment. PROTECT is used also to set accessibility standards for users trying to access data on file levels and field levels.

Finally, you learned how to control transaction processing so that any changes made to data files can be reversed if an error or system-wide failure occurs.

Chapter 16 explains how to use the RunTime module to distribute your programs to users who do not have dBASE IV.

16

Distributing Programs with the RunTime Module

Thus far, all the techniques and features presented in this book are available to you regardless of which version of dBASE IV you have. The RunTime module presented in this chapter and the dBASE IV Template Language presented in Chapter 17, however, are available to you only if you own the Developer's Edition of dBASE IV.

In this chapter, you will become acquainted with the RunTime module, which enables you to distribute your applications to users who do not have dBASE IV. You also will see how the bicycle shop application, presented in Chapter 13, can be readied for RunTime distribution.

The RunTime module is a special version of dBASE IV that can be accessed only by programs. A few commands cannot be included in an application designed to run under the RunTime module. These commands are listed in table 16.1.

Table 16.1
Commands Not Supported by RunTime

```
ASSIST
COMPILE
CREATE/MODIFY FILE
CREATE/MODIFY LABEL
CREATE/MODIFY QUERY
CREATE/MODIFY REPORT
CREATE/MODIFY SCREEN
```

Table 16.1—*Continued*

```
CREATE/MODIFY STRUCTURE
CREATE/MODIFY VIEW
HELP
HISTORY
RESUME
SET   (The menu-driven form of SET)
SET DEBUG
SET DOHISTORY
SET ECHO
SET HISTORY
SET INSTRUCT
SET SQL
SET STEP
SET TRAP
SUSPEND
```
Macro substitution (&) of command verbs

Note: Some other types of macro substitution involving file names are limited.

You can distribute your applications with the RunTime module files on a royalty-free basis. In other words, you do not have to pay a royalty to Ashton-Tate when you provide the RunTime files to your users, even if you are charging a fee for your programming services. Of course, you cannot distribute the rest of the dBASE IV package, as this is a violation of your license agreement and an act of piracy.

Two responsibilities rest squarely on your shoulders when you distribute applications with the RunTime module: you must provide documentation and support for your applications. The Ashton-Tate Technical Service staff cannot provide these services to your users.

The following seven files make up the RunTime system:

RUNTIME.EXE
RUNTIME1.OVL
RUNTIME1.OVL
RUNTIME3.OVL
RUNTIME4.OVL
DBASE1.RES
RPROTECT.OLV

The RPROTECT.OVL file is optional. You include it only when you want your users to be able to adjust access levels within the application, or when your users want to add new users or files. If your application does not contain the PROTECT command, you do not need to provide the RPROTECT.OVL file with the RunTime system files. If your application is PROTECTed, you will need either to use the PROTECT command from within the application to create the DBSYSTEM.DB file, or to provide a copy of the DBSYSTEM.DB file that will control access to the application.

Understanding the RunTime Module

The easiest way to understand what the RunTime module does is to consider what it doesn't do. The RunTime module does not give the user a dot prompt or provide the Control Center. RunTime does not create report form files, label form files, or data files. Nor can the RunTime module be used for developing databases or database applications.

Except for these limitations, the RunTime module does everything that the full dBASE IV package does (RunTime even includes the SQL commands). The only difference is that RunTime performs under the control of your programming. In effect, the RunTime module does only what your application tells it to do.

The RunTime module offers three main advantages. First, it enables you to provide sophisticated data-management applications to your users so that they won't have to buy dBASE IV. If you are free-lancing, you can thus sell an application more easily to a potential client. Obviously, you will have more difficulty in selling your programming services when that client must also spend as much, or more, for the software that *your* software runs under. With RunTime, you do not have to worry about whether your user owns a copy of dBASE IV. In all likelihood, the user will decide eventually to buy the full version of dBASE IV, for maintaining data files, creating new ones, and so on. RunTime severs the link that makes that purchase absolutely necessary.

Second, the RunTime module can operate in a multiuser mode without any special installation. This advantage can save money for your users, for they do not have to purchase LAN packs to add new users to the system. Again, a client may decide to install multiuser dBASE IV at a later time in order to give users the ability to access the dot prompt or Control Center.

Third, and most important, your applications will run faster with RunTime. Although this claim has not been accurately benchmarked in formal tests, all the sample applications tested in assembling this chapter ran with less overhead and accessing of the hard disk drive with RunTime. Furthermore, faster run times are ensured if you use the BUILD and DBLINK utilities to turn the application into one large .DBO file. That way, fewer files need to be accessed.

Taking Advantage of the BUILD and DBLINK Utilities

The DBLINK and BUILD utilities prepare your application for RunTime distribution. They can be used separately, or you can run DBLINK from the menu structure of the BUILD utility. DBLINK places all your executable code into one .DBO file, whereas BUILD is used to package your application, even putting the necessary files on diskettes for you.

Before using either of these utilities, your application must be thoroughly tested and ready for distribution. Remember that you are responsible for providing training, documentation, and support for your application; make sure that it is ready before distributing it.

Using DBLINK as a Stand-Alone Utility

DBLINK is a utility that will combine (link) all the executable files (.DBO, .FMO, .LBO, and so on) in your application into one large .DBO file. This utility can be invoked either manually at the DOS prompt or automatically by BUILD.

Using DBLINK has two advantages and one disadvantage. The advantages have already been mentioned—you have fewer files to access and distribute, and less accessing of the hard disk drive means that execution times will be faster. The disadvantage is that you have to relink the entire application whenever you want to make a change. If you supply the application in its separate parts, you will have to recompile only those parts when changes are made.

For most applications the advantages to using DBLINK outweigh the disadvantage. In some circumstances, though, you cannot use DBLINK. For instance, DBLINK will not work with applications that exceed 65,520 bytes per procedure or 1,170 procedures per compiled program file (.DBO). As these limitations apply to applications running from the dot prompt, you will know about either condition before you attempt to use DBLINK. More commonly, you cannot use DBLINK if any of the .DBO files are too large to fit on a diskette.

To link all the files together with DBLINK, issue the following command at the DOS prompt:

```
DBLINK <main program name> /L /D
```

The /L and /D switches are optional. The /L switch creates a listing of all the files that are linked, along with any files that are referenced in the programs but not included in the link. In other words, the /L switch puts on the disk a report indicating what happened during the linking process. You can then find and correct any errors that occurred. The /D switch turns on the display, letting you see on-screen that each pass of the linker has occurred.

For DBLINK to work properly, you must compile all the executable files by running them in dBASE IV or by using the COMPILE command from the dot prompt.

The syntax information is offered here for completeness only, for the BUILD utility will automatically invoke DBLINK if you so choose. By using BUILD, you can make the entire process menu-driven.

Compiling Files with the Menu-Driven BUILD Utility

The BUILD utility is a menu-driven program that enables you to compile and link your programs, as well as place all the needed files onto your distribution diskettes. You should be aware of two facts about the BUILD utility. First, early versions of BUILD are extremely fragile with respect to RAM-resident (TSR) software. Before beginning to use BUILD, you need to make sure that such programs are not in memory. Otherwise, you are likely to have problems with machine hang-ups and incomplete execution. Second, early versions of BUILD will make your video card go into monochrome mode. To test a program that uses color, you will have to reboot your machine to restore the video mode to its normal default.

You also need to be aware that both DBLINK and BUILD recognize references to external executable files only. If you have references to procedures and user-defined functions in other files, DBLINK and BUILD will display error messages.

A good example of this limitation is found in the menu-definition section of the bicycle shop application, first presented in Chapter 13. One of the ON SELECTION commands in the file MAIN.PRG references the PROCEDURE add_inv, which is found in the INVEN.PRG module of that application. Unless you declare this program (containing the procedure) to the BUILD utility before MAIN.PRG is compiled, you will get an error message telling you that ADD_INV.PRG was not found.

The way to declare relationships among program files is to add to the main program (the highest-level module) a special comment telling BUILD that other program files contain procedures and user-defined functions to be included in the application. The syntax for this comment is

    **MODULE ‹*program name*›[,‹*program name*›[,...]]

The comment must be preceded by two asterisks, and the word MODULE cannot be abbreviated. The list of program names should include all the executable files that will be part of the application, including files with the extension .PRG, .PRS, .FMT, and so on. By including a MODULE statement at the beginning of your highest-level program, you are telling the compiler that other files may contain the code for procedures and user-defined functions.

You can include in your application's program files two other special comments: the EXTERNAL comment and the MACRO comment. The EXTERNAL comment tells the BUILD utility what data files to copy to the distribution diskettes. All the files in the list will be copied to the diskette or directory specified in the **Build** menu. The syntax for the EXTERNAL comment is

    **EXTERNAL ‹*data file*›[,‹*data file*›[,...]]

The MACRO comment differs in syntax from the other two in that at least two lines are needed. Look at the following example:

    **MACRO USE inv ORDER part
    **MACRO USE invoice ORDER in_no
    **MACRO USE customer ORDER acct
    USE &fil ORDER &tag_nam

Here you are telling the compiler that three possible combinations of RunTime values could result from the command shown on the fourth line. BUILD tosses out the **MACRO portion of the first three lines and processes each of the commands that can result from the macro expression given to BUILD as a guide. The guide statement is then left out of the program.

To invoke the BUILD utility, you simply issue the following command at the DOS prompt:

    BUILD

You will be presented with the **Build** menu shown in figure 16.1.

From this menu, you can provide BUILD with the name of the highest-level module, indicate whether you want DBLINK to be automatically linked once the programs are compiled, and tell where you want the distribution files to be written. The fourth choice on the menu, **Perform BUILD**, sets the process in motion.

Before setting the BUILD process in motion, you may want to change some settings on the **Options** menu. Figure 16.2 shows the structure of this menu.

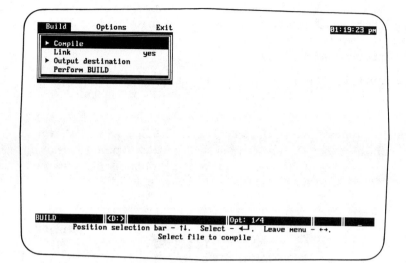

Fig. 16.1

The BUILD work surface.

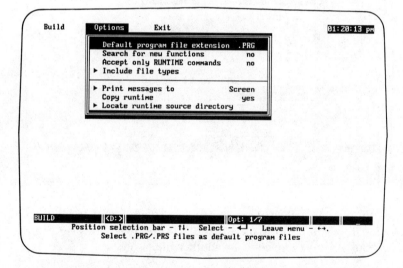

Fig. 16.2

The Options dialog box of the BUILD work surface.

The **Options** menu offers several choices about the way your application is to be handled by BUILD, as well as the copy process that creates your RunTime diskettes. The first menu option, **Default program file extension**, lets you specify the default extension for program files (such as .PRG and .PRS), for which BUILD should look.

The **Search for new functions** option tells BUILD whether to display a listing of all the functions used in the application. You use this option when you are building applications originally written in another dialect of dBASE, such as

Clipper or Foxbase, in which you may have some user-defined functions with identical names as native dBASE IV functions. If a UDF has the same name as a native function, the native function's code is compiled into the program, and the UDF's programming is lost.

Accept only RunTime commands parses the application to make sure that no commands which are prohibited in RunTime will be included in the application.

The **Include file types** option produces a screen similar to that shown in figure 16.3. With this submenu, you can tell BUILD which types of files in the current subdirectory should be copied to your distribution diskettes once the BUILD and DBLINK portions of the process are completed.

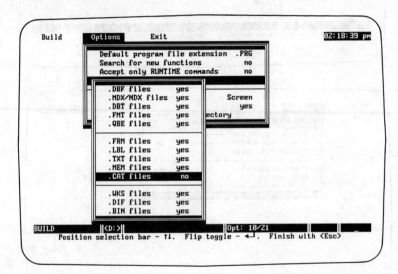

Fig. 16.3

The Include file types option of the Build menu.

Print messages to lets you tell BUILD where to write messages. In all cases dBASE IV messages are written to the file BUILD.TXT. You may, however, want the messages to echo also to the printer or another file.

The **Copy RunTime** option tells BUILD whether you want the RunTime files copied to the distribution diskettes automatically.

Finally, the **Locate RunTime source directory** option lets you specify the disk drive and path name where the RunTime files can be found. The directory is usually the same as that which contains your dBASE IV system files.

Preparing Your Application for RunTime Distribution

Preparing your application is quite simple. You set from the **Options** menu the options you want for the files to be copied, indicating whether BUILD should copy RunTime files to the distribution diskettes. Then you return to the **Build** menu and highlight **Compile**. By pressing F1 (PICK), you can use a pick list to highlight the highest-level module of the application. Next, you indicate whether you want the application linked and then specify the output destination. If you do not specify an output destination, all the files created by BUILD will be placed in the current subdirectory. Finally, you highlight **Perform BUILD** and press Enter.

BUILD will then compile the highest-level module, any program files referenced by the application (according to the default extension you chose at the **Options** menu), and any files specified by a `**MODULE` statement in the highest-level module.

BUILD actually writes a program called _BUILD.000, then calls dBASE IV, and uses it to compile the different modules of the application. Once the compilation takes place, control is returned to BUILD so that the process can be completed.

If you have set the **Build** menu to **Link**, the DBLINK utility is then called, and all the modules of the application are linked in a file with the same name as that of your highest-level module and with the extension .DBO. This is the only .DBO file that you will have to give to your users for the application to run.

Finally, if you have supplied an output destination, the files you specified at the **Options** menu—such as RunTime files and application files—will be copied to that destination. If the destination is a diskette drive, make sure that you have a supply of formatted diskettes handy.

BUILDing a Sample RunTime Application

Essentially the BUILD utility compiles the application one last time and then creates the diskettes to be given to end users. As indicated previously, the DBLINK utility also can be invoked automatically from the BUILD utility.

The bicycle shop application presented in Chapter 13 is typical of the kind of application you will want to distribute through the RunTime module. In the highest-level module for the application, you simply add one line telling the compiler that other executable files need to be created.

The following excerpt from MAIN.PRG shows just the first few lines of program code. The third line shows the only change you make in using the BUILD utility to create the RunTime diskettes:

```
*****  Program: MAIN.PRG  *****
* Main module for Belinda's Bike Boutique
**MODULE repo,sell,inven,sales.frg,IN_stat.frg

SET TALK OFF
```

The inclusion of the **MODULE line in the highest-level module of the application alerts the compiler to the other program files that contain the procedures and user-defined functions referenced in the program code (mainly in ON SELECTION commands during menu creation).

For example, one of the ON SELECTION PAD commands in the menu-creation section of code ends with DO add_inv. This reference to the procedure will cause the compiler to look for ADD_INV.PRG. Unless instructed with a **MODULE line, the compiler will not know to look in a file called INVEN.PRG to find the command PROCEDURE add_inv.

All the files referenced in the **MODULE line are the executable files associated with the application. The first three files mentioned (repo, sell, and inven) are the program modules bearing the extension .PRG. You do not have to include the extension in the **MODULE command if the file is a program, for .PRG is the default. The two .FRG files that are listed contain the code written by the report format generator. By including these files to be compiled, you eliminate the need for including the .FRM files with your application. The code for the reports will be contained in the file MAIN.DBO once the files are compiled and DBLINKed.

After you add the **MODULE line to the highest-level program file (in this case, MAIN.PRG), the compiler can find all the PROCEDURE and FUNCTION commands in all files that are part of the application. You are now ready to put the package together.

Change DOS directories so that you are logged into the subdirectory where your program and data files for the application are written. Assuming that you have set a DOS PATH that points to the subdirectory where the dBASE IV system files are written (per the dBASE IV installation instructions), you just type the command BUILD at the DOS prompt. Make sure that you have plenty of formatted diskettes before calling the BUILD utility if you are going to have the RunTime package written to diskettes during the BUILD operation.

To BUILD and DBLINK the bicycle shop application, fill in the **Build** menu as it is shown in figure 16.4. Then fill in the **Options** menu as shown in figure 16.5.

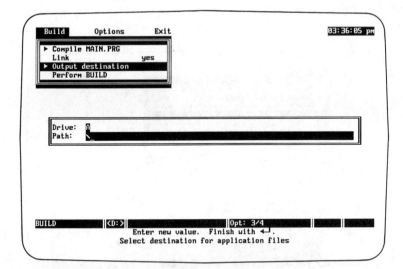

Fig. 16.4

Accessing the menu to determine where the package will be output.

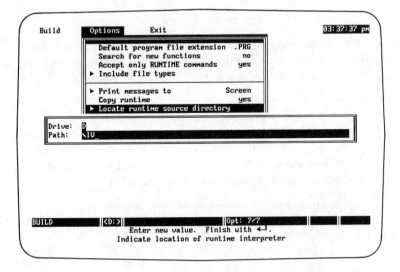

Fig. 16.5

Accessing the menu to tell BUILD where the RunTime files are located.

Be sure to access in the **Build** dialog box the menu item that directs the output to diskette, as well as the item under **Options** that directs BUILD to the subdirectory where the RunTime files are stored.

Also access in the **Options** dialog box the **Include file types** option to set the types of files that should be transferred to the diskettes as part of the BUILD package (see fig. 16.6). Certainly you will want .DBF and .MDX files to be copied to the diskettes. You will need to make decisions about the other types of files as well.

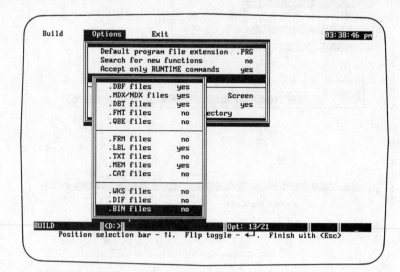

Fig. 16.6

Telling BUILD what files to include in the package.

Note one caution. Files to be copied are identified by extension. If you have in the subdirectory where you are working the files of more than one application, you might accidentally include files that don't belong to the application in the package.

To create the package, you simply return to the **Build** menu and execute the **Perform BUILD** prompt. The BUILD utility will then create a new set of .DBO files. If the DBLINK option is active, the .DBO files will be combined into one large file with the same first name as that of the highest-level program (in this case the program will be completely contained in MAIN.DBO).

The BUILD utility will then create the diskettes you can use as masters to produce the individual copies of the application. These are the copies to be distributed to end users.

Running the Application

To run the application, you simply copy the files from the distribution diskettes onto the hard disk drive of the system on which the application will run. If you did not include the RunTime files on the distribution diskettes, you also will need to copy those files onto the hard disk drive. Generally you will want all the files to reside in the same subdirectory. However, if you are supplying the user with more than one application, you may want to put the RunTime files in a directory (made accessible with the DOS PATH command) and place the applications in subdirectories under the RunTime directory.

To start the application, have the user enter the following command at the DOS prompt, or have the command issued by a batch file:

    RUNTIME *appname*

The parameter *appname* is the name of the highest-level module of the application. For the bicycle shop application, you type

    RUNTIME main

An alternative is to call RunTime with the /T switch:

    RUNTIME /T *appname*

The /T switch suppresses the elaborate sign-on banner that dBASE IV displays (by default) before painting the license agreement on-screen. This switch causes both dBASE IV and RunTime to bypass these screens in favor of a more subdued copyright sign-on banner that disappears after a few seconds. As a result, the dot prompt or the RunTime application appears more quickly.

Once the main menu of the application is displayed, the application will run just as it does under the full version of dBASE IV. If you provide a CONFIG.DB file with your application, that file can be used to control the environment settings for each individual user's system. You can therefore accommodate systems with different peripherals—such as monochrome displays, color monitors, and various printers—without having to modify the application code for each system that will run the application.

Summary

In this chapter, you were introduced to the RunTime module, a feature available only with the Developer's Edition of dBASE IV. The RunTime module enables you to provide your applications to users who do not own a copy of dBASE IV.

You learned what commands to avoid in a RunTime application and what files are necessary to make the RunTime module work properly. You learned also how to use the DBLINK and BUILD utilities in preparing your applications for RunTime distribution, as well as how to set up your user's system to run an application under RunTime.

The final chapter introduces the dBASE IV Template Language, another feature available with the Developer's Edition of dBASE IV.

17

Using the dBASE IV Template Language

The dBASE IV Template Language, supplied with the Developer's Edition of dBASE IV, enables you to control the generation of objects designed on the reports, labels, and forms design screens, or with the dBASE IV Applications Generator. With the Template Language, you can generate program versions of these design objects, or documentation to describe them.

This chapter is not intended to be a complete tutorial on the Template Language. Its techniques could fill an entire book, and still the subject would not be exhausted. Instead, the chapter provides a "quick peek" at one of the most advanced topics in dBASE IV so that you can better understand the processes that occur when a design object is generated. Later, when you become more comfortable with the structure of dBASE IV's design objects, you will want to use the Template Language to customize the way an object is generated.

Understanding the Template Language

The dBASE IV Template Language uses many of the same commands and functions that the dBASE IV command language uses. A Template Language program interacts with data from a design object to create a dBASE program in much the same manner that a command language program interacts with user input to create a report. As you make choices and entries in the Applications Generator or in any of the other object generators, your choices and entries are recorded in the design object file as variables (or selectors, as they are called in the Template Language).

Each of the selectors that represents a choice or entry is used by the template to determine what will be written to the output file. When you choose **Save** from the work surface menu, or **Generate** from the main menu of the Applications Generator, the template controls the code generation based on the values of the selectors.

If the template's contents are dBASE language commands, the file created will be a dBASE program. If the contents are text, documentation of the object will be created.

A *template* is a standard ASCII file (with the extension .COD) that contains four elements: comments, introduction, text, and commands. These elements are described in the next several sections.

The Template Comments

Comments in a template are preceded by two slashes (//). Comments must start in the first column if they are outside the command braces ({}). Inside the command braces, they can start in any column. Multiple lines of comments require the double slashes at the beginning of each line. Comments are extremely useful in documenting sections of your template code to ensure that you will be able to maintain or modify the code at a later date. In figure 17.1, comments outside the braces are shown in the first three lines. Comments embedded within command braces are shown with the first command.

Fig. 17.1

A sample of Template Language code.

```
// TEST.COD   A sample of the Template Language Code
//            These lines are comments and will be ignored by
//            the Template Compiler.
This is the template introduction, which will be included in the
output file in ASCII format. You can view this material with the
dBASE or DOS TYPE command. This material is considered to be
the introduction because no template commands have been given
at this point.
{INCLUDE builtin.def;   //This is an embedded comment.
CREATE("test.doc")}
This file was created on {Date()}
{RETURN 0;}
// End of template
```

The Template Introduction

Any text, other than comments, that precedes the first command line in a template is considered the introduction. When the template is compiled, this material is kept in its ASCII form and written to the output file as a header. You can read the introductory material by using the DOS TYPE command at the DOS prompt or the dBASE TYPE command at the dot prompt. The introduction for the sample template in figure 17.1 begins with line 4 and ends with line 8. Introductions may be up to 4K in size.

The Template Text

After the first braced command, any material not included in command braces is passed unchanged to the output file. (Remember that the text before the first set of braced material is considered an introduction.) Line 11 of the sample template in figure 17.1 shows an example of text. This file was created on is passed directly to the output file.

If you are creating a template to produce dBASE programs, the text will be dBASE commands. If you are creating a template to produce documentation, the text will be descriptive information. If you intend to produce dBASE programs, make sure that your text contains the correct syntax to avoid errors when the program is compiled by dBASE IV.

The Template Commands

dBASE IV Template Language commands and functions are enclosed in braces ({ }). Anything inside the braces is considered a template expression and is therefore evaluated. The results of the evaluation are included in the output file. If you look again at line 11 of the sample template in figure 17.1, you will see the DATE() function enclosed in braces. The template compiler will evaluate the function and write the result—today's date—to the output file.

At times—for instance, when an internal variable is evaluated—the result of the evaluation should not be placed in the output file. To prevent the result from being output, you place a semicolon (;) in front of the closing brace. The template compiler then considers the expression to be internal to the template, and the result of the command expression will not be output.

Understanding the Design Object

Templates use information from design objects to produce dBASE code or documentation. This information is located in the file that is created when you design the object. You create design files for reports, labels, and forms by choosing the <**create**> option in the associated panel in the Control Center or by using the CREATE/MODIFY command at the dot prompt. The design files have the following file extensions: reports (.FRM), labels (.LBL), and forms (.SCR). The Applications Generator uses a number of design objects in addition to reports, labels, and forms. Table 17.1 shows the file extensions used by the various Applications Generator design objects.

Table 17.1
File Extensions for Applications Generator Design Objects

Object	File Extension
Application	.APP
Pop-up	.POP
Bar	.BAR
File	.FIL
Structure	.STR
Values	.VAL
Batch	.BCH

Design data is stored in files with these specific extensions, one file per object. Each object file contains information about the design in a record structure called an *element*. You can draw an analogy between design objects and data files. Each design object is like a database which contains information about that design object. Elements are to design objects what records are to data files; attributes are to elements what fields are to records. The analogy fails, however, in one respect: not all elements have the same attributes in the way that all records in a data file have the same fields. The number of attributes assigned to an element can differ from element to element.

Different kinds of elements can be found in design objects. Each of these elements specifies the actions for different parts of a particular object. Not all objects contain all the different elements, and some elements are found only in one type of design object. The following list includes some types of design elements that are available:

Attribute
Element
DOS_File
Tree
Group
Field
Text
Band
Box
Frame
Ruler
Paragraph
Page_Break

The value of an element or attribute is attached to a selector. A *selector* is a special type of variable initialized with the SELECTOR command. Each selector is given a unique numeric code called its IID (item identification), which is used to identify that selector. In addition to identifying elements and attributes, selectors identify Template Language functions, such as DATE( ); and miscellaneous names, such as Tree and DOS_File shown in the preceding list.

Five standard selector files are provided with the Template Language. You can examine these files to discover the different elements that make up each design object. The selector files available are the following:

APPLCTN.DEF	For Applications Generator objects
BUILTIN.DEF	For Template Language functions and miscellaneous declarations
FORM.DEF	For forms (screens)
LABEL.DEF	For labels
REPORT.DEF	For reports

You can use the INCLUDE command to import these standard selector files into your templates. Most templates will require BUILTIN.DEF because this file provides access to the Template Language functions. This file can be used with any of the other .DEF files. Templates used with the Applications Generator design files should include APPLCTN.DEF, and templates for reports, labels, or forms should include the appropriate .DEF file. However, you cannot use the APPLCTN.DEF file with the three .DEF files for reports, labels, or forms because the Applications Generator declares the same selector numbers declared in the other three files, but the numbers may represent different elements.

Using a selector within a template returns the information about the item referenced. Most selectors return strings or constants when used. The `Fld_fieldname` selector, for example, refers to the attribute assigned to the name of a field used in a form's definition. If you use a field named `ADDRESS` in a data-entry form, the `Fld_fieldname` selector will return the value `ADDRESS` when referencing that field in your template.

Understanding Template File Names

Each design object, by default, requires a template with a specific name. If you intend to make modifications to these default templates, you can proceed in one of two ways. First, you can simply use for your modified template the name of the default template for the design object. Make sure that you have a copy of the original template file for future use. Second, and preferably, you can use the DOS `SET` command with the appropriate environment variable to redirect the object generator to your modified template.

You can create a DOS environment variable with the following command syntax:

```
SET <var name> = <expC>
```

To list the environment variables that are in effect, you issue the `SET` command without an argument. All the variables established will be listed on-screen.

Table 17.2 shows the default file names for each of the three types of design objects, as well as the DOS environment variables to be used to redirect the compiler from the defaults.

Table 17.2
Default File Names for Design Objects

Design Object	Default File	DOS Variable
Forms	FORM.GEN	DTL_FORM
Labels	LABEL.GEN	DTL_LABEL
Reports	REPORT.GEN	DTL_REPORT

If, for example, you want to use a template named MYFORM.GEN instead of the default FORM.GEN, you issue the following `SET` command at the DOS prompt:

```
SET DTL_FORM = MYFORM.GEN
```

Inside the Applications Generator, the template used is selected from the **Generate** menu; no environment variables are therefore needed to redirect from the default. You simply select your modified template from the displayed list.

Using Template Language Commands and Functions

As indicated earlier, the Template Language commands and functions interact with data from the design object files to produce either dBASE command language programs or documentation files. The Template Language has 75 functions for evaluating design object information, but only 17 commands. These commands fall into four categories: compiler directives, definition commands, program flow commands, and loop commands.

Compiler Directives

Five Template Language commands control three options at compile time. These commands enable you to combine external files (such as BUILTIN.DEF) with your template and to control list output and assembler statements in the compiler listing. Following are the command syntaxes for the five commands:

{INCLUDE <filename>;}	This command includes information from the named file.
{#LSTON} or {#LSTOFF}	These commands control output to the list file if –l was used in the command line when the compiler was invoked. The *list file* contains the source lines, including the line numbers. Such a file is useful for debugging.
{#CODON} or {#CODOFF}	These commands allow or suppress assembler statements in the compiler listing.

Definition Commands

Definition commands define variables and user-defined functions for use within the template. The three definition commands are DEFINE, ENUM, and VAR.

DEFINE

The DEFINE command declares a user-defined function for use within the Template Language. Note that because the command language is not compatible with the Template Language, these user-defined functions cannot be used outside the template. The command syntax is

```
DEFINE <udf_name> ([<varname>,<varname>...]) ... RETURN
ENDDEF
```

User-defined functions must begin with DEFINE and end with ENDDEF. If values are passed to a user-defined function, the values must be listed within parentheses following the function name. Values can be returned from the user-defined function either explicitly (by specifying the variable name immediately following the RETURN) or implicitly (by passing back as the return value any pending value when RETURN/ENDDEF is reached). Any variable defined within the user-defined function is local to that function.

Figure 17.2 shows a sample user-defined function that converts a null value to zero. This UDF is taken from the FORM.COD template supplied with the Developer's Edition. Note that the variable numbr is returned explicitly in this function.

Fig. 17.2

A sample user-defined function.

```
{
DEFINE nul2zero(numbr);
// If number is nul and you are expecting a zero, convert it.
IF !numbr THEN numbr=0 ENDIF;
RETURN number;
ENDDEF
}
```

ENUM

The ENUM command substitutes a string or numeric constant for a symbolic name at compile time. This helps to make the template more readable because you can use the symbolic name in the template and then have the compiler replace that name with the correct string or numeric constant at compile time. The command syntax of the ENUM command is

```
ENUM <sym_name> = <exp>, [<sym_name> = <exp>] ...
```

After the first numeric assignment is made to a symbolic name, the remaining names are assigned sequentially until a new numeric assignment restarts the sequence. A sample ENUM definition, taken from BUILTIN.DEF, lists the possible values for the type of monitor in use (see fig. 17.3).

```
{
ENUM mono = 0,
cga,
ega25,
mono43 = 4,
ega43 = 6;
}
```

Fig. 17.3

A sample ENUM definition.

In this example, the symbolic name `mono` is assigned a value of 0, `cga` is assigned a value of 1, and `ega25` is assigned a value of 2. The name `mono43` would have been assigned a value of 3, except that `mono43` has been explicitly assigned a value of 4. This `ENUM` construct enables you to check for a condition like `display > ega25`, rather than `display > 2`, thus making your template program easier to read.

VAR

All variables referenced in the template must be declared with the `VAR` command before they can be used. The syntax of the `VAR` command is

    VAR <varname>, [<varname>] ...

The variable name, which must begin with a letter or an underscore, can contain up to 200 characters. You can use letters, numbers, or the underscore character for the rest of the variable name. Remember that variables declared within a user-defined function are local to that function. Those declared outside a user-defined function are global to the template. Figure 17.4 shows a sample variable declaration.

```
{
VAR temp_cnt, x, y, z;
}
```

Fig. 17.4

A sample variable declaration.

Program Flow Commands

Template Language commands that control the flow of the program are typically the ones you find in most programming languages. These commands are `CASE...ENDCASE`, `GOTO`, `IF...THEN...ENDIF`, and `RETURN`.

CASE...ENDCASE

The CASE...ENDCASE command enables you to define a set of alternative commands that are executed depending on the value of a selector. The syntax of CASE...ENDCASE is

```
CASE <exp> OF [CASE] <n:> <commands> ...
[OTHERWISE <commands>] ENDCASE
```

The CASE selectors (*n*:) must be numeric unless the CASE command is preceded by an ENUM command. The OTHERWISE clause enables you to specify default commands to be performed if the values of the selectors you have defined are not matched. Figure 17.5 shows a sample CASE construct.

Fig. 17.5

A sample CASE construct.

```
{
// Set background color
CASE background OF
0: incolor = incolor + "n";
1: incolor = incolor + "b";
2: incolor = incolor + "g";
ENDCASE;
}
```

GOTO

The GOTO command branches the program to a specified labeled statement. The label name must appear on a command line by itself and must have a colon (:) as its last character. The syntax of the GOTO command is

```
GOTO <label>
```

Although use of the GOTO command is not considered good structured programming, the command is convenient to use with an IF...THEN test to bypass sections of code when the specified condition is met. The FORM.COD template uses a GOTO to exit if the design object is not a form (see fig. 17.6).

If the design object is not a form, an error message is issued with the PAUSE command, and program flow is branched to the nogen: label at the end of the template.

IF...THEN...ENDIF

IF...THEN...ENDIF evaluates an expression for a True or False condition and executes the corresponding commands. The nesting rules for this command are

```
{
IF Frame_class != form THEN
PAUSE(wrong_class + any_key);
GOTO nogen;
ENDIF
   .
   .                  (The commands for form generation are here.)
   .
nogen:
RETURN 0;
}
```

the same as those for the IF...ENDIF command of the dBASE IV command language. The syntax is

>   IF <*cond*> [THEN] <*commands*> [ELSE <*commands*>] ENDIF

The ELSE clause is optional and specifies commands to be executed when the
condition is False. Figure 17.7 shows an example of an IF...THEN...ENDIF
construct.

```
{
IF display > ega25 THEN
scrn_size = 39
ELSE
scrn_size = 21
ENDIF;
}
```

RETURN

The RETURN command is used in the template to terminate the template run.
This command may be used also inside a user-defined function to exit the function and provide the pending value. If RETURN is not used inside a user-defined
function, any pending value is implicitly returned when ENDDEF is reached. The
syntax of the RETURN command is

>   RETURN [<*exp*>]

When RETURN is used outside a user-defined function to terminate a template
run, you must specify RETURN 0 to prevent any pending values from being
implicitly returned. A value other than zero will indicate an error condition to
dBASE. Figure 17.8 shows a simple user-defined function containing the RETURN
command.

Fig. 17.8

Using the RETURN command in a user-defined function.

```
{
DEFINE twice(x)
RETURN 2*x;
ENDDEF
}
```

Loop Commands

Three loop constructs are available within the Template Language: DO...WHILE/UNTIL...ENDO, FOR...NEXT, and FOREACH...NEXT. The commands EXIT and LOOP are used to control execution of these constructs. The first two loop constructs are similar to their command language counterparts.

DO...WHILE/UNTIL...ENDO

This construct enables you to repeat a command, or a group of commands, while the specified condition is met. The syntax is

DO [*<commands>*] WHILE/UNTIL [*<cond>*] ENDDO

The commands that appear between the DO and the WHILE will be executed at least once, and repeated as long as the condition is met. If WHILE is specified, the condition must be True for the commands to be repeated. If you place commands between the WHILE and the ENDDO, those commands will be executed after the condition is evaluated. If the condition is False, the commands will not be executed.

If UNTIL is specified, the condition must be False for the DO commands to continue repeating. Statements between UNTIL and ENDDO are executed before the condition is evaluated, and those statements will be executed at least once, even if the condition is not met.

FOR...NEXT

The FOR...NEXT construct is used for incremental looping (remember the DO LOOP from FORTRAN 101?). The syntax of FOR...NEXT is

FOR *<var>* = *<expN1>* TO *<expN2>* [STEP *<constant>*]
<commands> NEXT [*<var>*]

As a counter, the variable is initialized to the value declared in *<expN1>*, and incremented for each iteration through the loop. If STEP is specified, the variable is incremented by STEP *<constant>*; otherwise, the variable is incremented by one.

At the beginning of each iteration through the loop, the incremented value of the variable is compared with the value specified by ⟨*expN2*⟩. As long as the variable is less than or equal to ⟨*expN2*⟩, the commands are executed. The loop may be executed many times or not at all, depending on the results of the test.

FOREACH...NEXT

The `FOREACH...NEXT` construct is extremely important to the Template Language. This construct allows easy access to elements and attributes found in design object files. The syntax of `FOREACH...NEXT` is

```
FOREACH <loop selector> [<cursor var>]
[IN <cursor var>] ... NEXT
```

The cursor variable is a pointer that references your position within a set of elements or attributes. The pointer is advanced each time the `NEXT` command is encountered, until the end of the data is reached. The loop is then terminated at that `NEXT` command. The cursor variable is defined implicitly by its inclusion in the `FOREACH...NEXT` command. If this variable is going to be referenced by another expression, the variable must be explicitly defined.

The loop selector identifies the element or attribute processed within the loop. Loop selectors common to all design objects are `Element`, `Box_element`, `Fld_element`, `Text_element`, and `Tree`. Figure 17.9 shows a `FOREACH...NEXT` construct, taken from the FORM.COD template, that processes the `Fld_element` loop selector in defining which fields to carry forward during an append operation.

Essentially this construct writes the command language's `SET CARRY TO` ⟨*fieldlist*⟩ command to the output file by using the `flds` cursor variable to index through the `Fld_element` loop selector. The total length of the field list is checked to ensure that it does not exceed the maximum allowed (1,000 characters). The length of each line set up to be written to the output file is also checked and written only when the length exceeds 75 characters.

EXIT

`EXIT` branches program execution to the first statement after the loop construct. This command may be used only within a loop construct.

LOOP

The `LOOP` command branches program execution to the next `WHILE` or `UNTIL` test within the loop. If no `WHILE` or `UNTIL` has been specified, execution is branched to the beginning of the loop construct.

Fig. 17.9

*A sample
FOREACH...NEXT
construct.*

```
SET CARRY TO \
{
carry_len = 13; carry_first = 0;
FOREACH Fld_element flds
    IF Fld_carry THEN
        carry_len = carry_len + len(Fld_fieldname + ",");
        carry_lent = carry_lent + carry_len;
        IF carry_lent > 1000 THEN
            PRINT(crlf + "SET CARRY TO ");
            carry_len = 13; carry_lent = 0;
        ENDIF
        IF carry_len > 75 THEN
            PRINT(";" + crlf + " ");
            carry_len = 2;
        ENDIF
        temp = lower(Fld_fieldname);
        IF !carry_first THEN
            PRINT(temp);
            carry_first = 1;
        ELSE
            PRINT("," + temp);
        ENDIF
    ENDIF
NEXT flds;
}
```

Template Language Functions

As mentioned previously, the Template Language contains 75 functions that can
be used to control both the execution of the template and the data written to
the output file. Many of these functions are identical to those found in the command language, but some are designed specifically for the Template Language.
It is beyond the scope of this chapter to discuss each function in detail. For
further information, refer to the reference manual provided with the Developer's Edition of dBASE IV.

Using a Sample Template

This section presents the FORM.COD template supplied with the Developer's Edition of dBASE IV. The template works with the form design object to create a dBASE program. FORM.COD is divided into four parts: (1) introduction and setup, (2) creation of the output file and the initial program code, (3) primary processing code, and (4) program code to complete processing. Although the template code appears exactly as it is supplied by dBASE, the comments have been edited for readability and consistency.

Setting Up the Template

The first portion of code, shown in figure 17.10, contains comments and introduction describing the general function of the template. Remember that you can view the introduction of a compiled template with the DOS or dBASE TYPE command.

```
//
// Module Name: FORM.COD
// Description: This module is for producing dBASE IV .FMT files.
//

Format (.fmt) File Template
---------------------------

Version 1.0
Ashton-Tate (c) 1987, 1988
```

Fig. 17.10

Comments and introduction for the FORM.COD template.

The next portion of code, shown in figure 17.11, contains the INCLUDE command, which copies in standard definitions for selectors used in dBASE form objects (FORM.DEF) and standard functions used in the Template Language (BUILTIN.DEF). As mentioned earlier, standard definition files (.DEF) are provided for labels, forms, and reports, as well as for the Applications Generator. By maintaining these definitions in a separate file and using the INCLUDE command, modifications need to be made just once instead of in each individual template. The templates need only to be recompiled.

```
{
include "form.def";    // Form selectors
include "builtin.def"; // Built-in functions
```

Fig. 17.11

Using the INCLUDE command to include definitions and functions.

The ENUM command, shown in figure 17.12, defines string constants for the template. These particular string constants issue error messages during object generation. By substituting the English error text with a foreign language—for instance, Spanish—you can generate code for your non-English speaking users.

```
//
// Enum string constants for international translation
//
enum wrong_class = "Can't use FORM.GEN on non-form objects. ",
     form_empty = "Form design was empty. "
   ;
   //
```

As an attribute of the design object, Frame_class identifies the object type. The lines of code shown in figure 17.13 check this attribute to ensure that you are using the template with the proper type of object—in this case, a form. If you were not processing a form, the GOTO command would branch to the end of the template after issuing the wrong_class error message defined in the code.

```
if Frame_class != form then // You are not processing a form object.
   pause(wrong_class + any_key);
   goto NoGen;
   endif
```

The variables required to process the form are defined with the VAR command (see fig. 17.14). After being defined, some variables are initialized. Note the names of the variables and the use of comments to describe each variable. If you select names that describe the variable (instead of using x, y, or z) and include comments like these, you can maintain your code at a later date without spending much time trying to remember what you were doing.

In the next section of code, you can check the type of display adapter in use and whether the status line is on or off to determine the size of the working area of the form (see fig. 17.15). The NUMSET() function returns the numeric value of the _flgcolor and _flgstatus selectors. These selectors are defined in BUILTIN.DEF, as are selectors for all dBASE IV internal settings. The variable scrn_size, defined in this template, is set to the appropriate value.

```
var  fmt_name,   // Format file name
      crlf,       // Line feed
      carry_flg,  // Flag to test carry loop
      carry_cnt,  // Count of the number of fields to carry
      carry_len,  // Cumulative length of carry line until 75 characters
      carry_lent, // Total cumulative length of carry line
      carry_first,// Flag to test "," output for carry fields
      color_flg,  // Flag to test if color should stay on same line
      line_cnt,   // Count for total lines processed (multiple page forms)
      page_cnt,   // Count for total pages processed (multiple page forms)
      temp,       // Temporary work variable
      cnt,        // Foreach loop variable
      wnd_cnt,    // Window counter
      wnd_names,  // Window names so that you can clear them
                  // at the bottom of file
      default_drv,// dBASE default drive
      dB_status,  // dBASE status before entering designer
      scrn_size,  // Screen size when generation starts
      display,    // Type of display screen you are on
      color;      // Color returned from getcolor function
```

Fig. 17.14

Defining variables with the VAR command.

```
//-------------------------------------------------
// Assign default values to some of the variables
//-------------------------------------------------
crlf = chr(10);
temp = "";
carry_flg = carry_first = carry_cnt = carry_len = carry_lent =
wnd_cnt = line_cnt =  color_flg = cnt = 0;
page_cnt = 1;
```

```
// Test screen size if display > 2 screen is 43 lines
display = numset(_flgcolor);
if display > ega25 then scrn_size = 39 else scrn_size = 21 endif;
```

Fig. 17.15

Checking the display adapter and the status line.

```
// Test to see if status was off before going into form designer
dB_status = numset(_flgstatus);
if scrn_size == 21 and !db_status then
scrn_size = 24;
endif
if scrn_size == 39 and !db_status then // Status is off
scrn_size = 42;
endif
```

Creating the Output File

The output file for the dBASE IV programming code is now created (see fig. 17.16). The default drive in effect is determined by using the STRSET() function to return the string constant assigned to _defdrive, which is another selector provided for internal dBASE IV settings. The drive and path information is added from the appropriate selectors, and the FILEOK() function ensures that a valid DOS file name has been provided. The file is then created with the CREATE() function. If the file creation fails, an error message is issued, and GOTO is used again to exit the template.

Fig. 17.16

Creating the output file.

```
//-------------------------------
// Create format file
//-------------------------------
default_drv = strset(_defdrive);  // Grab default drive from dBASE

fmt_name = frame_path + name;
if not FILEOK(fmt_name) then
if !default_drv then
fmt_name = name;
else
fmt_name = default_drv + ":" + NAME;
endif
endif
fmt_name = upper(fmt_name);
if not create(fmt_name+".FMT") then
pause(fileroot(fmt_name) +".FMT" + read_only + any_key);
goto nogen;
endif
}
```

Now that the output file is created, the template begins generating the dBASE IV program and writing the code to the file. Remember that text outside command braces ({ }) is written unchanged to the output file. Figure 17.17 shows the initial lines written.

First are command language comment lines (note the * in the first column) giving the name, date of generation, and so on. In your templates, you can include your name and copyright notice so that they will appear in all generated code as well.

```
//
{print(replicate("*",80)+crlf);}
*-- Name....: {filename(fmt_name)}FMT
*-- Date....: {ltrim(SUBSTR(date(),1,8))}
*-- Version.: dBASE IV, Format {Frame_ver}.0
*-- Notes...: Format files use "" as delimiters!
{print(replicate("*",80)+crlf);}
//


*-- Format file initialization code -----------------------------

IF SET("TALK")="ON"
    SET TALK OFF
    lc_talk="ON"
    ELSE
    lc_talk="OFF"
    ENDIF
    {   case display of
    mono:    temp="MONO";
    cga:     temp="COLOR";
    ega25:   temp="EGA25";
    mono43:  temp="MONO43";
    ega43:   temp="EGA43";
    endcase
    }


*-- This form was created in {temp} mode
SET DISPLAY TO {temp}
{   temp="";}


lc_status=SET("STATUS")
*-- SET STATUS was \
{if dB_status then}
ON when you went into the Forms Designer.
IF lc_status = "OFF"
    SET STATUS ON
    {else}
    OFF when you went into the Forms Designer.
    IF lc_status = "ON"
    SET STATUS OFF
    {endif}
    ENDIF
```

Fig. 17.17

*Generating the
dBASE IV program.*

Next is the code for storing the current TALK and STATUS values (so that they can be restored later) as well as the code for turning them off. A CASE statement that uses the display variable assigns the appropriate string to a temporary variable (temp) so that you can write the correct SET DISPLAY TO command to the output file.

Note the backslash (\) used in writing the command language comment for the STATUS value. The backslash prevents a carriage return from being written to the output file after the first part of the comment line output. You use the value of dB_status to determine the rest of the comment line to be output.

The FOREACH...NEXT construct is used to write WINDOW and SET CARRY commands to the output file (see fig. 17.18). Both these commands use the Fld_element selector with the flds cursor variable to process each field in the form design object. For each memory variable encountered, an editing window is defined with Box attributes determining the dimension of the window. The construct for the SET CARRY command was discussed in the earlier section on LOOP commands.

Fig. 17.18

Using the FOREACH...NEXT construct.

```
//--------------------------------------------------------------------
// Process fields to build "SET CARRY" and WINDOW commands
//--------------------------------------------------------------------
{
       foreach Fld_element flds
       if Row_positn-line_cnt > scrn_size then
       line_cnt = line_cnt+scrn_size+1;
       endif
       if Fld_carry then carry_flg = 1; ++carry_cnt; endif
       if chr(Fld_value_type) == "M" and Fld_mem_typ and wnd_cnt < 20 then
       ++wnd_cnt; wnd_names = wnd_names + "Wndow" + wnd_cnt + ",";
       }

*-- Window for memo field {lower(Fld_fieldname)}.
DEFINE WINDOW Wndow{wnd_cnt} FROM {nul2zero(Box_top) - line_cnt},\
{  nul2zero(Box_left)} TO \
{  temp = nul2zero(Box_top) + Box_height - line_cnt - 1;
       if temp > scrn_size then scrn_size else temp endif},\
       { nul2zero(Box_left) + Box_width - 1} \
       { outbox(Box_type, Box_special_char);
       color = getcolor(Fld_display, Fld_editable);
       outcolor();
       endif
       next flds;
```

Fig. continues

Fig. continued

```
                print(crlf);
                if carry_flg then
                }

        lc_carry = SET("CARRY")
        *-- Fields to carry forward during APPEND.
        SET CARRY TO \
        {  carry_len = 13; carry_first = 0;
            foreach Fld_element flds
            if Fld_carry then
            carry_len = carry_len + len(Fld_fieldname + ",");
            carry_lent = carry_lent + carry_len;
            if carry_lent > 1000 then
            print(crlf + "SET CARRY TO ");
            carry_len = 13; carry_lent = 0;
            endif
            if carry_len > 75 then print(";" + crlf + "  "); carry_len = 2; endif
            temp = lower(Fld_fieldname);
            if !carry_first then
            print(temp);
            carry_first = 1;
            else
            print("," + temp);
            endif
            endif
            next flds;
            print(" ADDITIVE" + crlf);
            endif
        }
```

Processing the @....SAY...GETs

Now you have reached the primary function of the form template: the setting up of the @...SAY...GET commands for the program. This section of the template also uses a FOREACH...NEXT construct to cycle through each field on the form. Within this construct, a CASE statement, which is based on the field type, is used to set up the command.

Figure 17.19 shows the first part of this section of the template. Two command language comments are written to the output file, variables for line count and window count are initialized to zero, and the top of the loop is defined by using the cursor variable k. In addition, the color of each element is determined, and screen size is checked. If you have exceeded the screen size, a READ is output, and a new page is set up.

Fig. 17.19

Setting up the @...SAY...GET commands.

```
*-- @ SAY GETS Processing. ----------------------------------------
*--   Format Page: {page_cnt}

{line_cnt = wnd_cnt = 0;
    foreach ELEMENT k
    color = getcolor(Fld_display, Fld_editable); // Get color of element
    if nul2zero(Row_positn) - line_cnt > scrn_size then
    line_cnt = line_cnt + scrn_size + 1;
    ++page_cnt;
    }
    READ

*--   Format Page: {page_cnt}

{  endif
```

Next, a comment line is output describing the field (based on the field type) and documenting the dBASE program being generated. In addition, the first part of the @...SAY...GET is set up, depending on the element type. The row and column positions specified in the @...SAY...GET are calculated from attributes from the design object file, and from the screen size, depending on the display type assigned earlier. These operations are shown in figure 17.20. Again note the backslash used to suppress the writing of a carriage return to the output file until the @...SAY...GET is completed.

A CASE statement determines the next portion of the @...SAY...GET, depending on the type of element being processed. Figure 17.21 shows the CASE statement and the template code for processing a Text element and a Box element. User-defined functions provide the color and line thickness for the Box element, which is determined by attributes from the design object file.

In the next section of code is a Field element. If the field is not editable, you set up a SAY and include a PICTURE (see fig. 17.22). Again, attribute information from the design object file is used to format the syntax for the command language line.

```
//
    if Element_type == @Text_element or Element_type == @Fld_element then
    if Fld_fieldtype == calc}
    *-- Calculated field: {lower(Fld_fieldname)} - {Fld_descript}
    {    endif
    if Fld_fieldtype == memvar then}
    *-- Memory variable: {lower(Fld_fieldname)}
    {    endif}
    @ {nul2zero(Row_positn) - line_cnt},{nul2zero(Col_positn)} \
    {  endif
    if ELEMENT_TYPE == @Box_element then}
    @ {nul2zero(Box_top) - line_cnt},{nul2zero(Box_left)} TO \
    {    temp = nul2zero(Box_top) + Box_height - line_cnt - 1;
    if temp > scrn_size then scrn_size else temp endif},\
    {    nul2zero(Box_left) + Box_width - 1} \
    {  endif}
    //
```

Fig. 17.20

*Calculating row
and column
positions.*

```
{  case ELEMENT_TYPE of
    @Text_element:
    // Certain control characters can cause dBASE problems, such
    // as ASCII(13,26,0). So the form designer will send them to
    // you either as a string if they are all the same character
    // or as individual characters if they differ. You handle this
    // by using the chr() function to "SAY" them in dBASE.
    }
    SAY \
    {    if asc(text_item) < 32 then
    if len(text_item) == 1 then}
    CHR({asc(text_item)}) \
    {    else}
    REPLICATE(CHR({asc(text_item)}), {len(text_item)}) \
    {    endif
    else}
    "{Text_Item}" \
    {  endif
        outcolor();
        @Box_element:
        outbox(Box_type, Box_special_char);
        outcolor();
```

Fig. 17.21

*Processing Text
and Box elements.*

Fig. 17.22

Setting up a SAY with a PICTURE clause.

```
@Fld_element:
if !Fld_editable then; // It's a SAY}
SAY \
{        if Fld_fieldtype == calc then
// Loop through expression in case it is longer than 237
foreach Fld_expression fcursor in k
Fld_expression}
{        next}
// Output a space after the Fld_expression and get ready for picture clause
\
{        else // Not an editable field
if Fld_fieldtype == dbf then temp = "" else temp = "m->" endif;
lower(temp + Fld_fieldname)} \
{        endif
temp = Fld_template;
if Fld_template && !(AT("DD",temp) | AT("HH",temp) | AT("MM",temp)
| AT("SS",temp) | chr(Fld_value_type) == "M") then}
PICTURE "{  if Fld_picfun then}@{Fld_picfun}\
{          if AT("S", Fld_picfun) then}{Fld_pic_scroll}{endif}\
{//leave this space}\
{          endif
if !AT("S", Fld_picfun) and !AT("M", Fld_picfun) then
Fld_template}\
{          endif}" \
{          endif
```

If the field is editable, you bypass the code shown in figure 17.22 and set up a
GET, including PICTURE, RANGE, VALID, ERROR, WHEN, DEFAULT, and MESSAGE
clauses as appropriate. This code is shown in figure 17.23.

You are now at the end of the code for processing the @...SAY...GET commands. As each portion of the command was set up, the backslash character
was used to prevent a carriage return from being written to the output file. A
blank line in the template is used to force a carriage return to be written to the
output file in order to complete the command, and the NEXT command is used
to loop back to FOREACH to process the next field. These operations are shown
in figure 17.24.

```
        else // It's a GET}
GET \
{        if Fld_fieldtype == dbf then temp = "" else temp = "m->" endif;
lower(temp + Fld_fieldname)} \
{        if chr(Fld_value_type) == "M" && Fld_mem_typ then
if wnd_cnt < 20  then ++wnd_cnt endif;
if Fld_mem_typ == 1}OPEN {endif}WINDOW Wndow{wnd_cnt} \
{        endif
temp = Fld_template;
        if Fld_template && !(AT("DD",temp) | AT("HH",temp) | AT("MM",temp)
        | AT("SS",temp) | chr(Fld_value_type) == "M") then}
        PICTURE "{if Fld_picfun then}@{Fld_picfun}\
{                if AT("S", Fld_picfun) then}{Fld_pic_scroll}{endif}\
{//leave this space}\
{        endif
        if AT("M", Fld_picfun)}{Fld_pic_choice}{endif}\
{        if !AT("S", Fld_picfun) and !AT("M", Fld_picfun) then
Fld_template}\
{        endif}" \
{        endif
        if Fld_l_bound or Fld_u_bound then color_flg = 1;}
        ;
        RANGE {Fld_l_bound}{if Fld_u_bound then},{Fld_u_bound}{endif} \
{        endif
        if Fld_ok_cond then color_flg = 1;}
        ;
        VALID {Fld_ok_cond} \
{        if Fld_rej_msg then}
        ;
        ERROR \
{        if !AT("IIF", upper(Fld_hlp_msg))}"{endif}{Fld_rej_msg}\
{        if !AT("IIF", upper(Fld_hlp_msg))}"{endif} \
{        endif

        endif // Fld_ok_cond
        if Fld_ed_cond then color_flg = 1;}
        ;
        WHEN {Fld_ed_cond} \
{        endif
        if Fld_def_val then color_flg = 1;}
        ;
        DEFAULT {Fld_def_val} \
{        endif
```

Fig. 17.23

Setting up a GET with the appropriate clauses.

Fig. continues

Fig. continued

```
        if Fld_hlp_msg then color_flg = 1;}
        ;
        MESSAGE \
        {               if !AT("IIF", upper(Fld_hlp_msg))}"{endif}{Fld_hlp_msg}\
        {               if !AT("IIF", upper(Fld_hlp_msg))}"{endif} \
        {       endif
        endif // Fld_editable
        outcolor();
        color_flg=0;
        otherwise: goto getnext;
```

Fig. 17.24

Forcing a carriage return and using NEXT.

```
        endcase
        }

// Leave the above blank line; it forces a line feed!
//-----------------
// End of @ SAY GET
//-----------------
{  ++cnt;
   getnext:
   next k;
   }
```

Completing the Template

Because the values of TALK and STATUS were stored, the code to restore them to their original states is written to the output file (see fig. 17.25). Code for releasing any windows and any "carry" fields is written as well.

At this point, the code for the design object has been generated, but you still have a couple of tasks to accomplish (see fig. 17.26). First, you need to check the field counter maintained during generation to ensure that the form was not empty. If it was empty, you issue an error message (form_empty).

```
*-- Format file exit code -----------------------------------------

*-- SET STATUS was \
{if dB_status then}
ON when you went into the Forms Designer.
IF lc_status = "OFF"      && Entered form with status off
   SET STATUS OFF         && Turn STATUS "OFF" on the way out
   {else}
   OFF when you went into the Forms Designer.
   IF lc_status = "ON"  && Entered form with status on
   SET STATUS ON         && Turn STATUS "ON" on the way out
   {endif}
   ENDIF
   {if carry_flg then}

IF lc_carry = "OFF"
   SET CARRY OFF
   ENDIF
   {endif}
   {if wnd_names then}

RELEASE WINDOWS {substr(wnd_names, 1, (len(wnd_names) - 1))}
{endif}

IF lc_talk="ON"
   SET TALK ON
   ENDIF

RELEASE {if carry_flg then}lc_carry,{endif}lc_talk,lc_fields,lc_status
*-- EOP: {filename(fmt_name)}FMT
```

Fig. 17.25

Restoring the values of TALK and STATUS.

```
{if cnt == 0 then
   pause(form_empty + any_key);
   endif;
   fileerase(fmt_name+".FMO");
   nogen:
   return 0;
```

Fig. 17.26

Completing the template.

You then erase the compiled version of the program just generated. When dBASE is run, the compiled version is used, if found. If the compiled version is not found, the program is recompiled and then run. If you do not erase the previous compiled version, dBASE will run it, and your changes will not be put into effect. Erasing that version forces dBASE to compile your new program source. After erasing the previous compiled version, you are finished.

This discussion of the FORM.COD has shown you many of the techniques available in the Template Language. For additional insights, you may want to study the other templates supplied with the Developer's Edition.

Using the Template Compiler

The dBASE IV template compiler is a stand-alone utility invoked at the DOS prompt. If you execute this program from the dot prompt with the RUN command, you will get an insufficient memory error.

The compiler is contained in the file DTC.EXE, which compiles .COD files into .GEN files. The .GEN files can then be used by the Applications Generator and the three object generators (reports, labels, and forms). By issuing the INCLUDE command in a template, you can combine several .COD and .DEF files into one compiled object file with the extension .GEN.

To invoke the template compiler, you issue the following command:

DTC ‹*arguments*›

The DTC command includes four possible arguments. Each is a single lowercase letter preceded by a dash. Spaces between the argument and the file name are optional. Full path names for the argument's file specification are honored. The four arguments include the following:

1. -i ‹*filename*›

   Specifies the .COD file to be compiled.

2. -o ‹*filename*›

   Specifies the output name of the object file. The file extension must be included as part of the file name. If this argument is omitted, the resulting object file will be given the first name of the input file and the extension .GEN.

3. -l ‹*filename*›

   Produces a listing of the source code (with added line numbers). If you do not specify a file with the -l argument, the listing is sent to the screen. You also can include in the source code (the .COD file) commands that will affect the action of the listing. These commands include the following:

```
#CODEON
#CODEOFF
#LISTON
#LISTOFF
```

4. -a

Causes the listing to contain assembly language translations in the listing output.

Using the Template Interpreter

In addition to providing the compiler, dBASE IV supplies a template interpreter. You can use the interpreter to test your templates instead of testing them with the actual object generators. The advantage of using the template interpreter for initial testing is that it includes a debugger that can help you find and document errors in your templates.

To invoke the template interpreter, you issue the following command at the DOS prompt:

```
DGEN <arguments>
```

Like the compiler, the arguments of the DGEN command begin with a dash followed by a single lowercase letter. DGEN's arguments include the following:

1. -t <filename>

This argument tells DGEN the name of the input file to process. This file is the -o file produced by the compiler.

2. -i <filelist>

This optional argument specifies the object files. To specify one or more object files, you use the wild-card characters * or ? (as in *.POP), or a comma-delimited list (such as PAR.POP,PAR.BAR, PAK.BAR).

3. -l <listfile>

With this argument, the debugger writes to disk a diagnostic listing of information.

4. -n

This optional argument is used to echo command-line arguments to the screen during processing.

Object files created by the Applications Generator can be used just as they are produced. Files created by the other object generators must be created as .NPI files in order to be used with DGEN. An .NPI file is controlled by an environment variable created with the DOS SET command. Three variables can be used with DGEN:

1. SET DTL_TRANSLATE = ON

   This variable tells dBASE IV to write .NPI files for use with DGEN when report formats, label formats, or screen formats are created.

2. SET DTL_NOGEN = ON

   This variable causes the creation of dBASE code to be suppressed when .NPI files are written. Usually the variable is used with DTL_TRANSLATE.

3. SET DTL_TRACE = ON

   This variable displays all elements and attributes that are lower than frame level, echoing the selectors contained in .DEF files.

Debugging the Template

You invoke the DGEN template debugger by including either the DEBUG() or BREAKPOINT() function in the source code for the template. Seven levels of debugging are available. You can access the appropriate level by including a numeric argument within the parentheses of the DEBUG() function. These arguments are listed in table 17.3.

Table 17.3
Numeric Arguments of DEBUG()

Argument	Meaning
0	The Debugger is OFF; it is not called.
1	Displays the generated text on-screen.
2	Displays the generated text on-screen and monitors the keyboard for an entry that will change the debug level.
3	Displays the generated text on-screen, monitors the keyboard for an entry that will change the debugging level, and displays the template commands as they are issued.

Table 17.3—*Continued*

Argument	Meaning
4	Displays the generated text on-screen, monitors the keyboard for an entry that will change the debugging level, displays the template commands as they are issued, and single-steps the execution of the template.
5	Displays the generated text on-screen, monitors the keyboard for an entry that will change the debugging level, displays the template commands as they are issued, and traces the stack and assembly code.
6	Displays the generated text on-screen, monitors the keyboard for an entry that will change the debugging level, displays the template commands as they are issued, single-steps the execution of the template, and traces the stack and assembly code.

For the debugging levels 3 through 6, the commands executed in the template are also printed to the file specified by the -1 argument.

The BREAKPOINT() function takes between its parentheses a character-string argument that echoes to the screen, and a prompt asking the user to specify a new debugging level. If the -1 argument was used to invoke DGEN, the BREAKPOINT message (added as an argument to the function) is printed to the listing file.

Summary

In this chapter, you were introduced to one of the most advanced topics in dBASE IV—the Template Language, which is supplied with the Developer's Edition.

You learned that templates are programs which interact with data from design objects to create dBASE programs or object documentation. You were shown the four basic parts of a template—comments, introduction, text, and commands. And, by examining the FORM.COD template, you saw how a template operates. In addition, you learned how the template compiler and interpreter work, as well as the two Template Language functions used for debugging.

The dBASE IV Template Language enables you to customize the generation of forms, labels, and reports used in your programs. By tailoring these design objects to your specifications, you can reduce the amount of hand coding done to produce your applications. Although the Applications Generator may never replace hand-generated code, the Template Language allows you to enhance the Applications Generator's capability to produce code that meets your specifications.

dBASE IV Commands and Functions

This appendix provides an alphabetical listing of dBASE IV commands and functions. A few of the commands are followed by italicized elements, such as *‹variable›* or *‹filename›*, which are enclosed in angle brackets (‹ ›). When you type these commands, you should substitute the appropriate information for each italicized element. Do not type the angle brackets (‹ ›).

Summary of Commands

?

Displays the contents of an expression on a new display line or print line.

```
? "Employee's name..."+FIRST_NAME+LAST_NAME
? HOURS*PAYRATE
? "Gross Pay..."+STR(GROSSPAY,7,2)
```

??

Displays output on the same display line or print line.

```
?? "Invoice number: "+INVNO
```

???

Outputs characters directly to the printer without changing the column and row position.

```
??? CHR(27) + "X"
```

@<row,column> GET

Displays user-formatted data at the screen location specified by *‹row,column›*.

```
@5,10 GET SSNO PICTURE "999-99-9999"
```

@<row,column> SAY

Displays user-formatted data on the screen or printer at the location specified by *‹row,column›*.

```
@5,10 SAY "Enter the Social Security Number "
@6,10 SAY mtotal PICTURE "$##,###.##"
```

@<row,column> SAY...GET <field name or variable>

Displays user-formatted data on the screen at the location specified by *‹row,column›*; used for appending or editing a data field or inputing data into a variable.

```
@5,10 SAY "Last name : " GET LAST_NAME
```

@ <row,column> CLEAR TO <row,column>

Clears a portion of the screen.

```
@ 3,10 CLEAR TO 12,20
```

@ <row,column> FILL TO <row,column> COLOR

Changes the color of an area of the screen.

```
@ 4,5 FILL TO 10,18 COLOR G/N
```

@ <row,column> TO <row,column>

Displays a box on the screen. DOUBLE specifies a double-line box, PANEL shows a solid border in inverse video, and COLOR attributes may be specified.

```
@ 4,6 TO 8,10 DOUBLE COLOR G/N
@ 4,6 TO 8,10 PANEL
```

ACCEPT

Assigns an alphanumeric string to a memory variable while displaying an optional prompt.

```
ACCEPT "Enter your last name..." TO LASTNAME
```

ACTIVATE MENU

Causes a defined bar menu to become activated. Optionally you may specify the default menu PAD.

```
ACTIVATE MENU mainmenu PAD lookup
```

ACTIVATE POPUP

Causes a defined pop-up menu to become activated.

```
ACTIVATE POPUP sysfile
```

ACTIVATE SCREEN

When a window is active, this command restores output to the entire screen, but existing window text remains.

ACTIVATE WINDOW

Directs screen output to a defined window. Use the ALL option to activate all defined windows.

```
ACTIVATE WINDOW mainwind
ACTIVATE WINDOW ALL
```

APPEND

Adds a data record to the end of the active database file and causes full-screen editing mode to activate using the current format.

```
USE EMPLOYEE
APPEND
```

APPEND BLANK

Adds a blank record to the end of the current database but does not activate full-screen editing mode.

```
USE EMPLOYEE
APPEND BLANK
```

APPEND FROM

Adds records from one database file to the current database file. The optional TYPE qualifier specifies the format of the source file if it is not a dBASE file.

```
USE HISTORY
APPEND FROM MONTHLY


USE NEWPARTS
APPEND FROM ADDLIST.TXT TYPE SDF FOR ACCT_NO="10123"
```

APPEND FROM ARRAY

Appends records to the database from values stored in an array.

```
APPEND FROM ARRAY empdata FOR lname="Jones"
```

APPEND MEMO

Places a text file into a specified memo field of the current record. The OVERWRITE option replaces the existing contents of the memo field with the new text.

```
APPEND MEMO remarks FROM letter.txt OVERWRITE
```

ASSIST

Activates the Control Center menu.

AVERAGE

Computes the average of a numeric expression and assigns the value to a memory variable or array, with or without a condition.

```
AVERAGE ANNUAL_PAY TO AVERAGEPAY
AVERAGE QTY_SOLD TO AVG_SALE FOR MODEL_NO="XYZ"
AVERAGE HOURS*PAYRATE TO ARRAY AVERAGEPAY FOR .NOT. MALE
```

BEGIN TRANSACTION

Begins transaction processing, logging to the transaction file all changes made to data so that data can be restored to its original state with the ROLLBACK command. See also END TRANSACTION.

BROWSE

Displays for review or modification records from the active database file in tabular format.

```
USE EMPLOYEE
GO TOP
BROWSE
```

BROWSE FIELDS

Browses selected data fields in the current database file.

```
USE EMPLOYEE
GO TOP
BROWSE FIELDS FIRST_NAME, LAST_NAME, PHONE_NO
```

CALCULATE

Calculates one or more statistical and financial functions on the entire database or on selected records, and optionally stores the results in a memory variable or an array.

```
CALCULATE AVG(Salary),MAX(Salary) FOR OFFICE="Chicago"
TO Avsal,Mxsal
```

CALL

Executes a binary program that has previously been put in memory with the LOAD command.

```
CALL mathpak
```

CANCEL

Terminates the processing of a program file and returns the control to the dot prompt.

```
IF EOF()
CANCEL
ENDIF
```

CHANGE

Displays the data records in a full-screen edit mode. `CHANGE` is identical to the `EDIT` command.

```
USE EMPLOYEE
CHANGE


USE EMPLOYEE
CHANGE FOR ZIP_CODE="46250"
```

CLEAR

Clears (erases) the screen and releases pending GETs.

CLEAR ALL

Closes all open database-related files (including .DBF, .NDX, .FMT, .CAT and .DBT files) and releases all memory variables, array elements, pop-up definitions, and window definitions.

CLEAR FIELDS

Releases the data fields that have been created by the `SET FIELDS TO` command.

CLEAR GETS

Clears all pending GETs that have not been satisfied by a `READ` command.

```
@5,10 SAY "Account number : " GET ACCT_NO
CLEAR GETS
@7,10 Say "Account name : " GET ACCT_NAME
READ
```

CLEAR MEMORY

Releases all memory variables and array elements.

CLEAR MENUS

Clears all user menus from the screen and from memory.

CLEAR POPUPS

Clears all pop-up menus from the screen and from memory.

CLEAR TYPEAHEAD

Empties the type-ahead buffer so that no unprocessed keystrokes remain.

CLEAR WINDOWS

Clears all windows from the screen and from memory.

CLOSE

Closes various types of files.

```
CLOSE ALL
CLOSE ALTERNATE
CLOSE DATABASES
CLOSE FORMAT
CLOSE INDEX
CLOSE PROCEDURE
```

COMPILE

Compiles a dBASE IV source code program file into an executable object code file.

CONTINUE

Resumes the search started with the LOCATE command.

```
USE EMPLOYEE
LOCATE FOR ZIP_CODE="46250"
DISPLAY
CONTINUE
DISPLAY
```

CONVERT

In multiuser applications, adds a field to the database structure for record locking.

COPY FILE

Duplicates an existing file of any type, using a new file name or path name.

```
COPY FILE MAINPROG.PRG TO MAIN.PRG
COPY FILE \TEMP\COST.FMT TO COST.FMT
COPY FILE ROSTER.FRM TO NAMELIST.FRM
```

COPY INDEXES

Used to convert index files (.NDX) to tags in a multiple index file (.MDX). The default .MDX file is the production index file.

```
COPY INDEXES NAME,STATE TO PERSONS
```

COPY MEMO

Copies the information in a memo field to a file. The ADDITIVE option appends the information to the output file.

```
COPY MEMO REMARKS TO INFO.DOC ADDITIVE
```

COPY STRUCTURE

Copies the data structure to another database file.

```
USE COST
COPY STRUCTURE TO NEWCOST
```

COPY STRUCTURE EXTENDED

Creates a database whose records contain the field structure of the current database.

```
COPY TO LAYOUT STRUCTURE EXTENDED
```

COPY TAG

Converts tags from a multiple index (.MDX) file to index (.NDX) files. The default .MDX file is the production index file.

```
COPY TAG LAST OF NAMES TO NAME.NDX
```

COPY TO

Copies selected fields of a source database file to a new file, with or without a qualifier. The TYPE clause specifies the format of the output file.

```
USE EMPLOYEE
COPY TO ROSTER FIELDS FIRST_NAME, LAST_NAME
COPY TO SALARY.TXT FIELDS LAST_NAME, ANNUAL_PAY
FOR MALE TYPE SDF
```

COPY TO ARRAY

Places the values of records into an array. The array must have been previously declared.

```
DECLARE PEOPLE[9]
COPY TO ARRAY PEOPLE NAME FOR NAME="Jones"
```

COUNT

Counts the number of records in the active database file and assigns the number to a memory variable.

```
USE EMPLOYEE
COUNT TO NRECORDS
COUNT FOR ANNUAL_PAY>="50000" .AND. MALE TO RICHMEN
```

CREATE

Sets up a new file structure and adds data records.

```
CREATE EMPLOYEE
```

CREATE APPLICATION

Activates the Applications Generator, allowing you to create a dBASE IV application.

```
CREATE APPLICATION NEWPROG
```

CREATE FROM

Creates a database from the structure stored in a file created with COPY STRUCTURE EXTENDED.

```
CREATE PEOPLE FROM NEWFILE
```

CREATE LABEL

Displays a design form to set up a label file (.LBL).

```
CREATE LABEL MAILLIST
```

CREATE QUERY

Displays the query design screen, which allows the user to create a new query file (.QBE).

```
USE EMPLOYEE
CREATE QUERY FINDEMPL
```

CREATE REPORT

Displays a design form to set up a report form file (.FRM).

```
CREATE REPORT WEEKLY
```

CREATE SCREEN

Creates a new screen file (.SCR) and format file (.FMT).

```
USE EMPLOYEE
CREATE SCREEN SHOWEMPL
```

CREATE VIEW

Creates a new view query file.

```
USE EMPLOYEE
CREATE VIEW SAMPLE
```

CREATE VIEW FROM ENVIRONMENT

Creates a view (.VUE) file that can be used with dBASE III Plus.

DEACTIVATE MENU

Erases an active menu bar from the screen, making it inactive.

DEACTIVATE POPUP

Erases an active pop-up menu from the screen, making it inactive.

DEACTIVATE WINDOW

Erases an active window from the screen, making it inactive.

DEBUG

Executes a dBASE IV program using the full-screen debugger.

```
DEBUG EMPLOY.PRG
```

DECLARE

Declares a one- or two-dimensional array of memory variables.

```
DECLARE PEOPLE[9]
```

DEFINE BAR

Defines a bar for a pop-up menu. The optional MESSAGE line is displayed at the bottom of the screen, and the SKIP option specifies when a bar is accessible.

```
DEFINE BAR 3 OF NAMEMENU PROMPT "Choose name"
MESSAGE "Please make a selection" SKIP FOR MALE
```

DEFINE BOX

Defines a box to be printed in a report.

```
DEFINE BOX FROM <column> TO <column> HEIGHT <lines>
SINGLE/DOUBLE
```

DEFINE MENU

Assigns a name and optional message to a menu.

```
DEFINE MENU NAMES MESSAGE "Please make a selection"
```

DEFINE PAD

Defines a pad for a bar menu.

```
DEFINE PAD UPDATE OF MENU1 PROMPT "Update" AT 1,15
MESSAGE "Make a selection"
```

DEFINE POPUP

Defines a pop-up window menu.

```
DEFINE POPUP UPDATE FROM 2,4 TO 6,10 PROMPT FIELD NAME
```

DEFINE WINDOW

Defines a screen window.

```
DEFINE WINDOW UPDATE FROM 4,6 TO 8,12 DOUBLE COLOR W,G
```

DELETE

Marks the records in the active database file with a deletion symbol.

```
USE EMPLOYEE
DELETE
DELETE RECORD 5
DELETE NEXT 3
DELETE FOR AREA_CODE="503"
```

DELETE TAG

Removes an index tag from a multiple index file (.MDX).

```
DELETE TAG L_NAME OF PEOPLE
```

DIR

Displays the file directory.

`DIR`	Displays .DBF files
`DIR *.* .PA`	Displays all files
`DIR *.PRG`	Displays program files
`DIR *.NDX`	Displays index files
`DIR X*.DBF`	Displays .DBF file names beginning with X
`DIR ??X???.PRG`	Displays .PRG file names that have six letters and X as the third character
`DIR ???.*`	Displays all file names that are three characters long

DISPLAY

Shows the contents of the data records one screen at a time.

```
USE EMPLOYEE
DISPLAY
DISPLAY RECORD 3
DISPLAY NEXT 2
DISPLAY LAST_NAME,FIRST_NAME
DISPLAY AREA_CODE,PHONE_NO FOR AREA_CODE="206"
```

DISPLAY FILES

Shows a directory of files.

DISPLAY MEMORY

Shows the contents of active memory variables.

DISPLAY STATUS

Shows the current processing situation, including the names of active files, the work area number, and so on.

DISPLAY STRUCTURE

Shows the data structure of an active database file.

```
USE EMPLOYEE
DISPLAY STRUCTURE
```

DISPLAY USERS

Shows users logged into a network using dBASE IV.

DO

Executes a program file.

```
DO MAINPROG
```

DO CASE...ENDCASE

A multiple-avenue branching command.

```
DO CASE
   CASE ANSWER="Y"
      ...
   CASE ANSWER="N"
      ...
   OTHERWISE
      ...
      RETURN
ENDCASE
```

DO WHILE...ENDDO

A program loop command.

```
DO WHILE .NOT. EOF()
...
...
ENDDO
```

EDIT

Displays a data record for editing.

```
USE EMPLOYEE
GOTO 5
EDIT

USE EMPLOYEE
EDIT RECORD 5
```

EJECT

Advances the printer paper to the top of the next page.

END TRANSACTION

Indicates the end of transaction processing and stops logging changes made to data so that data can no longer be restored to its original state with the ROLLBACK command. See also BEGIN TRANSACTION.

ERASE

Removes a file from the directory. The file to be erased must be closed.

```
ERASE SALE.DBF
ERASE SAMPLE.PRG
```

EXIT

Exits from a program loop, as in the following loop created with DO WHILE...ENDDO.

```
DO WHILE .T.
   ...
   IF EOF()
      EXIT
   ENDIF
   ...
ENDDO
```

EXPORT TO

Converts a dBASE IV file to another file format specified in the TYPE clause, such as PFS, DBASEII, FW2 (Framework II), or RPD (RapidFile).

```
EXPORT TO NEWNAMES TYPE FW2
```

FIND

Searches for the first data record in an indexed file with a specified search key.

```
FIND "206"
```

FUNCTION

Indicates the beginning of a user-defined function.

```
FUNCTION SALARY
```

GO BOTTOM

Positions the record pointer at the last record in the database file.

```
USE EMPLOYEE
GO BOTTOM
```

GO TOP

Positions the record pointer at the first record in the database file.

```
USE EMPLOYEE
GO TOP
```

GOTO

Positions the record pointer at the indicated record in the database file.

```
USE EMPLOYEE
GOTO BOTTOM
GO TOP
GOTO 4
```

HELP

Calls up the help screens; can be used with a keyword to specify the subject.

```
HELP
HELP CREATE
HELP JOIN
```

IF...ELSE...ENDIF

A conditional branching construction.

```
IF CHOICE="Q"
   RETURN
ELSE
   ...
   ...
ENDIF
```

IMPORT FROM

Converts another file format to a dBASE IV file. See also EXPORT TO.

```
IMPORT FROM OLDFILE TYPE PFS
```

INDEX

Creates a key file in which all records are ordered according to the contents of the specified key field. The records can be arranged in alphabetical, chronological, or numerical order. If you are specifying a tag of a multiple index file (.MDX) instead of an index file (.NDX), the descending order option may be used.

```
INDEX ON NAME TO TAG NAME OF PEOPLE DESCENDING
```

INPUT

Assigns a data element to a memory variable using information entered from the keyboard.

```
INPUT PAYRATE
INPUT "Enter units sold :" TO UNITSSOLD
```

INSERT

Adds a new record to the database file at the current record location. The BEFORE option adds a record in the position just before the current position of the record pointer.

```
GOTO 4
INSERT
GOTO 6
INSERT BEFORE
GOTO 5
INSERT BLANK
```

JOIN

Creates a new database file by merging specified data records from two open database files.

```
SELECT A
USE NEWSTOCKS
SELECT B
USE STOCKS
JOIN WITH NEWSTOCKS TO ALLSTOCK FOR STOCK_NO=A->STOCK_NO
```

LABEL FORM

Displays data records with labels specified in a label file.

```
LABEL FORM ROSTER FOR AREA_CODE="206" .AND. MALE
```

LIST

Shows the contents of selected data records in the active database file.

```
USE EMPLOYEE
LIST
LIST RECORD 5
LIST LAST_NAME,FIRST_NAME
LIST LAST_NAME,FIRST_NAME FOR AREA_CODE="206" .OR. MALE
```

LIST FILES

Shows a directory of files.

LIST HISTORY

Shows a list of commands stored in the HISTORY buffer.

LIST MEMORY

Shows name, type, and size of each active memory variable; also shows the amount of memory allocated to and used by dBASE IV.

LIST STATUS

Lists the current processing situation, including the names of active files, work area number, and so on.

```
LIST STATUS
LIST STATUS TO PRINT
```

LIST STRUCTURE

Displays the data structure of the active database file.

```
USE EMPLOYEE
LIST STRUCTURE
LIST STRUCTURE TO PRINT
```

The IN clause specifies an unselected work area.

```
LIST STRUCTURE IN NAMES TO FILE STRUC.TXT
```

LIST USERS

Shows the users logged into a dBASE IV network.

LOAD

Loads a binary program file into memory.

LOCATE

Sequentially searches data records of the active database file for a record that satisfies a specified condition.

```
LOCATE FOR LAST_NAME="Smith"
```

LOGOUT

In a network, logs a user out of the program.

LOOP

Transfers execution from the middle of a program loop to the beginning of the loop.

```
DO WHILE .T.
...
...
IF ...
LOOP
ENDIF
...
ENDDO
```

MODIFY COMMAND/FILE

Invokes the text editor to create or edit a program file (.PRG), a format file (.FMT), or a text file (.TXT). The default file extension is .PRG. With the command MODIFY FILE, no default file extension is provided.

```
MODIFY COMMAND MAINPROG
MODIFY COMMAND BILLING.PRG
MODIFY COMMAND EMPLOYEE.FMT
MODIFY COMMAND TEXTFILE.TXT
```

MODIFY APPLICATION

Uses the Applications Generator to change an existing application.

MODIFY LABEL

Creates or edits a label file (.LBL) for the active database file.

```
USE EMPLOYEE
MODIFY LABEL MAILLIST
```

MODIFY QUERY/VIEW

Creates or edits a query file.

```
USE EMPLOYEE
MODIFY QUERY FINDEMPL
```

MODIFY REPORT

Creates or edits a report form file (.FRM) for the active database file.

```
USE QTYSOLD
MODIFY REPORT WEEKLY
```

MODIFY SCREEN

Creates or edits a screen file (.SCR).

```
USE EMPLOYEE
MODIFY SCREEN SHOWEMPL.SCR
```

MODIFY STRUCTURE

Displays for modification the structure of the active database file.

```
USE EMPLOYEE
MODIFY STRUCTURE
```

MOVE WINDOW

Relocates a window on the screen. The BY clause specifies movement relative to the current position.

```
MOVE WINDOW UPDATE TO 5,8
MOVE WINDOW UPDATE BY 6,1
```

NOTE

Marks the beginning of a remark line in a program.

```
SET TALK OFF
SET ECHO OFF
NOTE Enter hours worked and payrate from the keyboard
INPUT "Enter hours worked ... " TO HOURS
INPUT "       hourly rate ... " TO PAYRATE
...
...
```

ON ERROR/ESCAPE/KEY

Specifies a command to execute if an error is detected or if the Esc key or any key is pressed.

```
ON ERROR DO FIX
ON ESCAPE DO PREVIOUS
ON KEY DO LEAVE
```

ON PAD

Specifies which pop-up menu to execute when a menu pad is selected.

```
ON PAD LOCATE OF MENU1 ACTIVATE POPUP FINDMENU
```

ON PAGE

Performs a certain command when a specified line is reached on the current page.

```
ON PAGE AT LINE 24 DO FOOTERS
```

ON READERROR

Performs a command when an error is encountered during a full-screen operation.

```
ON READERROR DO WARNING
```

ON SELECTION PAD

Specifies a command to execute when a certain bar menu pad is selected.

```
ON SELECTION PAD SEARCH OF MENU1 DO GOFIND
```

ON SELECTION POPUP

Specifies a command to execute when a selection is made from a pop-up menu. The ALL option performs the command for all pop-up menus.

```
ON SELECTION POPUP NAMES DO GOFIND
ON SELECTION POPUP ALL DO GOFIND
```

PACK

Removes data records marked for deletion by the DELETE command.

```
USE EMPLOYEE
PACK
```

PARAMETERS

Assigns local variable names to data items that are to be passed from a calling program module.

```
*****  Program: MULTIPLY.PRG  *****
* A program to multiply variable A by variable B
PARAMETERS A,B,C
C = A*B
RETURN
```

The preceding program is called from the following main program:

```
* The main program
HOURS = 38
PAYRATE = 8.5
DO MULTIPLY WITH HOURS,PAYRATE,GROSSPAY
? "Gross Wage =",GROSSPAY
RETURN
```

PLAY MACRO

If a keyboard macro has been created, this command executes the specified macro.

PRINTJOB/ENDPRINTJOB

These two commands indicate the beginning and end of a print job.

PRIVATE

Declares private variables in a program module.

```
PRIVATE VARIABLEA, VARIABLEB, VARIABLEC
```

PROCEDURE

Identifies the beginning of each procedure in a procedure file.

PROTECT

In a network, used for data security by allowing for password protection and data encryption.

PUBLIC

Declares public variables or arrays to be shared by all program modules.

```
PUBLIC VARIABLEA, VARIABLEB, VARIABLEC
PUBLIC ARRAY <elements>
```

QUIT

Closes all open files, terminates dBASE IV processing, and exits to DOS.

READ

Activates all the @...SAY...GET commands issued since the last CLEAR, CLEAR ALL, CLEAR GETS, or READ was issued.

```
@6,10 SAY "First name : " GET FIRST_NAME
READ
```

RECALL

Recovers all data records marked for deletion.

```
RECALL
RECALL ALL
RECALL RECORD 5
```

REINDEX

Rebuilds all active index files (.NDX) and multiple index files (.MDX).

```
USE EMPLOYEE ORDER AREACODE
REINDEX
```

RELEASE

Deletes all or selected memory variables. Also used to release assembly language program modules, menus, pop-up menus, and windows from memory.

```
RELEASE ALL
RELEASE ALL LIKE NET*
RELEASE ALL EXCEPT ???COST

RELEASE MODULE ASMPROG
RELEASE MENUS NEWNAME
```

RENAME

Changes the name of a disk file.

```
RENAME XYZ.DBF TO ABC.DBF
```

REPLACE

Changes the contents of specified data fields in an active database file.

```
USE EMPLOYEE
REPLACE ALL ANNUAL_PAY WITH ANNUAL_PAY*1.05
```

REPORT FORM

Displays information from the active database file with the custom form specified in the report form file (.FRM).

```
USE QTYSOLD
REPORT FORM WEEKLY TO PRINT
```

RESET

Used with the transaction processing commands BEGIN TRANSACTION, END TRANSACTION, and ROLLBACK, this command resets the integrity flag for a file that the user does not want to ROLLBACK.

RESTORE FROM

Retrieves memory variables from a memory file (.MEM).

```
RESTORE FROM MEMLIST.MEM
RESTORE FROM MEMLIST ADDITIVE
```

RESTORE MACROS FROM

Retrieves macros stored in the current macro library.

RESTORE WINDOW

Retrieves window definitions from a file.

RESUME

Resumes execution of a program or procedure after it has been stopped by the SUSPEND command.

RETRY

Reexecutes a command that caused an error.

RETURN

Terminates a program and either returns to the dot prompt or transfers execution to the calling program module.

ROLLBACK

Used to restore the contents of a database during transaction processing. See also BEGIN TRANSACTION and END TRANSACTION.

RUN

Executes an .EXE DOS disk file, a .COM DOS disk file, or a .BAT DOS disk file from within dBASE IV.

```
RUN B:XYZ
```

XYZ.EXE, XYZ.COM, or XYZ.BAT is an executable disk file in a DOS directory.

SAVE TO

Stores all or selected memory variables to a memory file (.MEM).

```
SAVE TO ALLVARS
SAVE TO VARLIST ALL LIKE COST????
```

SAVE MACROS

Stores macros to a disk file.

```
SAVE MACROS TO MACFILE
```

SAVE WINDOW

Stores window definitions to a file.

```
SAVE WINDOW UPDATE,SEARCH TO WINDO_FIL
```

SCAN

Searches a file and performs a command on records that meet a specified condition.

```
SCAN NEXT 100 FOR NAME="Jones" WHILE STATE="MN"
REPLACE MAILED WITH "Y"
ENDSCAN
```

SEEK

Searches an indexed database file for the first data record containing the specified key expression.

```
MKEY="206"
SEEK MKEY
```

SELECT

Makes one of 10 database work areas active.

```
SELECT 1
USE EMPLOYEE
SELECT A
USE COSTS
```

SET

Sets control parameters for processing. The default settings (indicated by uppercase letters) are appropriate for most purposes.

SET ALTERNATE on/OFF

Creates a text file, as designated by the SET ALTERNATE TO command, to record the processing activities.

SET AUTOSAVE on/OFF

When ON, saves each record to disk as it is entered. When OFF, saves records when the record buffer is filled.

SET BELL ON/off

Turns on/off the warning bell.

SET BELL TO <frequency,duration>

Specifies how the bell will sound.

SET BLOCKSIZE TO

Specifies the default block size of memo files. Up to 32 blocks of 512 bytes may be used.

SET BORDER TO

Specifies the default border for menus and windows.

SET CARRY on/OFF

Carries the contents of the previous record into an APPENDed record.

SET CARRY TO <field list>

Specifies fields to carry forward when SET CARRY ON is in effect.

SET CATALOG ON/off

Adds files to an open catalog.

SET CATALOG TO

Creates, opens, and closes a catalog file.

SET CENTURY on/OFF

Shows the century in date displays.

SET CLOCK on/OFF

Turns on/off the clock display.

SET CLOCK TO <row,column>

Specifies the location of the clock display.

SET COLOR ON/OFF

Sets output display to color/monochrome monitor. The default is the mode from which dBASE IV is started.

SET COLOR TO

Sets color screen attributes. The following list shows available colors and their letter codes.

Color	Letter
Black	N
Blue	B
Green	G
Cyan	BG
Blank	X
Red	R
Magenta	RB
Brown	GR
White	W

With these codes, you can use an asterisk (*) to indicate blinking characters and a plus sign (+) to indicate high intensity. Format of the command is

```
SET COLOR TO <standard,enhanced,border,background>
```

For example, the following command sets standard video to yellow characters on a red background, and enhanced video to white letters on a red background with a yellow screen border:

```
SET COLOR TO GR*/R,W/R+,GR
```

SET CONFIRM on/OFF

When OFF, the cursor automatically moves to the next entry field when the current field is filled.

SET CONSOLE ON/off

Turns on/off the video display.

SET CURRENCY TO

Specifies the symbol for currency unit used.

SET CURRENCY LEFT/right

Specifies the location of the currency symbol.

SET DATE

Specifies the format for date expressions.

```
SET DATE AMERICAN        (mm/dd/yy)
SET DATE ANSI            (yy.mm.dd)
SET DATE BRITISH         (dd/mm/yy)
SET DATE ITALIAN         (dd-mm-yy)
SET DATE FRENCH          (dd/mm/yy)
SET DATE GERMAN          (dd.mm.yy)
SET DATE USA             (mm/dd/yy)
SET DATE DMY             (dd/mm/yy)
SET DATE YMD             (yy/mm/dd)
```

SET DEBUG on/OFF

Traces the command errors during processing. When DEBUG is ON, messages from SET ECHO ON are routed to the printer.

SET DECIMALS TO

Sets the number of decimal places for values.

```
SET DECIMALS TO 4
```

SET DEFAULT TO

Designates the default disk drive.

```
SET DEFAULT TO B:
```

SET DELETED on/OFF

Determines whether data records marked for deletion are to be ignored.

SET DELIMITERS on/OFF

Marks field widths with the delimiter defined with the SET DELIMITERS TO command.

SET DELIMITERS TO

Specifies the characters for marking a field.

```
SET DELIMITERS TO '[]'
SET DELIMITERS ON
```

SET DESIGN ON/off

When OFF, prevents a user from entering design mode.

SET DEVELOPMENT ON/off

Compares the date and time stamp on .PRG and .OBJ files and recompiles .PRG files if the date has changed. When OFF, the date and time are not checked.

SET DEVICE TO SCREEN/PRINTER/FILE <filename>

Directs output from @...SAY commands to the device specified.

SET DISPLAY TO

Specifies the monitor and number of display lines used: MONO, COLOP, EGA25, EGA43, MONO43.

SET ECHO on/OFF

Displays instructions during execution.

SET ENCRYPTION on/OFF

When ON, allows for encryption of a new database file when PROTECT is used.

SET ESCAPE ON/off

Controls the capability of aborting execution with the Esc key. When ESCAPE is ON, pressing Esc aborts execution of a program.

SET EXACT on/OFF

Determines how two alphanumeric strings are compared.

SET FIELDS on/OFF

Activates the selection of data fields named with the SET FIELDS TO command.

SET FIELDS TO

Selects a set of data fields to be used in one or more files.

```
USE EMPLOYEE
SET FIELDS TO LAST_NAME, FIRST_NAME
SET FIELDS ON
```

SET FILTER TO

Defines the filter conditions.

```
USE EMPLOYEE
SET FILTER TO AREA_CODE="216"
```

SET FIXED on/OFF

Sets all numeric output to the fixed number of decimal places defined by SET
DECIMALS TO.

SET FORMAT

Selects a custom format defined in a format file (.FMT).

SET FULLPATH on/OFF

Returns a full file and path name in functions returning file names, such as
MDX(), NDX(), and DBF().

SET FUNCTION

Redefines a function key for a specific command.

```
SET FUNCTION F10 TO "QUIT;"
```

SET HEADING ON/off

Uses field names as column titles for display of data records with the
DISPLAY, LIST, SUM, and AVERAGE commands.

SET HELP ON/off

Determines whether the Help screen is displayed.

SET HISTORY ON/off

Turns on/off the HISTORY feature.

SET HISTORY TO

Specifies the number of executed commands to be saved in the HISTORY buffer.

```
SET HISTORY TO 10
```

SET HOURS TO 12/24

Selects the time display format.

SET INDEX TO

Opens the specified index files or sets the index order using tags in multiple index files.

```
SET INDEX TO NAME.NDX
SET INDEX TO NAME.NDX ORDER TAG NAMES OF LIST.MDX
```

SET INSTRUCT ON/off

Determines whether instruction boxes will appear during full-screen operations.

SET INTENSITY ON/off

Displays data fields in reverse video with the EDIT and APPEND commands.

SET LOCK ON/off

In a multiuser system, determines whether records are locked.

SET MARGIN TO

Adjusts the left margin for all printed output.

```
SET MARGIN TO 10
```

SET MEMOWIDTH TO

Defines the width of memo field output. The default is 50.

```
SET MEMOWIDTH TO 30
```

SET MESSAGE TO

Displays an alphanumeric string in the message window.

```
SET MESSAGE TO "Hello!"
```

SET NEAR on/OFF

When a search is unsuccessful, setting NEAR to ON positions the record pointer at the expression nearest to the one sought instead of at the end of the file.

SET ODOMETER TO

Specifies how often the record counter display is updated; may be set from 1 (default) to 200.

SET ORDER TO

Sets up an open index file as the controlling index file, or specifies a tag in a multiple index file.

```
SET ORDER TO 2
SET ORDER TO TAG NAME OF LIST.MDX
```

SET PATH TO

Defines the search directory path.

```
SET PATH TO C:\DBDATE\SALES
```

SET PAUSE on/OFF

Displays the result of SQL SELECT commands one screen at a time.

SET POINT TO

Changes the character used for the decimal point.

SET PRECISION TO

Sets the range, from 10 to 20, for the number of digits used for precision in numeric operations. The default is 16.

SET PRINTER on/OFF

When ON, directs output not generated with @...SAY commands to the printer or a file.

SET PRINTER TO

Specifies printer device name.

SET PROCEDURE TO

Opens a specified procedure file.

SET REFRESH TO

On a network, determines how often the screen is refreshed.

SET RELATION TO

Links two open database files according to a common key expression.

SET REPROCESS TO

On a network, sets the number of times that a file is retried.

SET SAFETY ON/off

Displays a warning message when overwriting an existing file.

SET SCOREBOARD ON/off

Displays or hides dBASE messages on the top line.

SET SEPARATOR TO

Changes the symbol for separating numbers. The default is the comma.

SET SKIP TO

When used with SET RELATION TO, allows record pointer in a related database to be updated before the active database record pointer is changed.

SET SPACE ON/off

Determines whether a space is printed between expressions when the ? and ?? commands are used.

SET SQL on/OFF

Accesses SQL mode.

SET STATUS ON/off

Displays or hides the status bar at the bottom of the screen.

SET STEP on/OFF

Causes execution to pause after each command.

SET TALK ON/off

Displays interactive messages during processing.

SET TITLE ON/off

Displays the catalog file title prompt.

SET TRAP on/OFF

Activates the debugger when an error occurs or the Esc key is pressed.

SET TYPEAHEAD TO

Specifies the size of the type-ahead buffer. Possible values are 0 to 32,000 characters; the default is 20 characters.

```
SET TYPEAHEAD TO 30
```

SET UNIQUE on/OFF

When ON, prepares an ordered list with the INDEX command, allowing only the first record with identical keys to be displayed.

SET VIEW TO

Selects the view file.

```
SET VIEW TO EMPLOY
```

SHOW MENU

Displays a bar menu, but does not make it active.

```
SHOW MENU SEARCH PAD NAMES
```

SHOW POPUP

Displays a pop-up menu, but does not make it active.

SKIP

Moves the record pointer forward or backward through the records in the database file.

```
USE EMPLOYEE
GOTO 3
DISPLAY
SKIP 3
DISPLAY
SKIP -1
DISPLAY
```

SORT

Rearranges data records on one or more key fields in ascending or descending order. The default setting is ascending order.

```
USE EMPLOYEE
SORT ON AREA_CODE TO AREACODE
SORT ON ANNUAL_PAY/D TO RANKED
SORT ON AREA_CODE, LAST_NAME /C TO PHONLIST FOR AREA_CODE="206"
```

STORE

Assigns a data element to a memory variable.

```
STORE 1 TO COUNTER
STORE "James" TO FIRSTNAME
```

SUM

Totals the value of a numeric expression and stores the total in a memory variable.

```
USE EMPLOYEE
SUM ANNUAL_PAY TO TOTALPAY
SUM ANNUAL_PAY*0.1 TO DEDUCTIONS
```

SUSPEND

Suspends the execution of a program or procedure.

TEXT

Displays a block of text on the screen or printer. TEXT is used in a program.

```
***** Program: BULLETIN.PRG *****
SET PRINT ON TEXT
This is a sample message to be displayed on the printer
when this program is executed.
ENDTEXT
```

TOTAL

Totals the numeric values of the active database file on a key field and stores the results to another file.

```
USE STOCKS
TOTAL ON MODEL_NO TO BYMODEL
TOTAL ON STOCK_NO TO BYSTOCNO FOR ON_HAND>="2"
```

TYPE

Displays the contents of a disk file to the screen or printer. The NUMBER option prints line numbers.

```
TYPE MAINPROG.PRG NUMBER
TYPE EMPLOYEE.FMT TO PRINT
```

UNLOCK

Makes records available to other users.

UPDATE

Uses records in one database file to update records in another file.

```
SELECT A
USE RECEIVED
SELECT B
USE STOCKS
UPDATE ON STOCK_NO FROM RECEIVED REPLACE ON_HAND WITH A->ON_HAND
```

USE

Opens an existing database file. The index file or index order can be specified, and the NOUPDATE option make the file read-only.

```
USE EMPLOYEE
USE EMPLOYEE ORDER TAG NAME NOUPDATE
```

WAIT

Causes execution to pause until a key is pressed.

```
WAIT
WAIT TO CHOICE
WAIT "Enter your answer (Y/N)? " TO ANSWER
```

ZAP

Removes all data records from the database file without deleting the data structure.

```
USE EMPLOYEE
ZAP
```

Summary of dBASE IV Functions

Functions usually return a value, either a logical value (`.T.` or `.F.`), a numeric value, or a character value. Most end in parentheses. Some functions require that one or more arguments (values) be included within the parentheses, whereas other functions require no argument or have a default argument. For example, to print the integer of 45.678, you could use the following function:

```
. ? INT(45.678)
   45
```

However, the end-of-file function returns a True or False value, and unless an alias is specified within the parentheses, the current database file in use is assumed.

```
. TEST = EOF()
. ? TEST
.F.
```

&

Macro substitution.

$

String is within another string.

ABS()

Absolute value.

ACCESS()

Access level of current user.

ACOS()

Angle in radians of a cosine.

ALIAS()

Alias name of the .DBF file in the specified work area.

ASC()

ASCII code of the first character of a string.

ASIN()

Arcsine, angle in radians for a sine.

AT()

Starting position of a string within another string.

ATAN()

Arctangent, angle in radians for a tangent.

ATN2()

Arctangent, when the cosine and the sine of point are specified.

BAR()

Most recently selected bar number from a pop-up menu.

BOF()

Beginning of file.

CALL()

Binary program module.

CDOW()

Day of week from a date.

CEILING( )

Smallest integer greater than or equal to value.

CHANGE( )

Record change.

CHR( )

Character value of a number.

CMONTH( )

Month name from date.

COL( )

Cursor column position.

COMPLETED( )

Transaction completion.

COS( )

Cosine for angle in radians.

CTOD( )

Converts string to a date.

DATE( )

System date.

DAY( )

Number of day of month.

DBF( )

Database in use.

DELETED( )

Record marked for deletion.

DIFFERENCE()

Difference between two strings.

DISKSPACE()

Bytes available on default drive.

DMY()

Converts to dd/mm/yy format from date expression.

DOW()

Number of day of week from date.

DTOC()

Converts date to a string.

DTOR()

Converts degrees to radians.

DTOS()

Converts date to a string in format CCYYMMDD.

EOF()

End of file.

ERROR()

Error message number.

EXP()

Exponent.

FIELD()

Field name from specified field number.

FILE()

File exists.

FIXED()

Converts floating point numbers to numeric decimals.

FKLABEL()

Function key label.

FKMAX()

Number of function keys.

FLOAT()

Converts numeric values to floating point.

FLOCK()

File locking.

FLOOR()

Largest integer less than or equal to value.

FOUND()

`LOCATE`, `SEEK`, or `CONTINUE` successful.

FV()

Future value.

GETENV()

DOS environment setting.

IIF()

Immediate `IF`. If condition is True, uses first value; otherwise, uses second value.

INKEY()

Key code of last key pressed.

INT( )

Integer.

ISALPHA( )

Character is alphabetic.

ISCOLOR( )

System will display color.

ISLOWER( )

Character lowercase.

ISMARKED( )

Database header marked for change.

ISUPPER( )

Character uppercase.

KEY( )

Key expression for index.

LASTKEY( )

ASCII value of last key pressed.

LEFT( )

Leftmost characters of a string.

LEN( )

Length of a string.

LIKE( )

Compares similarity of strings.

LINENO( )

Line number of command.

LKSYS( )

Log-in name of user, date, and time of record/file lock.

LOCK( )

Locks multiple records.

LOG( )

Natural logarithm.

LOG10( )

Common log to base 10.

LOOKUP( )

Searches for record and returns value from a field.

LOWER( )

Converts to lowercase.

LTRIM( )

Removes leading blanks.

LUPDATE( )

Date of last update.

MAX( )

Larger of two expressions.

MDX( )

Multiple index file name.

MDY( )

Converts date to Month Day, Year format (such as May 21, 1989).

MEMLINES( )

Number of lines in a memo field.

MEMORY()

Available RAM in kilobytes.

MENU()

Active menu name.

MESSAGE()

Error message.

MIN()

Smaller of two values.

MLINE()

Extracts text line from memo.

MOD()

Remainder from division of two numbers.

MONTH()

Month number from a date.

NDX()

Index file name.

NETWORK()

System running on network.

ORDER()

Index order file or tag.

OS()

Operating system name.

PAD()

Name of last pad selected.

PAYMENT()

Payment for amortized loan.

PCOL()

Printer column position.

PI()

Pi, 3.14159.

POPUP()

Name of active pop-up menu.

PRINTSTATUS()

Printer ready (.T. if ready; .F. if not).

PROGRAM()

Program or procedure executing when error occurred.

PROMPT()

Prompt of last pop-up or menu option selected.

PROW()

Printer row position.

PV()

Present value.

RAND()

Random number.

READKEY()

Number for key pressed to exit a full-screen command.

RECCOUNT()

Number of records in database.

RECNO( )

Current record number.

RECSIZE( )

Record size.

REPLICATE( )

Repeats character.

RIGHT( )

Rightmost characters of a string.

RLOCK( )

Locks multiple records.

ROLLBACK( )

Rollback successful.

ROUND( )

Round number.

ROW( )

Cursor row position.

RTOD( )

Converts radians to degrees.

RTRIM( )

Removes trailing blanks.

SEEK( )

Finds expression in indexed database.

SELECT( )

Highest unused work area.

SET()

Status of SET commands.

SIGN()

Positive or negative sign of number.

SIN()

Sine of an angle.

SOUNDEX()

Phonetic match.

SPACE()

String of blanks.

SQRT()

Square root.

STR()

Converts number to a string.

STUFF()

Replaces a portion of a string with another string.

SUBSTR()

Extracts characters from a string.

TAG()

Index tag name.

TAN()

Tangent of an angle.

TIME()

System time.

TRANSFORM()

PICTURE formatting of data.

TYPE()

Data type.

UPPER()

Converts to uppercase.

USER()

Log-in name of user.

VAL()

Converts character numbers to numeric values.

VARREAD()

Name of field or variable being edited.

VERSION()

dBASE IV version number.

YEAR()

Numeric value of year from a date.

B

Menu Structure of the Applications Generator

Each of the menus presented by the Applications Generator has a specific purpose. Appendix B presents these menu types and explains the functions of the menu options.

When the application object is the only object on the work surface, the **Application** dialog box is available for use. If you open a bar or pop-up menu object, the **Application** option is replaced with the **Menu** and **Item** options. If you open one of the three special types of pop-up objects (Structure, Files, or Values), the **List** dialog box becomes available. A **Batch process** prompt and **Batch** dialog box become active when the object you are working with is a batch process.

Menu Options at a Glance

The Preset dialog box
- Sign-on defaults
- Display options
- Environment settings
- Application drive/path

The Application dialog box
- Name and describe
- Assign main menu
- Display sign-on banner
- Edit program header comments
- Modify application environment
  - Display options
  - Environment settings
  - Search path
  - View/database and index
- Generate quick application
- Save current application definition
- Clear work surface

The Design dialog box
- Horizontal bar menu
- Pop-up menu
- Files list
- Structure list
- Values list
- Batch process

The Menu dialog box
- Name and describe
- Override assigned database or view
  - ABOVE
  - BELOW
  - IN EFFECT AT RUN TIME
- Write help text
- Modify display options
- Embed code
- Attach pull-down menus
- Save current menu
- Put away current menu
- Clear work surface

The Item dialog box
- Show item information
- Change action
  - Text (no action)
  - Open a menu
  - Browse
    - Allow record ADD?
    - Allow record EDIT?
    - Allow record DELETE?
    - KEEP image on exit?
    - Display Browse MENU?
    - Use PREVIOUS Browse table?
    - FOLLOW record after update?
    - COMPRESS display?
  - Edit form
  - Display or print
    - Report (Print a Report)
      - Report format
      - Heading format
      - Before printing
      - Send output to
      - FILTER, SCOPE, FOR, and WHILE
    - Labels (Print Labels)
    - Display/list
  - Perform file operation
  - Run program
    - Do dBASE program
    - Execute BATCH process
    - Insert dBASE code
    - Run DOS program
    - Load/call binary file
    - Play back macro
  - Quit
- Override assigned database or view
- Embed code
- Bypass item on condition
- Position record pointer
- Reassign index order
- Define logical window
- Write help text
- Assign message line prompt

The List dialog box
- Identify files in list
- Identify fields in list
- Identify field values in list

The Batch dialog box

The Generate dialog box
- Begin generating
- Select template
- Display during generation

The Exit dialog box
- Save all changes and exit
- Abandon all changes and exit

►The Preset Dialog Box

With the menu options displayed in the **Preset** dialog box, you can establish default settings for all future applications as well as the application you are currently generating. The options in this dialog box enable you to enter values for the default conditions of any application you create. When you change the information screens presented by these options, the changes are written to disk and used whenever the Applications Generator is invoked. The following options are available from the **Preset** dialog box:

Sign-on defaults
Display options
Environment settings
Application drive/path

Sign-on defaults

When you choose **Sign-on defaults**, three fields are displayed in the information screen. You fill in these fields with the text that appears in the application object when you create an application. Usually you will want to supply your name, a copyright notice, and the version of dBASE you used to create the application. You may want instead to put default values here for a sign-on banner.

After finishing, you press Ctrl-End to accept the values, or the Esc key to return to the menu without making any changes. Changes are saved to disk for use whenever you call the Applications Generator.

Display options

Display options presents the standard dBASE IV interface for choosing screen-display colors (represented in the command language by the SET COLOR TO and SET COLOR OFF commands). This information screen is the same one you see if you issue the SET command at the dot prompt and choose DISPLAY. To choose the color combinations for your application, you select the appropriate options from the **Display options** screen.

When you are finished, just press Ctrl-End to accept the entry, or Esc to return to the menu without making any changes. Again, any changes will be saved to disk and used as application defaults the next time you create an application.

Environment settings

By choosing **Environment settings**, you can control the major environment settings (established with the SET command) that affect your application. These settings include the following:

```
SET BELL
SET CARRY
SET CENTURY
SET CONFIRM
SET ESCAPE
SET SAFETY
SET DELIMITERS
```

Once you have established your default settings for the environment, you press Ctrl-End to save the changes, or Esc to return to the menu without making any changes. These settings also are recorded for future use.

Application drive/path

When you choose **Application drive/path**, you can enter the default drive designation and the path name for your application. Afterward, you press Ctrl-End to save the changes, or Esc to return to the menu without making any changes.

➤ The Application Dialog Box

From the **Application** dialog box, you can change certain aspects of your application. The choices you make affect the entire application you are generating. Your selections are not recorded to disk for use with future applications, however. The following options are available from the **Application** dialog box:

Name and describe
Assign main menu
Display sign-on banner
Edit program header comments
Modify application environment
Generate quick application
Save current application definition
Clear work surface

Name and describe

When you choose **Name and describe** from the **Application** dialog box, you are presented with an information screen. Here you can modify the first two entries (the application name and the description line) you made in the information screen that was presented when you first began to create the application. Make whatever changes are necessary and press Ctrl-End to save the changes, or Esc to return to the menu without making any changes.

Assign main menu

By choosing **Assign main menu**, you can change the type of menu used and the name of that menu; you entered this information in the information screen that was presented when you first began to create the application. In the first field, you use the space bar to cycle through the POPUP, BAR, and BATCH (process) menu types. In the second field, you en r the name of the menu. Afterward, you press Ctrl-End to accept entry, or Esc to return to the main menu without making any changes.

Display sign-on banner

With **Display sign-on banner**, you can display the application object as a sign-on banner. You can supply a message for the user to see before the application actually begins running in the application object. The sign-on banner is placed on-screen for several seconds (or until the user presses a key) before the main menu appears.

Edit program header comments

When you choose **Edit program header comments**, you are presented with the same information screen you see when you choose **Sign-on defaults** from the **Preset** dialog box. With **Edit program header comments**, you can change the defaults for the application you are developing. These changes become a part of the current application but are not applied to future applications.

Modify application environment

Modify application environment presents a submenu from which you can change four aspects of the application environment. The following options are available:

Display options
Environment settings
Search path
View/database and index

Display options

Display options enables you to override the default **Display options** you selected from the **Preset** dialog box. Any changes that you make here are applied to the current application only.

Environment settings

Environment settings enables you to override the default **Environment settings** you selected from the **Preset** dialog box. Again, any changes that you make here are applied to the current application only, not to future applications.

Search path

Search path lets you override the default search path. The information you enter here is included in the application as a SET PATH command and applies only to the current application.

View/database and index

View/database and index lets you modify the information you entered in the information screen that was presented when you first began the application. Here you can make any necessary changes concerning the database/ view, index, and order items. When you are finished, you press Ctrl-End to write the changes to disk, or Esc to return to the menu without making any changes.

Generate quick application

The dBASE IV Applications Generator, as it is shipped from the factory, contains QUICK.GEN, which is activated when you select **Generate quick application**. QUICK.GEN is a template that creates a simple application enabling the user to provide data entry in a data file, print one report, and print one set (style) of mailing labels. You also can include a screen form file to control the display of the data-entry screens. Further customization, however, is not available.

Save current application definition

When you choose **Save current application definition**, all the settings and actions that you have assigned to the application are saved to disk. You are then returned to the **Application** dialog box so that you can continue creating the application.

The **Save current application definition** is similar to a save-and-resume command in a word processing package. You can save your work so that you will not lose it if power is interrupted or if some other minor disaster occurs.

Clear work surface

If you choose **Clear work surface**, all the settings and actions you have assigned to currently active objects are written to disk, and they are put away. The work surface is cleared of all objects except the application object.

▶The Design Dialog Box

You use the **Design** dialog box to create menus and batch processes. Six different object types can be created with this menu. The following options are available from the **Design** dialog box:

Horizontal bar menu
Pop-up menu
Files list

Structure list
Values list
Batch process

Horizontal bar menu

The **Horizontal bar menu** option offers a BAR menu with all its prompts on one line of the screen. Surrounding the menu is a border frame. The user moves through a BAR menu with the left- and right-arrow keys and makes choices with the Enter key.

Pop-up menu

Pop-up menu offers a POPUP menu, which is similar to a BAR menu except that a POPUP's orientation is vertical. All the prompts are stacked vertically within a border frame. A user moves through a POPUP menu with the up- and down-arrow keys and makes selections with the Enter key.

Files list

The **Files list** option offers a Files list menu, which is similar to a POPUP except that the prompts in a Files list menu are always file names. Unlike POPUPs, a Files list menu is dynamic; that is, it changes when new files are added to or erased from the disk.

Structure list

Structure list offers a menu similar to a POPUP. The prompts in a Structure list menu, however, are always field names that you may want to include in a LIST/DISPLAY. Unlike a POPUP menu, a Structure list menu enables you to select more than one prompt. You first use the Enter key to mark the prompts you want, and then press Ctrl-End to accept the entry.

Values list

Values list offers a menu similar to a POPUP. In a Values list menu, however, the prompts are the values of a particular field. A prompt is available for each record, and the prompt string is the value in the data file for that field. A Values list menu is extremely useful in letting a user scroll through a list of values to find a particular record.

Batch process

The **Batch process** option provides a method for having more than one dBASE IV command execute. **Batch process** works in the background and is invisible to the user. In many ways, using **Batch process** is like running a small program. This option will become more useful to you as your knowledge of dBASE IV programming increases.

▶ The Menu Dialog Box

When you have a BAR or POPUP menu active on the work surface, the **Menu** option is displayed next to the **Design** option of the main menu. When you select **Menu**, the choices available from the **Menu** dialog box control the attributes of the menu you are generating. These attributes can be passed to the objects used by the menu if they have been set to inherit the database or view **IN EFFECT AT RUN TIME**. The following options are available from the **Menu** dialog box:

Name and describe
Override assigned database or view
Write help text
Modify display options
Embed code
Attach pull-down menus
Save current menu
Put away current menu
Clear work surface

Name and describe

Name and describe enables you to modify the entries you made initially in the information screen for the current object. You can change the name of the menu, its description, or the message line prompt of the current object.

Override assigned database or view

With **Override assign database or view**, you can specify that the menu open a different database or view from the one specified for the entire application. When you choose this option, the screen presents a set of choices for specifying how the database or view is to be set. An entry screen is presented showing the current database or view in the top half of the window, along with a multiple-choice field for specifying which view to use. You can specify one of the following options:

ABOVE
BELOW
IN EFFECT AT RUN TIME

ABOVE

ABOVE, which is the default condition for this entry screen, causes the settings specified in the top half of the frame to remain in effect while the current object is active.

BELOW

BELOW lets you enter database/view information in the bottom half of the frame in order to provide values that are in effect while the current object is active.

IN EFFECT AT RUN TIME

If you have designed the application so that the object which activates this menu has modified the database/view settings, **IN EFFECT AT RUN TIME** retains the settings in effect when the object is activated. In this way, you can create a menu that is usable by different modules requiring different data settings.

Write help text

Choosing **Write help text** from the **Menu** dialog box enables you to open a frame and provide help messages. When the object is active, the messages are displayed whenever the user presses the F1 key.

Modify display options

Modify display options lets you change color/display settings for the menu you are generating and for any object that might, in turn, be called by this object. When you choose this option, you will be presented with the standard dBASE IV color selection menu. You use the left- and right-arrow keys for setting the foreground and background colors, and the up- and down-arrow keys for the individual color settings. Once you have chosen your colors, just press Ctrl-End to save those choices, or Esc for the previous settings to remain in effect.

Embed code

The **Embed code** option enables experienced dBASE IV programmers to insert segments of program code that add actions not offered from the menu-driven Applications Generator. The difference between embedded code and a batch process is that a batch process often can be used by more than one object, whereas embedded code is generally reserved for modifying a specific situation. Embedded code can be specified to run both before and after the object is activated and deactivated.

Attach pull-down menus

Attach pull-down menus is available only when the current object is a BAR menu. This option lets you specify whether a POPUP menu associated with a BAR menu prompt should be automatically displayed when that prompt is highlighted.

Save current menu

Save current menu is essentially a save-and-resume command. Work that you have done on the menu thus far is stored to disk, but the current object remains open so that you can continue working with the menu after the save is completed.

Put away current menu

Having too many objects open on the work surface during the generation of an application can become confusing. **Put away current menu** deactivates the menu after saving it to disk (if any changes have been made) and then removes the menu from the work surface.

Clear work surface

Clear work surface closes all open objects on the work surface and saves them to disk. Only the application object will remain on the work surface.

▰The Item Dialog Box

You use the **Item** dialog box to specify the actions of the individual prompts found in the active menu. The following options are available from the **Item** dialog box:

Show item information
Change action
Override assigned database or view
Embed code
Bypass item on condition
Position record pointer
Reassign index order
Define logical window
Write help text
Assign message line prompt

Show item information

Show item information identifies the currently selected menu item, the object to which the item belongs, the database/view and index information scheduled to be in effect when the item is activated, and the action the item performs.

Change action

Like other options that invoke a submenu, **Change action** is designated with a triangular flag. The submenu offers the following choices:

Text (no action)
Open a menu
Browse
Edit form
Display or print
Perform file operation
Run program
Quit

Text (no action)

The first line of the frame shows the action attached to the currently selected menu item. If no action has yet been chosen, however, this line will read **Text (no action)**. Highlighting this choice and pressing Enter will produce a miniature version of the **Show item information** screen that pertains to this particular menu item only.

Open a menu

Open a menu activates another submenu. A small frame pops up, prompting you to enter the menu type and the menu name. When the cursor is in the **Menu name** field, you can use Shift-F1 (Pick) to call up a list of available menus of the type specified.

Browse

Browse enables you to attach the BROWSE command to the current item of the menu. When you select **Browse**, a window is presented that enables you to control the settings for the BROWSE.

First, you may specify a list of fields to be included in the BROWSE. Only those fields that are included are shown on-screen. If you leave **Fields** blank, all the fields in the data file will be part of the BROWSE. You also can enter filter information, which causes only certain records to be included in the BROWSE.

Next, you can indicate the number of fields from the left margin to be LOCKed on-screen. If you specify three fields in the LOCK, the first three fields presented in the BROWSE will always remain on-screen. You can move through the rest of the fields by pressing Tab and Shift-Tab (to tab backward).

If you choose, you can freeze the highlight bar in a particular field, thus allowing entry into that field only.

In the **Browse** screen, you also can specify the maximum width of any individual column in the BROWSE. If the field is wider than the column width you have specified, the field data scrolls within the column. You also can specify a form file that determines how the BROWSE is presented to the user.

Eight additional options are available in the **Browse** screen, each of which is a question requiring a Yes or No answer. To change the current setting, you place the cursor in the appropriate field and press the space bar to toggle between the choices. The questions include the following:

Allow record ADD?
Allow record EDIT?
Allow record DELETE?
KEEP image on exit?
Display Browse MENU?
Use PREVIOUS Browse table?
FOLLOW record after update?
COMPRESS display?

Allow record ADD?

Allow record ADD? determines whether a user can add new records to the data file. Selecting this option is the same as using the `NOAPPEND` argument of the `BROWSE` command at the dot prompt.

Allow record EDIT?

Allow record EDIT? determines whether a user can edit records currently in the data file. Setting the response to `NO` is the same as using the `NOEDIT` argument of the `BROWSE` command at the dot prompt.

Allow record DELETE?

The **Allow record DELETE?** option establishes whether a user can delete (mark for deletion) records currently in the data file. Setting the response to `NO` is the same as using the `NODELETE` argument of the `BROWSE` command at the dot prompt.

KEEP image on exit?

KEEP image on exit? determines whether the image of the `BROWSE` is cleared from the screen when the `BROWSE` terminates. Setting the response to `NO` is the same as using the `NOCLEAR` argument of the `BROWSE` command at the dot prompt.

Display Browse MENU?

Display Browse MENU? determines whether the **Browse** menu is displayed while the `BROWSE` is active. Setting the response to `NO` is the same as using the `NOMENU` argument of the `BROWSE` command at the dot prompt.

Use PREVIOUS Browse table?

The **Use PREVIOUS Browse table?** option establishes whether the `BROWSE` command reinitializes the entry table when it is invoked. Setting the response to `NO` is the same as using the `NOINIT` argument of the `BROWSE` command at the dot prompt.

FOLLOW record after update?

FOLLOW record after update? establishes how the record pointer behaves when a user makes an entry that changes the key expression on which the file is currently indexed. Answering `YES` causes the record pointer to follow the edited record to its new location in the index. For example, if the database/view is currently indexed on the last-name field and the user changes *Thomas* to *Adams*, the record pointer follows the record back to the top of the file.

If you answer NO to this option, once the user is finished editing a record, it repositions itself at the appropriate place in the index, but the record pointer remains in the vicinity, pointing to the next record in the data file.

COMPRESS display?

COMPRESS display? determines whether to use the compressed format of the BROWSE command in order to fit as many fields as possible on-screen. Answering YES is the same as using the COMPRESS argument of the BROWSE command at the dot prompt.

Once you have marked all the settings for the BROWSE command, you press Ctrl-End to accept your entries. Pressing Esc cancels any entries you have modified and returns you to the previous menu, with all settings remaining as they were before the menu was invoked.

Edit form

Edit form presents a screen that enables you to determine how records are appended and edited in the database. This screen is similar to the one displayed by the **Browse** option. While working in the **Edit form** screen, you can specify a form file that controls the display of the data-entry screen. You also can determine whether the action is an APPEND or an EDIT.

If you are not specifying a form file but are using the "standard" EDIT screen, you can include a list of fields for the APPEND/EDIT. If you have chosen EDIT mode, you also can specify a FILTER to supply a condition that must be met in order for the record to be included in the EDIT. In addition, you can specify a SCOPE that determines how many records are to be included in the EDIT. If you do not specify the scope, the default includes all records. You also can specify a FOR condition that must be met in order for the record to be included in the EDIT, and a WHILE condition that determines when the EDIT terminates.

At the bottom of the **Edit form** screen are seven of the eight options that were available in the **Browse** screen. (The only option missing is the one for determining whether the BROWSE reinitializes.) Here each option has the same parameters as those of its counterpart in the **Browse** screen

Once you have set the APPEND/EDIT actions, you press Ctrl-End to accept the entries. Pressing Esc returns you to the previous menu without changing any of the entries.

Display or print

You select **Display or print** to determine which of three actions will take place. A submenu appears offering these choices:

Report (Print a Report)
Labels (Print Labels)
Display/list

Print a Report

When you choose **Report**, a **Print a Report** screen displays a field in which you can enter the name of the form to be used in printing the report. To see a pick-list menu of the report forms on disk, just press Shift-F1 (Pick). Also included on this pick-list menu is the <**create**> option for creating reports on-the-fly.

The report-entry screen also contains a field in which you can type a header to be included at the top of each page of the report. Providing a header here is equivalent to using the heading argument with the REPORT FORMAT command at the dot prompt.

In addition, you can use the following fields to control the printing of the report:

Report format
Heading format
Before printing
Send output to
FILTER, SCOPE, FOR, and WHILE

Report format

In the **Report format** field, you specify whether detail lines should be printed as part of the report (select **FULL DETAIL**), or whether a summary report should be printed (choose **SUMMARY ONLY**).

Heading format

Heading format enables you to choose either a plain heading or a heading that includes the current date and page numbers.

Before printing

Before printing determines whether a page eject should be issued before printing commences.

Send output to

Send output to specifies where the report is to be sent. You can choose **PRINTER**, **SCREEN**, **DISK FILE**, or **ASK AT RUN TIME**. The last choice determines where the report should be directed at the time it is run.

FILTER, SCOPE, FOR, and WHILE

In the **Print a Report** screen, you can indicate FILTER and SCOPE arguments, as well as FOR and WHILE conditions, for determining which records in the database/view are to be used in the report.

Print Labels

When you choose **Labels**, a **Print Labels** screen appears in which you can specify which label form file to use during printing. Here the **Send output to** option follows the same parameters as those of its counterpart in the **Print a Report** screen. In the **Print SAMPLE** field, you determine whether sample labels (printed images of the label output, which are used for printer alignment) are to be printed before the labels are begun. You also can specify FILTER and SCOPE arguments, as well as FOR and WHILE conditions.

Display/list

If you do not have a label or report form for your application's output, you can use **Display/list** to display records from the data file. When you select **Display/list**, you are presented with a screen for specifying the parameters of the LIST/DISPLAY.

The first option lets you indicate whether output is to be paused automatically when the screen or page is full. The **Send output to** option is exactly the same as its counterparts in the preceding two screens. **Include RECORD NUMBERS?** lets you determine whether the record numbers are to be included as part of the display.

In this screen, you also can specify a field list that determines which fields in the database file/view are to be included in the display. In addition, you can specify FILTER, SCOPE, FOR, and WHILE conditions, as in the other two screens.

Perform file operation

The **Perform file operation** option from the **Item** dialog box presents 12 options in a submenu. Each option performs a specific file maintenance task with a dBASE command, such as `PACK`ing the data file, generating index files, `COPY`ing files, and performing physical `SORT`s.

Each choice then presents a POPUP menu for entering the arguments for that particular command (if the command can accept arguments). When the application code is actually generated, the Applications Generator includes the information you supply here as arguments to the command. The command, as it is assembled by the Applications Generator, is the action attached to the item on the menu you are currently designing.

Run program

Run program is an option that enables you to attach six different actions to the menu item you are specifying. The actions you can attach include the following:

Do dBASE program
Execute BATCH process
Insert dBASE code
Run DOS program
Load/call binary file
Play back macro

Do dBASE program

Do dBASE program attaches as an action to the current menu item a `DO` command that specifies the dBASE program to execute. The specified program can be as simple as a few lines of code or as complex as another application. The Applications Generator allows you to nest as many as four applications.

Execute BATCH process

Execute BATCH process attaches as a menu item's action a batch process you created by using the **Design** option from the main menu.

Insert dBASE code

Insert dBASE code opens an editing window for entering dBASE commands. This option should be used sparingly (if at all) by novice programmers, for they may be likely to introduce programming errors into the application. Furthermore, including code on-the-fly is never something to take lightly; in fact, it conflicts directly with the recommended practice of preplanning.

Run DOS program

Run DOS program lets you attach as a menu item's action the calling of a DOS program or the provision of a DOS shell. A note of caution is necessary, however. The success of using this option depends greatly on the amount of free memory available in the computer system at the time the specified DOS program is run.

To present your user with a temporary DOS environment, specifying COMMAND will cause a new version of COMMAND.COM to be loaded into memory and invoked. To return to executing the dBASE IV application, the user must type EXIT at the DOS prompt. This will cause the most recent version of COMMAND.COM to be unloaded from memory, and program control is passed back to the application.

Load/call binary file

Load/call binary file enables you to specify a binary .BIN program file to be loaded into memory and called into action. You can supplement dBASE IV applications with routines created in other programming languages. **Load/ call binary file** should be avoided by novice dBASE IV programmers, unless they are experienced in other languages.

Play back macro

Play back macro lets you specify the name of a macro (but not the keystrokes necessary to invoke it). By specifying a valid macro name, this menu item plays back that macro and causes the stored keystrokes to be executed as if they were being typed at the keyboard. The macro library will have to be loaded with **Embed code** or a batch process before this choice can be run.

Quit

Quit, the final entry on the **Change action** menu, determines how the user will exit the application. Two choices are available. The first option is to issue a RETURN, which causes the application to terminate and then returns control to a calling program, the dot prompt, or the Control Center. The second option is to have dBASE IV terminate when the user quits the application. In that case, the user is returned to the DOS prompt.

Override assigned database or view

Override assigned database or view from the **Item** dialog box presents a data-entry screen similar to that presented by a similar option from the **Menu** dialog box. Instead of determining the database/view and/or index order while the menu is active, this choice enables you to alter the database/view during the execution of this particular menu item only.

Embed code

The **Embed code** option uses the same parameters as those of the **Embed code** option from the **Menu** dialog box. Here the selection differs in that the embedded code is executed before and/or after this particular menu item executes, rather than before and/or after the menu itself executes.

Bypass item on condition

Bypass item on condition specifies a logical condition that determines whether the highlight bar can be moved to this menu item and thus whether this menu item can be selected. For example, if you wanted to turn off the edit/delete prompt on a data-entry menu when no records are in the data file, you would specify the condition RECNO() = 0. If no records are in the data file, this menu option is inactive.

Position record pointer

Position record pointer determines how the record pointer is to be positioned in the database/view before the current item on the menu is executed. You can choose only one of the items offered on this entry screen.

The first option indicates whether the positioning menu should be presented to the user at run time. Generally this choice should be avoided, for the user is required to know at least some dBASE IV commands and syntax in order to use the screen effectively.

The second option lets you enter a value as the argument to a SEEK command. This command can be used to determine whether a particular key expression can be found within the currently active index.

In the **GOTO** field, you can enter either TOP or BOTTOM as the argument. Or you can supply a numeric expression, which evaluates to a record number that is used to position the record pointer.

The last option involves setting up the information necessary for a LOCATE. You can specify SCOPE, FOR, and WHILE conditions. To execute properly, the LOCATE must be given a valid FOR condition.

Reassign index order

The **Reassign index order** option from the **Item** dialog box lets you specify which index or index tag to use in providing a logical sort for the database/view.

Define logical window

Define logical window specifies a window or frame to contain the action for the current menu item. When the user chooses the item, a window is displayed on-screen, and all the actions associated with that menu item take place within this window. When the item is finished processing, the window is cleared from the screen.

When you select this option, an entry screen is displayed for entering the specifications for the window. You first need to name the window, for all windows activated in dBASE IV must be named.

The next field lets you specify how the window border is to be displayed—as a single or double line, a panel, or a custom border made up of characters. You also can specify NONE, in which case the frame is actually the normal background color.

In the next field, you specify a list of custom line-drawing symbols to be used in making the frame. The **Colors** prompt is used to specify the screen attributes of this window. Finally, two pairs of coordinates are needed to specify the upper left and bottom right corners of the window.

Once you have set the parameters in this information screen, you press Ctrl-End to accept the entries, or Esc to return to the **Item** dialog box without changing the choices.

Write help text

The **Write help text** option from the **Item** dialog box opens a window in which you can enter text to be displayed when the currently selected menu item is highlighted and the user presses F1. This option has exactly the same parameters as those of the **Write help text** option from the **Menu** dialog box. Specifying a help text for an individual item, however, supersedes any help text that may be attached to the parent menu while that item is highlighted.

Assign message line prompt

Assign message line prompt enables you to attach a message to the menu item that is displayed whenever the menu prompt you are specifying is highlighted during the running of the application. If a message has been specified from the **Menu** dialog box for the entire menu, the new entry replaces that message whenever this menu prompt is highlighted.

▶The List Dialog Box

The **List** dialog box is nearly identical to the **Menu** dialog box. They differ only in wording and in one option. The options of the **List** dialog box simply substitute the word *list* for the word *menu* when the **List** dialog box is displayed. For example, the **Put away current menu** option from the **Menu** dialog box reads **Put away current list** in the **List** dialog box.

Instead of offering the **Attach pull-down menus** option of the **Menu** dialog box, the **List** dialog box displays one of the following options, depending on the list being created:

Identify files in list
Identify fields in list
Identify field values in list

Identify files in list

Identify files in list (which replaces **Files list** from the **Design** dialog box) presents a window for entering a file skeleton that controls the types of files displayed in the Files list POPUP menu. For example, entering *.DBF causes the Files list menu to display only data files.

Identify fields in list

Identify fields in list (which replaces **Structure list** from the **Design** dialog box) presents a window for entering a list of the fields that should be included in the menu. You separate the field names with a comma. You can use Shift-F1 (Pick) to highlight the field names that you want to appear in the menu instead of typing them.

Entering no names in the fields list allows the user to pick any field in the database, unless the SET FIELDS command has been issued. If a SET FIELDS is in effect, the menu is limited to those fields specified by that command. But if you have specified that the menu be attached to the prompt with the **Attach pull-down menus** option of the **Menu** dialog box, all fields are displayed in the POPUP menu.

Identify field values in list

Identify field values in list (which replaces **Values list** from the **Design** dialog box) presents a window for entering the name of the field contained in the database/view that provides each of the menu prompts with its value. Each record in the database/view creates a prompt that is the value of the specified field in the record.

➤ The Batch Dialog Box

Because batch processes execute in the background, the **Batch** dialog box omits the choices for changing the screen-display attributes. Furthermore, you cannot enter a help message in this dialog box. Otherwise, the **Batch** dialog box is similar to the **Menu** dialog box.

➤ The Generate Dialog Box

The following options are presented when you access the **Generate** dialog box:

    Begin generating
    Select template
    Display during generation

Begin generating

Begin generating sets into motion the code-creation functions of the Applications Generator.

Select template

Select template enables you to choose a template that controls the actions of the Applications Generator. The default is the template MENU.GEN (supplied as part of the dBASE IV package). Once you become familiar with the dBASE IV Template Language, you can create templates that personalize the actions of the Applications Generator.

Display during generation

Display during generation determines whether the code that is generated by the Applications Generator is displayed on-screen while the code is being created.

▶The Exit Dialog Box

The following options are available from the **Exit** dialog box:

Save all changes and exit
Abandon all changes and exit

Save all changes and exit

Save all changes and exit lets you save to disk all changes made to active objects. You then exit the Applications Generator.

Abandon all changes and exit

Abandon all changes and exit lets you abandon all changes made to any objects on the work surface since they were last saved. No changes since the last save will be written to disk. You then exit the Applications Generator.

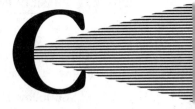

Sample Code from the Applications Generator

This appendix contains a printout of sample code generated by the Applications Generator. The program code is the same as the code you produced in the demonstration in Chapter 3. Minor differences may be noticeable if you have used other names for menus or screen formats. Theoretically these pages could be scanned into an ASCII text file and run.

A "play-by-play" description of the action taken by each set of commands and functions has been provided in program comments. Comments included by the Applications Generator have been edited for readability and consistency.

With your *Language Reference* manual handy, begin reading at the top of the code. Whenever you encounter a command you do not recognize or understand, take the time to look it up in the manual.

Code does not read like a book. Don't expect to read from top to bottom as you would a story. Whenever you encounter a DO command, skip down through the code listings to find either a PROCEDURE command that uses the name following the DO command, or another .PRG file listing that contains the name referenced in the DO.

If you encounter an unfamiliar function (remember that functions always have parentheses behind the name), look up the function in the *Language Reference* manual. If the name of the function does not appear in the manual, you can assume that the function is a user-defined function.

545

When IFs and CASE statements present different paths for program branching, follow each path in order.

As you follow the code through the DO references, proceed until you reach a RETURN command that sends you back to the calling module. Follow the return to the program line that sent you off looking for other code. Each time the program branches to a code segment, follow it and then come back. Eventually you will cover all the code in the application.

This process is difficult at first, but don't give up. If you find a section of code that is completely over your head, mark it and come back later. Getting a feel for the code above and below the section you don't understand often helps you grasp what is happening in that section.

By following this pattern, you will see the code in approximately the same order in which dBASE executes it. That way, you can better understand how the code is executed and in what order.

Remember that each time a DO command is executed, program control passes to a lower level. Try to keep track of which memory variables are used and what happens to them when the module in which they are found is terminated.

Program Listing of VENDOR.PRG

```
* These next lines are a program header. Because each begins with
* an asterisk, the line is ignored by the compiler and is not
* executed. Place any information in the header that will be of
* use to you when you need to come back to the file. Include any
* special conditions that apply specifically to the application
* or anything that is not a normal part of the applications you
* write.
*****************************************************************
* Program......: VENDOR.PRG
* Author.......: Ed Tiley
* Date.........: 1-16-89
* Notice.......: 1989  Que Corporation
* dBASE Ver....: dBASE IV Developer's Edition
* Generated by.: APGEN version 1.0
* Description..: An application to track vendor information

* This next header describes the code to follow.
* Description..: Main routine for menu system
*****************************************************************
```

```
*-- Setup environment
SET CONSOLE OFF              && Disables screen echoing of certain
                            && types of messages and report
                            && output

IF TYPE("gn_ApGen")="U"     && Tests to see whether another
                            && application is already running
                            && Applications created by the
                            && Applications Generator create this
                            && variable. The TYPE() function tests
                            && to see if it exists. U = undefined.
    CLEAR ALL               && These CLEAR commands close all and
    CLEAR WINDOWS           && clear all objects from memory.
    CLOSE ALL               && Memory variables are not RELEASED.
    CLOSE PROCEDURE
    gn_ApGen= 1             && Since the variable didn't exist,
                            && this creates it.

ELSE
    gn_ApGen=gn_ApGen+1     && If it did exist, this makes sure
    IF gn_ApGen > 4         && that no more than four applications
                            && are in memory at once. Remember that
                            && a whole application can be attached
                            && to a menu prompt action.
*
* If too many applications are in memory, do the PAUSE PROCEDURE.
* The WITH clause passes a parameter to the PAUSE, which in this
* case is the error message to be displayed.
    Do Pause WITH "Maximum level of Application nesting exceeded."
        RETURN              && Since the application can run, this
                            && passes control back to what called
                            && the application to run.
    ENDIF                   && Ends the second IF structure
*
* The creator of this template decided to give environmental
* variables a code to designate what they do and where.
*    gc_ means GLOBAL CHARACTER TYPE
*    gn_ means GLOBAL NUMERIC TYPE
*    ln_ means LOCAL NUMERIC TYPE
*    lc_ means LOCAL CHARACTER TYPE
*
```

```
* In the developer's mind GLOBAL means throughout the application,
* and LOCAL means in the currently executing module (or any
* module below it in the chain) of the current application.
* By making the variables PRIVATE here, no variable by the same
* name in a higher-level module will be affected by any changes
* while this application runs. These variables are used to store
* the environment condition so that it can be restored before
* the application terminates.
    PRIVATE gc_bell, gc_carry, gc_clock, gc_century, gc_confirm, gc_deli,;
            gc_instruc, gc_safety, gc_status, gc_score, gc_talk, gc_key

    ENDIF                      && Ends the first IF structure

*-- Store some sets to variables
gc_bell   =SET("BELL")
gc_carry  =SET("CARRY")
gc_clock  =SET("CLOCK")
gc_century=SET("CENTURY")
gc_confirm=SET("CONFIRM")
gc_deli   =SET("DELIMITERS")
gc_instruc=SET("INSTRUCT")
gc_safety =SET("SAFETY")
gc_status =SET("STATUS")
gc_score  =SET("SCOREBOARD")
gc_talk   =SET("TALK")
* The previous environment is tucked away in memory, and you know
* that you are not too many applications deep in memory. It's time
* for this one to start.

SET CONSOLE ON            && SETs the environment for this
SET BELL ON               && application
SET CARRY OFF
SET CENTURY OFF
SET CLOCK OFF
SET CONFIRM OFF
SET DELIMITERS TO ""
SET DELIMITERS OFF
SET DEVICE TO SCREEN
SET ESCAPE ON
SET EXCLUSIVE OFF
SET ECHO OFF
SET LOCK ON
SET MESSAGE TO ""
```

```
SET PRINT OFF
SET REPROCESS TO 4
SET SAFETY ON
SET TALK OFF


* Comments about the memory variables are provided by the
* Applications Generator, but have been edited.
*-- Initialize global variables
gn_error=0          && 0 if no error. Otherwise, error occurred.
gn_ikey=0           && Keypress returned from the INKEY() function
gn_send=0           && Return value from popup of position menus
gn_trace=1          && Sets trace level. However, you need to
                    && change template.
gc_brdr='1'         && Border to use when drawing boxes
gc_dev='CON'        && Device to use for printing (see Proc. PrintSet)
gc_key='N'          && Leaves the application
gc_prognum=' '      && Internal program counter to handle nested menus
gc_quit=' '         && Memvar for return to caller
listval='NO_FIELD'  && Pick list value


*-- remove asterisk to turn clock on
* SET CLOCK TO
SET INSTRUCT OFF        && Does not show menu during BROWSE, etc.


*-- Blank the screen
SET COLOR TO
CLEAR
SET SCOREBOARD OFF      && Takes control of lines 0 and 21 away
SET STATUS OFF          && from dBASE and gives it to the program


*-- Define menus
DO MPDEF                && Executes Menu Process DEFinition


*-- Execute main menu
DO WHILE gc_key = 'N'   && This line opens the loop that keeps
                        && the application open. As soon as the
                        && value of this variable changes, the
                        && application will do the termination
                        && code after the ENDDO.

    DO MAIN WITH "B00"   && Calls the PROCEDURE called MAIN and
                        && passes a parameter similar to
                        && gc_prognum
```

```
* This code executes when MAIN passes control back and determines
* whether the application needs to be exited.
   IF gc_quit = 'Q'      && If the variable has the value Q, this
      EXIT               && drops to the line just below the ENDDO
                         && and gets out, no questions asked.
   ENDIF                 && Closes the IF
   ACTIVATE WINDOW Exit_App    && If gc_quit <> Q, this asks the
                               && question, "Do you want to quit?"
                               && This paints the window on-screen.
   lc_conf=SET("CONFIRM")      && In case the user doesn't, this
   lc_deli=SET("DELIMITER")    && stores environmentals that affect
   SET CONFIRM OFF             && how the question is asked, and
   SET DELIMITER OFF           && then sets them the way they are
                               && needed.

* This paints the question on-screen in the window. The dollar
* sign in the VALID clause means "contains" and limits the
* response to Y or N.
   @ 1,2 SAY "Do you want to leave this application?" ;
         GET gc_key PICT "!" VALID gc_key $ "NY"
   READ      && Takes the entry. If the value of gc_key is not "N,"
             && the loop terminates to the first line of the code
             && following the ENDDO. Good-bye.
   SET CONFIRM &lc_conf.       && If the answer was No, this
   SET DELIMITER &lc_deli.     && resets the environmentals the
   RELEASE lc_conf, lc_deli    && way they were and drops them
                               && from memory.
   DEACTIVATE WINDOW Exit_App  && Closes the window. Since no
                               && command has dropped you out of
                               && the loop, this does it again.
ENDDO                          && Closes the loop

*-- Reset environment

gn_ApGen=gn_ApGen-1         && Cleans up and terminates the
SET BELL  &gc_bell.         && application, and restores the
SET CARRY &gc_carry.        && environment to the way it was
SET CLOCK &gc_clock.        && before the application began
SET CENTURY &gc_century.
SET CONFIRM &gc_confirm.
SET DELIMITERS &gc_deli.
SET INSTRUCT &gc_instruc.
SET STATUS &gc_status.
```

```
SET SAFETY &gc_safety.
SET SCORE  &gc_score.
SET TALK   &gc_talk.

IF gn_Apgen < 1           && Tests to see if this is the "highest-
                          && level" application in memory

    ON KEY LABEL F1
    CLEAR ALL
    CLEAR WINDOWS         && If so, this clears everything,
    CLOSE ALL             && closes all files, and releases all
    CLOSE PROCEDURE       && memory variables. Memory is returned to
    SET CLOCK OFF         && the way it was when dBASE first came up.
    SET ESCAPE ON
    SET MESSAGE TO ""
    CLEAR
ENDIF                     && Closes the IF
RETURN                    && This is the last line of code in the
                          && application that will execute. This
                          && line passes control back to the dot
                          && prompt, the Control Center, or whatever
                          && program called the application in the
                          && first place.


* From this point until the end of the file, all the code
* contained is in the form of subroutines (PROCEDURES).
* Unfortunately, no FUNCTIONs are included in the application,
* but their code would follow the same general pattern as that of
* a procedure.


********************************************************************
* Description..: Procedure files for generated menu system
* The programs that follow are common to main routines.
* The last procedure is the Menu Process DEFinition.
********************************************************************
PROCEDURE Lockit
PARAMETER ltype
IF NETWORK()
    gn_error=0
    ON ERROR DO Multerr   && LOCKIT provides multiuser
    IF ltype = "1"        && capabilities. See Chapter 15 on
      ll_lock=FLOCK()     && networking for more information.
    ENDIF
    IF ltype = "2"
```

```
        ll_lock=RLOCK()
    ENDIF
    ON ERROR
ENDIF
RETURN


PROCEDURE Info_Box        && Defines the procedure's name
PARAMETERS lc_say         && Takes a parameter that is passed by
                          && the module calling this one
? lc_say                  && Outputs the message that was passed
? REPLICATE("-",LEN(lc_say))  && Draws a line of dashes under it
                          && REPLICATE() repeats the
                          && character. LEN() determines how
                          && many times.
?                         && Adds a blank line
RETURN                    && Terminates
* EOP: Info_Box


PROCEDURE get_sele        && Defines the procedure
*-- Get the user selection  && Stores BAR() into variable

* BAR() returns the line number of the last prompt chosen in a
* POPUP menu. The next line simply takes that value and places it
* in a memory variable.
gn_send = BAR()           && Variable for print testing
DEACTIVATE POPUP          && Pulls the POPUP off the screen
RETURN                    && Terminates


* None of the actions in the VENDOR application use this routine.
* It is used to determine which choice is made from a values
* list or a files list.
PROCEDURE ShowPick        && Defines the name and stores the
listval=PROMPT()          && prompt string to a variable
IF LEFT(entryflg,1)="B"   && If the entry flag variable string
    lc_file=POPUP()       && begins with "B", this stores the
    DO &lc_file. WITH "A" && name of the POPUP to a variable and
    RETURN                && will DO a program of that name,
                          && passing the parameter "A".
ENDIF
IF TYPE("lc_window")="U"  && If no window is specified,
    ACTIVATE WINDOW ShowPick  && this uses the window SHOWPICK.
ELSE                      && Otherwise, this uses the
    ACTIVATE WINDOW &lc_window.  && specified window.
```

```
      ENDIF
      STORE 0 TO ln_ikey,x1,x2    && Inits three variables to 0
      ln_ikey=LASTKEY()           && Gives ln_ikey the value of the
                                  && last keypress
      IF ln_ikey=13               && Tests to see that Enter was
                                  && pressed
    * If so, this stores the starting character position of the
    * prompt in the field list.
         x1=AT(TRIM(listval)+',',lc_fldlst)
         IF x1 = 0        && If the string is not in the field list,
            lc_fldlst=lc_fldlst+TRIM(listval)+',' && the field list is
                                              && the list variable
                                              && plus the prompt
                                              && and a comma.

         ELSE
    * If the string is contained in the field list, this finds out
    * what position the comma occupies and inserts that many
    * characters into the variable.
            x2=AT(',',SUBSTR(lc_fldlst,x1))
            lc_fldlst=STUFF(lc_fldlst,x1,x2,'')
         ENDIF
         CLEAR                && Clears the window
         ? lc_fldlst          && and displays the choice
      ENDIF
      ACTIVATE SCREEN         && Allows the program to use the full
                             && screen, not just the window, and then
      RETURN                 && terminates
    * EOP: ShowPick


      PROCEDURE Cleanup       && Declares procedure name
    * This procedure resets conditions after a report has printed.
    *-- test whether report option was selected.
      DO CASE                 && Opens a multiple branch
      CASE gc_dev='CON'       && If the user had the report go to the
         WAIT                 && screen, this just pauses until a key is
      CASE gc_dev='PRN'       && pressed. If the printer was selected,
         SET PRINT OFF        && this ends output to the printer and
         SET PRINTER TO       && closes any file to which it was
                             && redirected.
      CASE gc_dev='TXT'       && If the user had it print to a text
         CLOSE ALTERNATE      && file, this closes the alternate file.
      ENDCASE                 && Ends the case construct
      RETURN                  && Terminates
    * EOP: Cleanup
```

```
PROCEDURE Pause        && This procedure is used to display an
PARAMETER lc_msg       && error message passed as a parameter.
*-- Parameters : lc_msg = message line
IF TYPE("lc_message")="U"    && If no message is passed,
   gn_error=ERROR()          && this STOREs the error number.
ENDIF
lc_msg = lc_msg        && This line is a mystery! It does nothing.
lc_option='0'          && Sets flag variable for after termination
ACTIVATE WINDOW Pause  && Window for display of error message
IF gn_error > 0        && If the ERROR() returns a value
   IF TYPE("lc_message")="U" && and no message has been passed,
                             && this paints the official dBASE IV error
                             && message.
      @ 0,1 SAY [An error has occurred !! - Error message: ]+MESSAGE()
   ELSE      && Otherwise, this paints the error message as stored in
             && the caller module.
      @ 0,1 SAY [Error # ]+lc_message
   ENDIF
ENDIF
@ 1,1 SAY lc_msg           && On the next line, this paints the
                           && parameter string.
WAIT " Press any key to continue..."
DEACTIVATE WINDOW Pause    && Closes the window and
RETURN                     && terminates
* EOP: Pause

PROCEDURE Multerr                  && This procedure is used
*-- set the global error variable  && for multiuser processing.
gn_error=ERROR()                   && See Chapter 15 on
*-- contains error number to test  && networking.
lc_erno=STR(ERROR(),3)+','
*-- option var.
lc_opt='T'
*-- Dialog box for options. Try again and Return to menu.
IF lc_erno $ "108,109,128,129,"
   ACTIVATE WINDOW Pause
   @ 0,2 SAY lc_erno+" "+MESSAGE()
   @ 2,22 SAY "T = Try again, R = Return to menu." GET lc_opt ;
PICTURE "!" VALID lc_opt $ "TR"
   READ
   DEACTIVATE WINDOW Pause
   IF lc_opt = "R"
      RETURN
   ENDIF
```

```
ENDIF
*-- Display message and return to menu.
IF .NOT. lc_erno $ "108,109,128,129,"
   DO PAUSE WITH ERROR()
   RETURN
ENDIF
*-- Reset global variable.
gn_error=0
*-- Try the command again.
RETRY
RETURN
* EOP: Multerr


PROCEDURE Trace    && This module is used in debugging. It is not
                   && used in this application.
* Desc: Trace procedure. This lets programmer know what module is
* about to execute and what module has executed.
PARAMETERS p_msg, p_lvl
*-- Parameters : p_msg = message line, p_lvl = trace level
lc_msg = p_msg
ln_lvl = p_lvl
lc_trp = ' '
IF gn_trace < ln_lvl
   RETURN
ENDIF
DEFINE WINDOW trace FROM 11,00 TO 16,79 DOUBLE
DO WHILE lc_trp <> 'Q'
   @ 2,40-LEN(lc_msg)/2 SAY lc_msg
   @ 4,05 SAY 'S - Set trace level, D - Display status, M - display Memory'
   @ 5,05 SAY 'P - Turn printer on, Q - to Quit'
   lc_trp = 'Q'
   @ 5,38 GET lc_trp PICTURE "!"
   READ
   DO CASE
   CASE lc_trp = 'S'
      @ 2,01 CLEAR
      @ 2,33 SAY 'Set trace level'
      @ 4,05 SAY 'Enter trace level to change to:' GET gn_trace PICTURE '#'
      @ 5,05 SAY '               '
      READ
      IF gn_trace=0
         @ 2,01 CLEAR
         @ 3,05 SAY 'Trace is now turned off..To reactivate Trace - Press [F3]'
         @ 4,05 say 'Press any key to continue...'
```

```
             WAIT ''
        ENDIF
     CASE lc_trp = 'D'
        DISPLAY STATUS
        WAIT
     CASE lc_trp = 'M'
        DISPLAY MEMORY
        WAIT
     CASE lc_trp = 'P'
        SET PRINT ON
     ENDCASE
ENDDO
SET PRINT OFF
@ 24,79 SAY " "
RELEASE WINDOW trace
RETURN
* EOP: Trace


PROCEDURE PrintSet   && Defines a procedure to set up printing
*-- Initialize variables
gc_dev='CON'         && Sets the default device to the console
lc_choice=' '        && Inits a variable to take user preference
gn_pkey=0            && Inits two variables to hold the actual
gn_send=0            && keypress made and the number of the
                     && selected prompt. gn_pkey will be used to
                     && see whether the user has pressed Esc to
                     && end the menu action.


DEFINE WINDOW printemp FROM 08,25 TO 17,56   && Names a window
                                             && and its place
                                             && on-screen


DEFINE POPUP SavePrin FROM 10,40    && Declares a POPUP menu and
                                    && places the upper left
                                    && corner
                                    && Lets dBASE IV calculate
                                    && the bottom left corner


* These next lines will define the prompts that appear in the
* menu. The argument SKIP is used to prevent the light bar
* from stopping on that prompt. The message will display on
* line 24 of the screen when the prompt is highlighted.
* Remember that the semicolon (;) is used to break one command
* onto two or more lines in the code for easier reading.
*
```

```
DEFINE BAR 1 OF SavePrin PROMPT " Send output to ..." SKIP
DEFINE BAR 2 OF SavePrin PROMPT ;
               REPLICATE(CHR(196),24) SKIP
DEFINE BAR 3 OF SavePrin PROMPT ;
     " CON:   Console" MESSAGE "Send output to Screen"
DEFINE BAR 4 OF SavePrin PROMPT ;
     " LPT1:  Parallel port 1 " MESSAGE "Send output to LPT1:"
DEFINE BAR 5 OF SavePrin PROMPT ;
     " LPT2:  Parallel port 2" MESSAGE "Send output to LPT2:"
DEFINE BAR 6 OF SavePrin PROMPT ;
     " COM1:  Serial port 1" MESSAGE "Send output to COM1:"
DEFINE BAR 7 OF SavePrin PROMPT ;
     " FILE = REPORT.TXT" MESSAGE "Send output to File Report.txt"
ON SELECTION POPUP SavePrin DO get_sele  && Specifies the action
                                         && to take when a
                                         && selection is made by
                                         && the user


ACTIVATE POPUP SavePrin    && Paints the menu and takes entry
RELEASE POPUP SavePrin     && Yanks the POPUP out of memory. The
                           && get_sele procedure has already
                           && DEACTIVATEd it.


IF gn_send = 7            && If the choice was "to file,"
   gc_dev = 'TXT'  && this SETs the device.
   SET ALTERNATE TO REPORT.TXT   && Turns on the alternate file
   SET ALTERNATE ON             && of choice
ELSE    && Otherwise....
   IF .NOT. (gn_send = 3 .OR. LASTKEY() = 27) && Tests if the
               && selection was anything other than the third
               && prompt or the Esc key. If the selection
               && was the third prompt, forget it; the device
               && is already set to CON. If the choice was
               && Esc, forget it, and no action will
               && happen other than the menu disappearing.

      gc_dev = 'PRN'           && Sends output to the printer
* This next command is cute! The prompts are arranged in such a
* way that the user can determine which device is to be used.
      temp = SUBSTR("  LPT1LPT2COM1 ",((gn_send-2)-1)*4,4)
      ON ERROR DO prntrtry   && Sets an error-trapping routine
                             && to be called if the printer is
                             && off-line when you do the
                             && redirection in the next line
```

```
        SET PRINTER TO &temp.      && Sets the printer to the string
                                   && extracted with the SUBSTR()
        IF gn_pkey <> 27           && As long as the last key pressed
                                   && wasn't Esc,
            SET PRINT ON           && this turns the redirection on.
        ENDIF
        ON ERROR                   && Releases the off-line error code
    ENDIF
ENDIF
RELEASE WINDOW printemp            && Closes the window, lets the
RETURN                             && output begin, and terminates to
                                   && the module that will be sending
                                   && the output


PROCEDURE prntrtry                 && Defines the procedure
PRIVATE lc_escape                  && Inits a variable, protecting any
                                   && other variables in higher-level
                                   && modules that have the same name
                                   && When this terminates, the
                                   && variable will release and any
                                   && others above it with the same
                                   && name will remain unaffected.
lc_escape = SET("ESCAPE")          && Stores the current setting of
                                   && the SET ESCAPE command
IF .NOT. PRINTSTATUS()             && If the printer is off-line...
    IF lc_escape = "ON"            && If ESCAPE is SET on,
        SET ESCAPE OFF             && this SETs it off.
    ENDIF
    gn_pkey = 0                    && Resets the variable to store the
                                   && keypress
    ACTIVATE WINDOW printemp       && Uses the window to pop up a
                                   && blank frame
    @ 1,0 SAY "Please ready your printer or"  && Tells the user to
    @ 2,0 SAY "    press ESC to cancel"       && get it on-line or
                                              && cancel the job

    DO WHILE ( .NOT. PRINTSTATUS()) .AND. gn_pkey <> 27  && Opens
                        && a loop that will cycle as long as
                        && the printer remains off-line or
                        && until the user presses a key
        gn_pkey = INKEY()    && Here is an interesting trick. You
                             && need to read for a keypress because
                             && the prompt advertises ESCAPE as a
```

```
                               && way out. A function cannot appear
                               && on a line by itself, so this does a
                               && variable store. The only thing that
                               && is done with the variable, however,
                               && is to make sure that the Esc key is
                               && not hit.
        ENDDO                  && Closes the loops
        DEACTIVATE WINDOW printemp  && Clears window off the screen
        SET ESCAPE &lc_escape. && Resets the SET ESCAPE to the way it
                               && was found
        IF gn_pkey <> 27       && If the keystroke wasn't Esc,
            RETRY              && this reissues the command that
                               && caused the error.

        ENDIF
    ENDIF
    RETURN                     && Terminates the procedure
    * EOP: PrintSet

    PROCEDURE Position         && Declares the procedure. This one is
                               && used to position the record pointer
                               && when that selection has been made
                               && in the Applications Generator. It
                               && is not used in VENDOR.
    IF LEN(DBF()) = 0          && Makes sure that a data file is open
        DO Pause WITH "Database not in use. "  && If not, this calls
                               && PAUSE with the error message passed
                               && as a parameter
        RETURN                 && and then aborts the procedure.
    ENDIF
    SET SPACE ON               && Turns on spacing in the ? command
    SET DELIMITERS OFF         && Loses any delimiters in effect


    * These comments are supplied with the code as it is generated,
    * but, again, they have been edited.
    ln_type=0                  && Sublevel selection
    ln_rkey=READKEY()          && Test for Esc or Return
    ln_rec=RECNO()             && DBF record number
    ln_num=0                   && For input of a number
    ld_date=DATE()             && For input of a date
    lc_option='0'              && Main option--that is, Seek, Goto,
                               && and Locate
    *-- Scope--ALL, REST, NEXT <n>
    STORE SPACE(10) TO lc_scp
```

```
*-- 1 = Character SEEK, 2 = For clause, 3 = While clause
STORE SPACE(40) TO lc_ln1, lc_ln2, lc_ln3
lc_temp=""                        && Inits a variable that will be used
                                  && for several different things


@ 0,00 SAY "Index order: "+ ;  && Looks up the IIF() function!
      IIF(""=ORDER(),"Database is in natural order",ORDER())
@ 1,00 SAY "Listed below are the first 16 fields."
lc_temp=REPLICATE(CHR(196),19)  && First uses it to paint a header
                                && on-screen with the line below
@ 2,0 SAY CHR(218)+lc_temp+CHR(194)+lc_temp+CHR(194)+lc_temp+CHR(194)+lc_temp

* This next section is slick. Mathematically it divides the
* screen and uses a very clever algorithm to paint the first
* 16 fields in the data file in 4 rows and in 4 columns across
* the screen. Take the time to work out the math to see why this
* works. It's actually worth generating an application that uses
* the feature to see it work. Modify the EDIT/DELETE vendor
* records to position the record pointer at run-time, then run
* it, and watch it work.
ln_num=240      && Inits a variable to hold an incremental value
DO WHILE ln_num < 560  && Does a loop until the value reaches 560
    lc_temp=FIELD( (ln_num-240)/20 +1) && Each time the variable
                && ln_num is incremented by 80, this value
                && increases by 1. The FIELD() function returns
                && the field name of the field pointed to by the
                && numeric argument to the function. For example,
                && FIELD(3) returns the name of the third field in
                && the file.
* The next line uses the relationships among the numbers to
* position the column-separator character and the name of the
* field (plus a padding of spaces) in the proper row/column.
* Also the data type is painted next to the field name by using
* the TYPE() function to determine which part of the string in
* the SUBSTR() to extract.
* Roll with the loop several times and calculate the numbers to
* see how this works. It is very slick.
* If there are fewer than 16 fields, blanks will be painted.

    @ (ln_num/80),MOD(ln_num,80) SAY CHR(179)+;
lc_temp+SPACE(11-LEN(lc_temp))+;
SUBSTR("= Char  = Date  = Logic = Num   = Float = Memo            ",;
AT(TYPE(lc_temp),"CDLNFMU")*8-7,8)
    ln_num=ln_num+20              && Increments the counter
```

```
ENDDO
ln_num=1                        && Resets the value of the
                                && counter


DEFINE POPUP Posit1 FROM 8,30   && Declares a POPUP and issues
                                && the specifications for the
                                && prompt
DEFINE BAR 1 OF Posit1 PROMPT " Position by " SKIP
DEFINE BAR 2 OF Posit1 PROMPT REPLICATE(CHR(196),15) SKIP
DEFINE BAR 3 OF Posit1 PROMPT ;
    " SEEK Record" MESSAGE "Search on index key" SKIP FOR ""=ORDER()
DEFINE BAR 4 OF Posit1 PROMPT ;
    " GOTO Record" MESSAGE "Position to specific record"
DEFINE BAR 5 OF Posit1 PROMPT ;
    " LOCATE Record " MESSAGE "Locate record for condition"
DEFINE BAR 6 OF Posit1 PROMPT ;
    " Return" MESSAGE "Return without positioning"
ON SELECTION POPUP Posit1 DO get_sele  && Provides an action when
                                && a selection is made


SET CONFIRM ON              && Forces a user to terminate a GET
                            && with an Enter keypress
DO WHILE lc_option='0'      && Opens a loop as long as no valid
                            && option has been chosen
   ACTIVATE POPUP Posit1    && Paints the POPUP and begins menu
                            && action


   lc_option = ltrim(str(gn_send))  && Prepares the return value
                                && from the get_sele procedure
                                && to be read by the upcoming
                                && DO CASE construct
   IF LASTKEY() = 27 .OR. lc_option="6"  && If Esc is pressed
                                && or the user decides
                                && not to select a
                                && position,
      GOTO ln_rec           && this leaves the record pointer on
      EXIT                  && record 1 and drops out of the loop.
   ENDIF
   DO CASE                  && Opens a CASE construct to determine
                            && what to do for each possible selection


   CASE lc_option='3'   && If the user selects a SEEK,
      *-- Seek
```

```
            IF LEN(NDX(1))=0 .AND. LEN(MDX(1))=0   && this traps the
                          && error that would occur if you tried to
                          && seek with no index open. This passes
                          && the error message to the error
                          && procedure as a parameter.
               DO Pause WITH "Can't use this option - No index files are open."
               LOOP         && After notifying the user of the error,
                          && this retries.
            ENDIF
            ln_type=1      && Inits variables to hold the data type
            lc_ln1=SPACE(40) && of the SEEK and the SEEK expression

* This next set of commands opens a window to take entry about
* the SEEK.
            DEFINE WINDOW Posit2 FROM 8,19 TO 15,62 DOUBLE
            ACTIVATE WINDOW Posit2
* Note that the positions of the @...SAYs are relative to the
* upper left corner of the window.
            @ 1,1 SAY "Enter the type of expression:" ;
                              GET ln_type PICT "#" RANGE 1,3
            @ 2,1 SAY "(1=character, 2=numeric and 3=date.)"
            READ         && Takes the entry

* If the user doesn't terminate the GET without an entry...
            IF .NOT. (READKEY() = 12 .OR. READKEY() = 268)
               SET CONFIRM ON
               @ 3,1 SAY "Enter the key expression to search for:"
               IF ln_type=3
                  @ 4,1 GET ld_date PICT "@D"  && GETs a date expression
               ELSE
                  IF ln_type=2
                     @ 4,1 GET ln_num PICT "##########" && A numeric
                  ELSE
                     @ 4,1 GET lc_ln1    && or character expression
                  ENDIF
               ENDIF
               READ                    && Activates the GET
               SET CONFIRM OFF
* If the user did not fail to enter a value....
               IF .NOT. (READKEY() = 12 .OR. READKEY() = 268)
                  lc_temp=IIF(ln_type=1,"TRIM(lc_ln1)", ;
                       IIF(ln_type=2,"ln_num","ld_date"))  && Trims the
                                                        && string
```

```
            SEEK &lc_temp.              && and performs the SEEK
        ENDIF
      ENDIF
      RELEASE WINDOWS Posit2        && Closes the window
    CASE lc_option='4'  && If the user chose a specific record...
        *-- Goto
* This defines a POPUP in which the user can specify the method
* of selecting the specific record.

ln_type=1
      DEFINE POPUP Posit2 FROM 8,30
      DEFINE BAR 1 OF Posit2 PROMPT " GOTO:" SKIP
      DEFINE BAR 2 OF Posit2 PROMPT REPLICATE(CHR(196),10) SKIP
      DEFINE BAR 3 OF Posit2 PROMPT " TOP" MESSAGE "GOTO Top of File"
      DEFINE BAR 4 OF Posit2 PROMPT
          " BOTTOM" MESSAGE "GOTO Bottom of File"
      DEFINE BAR 5 OF Posit2 PROMPT ;
          " Record # " MESSAGE "GOTO A Specific Record"
      ON SELECTION POPUP Posit2 DO get_sele
      ACTIVATE POPUP posit2
      ln_type = gn_send
      IF LASTKEY() <> 27   && Only goes through the evaluation
                           && if the user didn't press Esc
          IF ln_type=5     && If the user wants a specific record
                           && by number, this opens a window and
                           && takes the entry to determine which
                           && one.
          DEFINE WINDOW Posit2 FROM 8,26 TO 13,50 DOUBLE
          ACTIVATE WINDOW Posit2
          ln_num=0
          @ 3,1 SAY "Max. Record # = "+LTRIM(STR(RECCOUNT()))
          @ 1,1 SAY "Record to GOTO" ;
                  GET ln_num PICT "######" RANGE 1,RECCOUNT()
          READ
* If the user didn't fail to make an entry, GOTO the record
          IF .NOT. (READKEY() = 12 .OR. READKEY() = 268)
             GOTO ln_num
          ENDIF
          RELEASE WINDOWS Posit2
          ELSE   && Otherwise, this uses the selection value of
                 && the menu prompt to choose top or bottom.
                 && This works because there are only two
                 && possible choices. If the choice isn't 3,
                 && GO BOTTOM.
```

```
            lc_temp=IIF(ln_type=3,"TOP","BOTTOM")
            GOTO &lc_temp.
         ENDIF
      ENDIF
   CASE lc_option='5'   && If the user wants to use a LOCATE...
      *-- Locate
* This opens a window and takes entry for the SCOPE and FOR/WHILE.
      DEFINE WINDOW Posit2 FROM 8,16 TO 14,66 DOUBLE
      ACTIVATE WINDOW Posit2
      @ 1,19 SAY "ie. ALL, NEXT <n>, and REST"
      @ 1,01 SAY "Scope:" GET lc_scp
      @ 2,01 SAY "For:  " GET lc_ln2
      @ 3,01 SAY "While:" GET lc_ln3
      READ
* If the user didn't fail to make an entry, this trims the entry
* and puts the strings together.
      IF .NOT. (READKEY() = 12 .OR. READKEY() = 268)
         lc_temp=TRIM(lc_scp)
         lc_temp=lc_temp + IIF(LEN(TRIM(lc_ln2)) > 0," FOR "+TRIM(lc_ln2),"")
         lc_temp=lc_temp + IIF(LEN(TRIM(lc_ln3)) > 0," WHILE "+TRIM(lc_ln3),"")
         IF LEN(lc_temp) > 0  && If at least one field was filled
                              && in with an entry....
            LOCATE &lc_temp.  && this does the locate. The period
                              && ending the substitution signals
                              && the end of the string.
         ELSE   && Otherwise, this traps an error.
            DO Pause WITH "All fields were blank."
         ENDIF
      ENDIF
      RELEASE WINDOW Posit2     && Closes the window and
   ENDCASE                      && ends the evaluation
   IF EOF()                     && If the record pointer ends up at
                                && EOF() as a result of the SEEK,
                                && LOCATE, etc., this traps the
                                && error and tells the user.
      DO Pause WITH "Record not found."
      GOTO ln_rec               && Positions the record pointer to
                                && the first record in the file
                                && according to any active index
   ENDIF
   IF READKEY()=12 .OR. READKEY()= 268 .OR. LASTKEY()=27  && Esc was hit.
      lc_option='0'        && Remember the DO WHILE condition? If
                           && the user abandoned one of the
```

```
                                && methods by pressing Esc, this rolls
                                && the loop again. Otherwise, the loop
                                && will terminate.
      ENDIF
   ENDDO
   SET DELIMITERS &gc_deli.     && Resets the environment and
   SET CONFIRM OFF
   RETURN                       && terminates the procedure after the
                                && loop quits

   * EOP: Position


   PROCEDURE Postnhlp
   ln_getkey=INKEY()            && This procedure is called if the
                                && user presses F1 while the Position
                                && procedure is executing.

   DO CASE
   CASE "SEEK" $ PROMPT()       && If the menu prompt that is
                                && highlighted contains the string
      HELP SEEK                 && SEEK, this issues a HELP command
                                && specifying SEEK.
   CASE "GOTO" $ PROMPT()       && Ditto for GOTO
      HELP GOTO
   CASE "LOCATE" $ PROMPT()     && Ditto for LOCATE
      HELP LOCATE
   ENDCASE
   RETURN
   * EOP: Postnhlp


   * This section is the menu-definition procedure. It is only
   * run once while the application is active. Here the menus that
   * you created in the Applications Generator are put into memory.
   *************************************************************
   * Program......: MPDEF
   * Author.......: Ed Tiley
   * Date.........: 1-16-89
   * Notice.......: 1989  Que Corporation
   * dBASE Ver....: dBASE IV Developer's Edition
   * Generated by.: APGEN version 1.0
   * Description..: An application to track vendor information

   * Description..: Defines all menus in the system
   *************************************************************
```

```
PROCEDURE MPDEF
IF ISCOLOR()                           && If the video card can do
   SET COLOR OF NORMAL TO W+/B         && color, this SETs them as
   SET COLOR OF MESSAGES TO W+/N       && specified.
   SET COLOR OF TITLES TO W/B
   SET COLOR OF HIGHLIGHT TO GR+/BG
   SET COLOR OF BOX TO GR+/BG
   SET COLOR OF INFORMATION TO B/W
   SET COLOR OF FIELDS TO N/BG
ENDIF
CLEAR

DEFINE WINDOW FullScr FROM 0,0 TO 24,79 NONE     && Defines windows
DEFINE WINDOW Savescr FROM 0,0 TO 21,79 NONE     && for various
DEFINE WINDOW Helpscr FROM 0,0 TO 21,79 NONE     && uses in the
DEFINE WINDOW Browscr FROM 1,0 TO 21,79 NONE     && application
IF gn_ApGen=1 && If this is the first application in memory...
   DEFINE WINDOW Exit_App FROM 11,17 TO 15,62 DOUBLE  && Defines
ENDIF                                   && the exit window
*-- Window for pause message box
DEFINE WINDOW Pause FROM 15,00 TO 19,79 DOUBLE  && Makes a window
                                            && for the error trapper
ACTIVATE WINDOW FullScr     && Opens the full-screen window
@ 24,00                     && Clears the bottom line
@ 23,00 SAY "Loading..."    && Says something while the appl. loads
SET BORDER TO DOUBLE
*-- Bar                      && Inits the main menu and specifies
                            && the prompts and messages for each
                            && Also specifies the actions for
                            && each of the prompts
DEFINE MENU MAIN MESSAGE 'Position with: '+ ;
       CHR(27)+CHR(26)+' - <Enter> to select choice - <F1> Help'
DEFINE PAD PAD_1 OF MAIN PROMPT "DATA" AT 1,3
ON SELECTION PAD PAD_1 OF MAIN DO ACT01
DEFINE PAD PAD_2 OF MAIN PROMPT "REPORTS" AT 1,10
ON SELECTION PAD PAD_2 OF MAIN DO ACT01
DEFINE PAD PAD_3 OF MAIN PROMPT "EXIT" AT 1,20
ON SELECTION PAD PAD_3 OF MAIN DO ACT01
?? "." && Paints a dot on line 23 to let the user know that the
       && application hasn't crashed while the user waits
SET BORDER TO DOUBLE
*-- Popup               && Does the same for the DATA POPUP menu
DEFINE POPUP DATA FROM 2,3 TO 9,27 ;
MESSAGE "Use the up/down arrow keys to"+ ;
```

```
"   highlight a selection and press ENTER"
DEFINE BAR 1 OF DATA PROMPT "Add Vendors"
DEFINE BAR 2 OF DATA PROMPT "Edit/Delete Vendors"
DEFINE BAR 3 OF DATA PROMPT "-=-=-=-=-=-=-=-=-=-"   SKIP
DEFINE BAR 4 OF DATA PROMPT "PACK Vendor file"
DEFINE BAR 5 OF DATA PROMPT "Rebuild Vendor Indexes"
DEFINE BAR 6 OF DATA PROMPT "BACKUP Vendor Data"
ON SELECTION POPUP DATA DO ACT02
?? "."            && Lets them know that no crash has happened
SET BORDER TO DOUBLE
*-- Popup         && Does the same for the REPORTS POPUP
DEFINE POPUP REPORTS FROM 2,10 TO 6,33 ;
MESSAGE "Choose a report with the up\down"+ ;
        " arrow keys and press ENTER"
DEFINE BAR 1 OF REPORTS PROMPT "Vendors by name"
DEFINE BAR 2 OF REPORTS PROMPT "Vendors by ID #"
DEFINE BAR 3 OF REPORTS PROMPT "Mailing labels by zip"
ON SELECTION POPUP REPORTS DO ACT03
?? "."
@ 23,00 CLEAR
RETURN
*-- EOP: MPDEF.PRG


PROCEDURE 1HELP1        && This procedure provides the user with
                        && context-sensitive help screens if you
                        && include them in your application.


ACTIVATE WINDOW Helpscr
SET ESCAPE OFF
ACTIVATE SCREEN         && This command lets the procedure ignore
                        && any active windows.
@ 0,0 CLEAR TO 21,79
@ 1,0 TO 21,79 COLOR GR+/BG
@ 24,00
@ 24,26 SAY "Press any key to continue..."
@ 0,0 SAY ""
ln_row=INKEY()
DO CASE
* This section evaluates whether you have entered help text for
* the menu you are on. If you have not entered help text, users
* are notified when they press F1.
*-- help for menu MAIN
CASE "01"=gc_prognum
```

```
        @ 2,2 SAY "No Help defined."
        ln_row=INKEY(0)
*-- help for menu DATA
CASE "02"=gc_prognum
        @ 2,2 SAY "No Help defined."
        ln_row=INKEY(0)
*-- help for menu REPORTS
CASE "03"=gc_prognum
        @ 2,2 SAY "No Help defined."
        ln_row=INKEY(0)
ENDCASE
SET ESCAPE ON
@ 24,00
DEACTIVATE WINDOW Helpscr
RETURN
*-- EOP: lHELPl


* This is the end of the VENDOR.PRG listing.


******************************************************************
* MAIN.PRG

* This section lists and documents those PROCEDURES that are
* specific to your VENDOR application.

******************************************************************
* Program......: MAIN.PRG
* Author.......: Ed Tiley
* Date.........: 1-16-89
* Notice.......: 1989  Que Corporation
* dBASE Ver....: dBASE IV Developer's Edition
* Generated by.: APGEN version 1.0
* Description..:

* Description..: Menu actions
******************************************************************
PROCEDURE MAIN       && Defines the procedure and gives it a name
PARAMETER entryflg   && Takes the parameter and calls it entryflg
PRIVATE gc_prognum   && Protects higher-level modules with a
gc_prognum="01"      && variable by the same name and gives it a
                     && value. The value is used to determine
                     && nesting depth.
```

```
DO SET01            && Goes out and performs the setup code
IF gn_error > 0     && If, when control is returned, an error
   gn_error=0       && was triggered, this resets the error flag
   RETURN           && and terminates this module because
                    && whatever was supposed to happen in SET01
                    && didn't.
ENDIF


*-- Before menu code


ACTIVATE MENU MAIN  && Paints the main menu and starts menu
                    && action

@ 0,0 CLEAR TO 2,27 && Clears the lines the menu occupied. The
                    && module called as a result of the user's
                    && selection has already DEACTIVATEd the
                    && menu.
*-- After menu

RETURN              && The main (highest-level) menu has been
                    && DEACTIVATEd, so this passes control back
                    && to the calling module. Depending on the
                    && values of the variables, either the
                    && application will be terminated or this
                    && module will be called again.
*-- EOP MAIN

PROCEDURE SET01           && This is the setup module.
ON KEY LABEL F1 DO 1HELP1 && This command tells dBASE what to do
                          && when the user presses the F1 key.
                          && In this case, the custom help
                          && screens are activated.
DO DBF01                  && Opens menu-level database
                          && This command opens the data file
                          && that you have specified in the
                          && Applications Generator by calling
                          && the module that does the work.
* There are those who would argue that opening the data file at
* this time is poor programming technique, and they have a point.
* Because minor changes to a data file are stored in memory
* buffers, a power failure, unintentional booting of the system,
* etc., could cause a loss of data. Users do have a tendency to
```

```
* walk away from the system with the menus still active. Avoid
* leaving data files open like this in the applications that you
* write from scratch.

IF gn_error = 0     && If no errors occurred opening the file....
    IF ISCOLOR()                        && this tests for a color card
        SET COLOR OF NORMAL TO W+/B     && If one is found, this SETs
        SET COLOR OF MESSAGES TO W+/N   && the color and screen
        SET COLOR OF TITLES TO W/B      && attributes.
        SET COLOR OF HIGHLIGHT TO GR+/BG
        SET COLOR OF BOX TO GR+/BG
        SET COLOR OF INFORMATION TO B/W
        SET COLOR OF FIELDS TO N/BG
    ENDIF

    SET BORDER TO                       && This command selects the
                                        && single-line default.
    @ 0,0 TO 2,27 DOUBLE COLOR GR+/BG   && Draws a border that
    @ 1,1 CLEAR TO 1,26                 && simulates the main menu
    @ 1,1 FILL TO 1,26 COLOR W+/N       && Cleans it up and paints
    @ 1,4 SAY "DATA" COLOR W+/N         && fake menu prompts in the
    @ 1,11 SAY "REPORTS" COLOR W+/N     && default colors
    @ 1,21 SAY "EXIT" COLOR W+/N
    @ 22,00                             && Clears (erases) line 22
ENDIF
RETURN                                  && Terminates


PROCEDURE DBF01                         && Declares the PROCEDURE
CLOSE DATABASES                         && name and closes any open
                                        && data files
*-- Open menu level view/database
lc_message="0"   && Sets the variable to hold error messages
* The next line tells dBASE to put the error number and the dBASE
* error message into a string when an error occurs.
ON ERROR lc_message=LTRIM(STR(ERROR()))+" "+MESSAGE()
USE VENDOR.DBF              && Opens the data file,
IF "" <> DBF()             && makes sure that the file opened
    SET INDEX TO VENDOR    && before opening the index(es), and
ENDIF
SET ORDER TO ID            && then chooses the proper index as
                           && the master
ON ERROR                   && Files are open by now, so this
                           && cancels the previous ON ERROR
                           && instructions.
```

```
    gn_error=VAL(lc_message)    && If error occurred, the value of the
                                && numeric part of the string is
                                && placed in the error flag. Any value
                                && other than 0 indicates that a
                                && problem occurred.
    IF gn_error > 0             && Tests to see if an error occurred
    * If so, this does the error routine, and passes the proper
    * message as a parameter.
       DO Pause WITH ;
       "Error opening VENDOR.DBF or index(es) VENDOR"
       lc_new='Y'              && Gives the variable the value of Y. This
                               && will serve as a flag later.
       RETURN                  && Terminates routine here if there is an
                               && error
    ENDIF
    lc_new='Y'                 && This section of code will execute only if
    RELEASE lc_message         && there has been no error.
    RETURN                     && If no error, here is where the
                               && termination occurs.


    PROCEDURE ACT01
    *-- Begin MAIN: BAR Menu Actions.
    *-- (before item, action, and after item)
    *
    PRIVATE lc_new, lc_dbf     && Inits flag variables to use for
    lc_new=' '                 && testing conditions and protects
    lc_dbf=' '                 && higher-level variables from change
    DO CASE                    && Uses CASE to determine which menu
    CASE "PAD_1" = PAD()       && choice was made. If the first pad
       lc_new='Y'              && is chosen,
       DO DATA WITH " 01"      && calls the PROCEDURE data, along with
                               && a parameter telling the application
                               && how deep the programs are nested

    CASE "PAD_2" = PAD()       && Does the same for the REPORTS menu
       lc_new='Y'
       DO REPORTS WITH " 01"
    CASE "PAD_3" = PAD()       && If the user chooses EXIT, this sets
       *-- Return to caller    && the variable that tells the highest-
       gc_quit='Q'             && level module to terminate.
       DEACTIVATE MENU && MAIN  && Deactivates the MAIN menu
       RETURN                  && Terminates this module
    OTHERWISE
```

```
   @ 24,00              && If there is a prompt that you have
                        && not attached an action to, this
                        && error coding is executed.
   @ 24,21 SAY "This item has no action. Press a key."
   x=INKEY(0)
   @ 24,00
ENDCASE


* This section of code executes after the prompt that was chosen
* terminates and returns control to this procedure. The section
* will also execute if an unattached prompt is chosen.
SET MESSAGE TO          && Clears whatever message might be
IF SET("STATUS")="ON"   && set and tests to see if SET STATUS
                        && is on
   SET STATUS OFF       && If so, this turns it off.
ENDIF
IF gc_quit='Q'          && If one of the lower-level procedures
                        && has set the quit flag to Q,
   DEACTIVATE MENU && MAIN    && this terminates the menu.
ENDIF
IF lc_new='Y'           && If the variable is set to flag
                        && an answer of Yes,
   lc_file="SET"+gc_prognum   && this resets the module-depth
                        && indicator.
   DO &lc_file.         && This does the SET??? procedure.
ENDIF
RETURN                  && Terminates the module


******************************************************************
* Program......: DATA.PRG
* Author.......: Ed Tiley
* Date.........: 1-16-89
* Notice.......: 1989  Que Corporation
* dBASE Ver....: dBASE IV Developer's Edition
* Generated by.: APGEN version 1.0
* Description..: POPUP menu for controlling data entry

* Description..: Menu actions
******************************************************************
PROCEDURE DATA      && This module sets up the environment to
                    && conform with the colors and database/view
                    && that you specified in the Applications
                    && Generator.
```

```
PARAMETER entryflg    && Takes the passed parameter and puts it in
                      && a variable called entryflg
PRIVATE gc_prognum    && Inits a PRIVATE variable that will store
                      && the depth of nesting of programs
gc_prognum="02"       && Stores it

DO SET02              && Calls the setup procedure that handles
                      && second-level setup
IF gn_error > 0       && If there was an error, this clears the
   gn_error=0         && error flag,
   RETURN             && terminates the procedure, and returns to the main
ENDIF                 && menu.

*-- Before menu code

ACTIVATE POPUP DATA   && Turns on the menu named DATA. The ON
                      && SELECTION commands attached to the menu
                      && will dictate what is done when a prompt
                      && is chosen. The menu will be DEACTIVATEd
                      && by that procedure.


*-- After menu

RETURN                && Terminates
*-- EOP DATA

PROCEDURE SET02                   && This procedure sets up the
                                  && second-level data file.
ON KEY LABEL F1 DO 1HELP1         && Turns on the custom help
                                  && so that when users press
                                  && F1, they get your help
                                  && prompts rather than the
                                  && regular help.
DO DBF02                          && Opens menu-level database

IF gn_error = 0                   && If there was no error
                                  && opening the file,
   IF ISCOLOR()                   && this tests for a color card.
      SET COLOR OF NORMAL TO W+/B     && If there is one, this sets
      SET COLOR OF MESSAGES TO W+/B && the screen attributes.
      SET COLOR OF TITLES TO W+/B
      SET COLOR OF HIGHLIGHT TO GR+/BG
      SET COLOR OF BOX TO GR+/BG
```

```
        SET COLOR OF INFORMATION TO B/W
        SET COLOR OF FIELDS TO N/BG
     ENDIF
     @ 22,00  && Clears line 22 just in case SET STATUS was ON
ENDIF
RETURN


PROCEDURE DBF02          && Because the database/view is the same
CLOSE DATABASES          && as in the DATA menu, this module is
                         && about the same as DBF01.
*-- Open menu level view/database.
lc_message="0"    && Inits a variable to hold error messages
ON ERROR lc_message=LTRIM(STR(ERROR()))+" "+MESSAGE()  && If an
                         && error occurs, this puts the number and
                         && message into the variable.
USE VENDOR.DBF           && Attempts to open the file
IF "" <> DBF()           && Tests to make sure that the file opened
                         && If the return value of DBF() is a null
                         && string, there was an error.
    SET INDEX TO VENDOR  && If there was no error, this opens
                         && index.
ENDIF
SET ORDER TO ID          && Activates the TAG to order the records
ON ERROR                 && Cancels the last ON ERROR
gn_error=VAL(lc_message) && Finds out if the error message has
                         && been altered. The VAL() function
                         && will return the error number if it
                         && was stored here as a result of the
                         && ON ERROR.
IF gn_error > 0          && If it has been altered, this does
   DO Pause WITH ;       && the ERROR module.
   "Error opening VENDOR.DBF or index(es) VENDOR"
   lc_new='Y'    && Alters the variable to show that the open was
   RETURN        && attempted and then terminates
ENDIF
lc_new='Y'               && Alters the variable to show that
RELEASE lc_message       && the open was attempted and then
                         && erases the variable that holds the
                         && error message
RETURN                   && Terminates


PROCEDURE ACT02          && This procedure performs the actions
                         && attached to the DATA menu prompts.
```

```
*-- Begin DATA: POPUP Menu Actions.
*-- (before item, action, and after item)
*
PRIVATE lc_new, lc_dbf      && Inits new versions of the flag
lc_new=' '                  && variables
lc_dbf=' '
DO CASE                     && Sets up a CASE to determine which
                            && prompt has been chosen by the user
CASE BAR() = 1              && If it was the first prompt,
   ACTIVATE WINDOW Browscr  && this opens the window in which
   SET SCOREBOARD ON        && editing is done and turns on the
                            && scoreboard to show the status of
                            && INS NUM.
   *-- Desc: attach format file VENDOR
   SET FORMAT TO VENDOR     && Specifies the screen format file
   APPEND                   && you attached and performs the APPEND
                            && new records function
   *-- close format file so as not to affect READ's
   SET FORMAT TO            && If you leave the format file open
                            && and try to READ a user response, the
                            && format screen is activated.
   SET SCOREBOARD OFF       && Turns off the INS NUM indicator line
   DEACTIVATE WINDOW Browscr && Closes the window covering the
                            && menus below
CASE BAR() = 2             && If the user chose EDIT/DELETE,
   ACTIVATE WINDOW Browscr  && this opens the window to cover the
   SET SCOREBOARD ON        && menu and turns on the INS NUM
                            && indicator line.
   *-- Desc: attach format file VENDOR
   SET FORMAT TO VENDOR     && Specifies the screen format to
   EDIT NOFOLLOW NOAPPEND   && use and performs the EDIT
   *-- close format file so as not to affect READ's.
   SET FORMAT TO            && Note that this section is the
   SET SCOREBOARD OFF       && same code as the APPEND with the
                            && exception that the BROWSE
   DEACTIVATE WINDOW Browscr && command is different.
CASE BAR() = 4             && If the user selects PACK,
   SET EXCLUSIVE ON         && this disallows multiuser access to the
                            && file.
   lc_message="0"           && Sets up the error handling
   ON ERROR lc_message=LTRIM(STR(ERROR()))+" "+MESSAGE()
   USE VENDOR.DBF           && Opens the file and tests
   IF "" <> DBF()           && to make sure that no error occurred
      SET INDEX TO VENDOR   && before opening index files
```

```
ENDIF
SET ORDER TO ID        && and setting the index order
ON ERROR               && Clears error handling, but tests to
gn_error=VAL(lc_message)   && see if any untrapped errors
IF gn_error > 0        && have occurred
   DO Pause WITH ;         && If so, calls the PAUSE procedure
   "Error opening VENDOR.DBF or index(es) VENDOR"
   gn_error=0
   lc_file="SET"+gc_prognum
   DO &lc_file.
   RETURN              && and then terminates
ENDIF
lc_new='Y'             && If no errors, this sets the flag
RELEASE lc_message     && and clears the error message.
SET EXCLUSIVE OFF
ACTIVATE WINDOW Savescr            && Opens a window and
lc_say='Looking for DELETED Records...'  && searches the file
DO info_box WITH lc_say            && for marked records
LOCATE FOR DELETED()
IF .NOT. EOF()    && IF any are found, this does the PACK.
   lc_say='Purging DELETED Records...'
   DO info_box WITH lc_say
   SET TALK ON
   PACK
   SET TALK OFF
   GO TOP
ENDIF

DEACTIVATE WINDOW Savescr  && Closes the window
CASE BAR() = 5             && If the user selects REINDEX,
   SET EXCLUSIVE ON        && this runs the same code to set up as
                           && before
   lc_message="0"
   ON ERROR lc_message=LTRIM(STR(ERROR()))+" "+MESSAGE()
   USE VENDOR.DBF
   IF "" <> DBF()
      SET INDEX TO VENDOR
   ENDIF
   SET ORDER TO ID
   ON ERROR
   gn_error=VAL(lc_message)
   IF gn_error > 0
      DO Pause WITH ;
      "Error opening VENDOR.DBF or index(es) VENDOR"
```

```
            gn_error=0
            lc_file="SET"+gc_prognum
            DO &lc_file.
            RETURN
      ENDIF
      lc_new='Y'
      RELEASE lc_message
      SET EXCLUSIVE OFF
      ACTIVATE WINDOW Savescr
      lc_say='Reindexing Database...'
      DO info_box WITH lc_say
      SET TALK ON
      REINDEX                       && Uses the REINDEX command
      SET TALK OFF                  && just like the PACK before

      DEACTIVATE WINDOW Savescr
CASE BAR() = 6                      && If the user chose the
      ACTIVATE WINDOW Savescr       && backup, this opens the
      RUN BACKUP D:\IV\APPS\*.DB? A:  && window and runs the
                                    && command.

      DEACTIVATE WINDOW Savescr     && Closes the window
ENDCASE
SET MESSAGE TO                      && Resets the environment to what
IF SET("STATUS")="ON"              && it was and terminates
      SET STATUS OFF
ENDIF
IF gc_quit='Q'                     && If the user has chosen to quit,
      DEACTIVATE POPUP && DATA     && this deactivates the menu and lets
ENDIF                              && the main module know to exit.
IF lc_new='Y'                      && If a new file was opened, this
      lc_file="SET"+gc_prognum     && resets the old one.
      DO &lc_file.
ENDIF
RETURN
```

```
* This is the code that is called when the user selects the
* REPORTS menu. It is similar in form to the DATA module.
*********************************************************************
* Program......: REPORTS.PRG
* Author.......: Ed Tiley
* Date.........: 1-16-89
* Notice.......: 1989  Que Corporation
* dBASE Ver....: dBASE IV Developer's Edition
* Generated by.: APGEN version 1.0
* Description..: A POPUP to control printing vendors


* Description..: Menu actions
*********************************************************************
PROCEDURE REPORTS       && Defines the procedure name,
PARAMETER entryflg      && accepts the passed parameter,
PRIVATE gc_prognum      && and sets the depth indicator after
gc_prognum="03"         && protecting those in higher procedures


DO SET03                && Does the setup procedure for the third
IF gn_error > 0         && level and then tests to see if an error
   gn_error=0           && occurred
   RETURN
ENDIF


*-- Before menu code

ACTIVATE POPUP REPORTS  && Turns on the menu

*-- After menu

RETURN                  && When the menu terminates
*-- EOP REPORTS

PROCEDURE SET03             && Third level set up
ON KEY LABEL F1 DO 1HELP1   && Turns on custom help


DO DBF03                    && Opens menu-level database
                            && Calls the data opening procedure

IF gn_error = 0             && IF no errors, this tests for color
   IF ISCOLOR()             && card and sets up display.
      SET COLOR OF NORMAL TO W+/B
      SET COLOR OF MESSAGES TO W+/N
      SET COLOR OF TITLES TO W/B
```

```
              SET COLOR OF HIGHLIGHT TO GR+/BG
              SET COLOR OF BOX TO GR+/BG
              SET COLOR OF INFORMATION TO B/W
              SET COLOR OF FIELDS TO N/BG
         ENDIF
         @ 22,00
    ENDIF
    RETURN


    PROCEDURE DBF03          && Procedure to open the data file
    CLOSE DATABASES          && Closes any now open
    *-- Open menu level view/database
    lc_message="0"           && Sets the error parameters
    ON ERROR lc_message=LTRIM(STR(ERROR()))+" "+MESSAGE()
    USE VENDOR.DBF           && Opens the file
    IF "" <> DBF()
        SET INDEX TO VENDOR  && If no errors, this opens the index.
    ENDIF
    SET ORDER TO ID          && Sets the order and
    ON ERROR                 && cancels the error trap
    gn_error=VAL(lc_message)
    IF gn_error > 0          && If there was an error, this displays
                             && it.
        DO Pause WITH ;
        "Error opening VENDOR.DBF or index(es) VENDOR"
        lc_new='Y'
        RETURN
    ENDIF
    lc_new='Y'
    RELEASE lc_message
    RETURN


    PROCEDURE ACT03          && Procedure to perform the actions
    *-- Begin REPORTS: POPUP Menu Actions.
    *-- (before item, action, and after item)
    *
    PRIVATE lc_new, lc_dbf   && Sets the file-handling flag variables
    lc_new=' '
    lc_dbf=' '
    DO CASE
    CASE BAR() = 1
        *-- Open Item level view/database and indexes.
        CLOSE DATABASES      && Closes the current data file and
        lc_dbf='Y'           && sets up error reporting
```

```
      lc_message="0"
      ON ERROR lc_message=LTRIM(STR(ERROR()))+" "+MESSAGE()
      USE VENDOR.DBF        && Opens the new data file
      IF "" <> DBF()
         SET INDEX TO VENDOR
      ENDIF
      SET ORDER TO COMPANY && Sets the ORDER
      ON ERROR             && Handles any errors
      gn_error=VAL(lc_message)
      IF gn_error > 0
         DO Pause WITH ;
         "Error opening VENDOR.DBF or index(es) VENDOR"
         gn_error=0
         lc_file="SET"+gc_prognum
         DO &lc_file.
         RETURN
      ENDIF
      lc_new='Y'
      RELEASE lc_message
      ACTIVATE WINDOW Savescr
      *-- Desc: Report
      SET PRINT ON                  && These three lines do the work
      REPORT FORM VEN_LIST NOEJECT  && of sending the report. The
      SET PRINT OFF                 && NOEJECT suppresses a page
      DEACTIVATE WINDOW Savescr     && eject before printing.
   CASE BAR() = 2                   && If the user selects the
      ACTIVATE WINDOW Savescr       && second report, this keeps the
      *-- Desc: Report              && same database/view.
      SET PRINT ON
      REPORT FORM VEN_LIST NOEJECT  && Just substitutes VEN_LIST
      SET PRINT OFF
      DEACTIVATE WINDOW Savescr
   CASE BAR() = 3                   && If the user selects labels,
      *-- Open Item level view/database and indexes.
      CLOSE DATABASES
      lc_dbf='Y'                    && this sets up error handling
      lc_message="0"                && and alters the database/view.
      ON ERROR lc_message=LTRIM(STR(ERROR()))+" "+MESSAGE()
      USE VENDOR
      IF "" <> DBF()
         SET INDEX TO VENDOR
      ENDIF
      SET ORDER TO ZIP
```

```
      ON ERROR
      gn_error=VAL(lc_message)
      IF gn_error > 0
         DO Pause WITH ;
         "Error opening VENDOR.DBF or index(es) VENDOR"
         gn_error=0
         lc_file="SET"+gc_prognum
         DO &lc_file.
         RETURN
      ENDIF
      lc_new='Y'
      RELEASE lc_message
      ACTIVATE WINDOW Savescr
      *--  Desc: LABEL command to call VEND_LBL
      SET PRINT ON
      LABEL FORM VEND_LBL SAMPLE      && Sends the labels to the
      SET PRINT OFF                   && printer
      DEACTIVATE WINDOW Savescr
ENDCASE
SET MESSAGE TO
IF SET("STATUS")="ON"               && Resets the environment and
   SET STATUS OFF                   && passes back control as before
ENDIF
IF gc_quit='Q'
   DEACTIVATE POPUP                 && REPORTS
ENDIF
IF lc_new='Y'
   lc_file="SET"+gc_prognum
   DO &lc_file.
ENDIF
IF lc_dbf='Y' .AND. .NOT. lc_new='Y'
   lc_file="DBF"+gc_prognum
   DO &lc_file.
ENDIF
RETURN
*****  End of code  *****
```

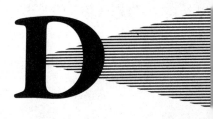

Major Differences between dBASE III Plus and dBASE IV

d BASE III Plus and dBASE IV differ in six major areas: general working environment, capacity, numeric data types, file types, built-in functions, and processing commands. Each of these areas is explored in this appendix.

General Working Environment

dBASE III Plus provides the Assistant to help users who need an easier method of using the program than is provided at the dot prompt. dBASE IV builds on the Assistant's ease of use and adds the Control Center, which provides additional integration of convenient management and productivity features. Even for power users, the Control Center represents an attractive alternative to dot prompt operations.

dBASE IV adds a powerful query-by-example (QBE) capability. With QBE, you can search and retrieve data from selective records by defining filter conditions. You can link files effortlessly by specifying their relationships with queries. Records generated from query operations can be saved to a database file.

dBASE IV adds DOS utilities to its program so that you can execute DOS commands without using the RUN command at the dot prompt or leaving dBASE IV. It also provides useful tools for managing disk files.

dBASE IV implements the Structured Query Language (SQL). You can issue SQL commands at the dot prompt for accessing the database created in dBASE IV.

dBASE IV incorporates an Applications Generator so that you can create programs by choosing the menu options from the generator instead of writing your own commands in an editor.

dBASE IV implements new label and report generators by using the "what you see is what you get" (WYSIWYG) approach. Labels and reports can be designed with the enhanced screen painter. Using the screen painter, you can place data fields on the design forms together with the necessary descriptive text.

After designing label and report forms, dBASE IV automatically generates the program listing for the forms and saves it as a program (.LBG or .FRG) file. The program files are compiled when they are put to use, and object codes are produced (saved as .LBO or .FRO files).

In dBASE IV, you can produce reports and labels by using records from multiple-database files that are linked or joined by means of a query operation. Records produced by the query can be saved as a database file or a view file. Reports and labels can be produced by using these records from the database file or from the query view.

dBASE III Plus uses individual index (.NDX) files for ordering records in a database file. Although these index files can still be used, in dBASE IV you can use a set of index tags in one or more multiple index (.MDX) files for arranging records. You need to reindex and rebuild individual index (.NDX) files yourself; index tags in a multiple index (.MDX) file are automatically updated whenever the contents of its database file are changed.

In dBASE IV, you must group your data files in file catalogs when you are in the Control Center. Once a file catalog is in use, all the data files subsequently created are automatically included in that file catalog.

dBASE IV supports multiple-child and multiple-file relationships in the database design. A database file can be linked to several database files simultaneously.

dBASE III Plus can be executed on a dual floppy system or a system with a hard disk; dBASE IV requires a hard disk to run the program once the program systems are installed. In dBASE IV, you are advised to organize your disk files in separate directories and subdirectories.

In dBASE IV, you can switch from Edit mode (displaying one record at a time) to Browse mode (displaying a set of records on-screen) by pressing a single keystroke (F2).

dBASE IV allows you to display the contents of a database file on the printer by using the quick report (Shift-F9) keystrokes.

dBASE IV provides a more powerful help screen system. Most help messages are context-sensitive—help messages are related to the operation being performed.

dBASE IV adds a macro capability, which allows you to save a series of key-strokes as a macro that can be played back later.

dBASE IV enhances the error-handling capability in dot prompt commands. When an error occurs, you can choose to re-edit the last command entered without retyping it.

dBASE IV allows you to encrypt your data for data security purposes. In addition, you can flag read-only files so that unintended deletions can be avoided.

dBASE IV allows you to use windows (up to 20) on the screen for displaying your output, menus, and messages.

Capacity

	dBASE III Plus	*dBASE IV*
Open data files allowed	10	99
Data fields per record	128	255
Command line length	256	1,024
Windows	N/A	20

Numeric Data Types

dBASE III used floating point numeric data type only (type N). dBASE IV supports floating point numeric data as type F. In addition, dBASE IV supports Binary Coded Decimal (BCD) as the default numeric data type (type N). Unlike floating point results, BCD results do not reflect rounding errors. BCD data type gives dBASE IV better handling of financial calculations where rounding errors would cause problems.

File Types

The following file types, not available in dBASE III Plus, are available in dBASE IV:

File Type	Description
.LBG	Program files for label form (.LBL)
.LBO	Object code files for label form (.LBL)
.FRG	Program files for report form (.FRM)
.FRO	Object code files for report form (.FRM)

.MDX	Multiple index files for holding index tags
.QBE	Query by Example files
.QBO	Object code files for query files

Built-In Functions

The dBASE IV functions that are either not available or different from those in dBASE III Plus are the following:

Mathematical and trigonometric functions:

ACOS()	COS()	RAND()
ASIN()	DTOR()	RTOD()
ATAN()	FLOOR()	SIGN()
ATN2()	LOG10()	SIN()
CEILING()	PI()	TAN()

Financial functions:

FV()	PAYMENT()	PV()

Memo field functions:

AT()	MEMLINES()	RIGHT()
LEFT()	MLINE()	SUBSTR()
LEN()		

Index file or tag functions:

KEY()	NDX()	SEEK()
MDX()	ORDER()	TAG()

Pop-up or bar-menu functions:

BAR()	PAD()	PROMPT()
MENU()	POPUP()	

Error-tracing and debugging functions:

LINENO()	PROGRAM()

Date conversion functions:

DMY()	MDY()

Other dBASE IV enhanced functions:

BOF()	FIELD()	LUPDATE()
CHANGE()	FOUND()	RECCOUNT()
DBF()	INKEY()	RECNO()
DELETED()	ISMARKED()	RECSIZE()
EOF()	LOOKUP()	

Other dBASE IV new functions:

ACCESS()	LASTKEY()	RLOCK()
ALIAS()	LIKE()	ROLLBACK()
CALL()	LKSYS()	SELECT()
COMPLETED()	LOCK()	SET()
DIFFERENCE()	MEMORY()	SOUNDEX()
DTOS()	NETWORK()	USER()
FIXED()	PICTURE()	VARREAD()
FLOAT()	PRINTSTATUS()	

Processing Commands

The dBASE IV commands that are either not available or different from those in dBASE III Plus are the following:

Commands for handling memo fields:

APPEND MEMO	SET BLOCKSIZE TO
COPY MEMO	SET WINDOW OF MEMO TO
REPLACE	

Commands for processing memory variables or arrays:

APPEND FROM ARRAY	DECLARE
COPY TO ARRAY	

Commands for performing index operations:

COPY TAG	INDEX...ON TO TAG
DELETE TAG	SET ORDER TO TAG

Commands for processing macros:

BEGIN TRANSACTION	RESTORE MACROS FROM
PLAY MACRO	ROLLBACK
RESET	SAVE MACRO TO

Commands for displaying data:

???	PRINTJOB...ENDPRINTJOB
ON PAGE	SET DESIGN

Commands for using pop-up or bar menus:

ACTIVATE MENU	DEFINE POPUP
ACTIVATE POPUP	ON PAD
DEACTIVATE MENU	ON SELECTION PAD
DEACTIVATE POPUP	ON SELECTION POPUP
DEFINE BAR	RELEASE POPUPS
DEFINE BOX	SHOW POPUP
DEFINE MENU	SHOW MENU
DEFINE PAD	

Commands for using windows:

ACTIVATE WINDOW	RELEASE WINDOWS
DEACTIVATE WINDOW	RESTORE WINDOW
DEFINE WINDOW	SAVE WINDOW

Commands for displaying foreign monetary values:

SET CURRENCY LEFT/RIGHT	SET POINT TO
SET CURRENCY TO	SET SEPARATOR TO

Commands for manipulating and displaying the date and time:

SET CLOCK ON	SET HOURS TO
SET CLOCK TO	SET MARK TO
SET DATE TO	

Other enhanced dBASE IV commands:

?	ON KEY LABEL
??	PUBLIC ARRAY
@	REINDEX
AVERAGE	REPORT FORM
BROWSE	RETURN TO MASTER
CALL	SET ALTERNATE TO
CHANGE	SET BELL TO
COPY TO	SET CARRY TO
CREATE	SET COLOR OF
DISPLAY	SET DEVICE TO
DISPLAY FILES	SET DO HISTORY
DISPLAY HISTORY	SET FIELDS TO
DISPLAY MEMORY	SET FIXED
DISPLAY STATUS	SET FUNCTION
DO	SET INDEX TO
EDIT	SET MENUS ON
EXPORT TO	SET PRINTER TO
IMPORT FROM	SET RELATION TO

LABEL FORM
LIST
LIST MEMORY
MODIFY COMMAND/FILE
MODIFY COMMAND
MODIFY STRUCTURE

SET VIEW TO
SKIP
SORT TO
SUM
TYPE

Other new dBASE IV commands:

ACTIVATE SCREEN
BUILD
CLEAR MENUS
CLEAR POPUPS
CLEAR WINDOWS
COMPILE
CONVERT TO
COPY INDEXES/TAG
CREATE APPLICATION
CREATE FROM
DEBUG
EJECT PAGE
FUNCTION
LOGOUT
MODIFY APPLICATION

MOVE WINDOW
ON READERROR
PROTECT
RELEASE MENUS
SET AUTOSAVE
SET BORDER TO
SET DISPLAY TO
SET EXCLUSIVE
SET LOCK ON
SET REFRESH TO
SET REPROCESS TO
SET SKIP TO
SET SPACE ON
SET TRAP
UNLOCK

dBASE IV Control Center
Command Menu

Data

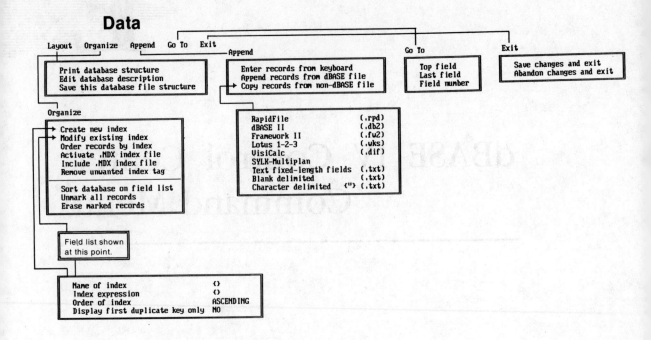

Layout Organize Append Go To Exit

```
Print database structure
Edit database description
Save this database file structure
```

Append

```
Enter records from keyboard
Append records from dBASE file
Copy records from non-dBASE file
```

Go To

```
Top field
Last field
Field number
```

Exit

```
Save changes and exit
Abandon changes and exit
```

Organize

```
Create new index
Modify existing index
Order records by index
Activate .MDX index file
Include .MDX index file
Remove unwanted index tag

Sort database on field list
Unmark all records
Erase marked records
```

```
RapidFile                    (.rpd)
dBASE II                     (.db2)
Framework II                 (.fw2)
Lotus 1-2-3                  (.wks)
VisiCalc                     (.dif)
SYLK-Multiplan
Text fixed-length fields     (.txt)
Blank delimited              (.txt)
Character delimited    (") (.txt)
```

```
Field list shown
at this point.
```

```
Name of index                       {}
Index expression                    {}
Order of index              ASCENDING
Display first duplicate key only  NO
```

Queries

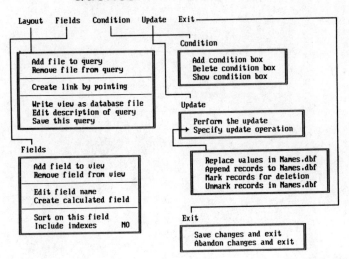

Layout Fields Condition Update Exit

```
Add file to query
Remove file from query

Create link by pointing

Write view as database file
Edit description of query
Save this query
```

Condition

```
Add condition box
Delete condition box
Show condition box
```

Update

```
Perform the update
Specify update operation
```

Fields

```
Add field to view
Remove field from view

Edit field name
Create calculated field

Sort on this field
Include indexes        NO
```

```
Replace values in Names.dbf
Append records to Names.dbf
Mark records for deletion
Unmark records in Names.dbf
```

Exit

```
Save changes and exit
Abandon changes and exit
```

Forms

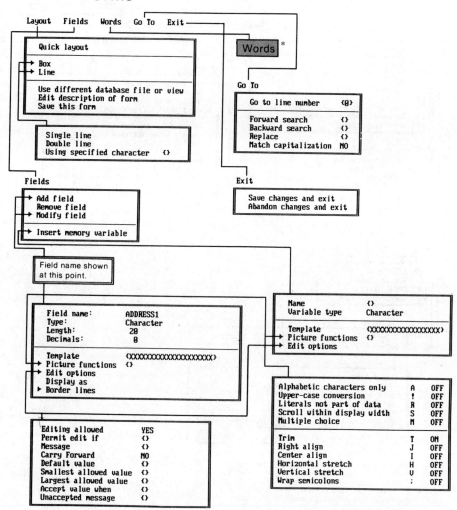

*See the Applications menu for a map of Words commands.

Reports

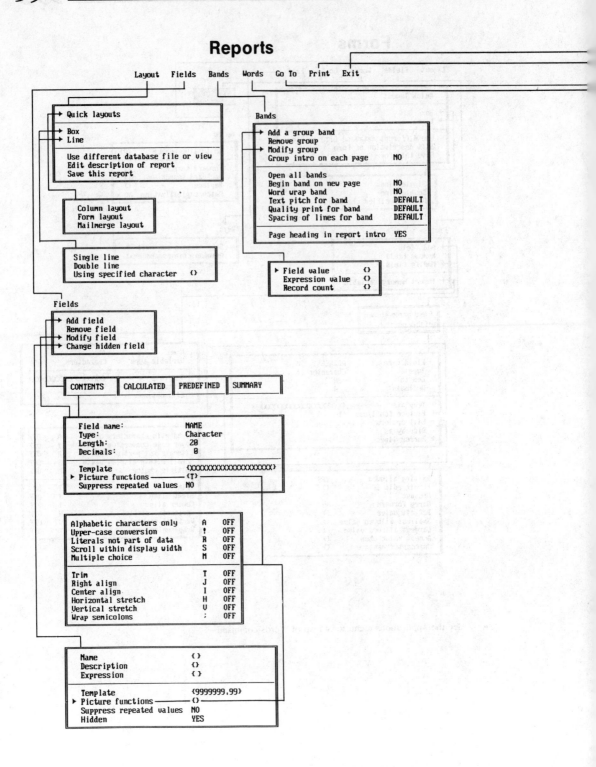

Layout   Fields   Bands   Words   Go To   Print   Exit

Quick layouts

Box
Line

Use different database file or view
Edit description of report
Save this report

Column layout
Form layout
Mailmerge layout

Single line
Double line
Using specified character   {}

Bands

Add a group band
Remove group
Modify group
Group intro on each page   NO

Open all bands
Begin band on new page   NO
Word wrap band   NO
Text pitch for band   DEFAULT
Quality print for band   DEFAULT
Spacing of lines for band   DEFAULT

Page heading in report intro   YES

Field value   {}
Expression value   {}
Record count   {}

Fields

Add field
Remove field
Modify field
Change hidden field

| CONTENTS | CALCULATED | PREDEFINED | SUMMARY |

Field name: NAME
Type: Character
Length: 20
Decimals: 0

Template   {XXXXXXXXXXXXXXXXXXXX}
Picture functions ———— {T}
Suppress repeated values   NO

Alphabetic characters only   A   OFF
Upper-case conversion   !   OFF
Literals not part of data   R   OFF
Scroll within display width   S   OFF
Multiple choice   M   OFF

Trim   T   OFF
Right align   J   OFF
Center align   I   OFF
Horizontal stretch   H   OFF
Vertical stretch   V   OFF
Wrap semicolons   ;   OFF

Name   {}
Description   {}
Expression   {}

Template   {9999999.99}
Picture functions ———— {}
Suppress repeated values   NO
Hidden   YES

Reports Continued

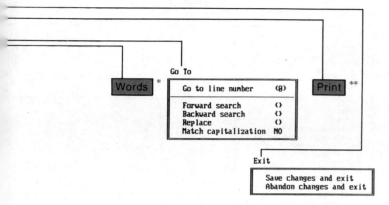

Words *

```
Go To
┌─────────────────────────────────┐
│ Go to line number        <0>    │
├─────────────────────────────────┤
│ Forward search           <>     │
│ Backward search          <>     │
│ Replace                  <>     │
│ Match capitalization     NO     │
└─────────────────────────────────┘
```

Print **

```
Exit
┌──────────────────────────────┐
│ Save changes and exit        │
│ Abandon changes and exit     │
└──────────────────────────────┘
```

*See the Applications menu for a map of Words commands.

**See the Applications menu for a map of Print commands.

Labels

Layout   Dimensions   Fields   Words   Go To   Print   Exit

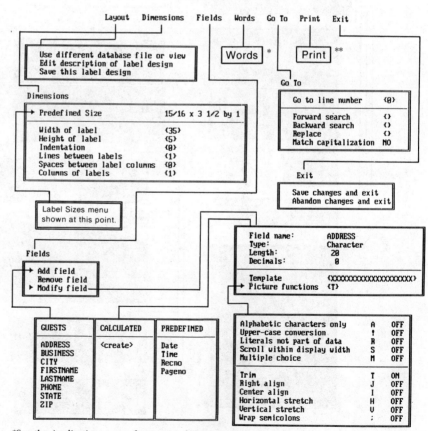

```
┌────────────────────────────────────────┐
│ Use different database file or view     │
│ Edit description of label design        │
│ Save this label design                  │
└────────────────────────────────────────┘
```

Words *

Print **

Dimensions
```
┌──────────────────────────────────────────────────┐
│→ Predefined Size          15/16 x 3 1/2 by 1       │
├──────────────────────────────────────────────────┤
│  Width of label           <35>                     │
│  Height of label          <5>                      │
│  Indentation              <0>                      │
│  Lines between labels     <1>                       │
│  Spaces between label columns  <0>                 │
│  Columns of labels        <1>                       │
└──────────────────────────────────────────────────┘
```

```
Go To
┌─────────────────────────────────┐
│ Go to line number        <0>    │
├─────────────────────────────────┤
│ Forward search           <>     │
│ Backward search          <>     │
│ Replace                  <>     │
│ Match capitalization     NO     │
└─────────────────────────────────┘
```

```
Exit
┌──────────────────────────────┐
│ Save changes and exit        │
│ Abandon changes and exit     │
└──────────────────────────────┘
```

```
┌──────────────────────────┐
│ Label Sizes menu         │
│ shown at this point.     │
└──────────────────────────┘
```

Fields
```
┌──────────────────────┐
│→ Add field           │
│  Remove field        │
│▶ Modify field        │
└──────────────────────┘
```

```
┌──────────────────────────────────────────────────┐
│ Field name:          ADDRESS                       │
│ Type:                Character                     │
│ Length:              20                            │
│ Decimals:            0                             │
├──────────────────────────────────────────────────┤
│ Template             <XXXXXXXXXXXXXXXXXXXX>        │
│→ Picture functions   <T>                           │
└──────────────────────────────────────────────────┘
```

GUESTS	CALCULATED	PREDEFINED
ADDRESS	<create>	Date
BUSINESS		Time
CITY		Recno
FIRSTNAME		Pageno
LASTNAME		
PHONE		
STATE		
ZIP		

```
┌──────────────────────────────────────────────────┐
│ Alphabetic characters only      A      OFF         │
│ Upper-case conversion           !      OFF         │
│ Literals not part of data       R      OFF         │
│ Scroll within display width     S      OFF         │
│ Multiple choice                 M      OFF         │
├──────────────────────────────────────────────────┤
│ Trim                            T      ON          │
│ Right align                     J      OFF         │
│ Center align                    I      OFF         │
│ Horizontal stretch              H      OFF         │
│ Vertical stretch                V      OFF         │
│ Wrap semicolons                 ;      OFF         │
└──────────────────────────────────────────────────┘
```

*See the Applications menu for a map of Words commands.

**See the Applications menu for a map of Print commands.

Applications

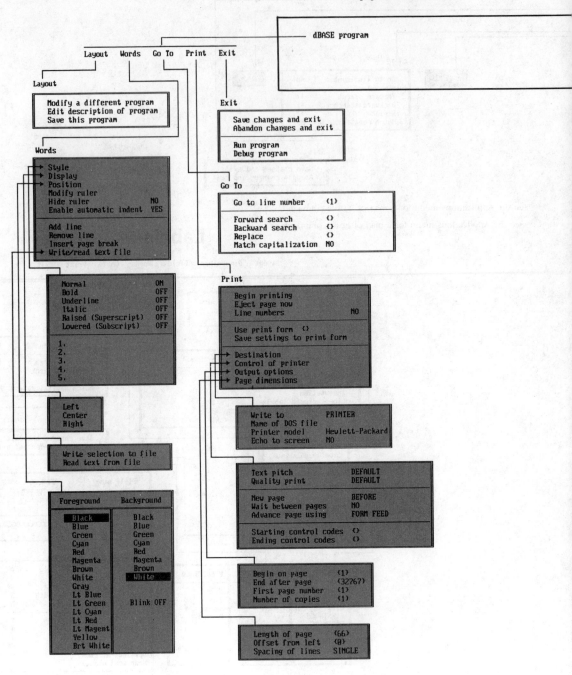

dBASE program

| Layout | Words | Go To | Print | Exit |

Layout

Modify a different program
Edit description of program
Save this program

Exit

Save changes and exit
Abandon changes and exit

Run program
Debug program

Words

→ Style
→ Display
→ Position
  Modify ruler
  Hide ruler   NO
  Enable automatic indent   YES

  Add line
  Remove line
  Insert page break
→ Write/read text file

Go To

Go to line number   {1}

Forward search   {}
Backward search   {}
Replace   {}
Match capitalization   NO

Normal	ON
Bold	OFF
Underline	OFF
Italic	OFF
Raised (Superscript)	OFF
Lowered (Subscript)	OFF

1.
2.
3.
4.
5.

Print

Begin printing
Eject page now
Line numbers   NO

Use print form   {}
Save settings to print form

→ Destination
→ Control of printer
→ Output options
→ Page dimensions

Left
Center
Right

Write to	PRINTER
Name of DOS file	
Printer model	Hewlett-Packard
Echo to screen	NO

Write selection to file
Read text from file

Text pitch	DEFAULT
Quality print	DEFAULT
New page	BEFORE
Wait between pages	NO
Advance page using	FORM FEED
Starting control codes	{}
Ending control codes	{}

Foreground	Background
Black	Black
Blue	Blue
Green	Green
Cyan	Cyan
Red	Red
Magenta	Magenta
Brown	Brown
White	White
Gray	
Lt Blue	
Lt Green	Blink OFF
Lt Cyan	
Lt Red	
Lt Magent	
Yellow	
Brt White	

Begin on page	{1}
End after page	{32767}
First page number	{1}
Number of copies	{1}

Length of page	{66}
Offset from left	{0}
Spacing of lines	SINGLE

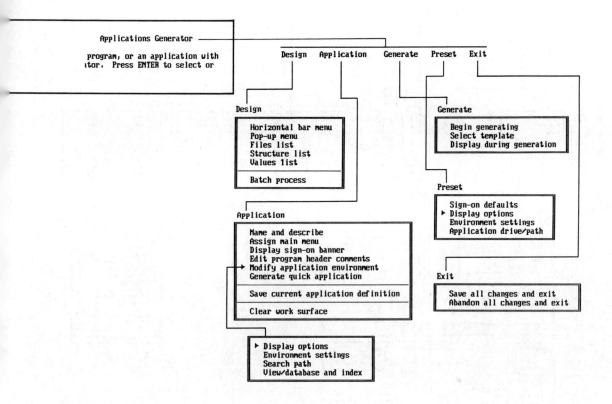

Applications Generator

program, or an application with
itor. Press ENTER to select or

Design   Application   Generate   Preset   Exit

Design

Horizontal bar menu
Pop-up menu
Files list
Structure list
Values list

Batch process

Application

Name and describe
Assign main menu
Display sign-on banner
Edit program header comments
→ Modify application environment
Generate quick application

Save current application definition

Clear work surface

→ Display options
Environment settings
Search path
View/database and index

Generate

Begin generating
Select template
Display during generation

Preset

Sign-on defaults
→ Display options
Environment settings
Application drive/path

Exit

Save all changes and exit
Abandon all changes and exit

Exit

Exit to dot prompt
Quit to DOS

Catalog

Tools

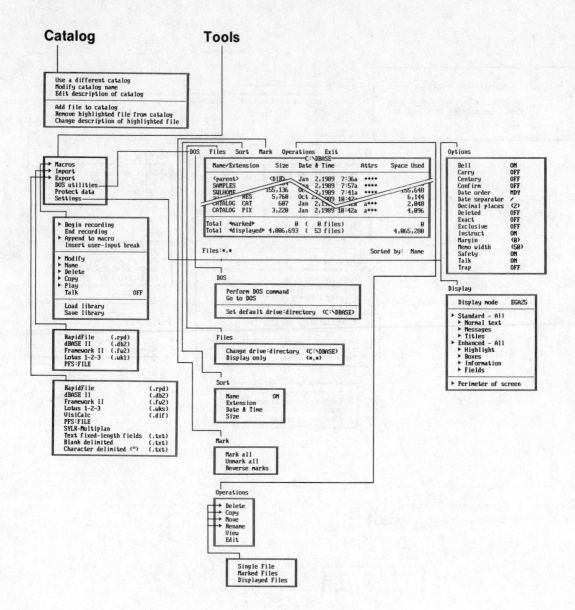

Index

D

E

F

G

H

I

J

K

More Computer Knowledge from Que

SELECT QUE BOOKS TO INCREASE
YOUR PERSONAL COMPUTER PRODUCTIVITY

dBASE IV Handbook, 3rd Edition

by George T. Chou, Ph.D.

Learn dBASE IV quickly with Que's new *dBASE IV Handbook*, 3rd Edition! dBASE expert George Chou leads you step-by-step from basic database concepts to advanced dBASE features, using a series of Quick Start tutorials. Experienced dBASE users will appreciate the extensive information on the new features of dBASE IV, including the new user interface, the query-by-example mode, and the SQL module. Complete with comprehensive command and function reference sections, *dBASE IV Handbook*, 3rd Edition, is an exhaustive guide to dBASE IV!

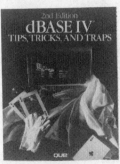

dBASE IV Tips, Tricks, and Traps, 2nd Edition

by George T. Chou, Ph.D.

Become a dBASE IV master with Que's informative *dBASE IV Tips, Tricks, and Traps*, 2nd Edition! This handy reference presents hundreds of hints and techniques that help you improve your dBASE IV efficiency. Organized by topic, this book will show you the best ways to use dBASE IV, from basic installation to advanced programming. Icons throughout the text highlight features new to dBASE IV, thus easing the transition to dBASE IV for previous dBASE users. Get more power from dBASE IV with *dBASE IV Tips, Tricks, and Traps*, 2nd Edition!

dBASE IV QuickStart

Developed by Que Corporation

The fast way to dBASE IV proficiency! More than 100 two-page illustrations show how to create common dBASE applications, including address lists and mailing labels. Readers are led step-by-step through dBASE IV basics, including many essential procedures and techniques. Simplify the complexity of dBASE IV with this visually oriented book—*dBASE IV QuickStart*!

dBASE IV Quick Reference

Developed by Que Corporation

Put dBASE IV commands and functions at your customers' fingertips with Que's *dBASE IV Quick Reference*. Whether they use laptop or desktop computers, this portable reference provides immediate access to information often buried in traditional text. This compact guide is an instant reference to often-used dBASE IV commands and functions.

ORDER FROM QUE TODAY

Item	Title	Price	Quantity	Extension
852	dBASE IV Handbook, 3rd Edition	$23.95		
873	dBASE IV QuickStart	19.95		
854	dBASE IV Tips, Tricks, and Traps, 2nd Edition	21.95		
867	dBASE IV Quick Reference	7.95		

Book Subtotal
Shipping & Handling ($2.50 per item)
Indiana Residents Add 5% Sales Tax
GRAND TOTAL

Method of Payment

☐ Check   ☐ VISA   ☐ MasterCard   ☐ American Express

Card Number _____ Exp. Date _____

Cardholder's Name _____

Ship to _____

Address _____

City _____ State _____ ZIP _____

If you can't wait, call **1-800-428-5331** and order TODAY.
All prices subject to change without notice.

FOLD HERE

Place
Stamp
Here

Que Corporation
P.O. Box 90
Carmel, IN 46032

REGISTRATION CARD

Register your copy of *dBASE IV Programming Techniques* and receive information about Que's newest products. Complete this registration card and return it to Que Corporation, P.O. Box 90, Carmel, IN 46032.

Name _____ Phone _____

Company _____ Title _____

Address _____

City _____ State _____ ZIP _____

Please check the appropriate answers:

Where did you buy *dBASE IV Programming Techniques*?
- ☐ Bookstore (name: _____)
- ☐ Computer store (name: _____)
- ☐ Catalog (name: _____)
- ☐ Direct from Que _____
- ☐ Other: _____

How many computer books do you buy a year?
- ☐ 1 or less   ☐ 6–10
- ☐ 2–5   ☐ More than 10

How many Que books do you own?
- ☐ 1   ☐ 6–10
- ☐ 2–5   ☐ More than 10

How long have you been using dBASE IV?
- ☐ Less than 6 months
- ☐ 6 months to 1 year
- ☐ 1–3 years
- ☐ More than 3 years

What influenced your purchase of *dBASE IV Programming Techniques*?
- ☐ Personal recommendation
- ☐ Advertisement   ☐ Que catalog
- ☐ In-store display ☐ Que mailing
- ☐ Price   ☐ Que's reputation
- ☐ Other: _____

How would you rate the overall content of *dBASE IV Programming Techniques*?
- ☐ Very good   ☐ Satisfactory
- ☐ Good   ☐ Poor

How would you rate *Chapter 2: Working with Macros*?
- ☐ Very good   ☐ Satisfactory
- ☐ Good   ☐ Poor

How would you rate the *examples of program code*?
- ☐ Very good   ☐ Satisfactory
- ☐ Good   ☐ Poor

How would you rate *Chapter 4: Using the Applications Generator*?
- ☐ Very good   ☐ Satisfactory
- ☐ Good   ☐ Poor

What do you like *best* about *dBASE IV Programming Techniques*?

What do you like *least* about *dBASE IV Programming Techniques*?

How do you use *dBASE IV Programming Techniques*?

What other Que products do you own?

For what other programs would a Que book be helpful?

Please feel free to list any other comments you may have about *dBASE IV Programming Techniques*.

_____
_____
_____
_____
_____

Place
Stamp
Here

_____
_____
_____
_____

Que Corporation
P.O. Box 90
Carmel, IN 46032